INFORMATION PROCESSING AND COGNITION
The Loyola Symposium

INFORMATION PROCESSING AND COGNITION
The Loyola Symposium

EDITED BY ROBERT L. SOLSO
LOYOLA UNIVERSITY OF CHICAGO

 LAWRENCE ERLBAUM ASSOCIATES, PUBLISHERS

1975   Hillsdale, New Jersey

DISTRIBUTED BY THE HALSTED PRESS DIVISION OF

JOHN WILEY & SONS
New York   Toronto   London   Sydney

Lawrence Erlbaum Associates, Inc., Publishers
62 Maria Drive
Hillsdale, New Jersey 07642

Distributed solely by Halsted Press Division
John Wiley & Sons, Inc., New York

Library of Congress Cataloging in Publication Data

Information processing and cognition.

Includes bibliographies and indexes.
1. Human information processing—Congresses.
2. Cognition—Congresses.   I. Solso, Robert L.,
1933–
BF455.I47   153   75-14324
ISBN 0-470-81230-3

Printed in the United States of America

CONTENTS

PREFACE

A friendly critic of mine recently told me that nothing was new in psychology and that the recent glamour of cognitive psychology was nothing more than "old wine in new bottles." I don't believe him, and after you read the contents of this book I think you too will share my impression that a new paradigm *is* emerging in psychology. That paradigm embodies more than substituting sentences for nonsense syllables, or using cathode ray tubes for memory drums, or developing models before the data are collected rather than after the numbers are all laid out, or allowing the experimental subject greater freedom than he has had in previous designs, or studying complex phenomena before simple phenomena are understood, or rapidly adjusting what to study in light of new investigatory tools. But this is part of it.

The provocative feature of the new paradigm, which permeates all of its polymorphistic attributes, is its special use of behavioral responses to fabricate elaborate models of internal representations of underlying structures. As the early physicists' preoccupation with the description of physical phenomena has given way to modern physics in which matter and time are conceptually interrelated, contemporary cognitive psychologists have come to view the description of behavioral phenomena as components of a larger conceptual entity that is logically interrelated. The major operational problem of all behavioral scientists is to translate fundamental sensory impressions to concepts of reason and to develop validating criteria for the percept and the process. No other problem is more critical to the applied epistemologist, of which experimental psychologists are exemplars. No other problem has been more persistently tracked; indeed, the history of experimental psychology is largely a history of refining the measurement of phenomena. Subjective impression of weight, time, distance, knowledge, learning, intelligence, attitudes, etc. have been carefully carved up into finer and finer gradations of objectively measured human attributes. However, no matter how sophisticated the conquest of measurement techniques (and the analytic hardware described in this book is impressive), it is in itself a hollow victory that leaves the contemporary scientist wanting. The new genre of cognitive psychologists are moving beyond the protocol domain of refined data collection. Behavioral measurements are not passé, but with the development of a sophisticated technology other topics are more actively addressed. Indeed, it is partly *because* a dazzling technology has emerged that a greater proportion of the scientist's energy can be devoted to the conceptual structure of the mind rather than the form of data-gathering procedures. The consequence is that observations are not viewed as scientific conclusions but as means to validate notions of rational order among operationally defined concepts. This volume, based on the last of a series of three symposia on cognitive psychology, monitors a bit of the above-mentioned scientific history.

The first of these symposia on cognitive psychology brought together representatives from the diverse corners of cognitive psychology; the second symposium convened specialists in memory and concept formation, whereas this book has chapters by scientists interested in cognition and information processing as it relates to the general topics of perception, memory, and language. This volume is based on the third Loyola Symposium on Cognitive Psychology held on April 30 and May 1, 1974 in Chicago. The format was similar to the preceding symposia in that distinguished psychologists were invited to present their current views on information processing and cognition during the two-day meeting. At the end of each day an informal exchange of ideas was held. An edited transcript of those discussions is presented in this book.

The topics of this symposium fall into three major groups, but I would not quarrel with another taxonomy. The first section is concerned with the issues of perception and initial processing of visual material; the second section is addressed to problems of storage, retrieval, and consciousness in memory; the final section is related to the processing of language. This organizational plan is suggestive of an overall information-processing model: starting at the perceptual stages through early processing of inmation, to memory stores and consciousness, and then including transformation of information into linguistic codes. This rude pattern of information processing and cognition is unrelated to any notion that some properties are basic and others are esoteric, but is only a convenient semantic organization based on a temporal structure.

In the first chapter Estes has proposed a serious model of how memory and perceptual factors influence single-letter identification. The nature of his model is that stimuli are processed through several interrelated filters and that contextual input "combines multiplicatively with stimulus input to determine the output of each level of the succession of filters, and thus to control response selection." Mark Mayzner's chapter on visual information processing, based on 10 years of research, is an ambitious and spectacular effort in which new perceptual–cognitive phenomena are disclosed. By using a computer-based cathode ray tube, Mayzner describes his discovery of specialized forms of sequential blanking, sequential displacement, dynamic visual movement, and subjective color experiences and has opened the door to a new concept in research technology based on stimuli completely foreign to the human subject. Chapter 3 by Posner and Snyder is on attention and cognitive control. They methodologically distinguish between automatic activation processes, which are the result of learning, and processes that are under current conscious control. This historically vexing distinction is given fresh insight as reflected in their data. The final chapter in the first section was written by Roger Shepard. It is Shepard's most comprehensive theoretical statement to date on internal representations and their transformations and represents a decade of research. I am delighted that Professor Shepard has allowed us to print this very important chapter in our series.

The second section of this book contains chapters by Bjork, Murdock and R. Anderson, Battig, and Mandler. Bjork looks at retrieval as a memory modifier in which negative recency is evaluated in terms of its modifying effect on retrieval. Murdock and R. Anderson consider the topic of encoding, storage, and retrieval of item information. Specifically, Murdock and Anderson are concerned with retrieval from subspan lists and superspan lists. Not only will the reader be interested in their detailed experiments, but they also will find a thorough review of retrieval literature. Battig's chapter admonishes us to beware of a "band-wagon" effect and not be seduced by a harpy's fair cry, only to discover the traditional investigatory procedures are based on valid assumptions. His article and defense of his position (see Discussion, Sections I and II) caused us all to reflect on the "new paradigm" in psychology. Finally, Mandler has reactivated the important and sometimes forgotten topic of consciousness and made us consider it as "respectable, useful, and probably necessary."

The final section of this books deals with the general topic of language and cognition. John Anderson has given us the opportunity to publish his first report in a new series of papers on computer simulation of a language acquisition system. By reducing the constraints of the relationships between sentences and their semantic referents, Anderson has developed a computer program in which language acquisition is, at least in part, simulated. In his presentation one can sense the agony and frustration in his attempt to specify the semantic features used to constrain the syntactic form of a natural language. Anderson's courage in tackling a complex problem may have been contagious, as Walter Kintsch in the previous chapter explores the labyrinth of text memory. His penetrating analysis may well serve as a much-needed bridge between memory theorists and verbal learners, with psycholinguists passing over the structure without a toll. Starting from the standpoint of a recognition model for list learning, he has concluded that list memory and text memory differ not in the memory process assumed, but only in the greater number of processing levels involved in text reading than in list reading. Kintsch's detailed analysis will provide a useful model for the intricate problem of memory for items and memory for text. Speech production of adults and children is the topic of David McNeill's chapter. He finds support for the theory that a child's minimal unit of speech production is organized by means of action schemas by which he acquires knowledge about his world. Tom Trabasso and Christine Riley's chapter on the construction and use of symbols in linear order deals with the representation and operation of knowledge, a central topic in cognitive psychology. Specifically, they are concerned with how subjects construct internal representations from partial knowledge and how subjects use the representation in solving a problem.

Loyola University solely supported this symposium and in so doing has reflected the highest ideals of education: to provide an open arena for the free discussion of ideas. The final editing of this book was done while I was a Visting Scholar at Stanford University, and I am indebted to Richard Atkinson, who not only made my visit to Stanford possible, but highly enjoyable.

Many friends assisted me in the symposium and the development of this book. Homer and Barbara Johnson constantly supported our efforts, Joe King attended to numerous details in the development of the symposium, and Christine Patelski, that Joan of Arc of secretaries, performed miracles on my behalf. The staff of LEA has labored diligently on this book, and their effort is appreciated. Finally, Mary O'Brien has assisted the editor in many ways from the first day of the symposium until the completion of the book. Her steadfast council is deeply appreciated.

I am most grateful to each of the 50 contributors to the symposia, and it is with no small degree of nostalgia that I close this series. I have tried to present a forum for the best ideas in cognitive psychology; now, it is in your hands.

ROBERT L. SOLSO
Stanford University

SECTION I

1

MEMORY, PERCEPTION, AND DECISION IN LETTER IDENTIFICATION

W. K. Estes
The Rockefeller University

INTRODUCTION

The process of reading doubtless seems to hold few mysteries from the viewpoint of a normal adult who ingests large quantities of printed material during almost every waking hour but who has never had occasion to study this form of behavior in the laboratory. A commonsense view which, up to a point, cannot be far from the truth would have it that one reads by seeing letters and remembering the meanings of combinations of letters which make up words. Ease of reading clearly depends on two classes of conditions: (1) physical parameters such as type size, illumination, and viewing time; and (2) familiarity of the material. What has been added to this account by nearly 100 years of experimental and theoretical research?

Two lines of investigation conducted essentially in parallel over the entire history of research on reading have served to quantify and spell out in detail the contributions of these two types of factors to performance.

1. Perceptual variables. The very first laboratory studies of reading established a fundamental fact that determined much of the subsequent course of investigation, namely, that a reader's eyes move along a line of type in a series of discrete jumps, "saccades," and that information intake is limited to the brief pauses between saccades (Erdmann & Dodge, 1898). The natural next step, an effort to measure the amount of information

3

processed during a brief exposure of printed material, yielded the surprising result that the maximum is much below what would be expected on the basis of properties of the visual system. When an array of 10–20 letters is exposed under conditions such that resolvable images of all of the letters are generated on the retina, only 4 or 5 can be reported.

There ensued an enormous volume of research, which we shall not attempt to review here, addressing this problem via the strategy of elucidating the determinants of perceptibility of an individual letter in a brief display. It has become clear that perceptibility is determined jointly by the distance of a letter from its neighbors and from the fixation point (Estes & Wolford, 1971; Korte, 1923; Ruediger, 1907; Shaw, 1969) and by the confusability on both stimulus and response dimensions between a given letter and others in the display (Eriksen & Eriksen, 1974; Eriksen & Hoffman, 1973; Estes, 1972a, 1974). The body of theory growing out of this work helps to explain the limitations on processing from single fixations of printed material, yet is grossly incomplete in that it does not take account of the type of material being processed.

2. Linguistic variables.   Some of the earliest studies of tachistoscopic perception showed level of report to depend on familiarity of the material. Thus Cattell (1885) showed that in an exposure of the order of 10 msec about 3–4 unrelated letters could be reported, 2 short unconnected words, or 4 short connected words; thus a variation of four to one in the number of letters effectively processed must be attributed to linguistic properties of the letter array.

Research conducted much later under the influence of information theory showed that the explanation of this variation need not depend on the familiarity of words as units but rather has to do with familiarity of constituent letter sequences. Miller, Bruner, and Postman (1954), studying tachistoscopic presentations of eight-letter pseudowords constituting varying degrees of approximation to English, showed that the number of letters reportable increased uniformly as a function both of order of approximation to English and of exposure duration. Continuation of this line of research has established that an individual who has extensive familiarity with the letter combinations that frequently occur in printed material is able to reconstitute these even when they are imperfectly perceived and thus, in effect, to overcome limitations of perception by sophisticated guessing strategies. A similar interpretation may well account for the effects of familiarity of background material on visual detection (Hermann & McLaughlin, 1973) and visual search (Krueger, 1970).

One implication of these studies of sequential constraints on letter combinations in meaningful text, which raises serious problems for research on perception, is that an individual who makes use of his familiarity with these constraints may often correctly identify letters that are embedded in words even when he cannot actually perceive them. This possibility is brought out clearly, for example, in a study of Lefton (1973) in which seven-letter strings of 0–4 order approximation to English were prepared, then a letter deleted at random from each string; subjects whose task was to guess the letter omitted from each string performed significantly above chance and with accuracy that increased systematically with the order of approximation to English of the string.

It is clear also that aspects of words other than sequential probabilities of their constituent letters can provide clues to recognition. A voluminous literature on tachistoscopic word perception (reviewed by Woodworth, 1938, and Neisser, 1967) has elucidated the role of such factors as word length, overall contours of upper- and lower-case letters, and internal pattern. If I am reading about animals in dim light and encounter a rather long word with an upward projecting letter near the beginning and a downward projecting letter near the end I may well come up with the correct identification of the word "antelope" even though I have seen none of the letters clearly.

There are doubtless many practical situations in which these inferential processes are a considerable aid to reading, yet it is equally sure that in many other situations reading must depend primarily upon the identification of individual letters. If my task is to make out the names of country towns on a road map or to discover how to spell unfamiliar words by perusing a dictionary, general linguistic and orthographic properties of words will have little to contribute, and I will have to depend largely upon the identification of individual letters.

But even in situations where inferential processes are of little account, linguistic context may facilitate reading by aiding the individual to overcome limitations of memory. Thus, Woodworth (1938) cites the persisting reports by subjects in tachistoscopic experiments that they have the impression of being able to see all of the letters of a long word or nonword letter string distinctly, even though they cannot always subsequently report all that they have seen. If the letters presented are unrelated, then some of them may be lost from memory during the interval when the individual is organizing his verbal report, whereas if the letters constitute a meaningful word the representation of the word in memory will be activated and can be readily maintained.

This presumed disparity between what is perceived and what can be reported has been more rigorously documented by the partial report technique of Sperling (1960) and others. On the other hand the disparities are not as large as subjects' introspective reports might have us believe.

Studies by Townsend, Taylor, and Brown (1971) and Estes, Allmeyer, and Reder (1974) show clearly that such factors as position of letters in the visual field and interletter spacing set distinct limits on what can be reported from a single fixation even with viewing time so prolonged that limitations of memory cannot be an appreciable factor.

From the main results of these two lines of investigation, running from the pioneering studies of Cattell in the 1880s down to the most recent extensive survey of the literature by Neisser in 1967, we could conclude that an individual's ability to identify letters in printed text is limited by a number of perceptual factors and that these limitations can be overcome to some extent by inferential processes based on knowledge of the linguistic and orthographic properties of the language. Also it had become clear that any task situation that can be used to evaluate performance in identifying letters or words involves memory as well as perception and that limitations of short-term memory may also be overcome in part by the utilization of linguistic context. But there remained the central question of whether perceptual and linguistic processes involved in reading are basically independent. That is, once the contributions of linguistic context by way of inferential processes and aids to short-term memory have been partialed out, is it the case that letters embedded in words can be more readily or more clearly perceived than letters that occur alone or in meaningless context?

APPARENT EFFECTS OF WORD CONTEXT
ON PERCEPTION OF LETTERS

By the early 1950s it seemed quite well established that the effects of linguistic variables on letter identification could be accounted for in terms of two factors: the function of these variables in providing the basis for inference that could supplement deficiencies of perception, and the function of helping to overcome limitations of short-term memory. This picture remained essentially undisturbed for more than a decade. Then interest in the possibility of some deeper interaction between linguistic and perceptual processes was sharply reawakened upon the appearance of the study of Reicher (1969). This investigation was the first to provide effective controls for the inferential role of redundancy and seemed to provide evidence that linguistic context could facilitate the perception of letters even when factors having to do with response strategies and limitations of memory were ruled out.

The procedure of Reicher's study involved only a slight modification of the partial report techniques that had proliferated since the innovations of Sperling (1960) and Averbach and Coriell (1961). On each trial the subject viewed for a few msec a display that comprised either a single letter, a four-letter word, or a string of four unrelated letters. Immediately after the exposure, the subject was queried as to which of two target letters he had seen in a designated location in the display. The essence of the design was a rule, which I shall denote the WW–NN control, for making up the word and nonword letter strings in such a way that the subject could not improve his performance by utilizing redundant information from the context of a word to improve his guesses on trials when he had failed clearly to perceive the target letter.

The control was achieved by making up the word and nonword displays in such a way that, in the former case, either of the two target letters offered as response alternatives on a trial would complete a word, whereas in the latter case, neither target letter would produce a word. Thus, if the target letters for a trial were M and R, an acceptable word display would be COME and an acceptable nonword display would be VTMU. With this technique Reicher found that target letters embedded in words were identified significantly more often than letters embedded in nonword strings or letters presented alone, the latter two conditions being approximately equal.

Various control measures included in Reicher's experiment, a systematic followup by Wheeler (1970), and continuations by Smith and Haviland (1972) and Baron and Thurston (1973) seemed to dispose of alternative interpretations in terms of effects of linguistic context on short-term memory, pronounceability of words versus nonwords, and the like. Also, the latter two studies showed that the word effect could not be attributed solely to redundant information in a word context but depended also on conformity to spelling rules and orthographic regularities that differentiate words from random letter strings. The only viable explanation of the word advantage seemed to be some variation of a "unitization hypothesis," that is, the idea that perception of features of words of a higher order than those of the constituent letters interacts with the lower-level process of extracting information from individual letters (Smith & Haviland, 1972; Wheeler, 1970).

DETECTION PROCEDURES AND REVIVAL OF THE REDUNDANCY HYPOTHESIS

However, alternative interpretations, even when laid to rest, often fail to rest quietly. In this instance the interpretation of the word advantage in terms of redundancy was brought back to life when several investigators

(Bjork & Estes, 1973; Massaro, 1973; Thompson & Massaro, 1973) noted that the adequacy of the WW–NN control employed in the studies of Reicher and successors depends on one's theoretical interpretation of the process of letter identification.

The control can be considered adequate if one is correct in assuming, as Reicher evidently did, that on trials when the subject receives only a degraded and therefore ambiguous input from the location of a target letter, he is able to maintain a representation of this ambiguous input in memory until the target alternatives for the trial are presented and he can determine which alternative best matches the ambiguous representation. Since, on this assumption, at the time when comparison is made the subject has been restricted to two response alternatives by the presentation of the postexposure cue, redundant information from context can contribute nothing further by way of restricting his choices. If the assumption is correct, it should also follow that the comparison between a memory representation and the target alternatives in the postcue will be more difficult if the latter are made more similar to each other. But Thompson and Massaro found no effect of similarity of the target alternatives.

The hypothesis arises, therefore, that the assumption is incorrect and that, rather, the subject must during or immediately following the display synthesize on the basis of information from the display a set of letters that are compatible with what he has seen and then maintain this set of "candidate" letters in short-term memory until the postcue appears and he carries out the comparison to determine whether either of the cued target letters is included in his candidate set. On this interpretation, information from linguistic context would be clearly of advantage, serving in the case of a word display to restrict the subject's candidate set to letters that would complete a word and thus to exclude from the candidate set other letters that would necessarily lead to errors. By restricting his choices to letters that, on the basis of context, might possibly be correct, the subject would do better when forced to guess than he would do in the absence of redundant information, as would be the case with nonword or single-letter displays.

An obvious implication of this alternative hypothesis is that if the target letters were known to the subject in advance of a trial, then redundant information would have nothing to contribute by way of restricting his response alternatives and the word advantage should disappear. A series of studies from several laboratories investigated the effect of presenting target alternatives in advance (a forced-choice detection procedure), and with one exception (the precue condition of Reicher, 1969) all yielded the result that the word advantage disappears and that letters presented alone are better detected than letters embedded in either word or nonword strings

(Bjork & Estes, 1973; Estes, Bjork, & Skaar, 1974; Massaro, 1973; Thompson & Massaro, 1973).

THE POSTEXPOSURE PROBE TECHNIQUE

Testing the Redundancy Hypothesis

Of the two hypotheses that seemed a year ago to be real contenders for an interpretation of the word advantage, that is, unitization and redundancy, the latter has the advantage of being relatively directly testable. The basic assumption is that the subject uses redundant information from context to restrict the response alternatives from which he chooses when information from the target location in the display is incomplete. With the forced-choice procedure of the preceding studies, whether the target alternatives are made known to the subject before or after the display on a trial, one can only infer via arguments based on one or another theoretical framework how the subject uses redundant information.

But suppose we change the usual procedure by presenting a display, then in the postcue simply indicating a position and asking the subject what he believes he saw there. Now, on trials when information from the target location is incompletely perceived, we can get a picture of the distribution of errors that subjects make and from the error distribution determine how the subjects restrict their guesses on the basis of redundant information.

This idea was the basis of an experiment recently conducted in my laboratory (Estes, 1975, Exp. IIA). In this study, the subject was presented during each 72-trial block with a sequence of displays in which words, nonwords, and single letters occurred equally often in a random sequence. The display types are illustrated in the left-hand column of Table 1. All trials began with the display of a row of noise characters that resembled $ signs, shown in the top row for each of the three conditions. Then on a single-letter (S) trial, a single letter appeared in one of the four locations, the other positions being filled with noise characters that resembled # signs, this display remaining in view for 50 msec. Then the display was replaced by the postmask, the same row of $ characters as the premask, except that an upward pointing arrow appeared under one of the four $s, indicating the location whose contents the subject was to report. On a word (W) trial, the sequence of events was the same except that during the 50-msec display, the row of $ characters was replaced by a four-letter word. Similarly, on nonword (N) trials, the 50-msec display presented a string of four unrelated letters.

The subject had no advance information as to what letter might be cued on any trial, except that it might be any letter of the alphabet. However,

TABLE 1
Design and Percentages of Correct Responses
by Display Condition for Probe Experiment
with Simultaneous Context

Trial	Condition	% Correct
S	$ $ $ $ # # L # $ $ $ $	59
W	$ $ $ $ C O L D $ $ $ $	69
NW	$ $ $ $ O D L C $ $ $ $	63

in the makeup of a display series, one-fourth of the trials, equally distributed over the three display types, were programmed as "L–R" trials. On these trials, the probed letter was either an L or an R, the two occurring equally often; on W trials in this subsequence, all displays were so chosen that either an L or an R would produce a word, and on N trials neither an L nor an R would produce a word. Thus for this subsequence of trials, the WW–NN control introduced by Reicher was in effect, and the analyses reported here will be based only on these trials.

The overall result in terms of percentage of correct reports for each display condition, shown in the right-hand column of Table 1, indicates only that with this probe procedure we reproduce closely the main result of the Reicher and Wheeler studies, namely, an advantage for words over both nonwords and single letters with the latter two conditions not differing significantly.

Proceeding to a finer analysis of the data, our first question is what happens on error trials with regard to the letters that subjects use as guesses. From the standpoint of the redundancy hypothesis, the W versus N comparison is of principal relevance. If the subjects utilize redundant information from context in generating their guesses on trials when information from the target location is ambiguous, they should so restrict their choices as to generate a higher proportion of Ls and Rs as errors on W trials than on N trials. This analysis of the data reveals the observed probabilities of occurrence of Ls and Rs as errors on W and N trials to be .02 and .04, respectively.

These values are not far from those that would be expected if the subjects were drawing letters at random from the full alphabet on these trials, and comparing W versus N, we find that the values do not even differ in the direction predicted by the redundancy hypothesis. Thus we have no shred of support for the idea that subjects utilize redundant information from W displays to restrict their choices to letters that would complete words. It appears then that the observed advantage for W over N displays signifies an interaction between linguistic and perceptual processes which cannot be accounted for on the basis of inference or response biases based on redundant information from context.

The Locus of Contextual Effects

To deal with the probe task, the subject must process item and position information, then collate this information and bring it to bear on his response decision. We might hope that further analysis of types of errors will provide clues as to the point in this sequence of events at which linguistic context exerts its effects.

The distribution of three principal types of errors, L-R errors, other intrusion errors, and omissions, for the W versus S comparison, shown in Fig. 1, seems to point in the direction of an effect at the level of interpretation or decision. Target letters embedded in words have no advantage

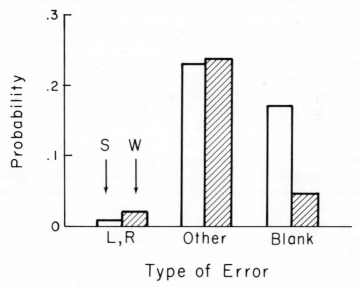

FIG. 1.   Analysis of errors in single-letter (S) versus word (W) comparison for postexposure probe experiment (Estes, 1975). Probability estimates are based on proportions of each type of error relative to total number of response opportunities.

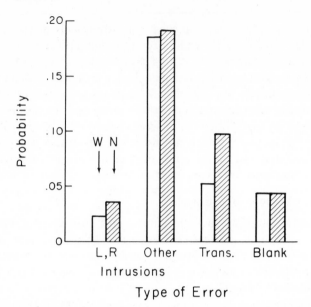

FIG. 2.   Error analysis for word (W) versus nonword (N) comparison of postexposure probe experiment (Estes, 1975).

over single letters with respect either to L–R errors or other intrusions. The advantage in terms of proportion of correct responses comes entirely from the difference in omission errors, suggesting that on S trials, in the absence of the context provided by adjacent letters in the W displays, the individual is less likely to generate letter name responses on the basis of incomplete information. On the other hand, on trials when the subject does generate a letter response to the postexposure probe, his likelihood of being correct is virtually equal on W and S trials.

A first glance at Fig. 2, showing the error breakdown for the W versus N comparison, might suggest that in this case the same interpretation does not apply, for the two types of displays do not differ with respect to frequency of omission errors. Neither, however, do they differ appreciably with respect to frequency of intrusion errors, which would be the principal index of change in discriminability or signal to noise ratio. The only significant difference between W and N displays, and one that accounts for a great part of the difference in correct responding, can be localized in the frequency of transposition errors.

As a first step toward interpreting these differences, we recall that the WW–NN control governed the displays on trials when the target was L or R. Consequently, the performance measure which, like the percentage of correct responses in Reicher's study, should be entirely free of effects of different response strategies, is the percentage of correct identifications on the L–R trials when the subject made either an L or an R response to the probe. This measure yields the strikingly high values of 99, 97, and 94, respectively, for the S, W, and N trials of the probe experiment— quite a different picture from the overall correct response percentages of Table 1.

This result presents us with a bit of a puzzle. A word context does not exert its effect by narrowing the subject's range of response alternatives as predicted from the redundancy hypothesis, but neither, evidently, does it increase the discriminability of the target alternatives. How, then, does the context enter into the process of response determination? An answer that appears to fit our entire pattern of findings is that context is a principal determiner of the extent to which the subject's response is based on stimulus input from the target location as opposed to other aspects of the display.

It might be thought that response to a position probe would always be based on the cued location, but there is substantial evidence to the contrary (Bjork & Estes, 1971; Eriksen & Hoffman, 1973; Eriksen & Eriksen, 1974). When, for example, subjects in a detection experiment are asked to indicate the location of the signal letter within a tachistoscopic display, they generate orderly uncertainty gradients which may span several degrees of visual angle around the true position (Bjork & Estes, 1971). Conversely, when a subject in a probe experiment is asked, following a display, to report what he saw in a specified location, there must be a gradient of uncertainty with regard to his memory for the positions of letters which appeared in or near the probed location.

Consider now the distribution of inputs that may occur on single-letter trials in the probe experiment. On some trials the input will be degraded but will still include some features of the target letter; since these features belong also to other letters, the result will be a mixture of correct responses and intrusion errors. On the remaining trials, the input will be uninterpretable and the response either a sheer guess or an omission error.

When the target letter is embedded in a nonword string, the situation is different. On a trial when the target letter yields an uninterpretable input, other letters in the display may be identified; and if the locations are ambiguous, the subject may reply to the probe with the name of a letter from a neighboring location, thus generating a transposition error.

When the display is a word and only letters other than the target are identified, these may constitute a regular orthographic pattern or spelling group, which will provide auxiliary information as to the location whose contents should be read out in response to the probe. In consequence, responses will more often be based on input from the correct location in the case of word than in nonword contexts.

A number of implications of this analysis are tested in a follow-up study recently conducted in my laboratory (Estes, 1975, Exp. IIB and IIC).

The idea was to change the display sequence on W and N trials in such a way as to make full information concerning the identities and positions of the nontarget letters available to the subject. The design and procedures were the same as in the experiment just described, except for the way in which the displays themselves and the postcue conditions were handled. In this experiment, the displays on all trials were identical to those of the S condition of the preceding experiment; that is, a target letter, which for the data to be reported was always an L or an R, was embedded in a row of # noise characters. The sequence of events on an S trial was the premask, consisting of a row of $s, then a 50-msec display, then the postmask, which was identical to the premask except that in the location corresponding to the target letter the $ was replaced by a #. For example,

$$\begin{array}{cccc} \$ & \$ & \$ & \$ \\ \# & \# & L & \# \\ \$ & \$ & \# & \$. \end{array}$$

A W trial was identical except for the postmask condition; the postmask comprised a four-letter word, except that the location corresponding to the target letter was filled with a #. For example,

$$\begin{array}{cccc} \$ & \$ & \$ & \$ \\ \# & \# & L & \# \\ F & O & \# & D. \end{array}$$

And similarly, on an N trial, the premask and display were identical, but the postmark consisted of a # in the position of a target character flanking by unrelated letters. For example,

$$\begin{array}{cccc} \$ & \$ & \$ & \$ \\ \# & \# & L & \# \\ D & F & \# & O. \end{array}$$

In all conditions the subject understood that his task at the end of each trial was to report the letter that had appeared in the position corresponding to the # in the postmask.

It was expected that, under these circumstances, positional uncertainty would be equalized over the S, W, and N contexts, since there would be no difference among conditions with respect to stimulus input during the exposure of the target letter. Neither would there be any basis for greater than chance incidence of transposition errors on N trials. Correct response frequency on W and N trials should diverge from the frequency obtaining on S trials only to the extent that the W and N contexts influence subjects'

TABLE 2
Percentages of Correct Responses by Condition
for Probe Experiment with Context
Following Exposure of Displays

	Context condition	
Display type	Immediately following	Delayed
S	57	68
W	61	66
NW	51	65

guessing strategies on trials when input from the display is too degraded to yield identification of the target letter.

The overall correct response data obtained for this procedure are given in the column of Table 2 labeled "Immediately following" under Context condition. As in the case of the preceding experiment, we limit consideration to the set of trials on which L or R were the target letters.

Again we have a substantial and significant advantage for target letters embedded in words over those presented alone or embedded in nonword strings. But the percentage of correct identifications on trials when the responses were either L or R yields a pattern differing appreciably from that obtained when the W or N context was simultaneous with the target letter. The value of 97 for S trials was virtually unchanged, as would be expected, but the values for W and N trials drop to 89 and 92, respectively. The reason for the drop is presumably a tendency on the part of the subjects to fill perceptual gaps by choosing response letters that complete words. Further evidence for this strategy is seen in the percentage of intrusion errors that were either Ls or Rs; this measure differed little from the preceding experiment for the S and N displays, 7 and 16%, respectively, but rose to 31% for W displays. The different expected frequencies of correct guesses entailed by the observed difference in L–R intrusion errors is sufficient to account entirely for the advantage of W over S displays with respect to percentage of correct responses.

Evidently we may conclude that subjects do employ the strategy of utilizing redundant information from context to guide response selection when the context is fully available at the time of choice. But they do not, perhaps cannot, do so when the context is available only during a brief tachistoscopic display, as in our probe experiment with simultaneous context and presumably also under the conditions of Reicher's study.

In the "Following" Context condition, the incidence of transposition errors was substantially reduced, as anticipated, but still differed significantly between W and N displays, 1 and 6%, respectively. Thus the advantage in correct responding for W and N displays apparently involves two distinct factors: the excess of L–R intrusions on W trials, presumably representing guesses based on redundant information, and a greater tendency for responses to be based on stimulus input from the target location in W than in N displays.

In the second part of this experiment, for which results are shown in the right-hand column of Table 2, we wished to determine whether the differences between S, W, and N conditions would disappear if the context were delayed until after the process of generating a letter name on the basis of display information was well under way. The design and procedures were idential to those of the first part of the experiment except that the postmask, which included the W or N context in those conditions, was delayed for 200 msec following the target display, the interval being filled with exposure of a row of $\#$ masks. Thus, for example, in the W condition, the sequence of events on a trial might be

$$\$ \; \$ \; \$ \; \$$$
$$\# \; \# \; L \; \#$$
$$\# \; \# \; \# \; \#$$
$$C \; O \; \# \; D.$$

It was expected that the process of generating a letter-name response would be initiated under identical conditions during the target display on S, W, and N trials, but that on occasions when the information from the target location was insufficient to identify the letter, the uncoded representation in memory would be lost during the 200-msec delay interval and that, since the subject's task was to report what he had seen, the process of generating a name response would not be restarted upon the appearance of the post-display context. The data show an overall increase in level of correct responding, doubtless owing to the ineffectiveness of a row of $\#$s as a post-mask (Bjork & Estes, 1973; Estes, Bjork, & Skaar, 1974), but the differences in performance among the three conditions disappear as do differences in the various types of errors.

AN INTERPRETATION OF THE ROLE
OF POSITIONAL UNCERTAINTY

In a provisional model I have outlined to account for the processing of feature information from letter displays, the positional uncertainty in subjects' reports is assumed to arise as a consequence of the limited number of input channels from the retina to feature detectors, the density of these channels decreasing from the fovea toward the periphery (Estes, 1972a). I would not, of course, identify these channels with fixed anatomical entities, but nonetheless the basic ideas of the model can be readily captured by thinking of channels as spatially distributed.

In these terms, feature information coming from locations that are sufficiently close together in the visual field must utilize the same channel, and in this event the individual will be uncertain as to the location of the source. Thus even when letters are clearly perceived at locations away from the fixation point, their relative positions may be uncertain. In the case of meaningful text, linguistic and orthographic rules help to resolve these uncertainties; but in the case of the unrelated letter strings often used in tachistoscopic experiments, errors representing inversions of the order of letters in a sequence should be expected to occur relatively frequently. Consequently, we should predict that linguistic context would selectively improve performance on ordered report as distinguished from item report.

This implication of our analysis can be illustrated in terms of some data from a study by Estes, Allmeyer, and Reder (1974). The study involved report of 4-letter strings presented tachistoscopically at locations slightly to the left or right of a fixation point. Display durations were 150 and 2400 msec, but with the subject being confined to a single fixation in the latter case by a procedure of monitoring eye movements. The three subjects were extremely experienced and understood that their task was to report all of the letters that they saw, even when uncertain, but not to make guesses that were not based on what they had seen. The displays were random strings of four consonants.

In the analysis of the report data that is immediately relevant, we considered all pairs of adjacent consonants in the display. For each of these digrams, we computed from the tables in Underwood and Shulz (1960) an index we might term a familiarity ratio (FR), indicating the relative frequency with which a given digram occurs in English text in the given order as compared to the reversed order. We expect that errors that result from inverting the order of letters in a digram will be systematically related to familiarity ratio, and such indeed proves to be the case.

To take a few examples, the digram comprising the letters C and H occurs virtually 100% of the time in the order CH in English text (FR = 1.00), and in our data occurrences of the diagram HC were incorrectly reported as CH 37% of the time by our subjects. Similarly for the digram CL (FR = .92) there were 22% inversion errors. On the other hand, the digrams TS and NR have FRs equal to .09 and .08, and these yielded inversion errors only 6 and 7% of the time, respectively. Considering a substantial block of data (pooled over exposure durations) constituting 22,680 observations from a total of 105 sessions, we obtained a point correlation of $-.27$ between FR and frequency of reversal errors, the associated χ^2 being significant at the 5% level. In contrast, a correlation of FR with frequency of report of the same digrams (scored only for correctness of the items without regard to order) yielded a correlation of virtually zero and a χ^2 that does not approach significance.

This result should of course be interpreted with regard to the experimental context. If subjects were encouraged or required to guess in the absence of perceptual information, they might well produce in their reports more digrams with high familiarity ratios. But when they understand the task to be that of reporting what they see in letter displays, then it appears that the identification of the constituent letters of digrams is independent of familiarity, but the accuracy in reporting these in the order actually presented is significantly related to the frequency of the particular digram order in English text.

LEVELS OF INFORMATION PROCESSING

On the basis of the preceding review of experimental approaches and results we can identify a number of clearly defined levels at which information abstracted from displays of characters is integrated and brought to bear upon decision and response selection.

1. Feature differences between two predesignated characters. In experiments conducted with the forced-choice detection procedure in which the target set is constant throughout a series of trials, it is not necessary for the subject actually to identify any characters in the display but only to arrive at a decision as to which of two already known alternatives is present. The task reduces to detection of the feature or features that differentiate the target characters. Studies utilizing this procedure have revealed no effects of linguistic context beyond those that clearly operate at the level of response bias (Estes, 1975).

2. Identification of letters. In a detection task with a pre- or postcue for the target item, the information required for a response is identification of a letter without regard to position. One of the few clear-cut examples in the literature is the study of Wheeler (1970) which yielded an advantage for word over single-letter displays. The interpretation of Wheeler's experiment is complicated by the fact that in two of his three conditions, the target letter appeared always at the fixation point, and, since no nonword displays were included, there was no control for possible facilitative effects of metacontrast (Matthews & Henderson, 1971).

Some studies of report of tachistoscopically presented letter strings may belong in the same category, particularly if the task orientation is strictly directed to the identification of letters rather than the identification of words as units. The study of Estes, Allmeyer, and Reder, cited above, meets these qualifications, and the data suggest that the identification of letters, as distinguished from letter sequences, may be independent of context.

3. Identification of letters in position. Procedures requiring this level of information integration include the report procedure, with scoring for items in position, and detection or probe procedures involving postexposure cues for position of the target element. Data obtained under these conditions quite uniformly reveal effects of linguistic context upon performance, even in the presence of controls for inferential processes and response bias.

4. Identification of letter groups. Studies involving the identification and report of spelling groups, syllables, or words (for example, Aderman & Smith, 1971; Baron, 1974) uniformly yield evidence of facilitating effects of linguistic context. Also, the most marked facilitating effects of context on the identification of single letters is observed in experiments in which the task orientation encourages subjects to identify words as units and to infer the presence of constituent letters in cued positions, even when these have not been individually clearly perceived (Johnston & McClelland, 1973).

A MODEL FOR LEVELS OF INFORMATION PROCESSING IN LETTER IDENTIFICATION

The Memory System:
Control Elements as Filters

I should like now to indicate at least in outline the form of a model that may provide an integrated interpretation of the effects of context at various levels of utilization of information. One of the principal considerations guiding this effort has been the avoidance of *ad hoc* mechanisms brought in solely to explain effects of linguistic variables. Rather, I have attempted to draw upon the body of theory already developed in connection with other phenomena, in particular the concepts of hierarchical associations and control elements (Estes, 1972b) and the interactive filter model of Anderson (1973), which has been proposed as a general framework relating neurophysiological and behavioral aspects of memory.

Some salient aspects of the present model are illustrated in Fig. 3. The control elements, C_F, C_L, C_G, at the levels of features, letters, and letter groups, respectively, correspond to the notion of abstract representations of these entities in long-term memory. However control elements should not be thought of as little pictures in the head but rather simply as control

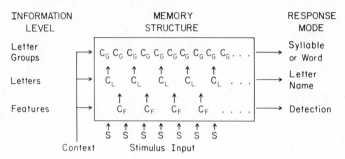

FIG. 3. Schema for memory structures and input–output relations in the multilevel filter model. Cs with subscripts represent control elements at levels of features, characters, and character groups in the memory system.

structures that are sensitive to particular combinations of inputs and which thus serve as gates or filters. The memory structure has somewhat the shape of an hourglass in that the infinite variety of stimulus inputs activates only a limited, and in fact rather small, number of feature detectors; then, proceeding upward, combinations of features activate a larger number of letter representations, and combinations of these in turn activate a much larger number of representations of letter groups.

The effects of stimulus input and context are assumed to combine multiplicatively to determine performance. The notion of context includes both prior events, for example instructions, which influence information processing on a given trial, and also current context, for example letters that surround a target letter in a display. The effects of context are less specific in that contextual variables serve to raise the level of activation of sets of control elements at a given level, the effects of stimulus input then determining which elements of the activated sets reach the threshold of initiating response processes. The information from the stimulus input is filtered through the successive levels of control elements, the output at each level providing a possible basis for response and also the input to the next higher level.

The set of control elements at each level constitutes an interactive filter in the sense of Anderson (1973). That is, a given control element embodies the traces in memory of previous experiences with a particular type of input. Once established, a control element yields output only if it is activated by appropriate contextual factors and at the same time receives a new input that matches the prior input whose traces are embodied in the control structure.

A small section of the schema of Fig. 3 is enlarged in Fig. 4 in order to bring out some properties of the activation process. The latter diagram represents some of the assumed events on a trial when stimulus input from a

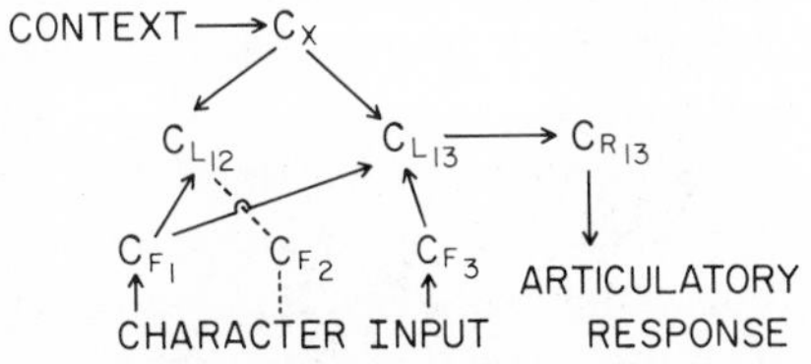

Fig. 4. Amplification of a segment of Fig. 3 with additional detail to illustrate the way in which context and stimulus input combine to determine response. Subscripts on control elements at the character level signify the elements at the feature level whose inputs must combine to yield character identification.

character location leads to activation of a particular letter representation in memory and occurrence of the corresponding naming response. Potential lines of transmission are indicated in the figure by dashed lines, and those actually active on the trial are illustrated by solid lines. Of the feature detectors F_1, F_2, and F_3, only the first and third are activated by the input from the character location. Of the two letter representations shown, $L_{1,2}$ requires inputs from F_1 and F_2, and $L_{1,3}$ inputs from F_1 and F_3; thus on the trial illustrated only $L_{1,3}$ yields an output. The input from the context determines the subset of letters, in this case $L_{1,2}$ and $L_{1,3}$, which constitute acceptable alternatives in the light of prior information, and the stimulus input selects one of these as the basis for a response. The input from context determines also the threshold or response criterion, that is, the level of stimulus input required to generate response output.

Functions of Linguistic Context

A basic assumption in the present model is that the encoding and filtering of stimulus information depends solely upon relationships between the stimulus input and the contents of memory. Context enters the picture as a factor in determining what memory comparisons will be made and in the interpretation of the output of the filtering system. In the process of letter identification, we can localize several specific points at which linguistic context should be expected to exert its effects.

1. Guessing strategies. When the stimulus input is too degraded to provide any basis for decision regarding the target letter, the subject's response may be determined by the context. Our results indicate that the strategy of filling a perceptual gap in a letter array by attempting to choose a letter that completes a word is utilized by subjects when a word context is available at the time of choice but probably cannot be used effectively when the context, as well as the target letter, is available only during a brief tachistoscopic exposure. Further, it appears that effects of this strategy on accuracy of letter identification are adequately excluded by the WW–NN control introduced by Reicher (1969).

2. Response threshold.   We must assume that subjects have a criterion or threshold for generating a letter-name response on the basis of incomplete or ambiguous stimulus input (as opposed to making an omission error or guessing on the basis of factors extrinsic to the stimulus information). Little is known concerning the variables that determine the response threshold, but surely one would expect it to be lower in a familiar context than in an unfamiliar context. Consequently, we assume that the presence of the orthographic regularities or familiar spelling groups of a word context will increase the likelihood that the subject will generate a letter-name response on the basis of ambiguous input from a target letter.

3. Positional uncertainty.   Following a brief display, the subject generally will have some uncertainty regarding both the identity and the location of the target letter, these aspects of the stimulus information having been encoded separately, and, in each case, fallibly. Consequently, at the point when the subject must collate and interpret the output of the filtering process, the regularities of a word context will serve to reduce positional uncertainty and increase the likelihood that the subject's response will be based on item information from the target location.

4. Setting factors.   Prior context, including the background situation and instructions, operates in terms of the model by preactivating the connections of sets of control elements to the response mechanism, and thus determining whether response selection will be based on filter output at the level of features, letters, or letter groups.

INTERPRETATIONS OF EMPIRICAL PHENOMENA

The Word Advantage in Detection and Probe Paradigms

How can the various phenomena having to do with effects of linguistic context be interpreted in terms of the model sketched above? Let us consider first the conditions under which the word advantage appears or fails to appear. We have noted that there is no facilitating effect of linguistic context, and in fact a uniform advantage for single letters over letters embedded in words, when the task is forced-choice detection with the target alternatives known in advance and fixed throughout a series of trials. Under these circumstances, in terms of the model, the control elements corresponding to critical features of the target letters are selectively preactivated by the experimental context, including instructions and effects of experience with preceding trials of a series. Thus the multiplicative effects of input from the context of a character display will be expected to yield a response as soon as a feature that differentiates the two target letters is encountered.

No differential effects of embedding target letters in words versus non-words can be expected because the level of letter identification is not reached before a response is initiated. On the other hand, a single-letter advantage is expected because in the case of single-letter displays there is no possibility that the response will be based on a differentiating feature that actually occurs in a position other than that of the target letter. In a multiple-letter display, it is possible that a feature that differentiates the two target letters may also occur in some of the noise letters, thus constituting a source of confusion errors not present in single-letter displays.

When the target letters vary from trial to trial, whether they are presented in postcues or in precues, and especially if they appear in a different orthography or modality from that of the display, then control elements at the level of letters will be preactivated by the background context and the response criterion will require letter identification. In terms of the model, linguistic context may play a role on trials when stimulus input from the location containing the target letter is ambiguous but input from some of the other locations is sufficient for letter identification. Under these circumstances, a letter group identified from a word context provides information as to which of the remaining locations is likely to contain a particular target letter. The function of the context, then, is to influence the likelihood that the subject's response decision will be based on input from the location that actually contains the target.

When the procedure includes a position cue, whether in a forced-choice or a probe paradigm, positional information from context must combine with feature input to generate a response which identifies a letter in a particular display position. Under this condition linguistic context should always be expected to be relevant, since various properties of words, including familiar letter sequences and orthographic patterns, provide cues to position. In effect the role of context here is to lower the subject's threshold for responding to the location actually containing the target and to raise his threshold for responding to noise locations, thus facilitating accurate performance.

In terms of the model, positional cues, as for example postcue indicators or spaces adjacent to characters, provide sources of contextual input; the amount of this input available to multiply the inputs from feature detectors varies over locations in the visual field and thus serves to influence the probability of responding on the basis of the correct display location on a given trial.

This factor may be modified in rather subtle ways by changes in display conditions. When a display is terminated by a postexposure pattern mask, cues to location of a target letter, particularly in the case of a single-letter display, are limited to those that can be processed during the exposure and maintained in memory until the appearance of a postcue. But if the display is not terminated by a mask, then persisting effects of the stimulus array in the visual system (for example, afterimages) provide additional cues to location and insure that feature input from the target location will have a greater probability of leading to a response than will input from nontarget locations. This differential in contextual input relating to target versus nontarget locations may account for the finding of Johnston and McClelland (1973) of a single-letter advantage when displays were terminated by a uniform bright field but a disadvantage for single letters, as compared to letters embedded in words, when displays were terminated by pattern masks.

Effects of Context on Level of Stimulus Coding

The interpretation of input from a combination of features as indicating the presence of a letter always depends upon both prior and current context. According to the present model the control elements at the letter level must be activated by context in order for response to be based on letter identification. A familiar phenomenon reflecting this aspect of the model is the "hidden figure" in which, for example, letters that fully qualify for identification in terms of their features are nonetheless effectively invisible when embedded in a picture—a context that does not activate control elements at the letter level in the system of interactive filters.

A more formal experimental demonstration of the effect of setting factors is exhibited in the study of Aderman and Smith (1971) in which identification of letters was shown to be better when the letters were embedded in regular spelling patterns than when they were not—provided that the instructions and context led the subjects to expect spelling patterns. In terms of the model, the effect appeared only when control elements at the level of letter groups were preactivated by the context.

It might be noted further that the largest facilitative effects of linguistic context upon detection performance have been reported from studies in which the instructions and the blocking of display types have been such as to encourage subjects to look for words in multiple-letter displays (Johnston & McClelland, 1973; Wheeler, 1970). According to our assumptions, these are the conditions under which control elements for higher-order letter groups will be most readily activated and thus available to provide auxiliary positional information regarding target location.

The various levels of organization of control elements in this system provide alternative routes whereby information originating in character displays can influence responding. In order to permit study of particular aspects of a potentially extremely complex process, it has been necessary to develop experimental paradigms in which instructions and task orientation effectively limit subjects to responding on the basis of a particular level. Thus in detection experiments, conditions are arranged to confine subjects, so far as possible, to responding on the basis of feature differences; in experiments involving either full or partial report of tachistoscopically displayed letter strings, the task orientation is normally chosen to yield responding on the basis of letter identification; and in studies of word identification, the emphasis in the task orientation is upon the identification of letter groups. In each case predisplay context is chosen so as to activate the desired level in the system and to adjust the subject's response criterion appropriately.

But modifications of the customary procedures can make alternative bases of response available in any of these types of experiments. Take for example the forced-choice detection paradigm, which normally leads uniformly to single-letter advantage and no difference between words and nonwords. We have interpreted the absence of effects of linguistic context in this paradigm as a consequence of the fact that input from nontarget locations is not processed to the level of letter identification prior to the initiation of a response based on feature differences. But in a recent study in my laboratory (Estes, 1975) we modified the procedures in the case of word and nonword strings simply by having the contents of nontarget locations remain in view until the subject made his response, although stimulation from the target location terminated at the end of the brief display. Under this circumstance, the characters in nontarget locations would all be processed to the level of letter identification; as anticipated, the result was an advantage for words over nonwords (but only on trials when the WW–NN control was not in effect).

Display Size and Category Effects

Setting factors, operating by way of contextual input, should be expected to provide major determiners of the signal–noise relationships in both detection and search experiments. It has been established by numerous studies that the detectability of a target letter decreases with the number of confusable noise letters present in the same display. And it can be shown that the detrimental effects of the noise letters on performance depend specifically upon the presence of features common to the noise letters and the targets (Estes, 1974).

The interpretation in terms of the filter model is quite straightforward. Suppose on a trial when L_1 is actually the target letter, control elements for two target letters L_1 and L_2 have been preactivated by the pretrial context and that, owing to an abbreviated or degraded display, the stimulus input from the target location activates only a portion of the features associated with L_1. If there were no other characters present in the display, L_1 would nonetheless lead to a response, though with a longer latency than on a trial when the input was not degraded. But if the display contains noise characters that include features associated with L_2, then the effect of an abbreviated display may be the activation of the control elements for both L_1 and L_2 and a consequent high likelihood of a confusion error. If, on the other hand, there were present only noise characters that did not share features with either of the target letters, the noise letters would have no effect, for their encoded inputs would go to control elements at the letter level which had not been preactivated by the prior context.

These considerations provide our interpretation of the finding from visual search experiments (for example, Egeth, Atkinson, Gilmore, & Marcus, 1973) that speed of detection of a target letter decreases as it is embedded in larger numbers of noise letters but is virtually independent of set size if it is embedded in backgrounds of varying numbers of digits. On the average, other letters would be more likely to share features with the target letter than would digits, and this aspect of the situation alone would lead to the observed result in terms of the model.

But, further, it is assumed in the present model that the sets of control elements associated with features of such highly familiar entities as letters and digits are organized into distinct systems. As a consequence, the set of control elements associated with the features of digits is preactivated by instructions or context which lead the subject to anticipate that he will be dealing with digits, and the set associated with features of letters is preactivated if the context has to do with letters. This organization of sets of features into systems that are preactivated as units would be particularly relevant to the study of Jonides and Gleitman (1972), in which a category effect similar to that of Egeth and co-workers was demonstrated, but with the additional feature that the display-size effect for the ambiguous target character O had the usual positive slope when the character was predesignated as a "zero" and embedded in a background of digits but a virtually zero slope when the same character was embedded in the same background but predesignated as a letter.

DISCUSSION

It is clear that even with relatively optimal viewing conditions, familiarity and linguistic properties of material constitute major determiners of performance in reading. How can we summarize the general picture resulting from more than 50 years of research on this problem? Perhaps the most critical and ubiquitous factor, identified by innumerable studies, is the role of prior information regarding the nature of the material. This "setting factor" determines just what entities (letters, letter groups, words) will be recognized as units.

But even during the fixation of a segment of text, properties of surrounding letters influence the speed and accuracy of identification of the letter in a particular position. It has long been known that a familiar context enables the filling in of perceptual gaps by guessing. A principal contribution of research of the last five years has been to show that the function of familiarity goes considerably deeper. A contribution of the present study has been to aid in localizing some specific points of interaction of stimulus and context. In particular, we have shown a role of current linguistic context in resolving uncertainty concerning the spatial location of characters and in furthering the organization of encoded stimulus input into higher units.

In the model proposed here to integrate the numerous findings concerning the role of context, it is assumed that stimulus input from a character display is processed through a series of interactive filters. These filters constitute assemblages of control elements embodying memory traces for features of characters, characters, or character groups that have been encountered in previous experience. Input from context, including both prior context (for example, instructions) and current linguistic context, combines multiplicatively with stimulus input to determine the output of each level of the succession of filters, and thus to control response selection.

In another paper I have presented a mathematical formulation of some aspects of the model (Estes, 1975). Although it must be considered only an exploratory effort, this formulation provides some evidence that the ideas developed here can generate quantitative accounts of error patterns on S, W, and N displays in detection and probe experiments. The task of constructing a formal theory really adequate to comprehend the diverse effects of linguistic variables on letter perception seems formidable to say the least, but it is encouraging to see that some progress can be made.

My principal concern in this essay has been to provide a framework that might permit a relatively uniform organization and integration of the more specific models and concepts that have emerged in current theoretical work to account for various segments of the array of phenomena reviewed here. To touch on a few specific examples, we might note first of all that Turvey's (1973) concurrent–contingent model for peripheral and central visual processes and my interactive channels model (Estes, 1972a) deal with the processing that occurs between the stimulus input and the level of control elements for features in the present model. That of Gardner

(1973) deals in more detail with the process of arriving at response decisions on the basis of outputs from control elements; as presently formulated, Gardner's model operates at the character level, but clearly it could readily be extended to other levels.

The model of Shiffrin and Geisler (1973) and the one just published by Rumelhart and Siple (1974) represent alternative formulations bearing particularly upon the role of confusability among characters in determining the limits of information transmission. Both of these models make assumptions concerning the process of feature extraction and the determination of response by ambiguous inputs, and these assumptions are generally compatible with those of the present model though differing in some details. These models do not take systematic account of effects of context, although Rumelhart and Siple allow subjects' expectations concerning the nature of material to influence the way in which they fill out their gaps in perception by sophisticated guessing. On the whole, there appears to be marked convergence among current theoretical approaches in the manner of distinguishing a number of levels of processing, from the registration of stimulus input through the action of feature detectors to character recognition.

A distinctive aspect of the model outlined here is that it handles in a uniform manner a wide variety of phenomena that have been assigned in the literature to an equally varied array of processes and mechanisms, for example, detection, identification, and recognition; feature detectors, letter representations, and coding of letters into higher-order units. The successive stages of encoding of stimulus information are conceived to arise from successive applications of the same filtering process with the output of each stage constituting the input for the next. And decision or response at each level is conceived to arise in the same way as a result of a process of matching encoded stimulus inputs with corresponding representations of previous inputs in memory. At each level, prior and current context determine the range of alternatives that will be acceptable as a basis for response, but stimulus information provides the basis for selection among these alternatives. Thus context and stimulus input always interact in the determination of response. Nonetheless, perception is in a sense independent of context in that the successive levels of encoding of stimulus information depend solely upon current input together with memory for past inputs and are not directly modified by current context.

ACKNOWLEDGMENTS

The ideas presented here have benefitted from continuing discussions of the problems in this area with many colleagues, in particular Elizabeth L. Bjork, Douglas L. Medin, Stephen M. Reder, and Richard M. Shiffrin.

Researches reported in this paper were supported in part by Grant MH23878 from the National Institute of Mental Health.

REFERENCES

Aderman, D., & Smith, E. E. Expectancy as a determinant of functional units in perceptual recognition. *Cognitive Psychology,* 1971, **2,** 117–129.

Anderson, J. A. A theory for the recognition of items from short memorized lists. *Psychological Review,* 1973, **80,** 417–438.

Averbach, E., & Coriell, A. S. Short-term memory in vision. *Bell Systems Technical Journal,* 1961, **40,** 309–328.

Baron, J. Successive stages in word recognition. In S. Dornic & P. M. A. Rabbitt (Eds.), *Attention and performance.* Vol. 5. New York: Academic Press, 1974.

Baron, J., & Thurston, I. An analysis of the word-superiority effect. *Cognitive Psychology,* 1973, **4,** 207–228.

Bjork, E. L., & Estes, W. K. Detection and placement of redundant signal elements in tachistoscopic displays of letters. *Perception & Psychophysics,* 1971, **9,** 439–442.

Bjork, E. L., & Estes, W. K. Letter identification in relation to linguistic context and masking conditions. *Memory & Cognition,* 1973, **1,** 217–223.

Cattell, J. McK. Über die Zeit der Erkennung und Benennung von Schriftzeichen. *Philosophische Studien,* 1885, **2,** 633–650.

Egeth, H., Atkinson, J., Gilmore, G., & Marcus, N. Factors affecting processing mode in visual search. *Perception & Psychophysics,* 1973, **13,** 394–402.

Erdmann, B., & Dodge, R. *Psychologische Untersuchungen über das Lesen auf experimenteller Grundlage.* Halle: M. Niemeyer, 1898.

Eriksen, B. A., & Eriksen, C. W. Effects of noise letters upon the identification of a target letter in a nonsearch task. *Perception and Psychophysics,* 1974, **16,** 143–149.

Eriksen, C. W., & Hoffman, J. E. The extent of processing of noise elements during selective encoding from visual displays. *Perception & Psychophysics,* 1973, **14,** 155–160.

Estes, W. K. Interactions of signal and background variables in visual processing. *Perception & Psychophysics,* 1972, **12,** 278–286.   (a)

Estes, W. K. An associative basis for coding and organization in memory. In A. W. Melton & E. Martin (Eds.), *Coding processes in human memory.* Washington, D.C.: Winston, 1972.   (b)

Estes, W. K. Redundancy of noise elements and signals in visual detection of letters. *Perception & Psychophysics,* 1974, **16,** 53–60.

Estes, W. K. On the locus of inferential and perceptual processes in letter identification. *Journal of Experimental Psychology,* General, in press, 1975.

Estes, W. K., Allmeyer, D. H., & Reder, S. Serial position functions for letter identification at brief and extended exposure durations. Unpublished manuscript, Rockefeller University, 1974.

Estes, W. K., Bjork, E. L., & Skaar, E. Detection of single letters and letters in words with changing versus unchanging mask characters. *Bulletin of the Psychonomic Society,* 1974, **3,** 201–203.

Estes, W. K., & Wolford, G. L. Effects of spaces on report from tachistoscopically presented letter strings. *Psychonomic Science,* 1971, **25,** 77–80.

Gardner, G. T. Evidence for independent parallel channels in tachistoscopic perception. *Cognitive Psychology*, 1973, **4**, 130–155.

Herrmann, D. J., & McLaughlin, J. P. Language habits and detection in very short-term memory. *Perception & Psychophysics*, 1973, **14**, 483–486.

Johnston, J. C., & McClelland, J. L. Visual factors in word perception. *Perception & Psychophysics*, 1973, **14**, 365–370.

Jonides, J., & Gleitman, H. A conceptual category effect in visual search. O as letter or as digit. *Perception & Psychophysics*, 1972, **12**, 457–460.

Korte, W. Über die Gestaltauffarsung im indirekten Sehen. *Zeitschrift für Psychologie*, 1923, 93, 17–82.

Krueger, L. E. Visual comparison in a redundant display. *Cognitive Psychology*, 1970, **1**, 341–357.

Lefton, L. A. Guessing and the order of approximation effect. *Journal of Experimental Psychology*, 1973, **101**, 401–403.

Massaro, D. W. Perception of letters, words, and nonwords. *Journal of Experimental Psychology*, 1973, **100**, 349–353.

Matthews, M. L., & Henderson, L. Facilitation of foveal letter recognition by meta-contrast. *Psychonomic Science*, 1971, **23**, 153–155.

Miller, G. A., Bruner, J. S., & Postman, L. Familiarity of letter sequences and tachistoscopic identification. *Journal of General Psychology*, 1954, **50**, 129–139.

Neisser, U. *Cognitive psychology*. New York: Appleton-Century-Crofts, 1967.

Reicher, G. M. Perceptual recognition as a function of the meaningfulness of the material. *Journal of Experimental Psychology*, 1969, **81**, 275–280.

Ruediger, W. C. The field of distinct vision. *Archives of Psychology*, 1907, Whole No. 5.

Rumelhart, D. E., & Siple, P. Process of recognizing tachistoscopically presented words. *Psychological Review*, 1974, **81**, 99–118.

Shaw, P. Processing of tachistoscopic displays with controlled order of characters and spaces. *Perception & Psychophysics*, 1969, **6**, 257–266.

Shiffrin, R. M., & Geisler, W. A. Visual recognition in a theory of information processing. In R. L. Solso (Ed.), *Contemporary issues in cognitive psychology: The Loyola symposium*. Washington, D.C.: Winston, 1973.

Smith, E. E., & Haviland, S. E. Why words are perceived more accurately than nonwords: Interference vs. unitization. *Journal of Experimental Psychology*, 1972, **92**, 59–64.

Sperling, G. The information available in brief visual presentations. *Psychological Monographs*, 1960, **74**(11, Whole No. 498).

Thompson, M. C., & Massaro, D. W. Visual information redundancy in reading. *Journal of Experimental Psychology*, 1973, **98**, 49–54.

Townsend, J. T., Taylor, S. G., & Brown, D. R. Lateral masking for letters with unlimited viewing time. *Perception & Psychophysics*, 1971, **10**, 375–378.

Turvey, M. T. On peripheral and central processes in vision: Inferences from an information-processing analysis of masking with patterned stimuli. *Psychological Review*, 1973, **80**, 1–52.

Underwood, B. J., & Schulz, R. W. *Meaningfulness and verbal learning*. New York: Lippincott, 1960.

Wheeler, D. D. Processes in word recognition. *Cognitive Psychology*, 1970, **1**, 59–85.

Woodworth, R. S. *Experimental psychology*. New York: Holt, 1938.

2

STUDIES OF VISUAL INFORMATION PROCESSING IN MAN

M. S. Mayzner
Loyola University of Chicago

INTRODUCTION

When our interest first began to seriously focus on problems of visual system behavior about ten years ago, it occurred to us that possibly the problem of space–time interactions in the visual system might provide a useful methodological strategy to study visual system performance and visual information processing mechanisms. Since at that time a computer-based cathode-ray tube (CRT) display system became available to us, it seemed inevitable that such a computer-based display system could provide us with the display flexibility we required, if we wished to examine space–time interactions and processing mechanisms in ways that had *never* been possible heretofore, because of hardware limitations. Quite specifically, it became increasingly obvious to us that a CRT display, under control of a digital computer, would allow us to present to the visual system strings of sequential stimuli or inputs, at display rates and in geometric configurations, that would be totally unique input events, never experienced before by man's visual system. In this sense then, our methodological strategy was unique, and suggested to us that if we conceptualized the visual system as an information processing system, a common strategy in visual research (DeValois, 1966; Rosenblith, 1961) with a given processing capacity, then it might become reasonable to expect that overloading or "stressing the system" in novel ways might produce a rich variety of space–time interactions.

For example, the most general paradigm for such overloading is to present the visual system with a pair or a string of sequential stimuli or inputs at a display rate that exceeds, the system's spatiotemporal resolving power. If a pair of stimuli is employed, some form of visual masking is typically implicated, whereas with a string of stimuli, interest is usually focused on such issues as the display rate that produces fusion, or on those display parameters that produce an experience of apparent movement. In all of these cases of space–time interactions, the central distinguishing feature is a breakdown of the visual system to provide an output that represents a veridical and isomorphic match to the input. In visual masking paradigms, space–time interactions are revealed by failures of the subject's visual output to match the input, such that, depending on the parameters under investigation, one or both of the inputs may be misperceived, or one input may not even be detected. With strings of stimuli, other types of input–output mismatches may occur, such that if the display rate is high enough and all the stimuli occur at the same location in space, total fusion will occur, or if the stimuli are displayed at different locations, all the stimuli will appear as if they have been displayed simultaneously, when in fact, they have been displayed sequentially. In brief, space–time interactions can produce a rich variety of input–output mismatches, for example: (1) failures of stimuli to be detected, (2) failures in the ability to detect sequential orderings of stimuli, (3) distortions in the spatial locations of stimuli, (4) distortion in the sharpness, clarity, or apparent duration of stimuli, (5) distortions in the relative subjective brightness of stimuli, (6) various experiences of apparent movement, and so on.

In approaches involving an information-flow diagram or model to visual system performance, one is attempting to both identify and conceptualize the "route" or "pathway" through the organism that links input or stimulus to output or response. Thus, in these models we find in the information-flow diagram notations representing the input, functions through which the input "passes" or is "processed," and finally an output. For example, to be specific, DeValois (1966) discusses visual information processing in the following terms:

> The neural activity evoked in the visual receptors by light passes through two or more synapses in the retina, one or more in the thalamus, and a dozen or more in the cortex. At each of these synapses there is a convergence of inputs and some sort of processing of the visual information. By the time the light stimuli are perceived and responded to, the information has passed sequentially through a great many stages of analysis. This fact is not generally considered in theories of vision, which often hypothesize in effect one or, at most, two stages of analysis. The types of data processing which take place at successive stages in the sequence can be investigated by single-cell recording from different levels in the visual system; it can also be tackled in psychophysical

experiments in which successively more complex stimuli and responses are involved. Our discussions of some of these experiments indicate that in the primate visual system one of the earliest, if not the first, stages involves the inhibition of each receptor by every other receptor of its type in the vicinity (adaptation and contrast). We know that in addition there is within the retinal portion of the visual system the summation of neighboring receptors of all types (brightness), and subtraction of the output of receptors of one class from the output of receptors of another class (color), and a simple concentric inhibitory and excitatory spatial organization of nearby cells. The more complex transformations which take place in the primate cortex are less well known but must involve processing with respect to form and movement, as we have mentioned [pp. 87–88].

As DeValois (1966) points out, data processing, or visual information processing, can be investigated at basic physiological levels or "tackled in psychophysical experiments in which successively more complex stimuli and responses are involved [p. 88]." For a variety of reasons we have chosen to employ in our research a large number of psychophysical procedures, varying from very simple reporting of subjective experiences, at one extreme, to more sophisticated procedures, such as the "staircase" method under computer control, at the other extreme, depending on the parameters under investigation, and the degree of quantification we wished to achieve. As Kahneman (1968) has remarked:

> Even informal reports may serve to illuminate complex results, as in Sperling's (1965) analysis of the masking function. Further, reports of subjective experience may become a source of data, as in the studies of metacontrast by Mayzner's group and by Kahneman. The high level of within-subject and between-subject reliability that is easily attained by naive observers justifies the use of this approach in studies of masking [p. 414].

In brief, in this contribution we shall report, selectively, on the major results of almost a decade of research on visual information processing, employing a computer-based CRT display system. Since we already have discussed at some length the earlier findings of our research including a model incorporating these findings (Mayzner & Tresselt, 1970b), I will review the earlier findings very briefly and devote most of my time today to our latest findings. Since the later results will probably require extensive revisions or extensions of our visual information processing model, I shall postpone this discussion for some future time. Before proceeding, however, with the substantive findings of our research over the past decade, it might be useful to describe very briefly our current hardware configuration and associated software package, which will perforce indicate previous hardware limitations and also disclose the very great flexibility of our current system for the study of novel space–time interactions in the visual system.

CURRENT HARDWARE SYSTEM
AND ASSOCIATED SOFTWARE PACKAGE

Our present system consists basically of a computer-based CRT display system. This system consists of a high-speed PDP-7 digital computer, which when appropriately programmed will display alpha-numeric characters, point light sources, or geometric configurations on some four CRT display consoles interfaced to the computer. The display surfaces of three of these consoles are coated with an ultrashort persistence phosphor (^{24}P), having a decay time on the order of a few microseconds. This essentially instantaneous decay of phosphor excitation coupled with a 20-kHz crystal clock in the computer permits input display times to go as low as 50 μsec per input and to vary upwards in 50-μsec increments. Inputs may be spatially located wherever desired on the CRT display surface. Thus, an extraordinary degree of space–time flexibility in the display of input configurations is made possible, far exceeding the capabilities of typical display systems of the past, such as tachistoscopes. A fuller description of this system may be found in our previous papers (Mayzner, 1968; Mayzner, Tresselt, & Helfer, 1967a).

Associated with this hardware system is a set of highly flexible display programs, which allows one to construct, by means of teletype inputs, an almost infinite variety of display configurations. For example, with our present display programs, any member of an alpha-numeric character set may be displayed in any one of the 1600 cells of a 40 $\times$ 40 cell matrix. This allows for a wide variety of display configurations, such as horizontal arrays, vertical arrays, oblique arrays, or any combinations thereof, and the number of individual inputs or characters displayed may vary from one to 100. The 100 individual inputs, in addition, all can be displayed sequentially, that is, one character at a time, each in a different cell of the 1600-cell matrix, or, if desired, they may also be displayed all in one cell, one input after another, or any mix of same or different cells desired. Further, subsets of characters may be displayed simultaneously, with subset size varying from 1 to 100, while preserving sequentially between subsets. Also, any mix of subsets and subset sizes may be displayed in any order, display location, or input rate required.

In addition, other display programs allow for the display of up to 100 point light sources or up to 100 straight-line segments, in a manner equivalent to the options available with the alpha-numeric program. In brief, this hardware display system and its associated software package allows an experimenter to construct almost any type of display configuration desired, very quickly and very easily, by simply typing in on the computer teletype console the desired display parameters.

We also should note that we just recently acquired a PDP-8E computer and associated VR-14 display console on which we plan to continue our research program, since the PDP-7 is now almost 10 years old, which is a very respectable age for a digital computer to retire these days. We have, in fact, already adapted the computer programs developed on the PDP-7 to the PDP-8E, adding additional new display options not easily available on the PDP-7 system, such as easy size changes of displayed characters, much greater ease of experimental tape production, and so forth, and many of the most recent experimental results I will discuss today were found employing the 8E system.

GENERAL RESEARCH STRATEGY

It is important to recognize that space–time interactions in the visual system have recently received increasing attention. For example, Kahneman (1968) has reviewed over 100 studies of visual masking and metacontrast in which spatiotemporal parameters are central, and most recently Turvey (1973) has provided an insightful analysis into peripheral and central processes in vision, again with a strong emphasis on space–time interactions. There is, however, one highly critical difference in the extensive work just alluded to and our own research strategy. Specifically, in the typical visual masking work, almost every study has employed experimental paradigms in which only two or at the most three stimuli or inputs are presented to the visual system. In marked contrast, our general research strategy for studying space–time interactions in the visual system involves presenting to the visual system increasingly longer and more complex spatiotemporal input configurations. It is our position, that a two or three input string presented to the visual system represents a highly special and limiting case of potential space–time interactions, and only N-input strings, where N varies from two up to 100 or more inputs, allows one to fully examine complex space–time interactions in the visual system. Thus, in the studies that we shall discuss in this paper, we shall be concerned basically with rather long input strings, and, in general, ask the question: "What information processing subroutines does the visual system bring to bear, when such long and complex input strings are presented to the visual system?"

The form this question takes is intended to make clear that our general theoretical approach to visual system operation is in terms of an information processing model of visual system behavior. Such information-processing approaches to visual system behavior, as previously indicated, have become increasingly popular of late (e.g., DeValois, 1966; Mayzner & Tresselt, 1970b; Mayzner, Tresselt, & Helfer, 1967b; Rosenblith, 1961;

Turvey, 1973, and the findings we shall discuss we believe can only be accommodated within such a theoretical framework. This position is a natural outcome of a very specific query, namely, "If one presents to the visual system a string of 20, 50, or even 500 inputs, arranged in some given spatial configuration, presents these inputs sequentially in time, and varies their input rate from very fast (e.g., 1 msec per input) to relatively slow (e.g., 50–200 msec per input), how does the visual system process such an input load and what is the resultant visual experience?" Thus, might it not be possible with such a technique of sequential presentation of inputs to probe in some depth into the internal information processing components and processing subroutines of the visual system, to expose to view, so to speak, the time course of the input string as it passes through successive data processing states of the visual system?

The experimental findings we shall discuss shortly will, in fact, demonstrate that such is indeed the case. By presenting long strings of sequential inputs at varying input rates and in varying geometric configurations, we have discovered a rich variety of novel perceptual phenomena, which only became apparent when this type of research methodology is employed. Some of these new perceptual effects, such as "sequential blanking" and "sequential displacement," have been described extensively elsewhere (Mayzner & Tresselt, 1970b; Mayzner, Tresselt, & Helfer, 1967a, b) and will be only briefly mentioned again, in order to discuss in more detail our latest findings in the areas of "dynamic visual movement" and subjective color experiences" resulting from highly complex spatiotemporal input configurations, and pattern recognition mechanisms with overprinting paradigms.

A BRIEF REVIEW OF SEQUENTIAL BLANKING AND DISPLACEMENT

Sequential blanking was the first new perceptual effect discovered in our laboratory, about 8 years ago, when we began to initially focus our attention on visual information processing mechanisms. The effect is most sharply observed under the following input conditions. Visualize, if you will, a linear array of 10 characters, for example, SOMERSAULT, in which the individual characters or letters are displayed sequentially (one at a time) in a display order from left to right (that is, 1, 2, 3, 4, 5, 6, 7, 8, 9, 10). If the input display rate is very fast, for example, 1 msec of display "on" time per letter with 1 msec of display "off" time between letters, then all 10 letters are clearly observed as occurring simultaneously, and all observers will readily report the word "somersault." If display "on" and "off" time now is slowly increased up to say 10–20 msec, observers continue to report seeing all 10 letters and the word "somersault," but now with a strong flowing movement of light from left to right. To produce sequential blanking, all one requires is to select "on" and "off" times of 10 msec, and then change the input display order. For example, if, instead of displaying the letters in an orderly progression from left to right, one selects an irregular order, such as 7, 5, 9, 2, 1, 10, 4, 3, 8, 6, that is, an order in which the letter in the fifth spatial location is displayed first, the letter in the fourth spatial location is displayed second, and so forth, then a most interesting event occurs; observers typically report seeing only five letters, namely S M S L T, with the five missing letters appearing as empty spaces on the display surface. If another irregular order is selected, for example, 1, 6, 2, 7, 3, 8, 4, 9, 5, 10, then again only five letters are observed, but this time the letters seen are O E S U T, with every other letter missing. At this point, one might conclude that since the missing five letters are always the first five letters displayed, then the first half of the input array is lost under sequential display conditions of this type. However, with the display order, 3, 1, 4, 2, 5, 7, 9, 6, 8, 10, the missing letters are those displayed second, fifth, sixth, seventh, and eighth, rather than the first five letters displayed. This finding, plus others discussed in much greater detail in earlier papers (Mayzner & Tresselt, 1970b; Mayzner *et al.*, 1967a, b), clearly demonstrated that sequential blanking phenomena have no simple ready-made explanation.

Furthermore, since work by Cumming (1971, 1973), Pollack (1972), and Uttal (1973, pp. 447–448), employing a variety of psychophysical procedures have clearly indicated that while the basic phenomena of sequential blanking can easily be replicated in other computer-based CRT display laboratories, if more sophisticated response indices are employed than simple reports of subjective experiences, then a new dimensional complexity is added. For example, Pollack (1972) reports:

> The primary result of Mayzner, Tresselt, and their associates is confirmed: within specified temporal-spatial limits, display elements may be perceptually blanked. Characteristics of perceptually blanked elements can, however, be revealed by forced-choice testing. The accuracy of tilt discrimination for perceptually blanked elements is equal to or better than that for unblanked elements. Perceptually blanked elements can also be distinguished from absent and from partially absent elements, presumably on the basis of a crude brightness discrimination [p. 121].

Cumming (1973) in the abstract of his dissertation also reports in a similar vein, namely:

> . . . converging experimental approaches were taken to discover what, if any, kinds of information about suppressed letters may be obtained by S. Classification, visual search, letter identification, letter matching, and subjective rating

tasks were used. The results showed clearly that although suppressed characters were "not seen" they could be classified as letters or digits with completely normal speed and accuracy. In visual search experiments, suppressed targets were detected with intermediate accuracy; they were detected more accurately if S set a lax criterion for a target and worked quickly. In letter identification experiments suppressed letters were poorly identified, but letters given in error tended to resemble the suppressed letters acoustically, suggesting that suppressed letters could sometimes be named but then visual information about them was lost. Converging findings led to the conclusion that detailed information about suppressed letters is available at first [p. III].

From the above, it appears evident that sequential blanking represents but one level of information processing as visual inputs pass through the visual system, and different psychophysical procedures "tap" different levels of the total visual information processing system.

Sequential displacement is perhaps an even more surprising phenomena than sequential blanking. In sequential displacement, if a display order such as 1, 3, 5, 7, 9, 2, 4, 6, 8, 10 is selected, the letters again being SOMER-SAULT, then, although all letters are clearly perceived, observers report seeing a large empty gap between the letter displayed ninth, R, and the letter displayed second, S. Our previous work (Mayzner & Tresselt, 1970b; Schoenberg, Katz, & Mayzner, 1970; Tresselt, Mayzner, Schoenberg, & Waxman, 1970) has clearly shown that several parameters affect sequential-blanking and displacement phenomena, among which are, at least, the following: (1) the number of total inputs displayed, (2) the input display order, (3) the input display rate, (4) the input content or geometry, (5) the input spacing, (6) the input size, and (7) the input luminance or intensity.

In the light of the number of parameters which affect blanking and displacement phenomena, we attempted a few years ago (Mayzner & Tresselt, 1970b; Mayzner et al., 1967b) to construct a visual information-processing model, involving as key constructs the lateral inhibition concepts of Hartline and Ratliff (Ratliff, 1965) and the receptive field concepts of Hubel and Wiesel (1968). Since that time our subsequent work, some of which I will describe shortly, has clearly shown that, while our original analysis might well have been in the right direction, a great deal of additional work will be required to "flesh out" the model and a number of further parameters will need to be accounted for by the model.

Although, this additional complexity demonstrates clearly that extensive revisions will probably be required in the original model, it also has shown that our initial choice of an information processing approach was most probably a sound one. In fact, as our work has progressed over the past three years, we have become increasingly convinced that an information-processing approach to the visual system, when exposed to complex spatiotemporal input configurations, is perhaps the most viable approach one can take at our present stage of theoretical development in the visual sciences.

DYNAMIC VISUAL MOVEMENT

I should like to turn now to a rich variety of totally new perceptual phenomena disclosed by our work during the past three years. The genesis of these phenomena may be found in Mayzner and Tresselt (1970a), In this paper, we become interested in pursuing certain ideas we had concerning illusory or apparent movement, but within a context quite different from past studies of apparent movement (Kolers, 1972). This interest resulted, in part, from reports of many observers who were exposed to our sequential blanking and displacement phenomena, reporting seeing various movement effects on the display, and, in part, from a study of Kahneman (1967) in which he attempted to explain metacontrast effects in terms of what he called "impossible motion."

In our initial study (Mayzner & Tresselt, 1970a), we discovered an input display order for a sequence of 20 input characters, at an input display rate of 5 msec "on" and 5 msec "off," and in which the display is continuously cycled, in which the subjects report seeing one of two perceptual organizations. In one perceptual organization, the subjects reported, with a linear array of 20 letter "Os," a line of 20 "Os" with a slight flicker present, but which could suddenly change to a second perceptual organization of from *only* four to five letter Os spaced equally apart across the width of the display surface (about 20 cm) and in continuous, totally smooth movement from left to right, just like "ducks in a shooting gallery."

Obviously, the crucial element in achieving the effect just described, apart from the proper input display rate, is the input display order. Specifically, the input display order needed is 1, 5, 9, 13, 17, 2, 6, 10, 14, 18, 3, 7, 11, 15, 19, 4, 8, 12, 16, 20. With this input display order one may readily observe four somewhat distinct temporal groupings of inputs with respect to spatial ordering, that is, 1, 5, 9, 13, 17, followed by 2, 6, 10, 14, 18, followed by 3, 7, 11, 17, 19, followed by 4, 8, 12, 16, 20. With such an input display ordering, combined with an input display rate of 5 msec "on" and 5 msec "off" per input, note that, in each of the four temporal groupings, for example, 1, 5, 9, 13, 17, 35 msec of time elapses between each successively displayed spatially adjacent input, except between inputs 17 and 2, 18 and 3, and 19 and 4, where 155 msec of time elapses between each successively displayed spatially adjacent input. These time constants, that is, 35 msec and 155 msec, are obviously at considerable variance with the time constants of typical apparent movement studies and perhaps more importantly instead of dealing with a display of typically just two flashing light sources (the usual apparent movement paradigm), we are dealing with a display of some 20 flashing light sources, being displayed in a complex spatiotemporal sequence.

Further, if the line of 20 Os is replaced with for example, O, —, /, !O, —, /, !, O, —, /, !, O, —, /, !, O, —, /, and !, then all subjects report a display which appears to consist of four Os moving from left to right, as before, except that now it appears as if each O had displayed within it, a—, /, and !. Such an organization represents, we believe, evidence that highly complex spatiotemporal codings of the input array are occuring within the visual system that reach far beyond the mechanisms encountered with simple two-flash apparent movement effects.

Pursuing the input display order parameter further in a subsequent study (Mayzner & Agresti, 1975), we displayed a linear array of 36 letter "Xs" in some seven different input display orders designed to vary the spatiotemporal grouping such that the subjects would report either 2, 3, 4, 6, 9, 12, or 18 moving Xs (note that 36 is divisible by 2, 3, 4, 6, 9, 12, and 18). For example, with the input display order 1, 3, 5, 9, 11 up to 35, and then 2, 4, 6, 8, 10 up to 36, two moving Xs are reported and two spatiotemporal groupings are found; with the input display order 1, 13, 25, 2, 14, 26, 3, 15, 29, etc., up to 12, 24, 36, 12 moving Xs are reported, and 12 spatiotemporal groupings are found. These findings demonstrate most sharply how the visual information processing system organizes a complex spatiotemporal input array into a perceptual organization involving what we have chosen to call *dynamic visual movement*.

Thus, it would appear that with linear arrays of up to at least 36 sequentially and discretely displayed inputs, if a given spatiotemporal ordering is employed, the visual system uniformly across subjects organizes or processes the input array in a rich variety of movement codings. At one extreme, the subjects report seeing 18 moving Xs out of 36 displayed; at the other extreme only 2 moving Xs, out of 36 displayed, are seen. The latter result, 2 Xs out of 36, represents a considerable reorganization of the displayed information and poses, we believe, a fundamental datum, which must be accommodated in any truly viable visual information processing model.

Complicating the above findings even further, we just completed a study that yielded results perhaps even more intriguing than those just described. In this most recent study, we displayed very thin vertical lines (about 10 cm high), with spatiotemporal orderings designed to yield perceptual groupings such as those just examined with the 36 letter "X" arrays, except that 48 vertical lines were displayed sequentially instead of 36 letter Xs. We selected 48 inputs, since we wished to create four perceptual groups each twice as big as the next, that is, groups of 3, 6, 12, and 24 inputs, respectively, moving from left to right across the display. Again, all subjects reported what was expected; depending on input display order, 3, 6, 12, or 24 vertical lines in smooth continuous movement were observed. We now added a further complication to the display. Specifically, 48 lines were displayed vertically while we simultaneously displayed another 48 lines horizontally, another 48 lines oriented obliquely to the right, and another 48 lines oriented obliquely to the left. The obliquely oriented lines varied in lengths such that they represented right and left diagonals of a square formed by the 48 vertical and 48 horizontal lines. We then displayed these four sets of 48 lines each in a spatiotemporal ordering such that four totally different perceptual groupings were perceived for each of the four orientations. Thus, all subjects (approximately 100) reported the following when observing this display: 24 vertical lines moving from the left to the right on the display, 6 horizontal lines moving from the bottom to the top of the display, 12 diagonals moving from the upper left corner to the lower right corner of the display, and 3 diagonals moving from the upper right corner to the lower left corner of the display. This perceptual experience is totally compelling; changes in fixation, distance from the display, variations in display intensity, and so forth in no way affected what the subjects reported. When the subjects were informed that, in fact, 48 lines were being displayed in each of four different orientations sequentially for a total display of 192 separate line inputs, the reaction was unvaryingly one of total disbelief.

Subsequent study has clearly demonstrated that by merely changing the input display order in any one of the four orientations of the above display (horizontal, vertical, diagonal right, or diagonal left) it is quite simple to change the number of perceived moving lines in any one of the orientations independent of the others, by any integer divisible into 48. Consider for a moment, the implications of this simple result. It means that at one extreme, if we employ the appropriate spatiotemporal input display ordering, 192 lines will be perceived, whereas at the opposite extreme only 8 lines (two lines per orientation) will be perceived in smooth continuous movement. Thus, merely by varying input display order, it would appear that the visual information processing subroutines underlying such visual experiences must undergo radical changes in their modes of operation to produce such massve reductions in visual output. Such massive reductions (that is, about 25 to 1) must continue to pose one of our most challenging findings and indicates again the remarkable flexibility of the visual information processing system when confronted with highly complex spatiotemporal input configurations.

One final input array merits particular attention, because of the very high frequency of depth perception experiences that are associated with this particular display. Specifically if we again employ with a 20-character input array the input display order and input display rate that yields four Os, or four Xs or four vertical lines, moving from left to right as "ducks in a shooting gallery", but employ 20 vertical lines, the heights of which vary from ¼ inch to say 3 or 4 inches, and intermix the various heights randomly across spatial location, a startling visual experience results. Namely, the subjects report, that instead of clearly perceiving only four moving vertical lines, they estimate perceiving about 12 vertical lines, but which now appear as if they were the polls on a merry-go-round in fairly rapid rotation, with the short polls or vertical lines near the observer and the longer polls or lines on the back face of the merry-go-round, with a very strong illusion of rotation movement plus depth. Thus, an instance of strong illusory movement combined with strong illusory depth is produced merely by presenting to the visual system the proper spatiotemporal input configuration. At this juncture one begins to wonder just how pliable and flexible the visual system is, if given the proper input array, and the following section of our paper, to which we now turn, suggests a truly remarkably pliable system.

SUBJECTIVE COLOR EXPERIENCES
ASSOCIATED WITH DYNAMIC VISUAL MOVEMENT

The phenomena we will now discuss represent some of our most recent work and were revealed quite by accident. Specifically, when we were examining linear arrays designed to yield "dynamic visual movement" effects, it occurred to us that, instead of employing only a linear array of characters, to position the characters such that with the input display order used previously of 1, 5, 9, 13, 17, 2, 6, 10, 14, 18, 3, 7, 11, 15, 19, 4, 8, 12, 16, 20, it might prove instructive to position the characters spatially to form the four sides of an enclosed square, so that across the top of the square, the characters 1, 5, 9, 13, 17 would appear; 2, 6, 10, 14, 18 would comprise the right side of the square; 3, 7, 11, 15, 19 would comprise the bottom side of the square; and 4, 8, 12, 16, 20 would comprise the left side of the square. With such a spatial positioning employing the letter X, and this input display order and display rates previously employed, with a linear array of 20 Xs four Xs are again reported by all observers (about 100) moving smoothly, as "ducks in a shooting gallery," around the perimeter of a square, with the Xs taking abrupt 90° right-angle turns at the four corners of the square. Now, while watching this display to see whether the visual system continued to process or track illusory movement around a square as it did with the linear array (and incidentally which it does with absolutely no spatial distortion of the square), the lights in the room were accidentally extinguished. Within 10–30 sec maximum, all subjects reported a very remarkable effect, the inside square area enclosed by the four moving Xs, which was initially completely black, began to undergo a very marked, vivid, and intense series of subjective color changes. A typical subject's protocol read as follows: "This is remarkable, what is happening. The inside area has suddenly changed from black to a dark green, no, now its blue, no wait a moment, its orange and so on." As long as the subject watched the display in the dark, this "flight of colors" persisted and, most important, was observed in an area on the display surface from which no radiation was coming. To make absolutely certain that no ancillary phosphor excitation could be stimulating the visual system a thick cardboard mask was placed on the CRT, permitting only the spatial path over which the Xs were moving to be exposed. This mask in no way attenuated the effect. Further, if the input display rate was increased to a degree where all 20 Xs appeared simultaneously, color effects were no longer observed. Similarly, if the input display rate was decreased so that no dynamic visual movement was apparent, but merely a clear, slow sequential presentation of the 20 Xs, again no color effects were observed.

Having demonstrated this effect with 20 Xs spatially positioned to yield dynamic visual movement of 4 Xs moving along the path of a square, the identical methodology was adopted to yield 4 X movement around the circumference of a circle. To further complicate the display two additional circles with dynamic visual movement of 4 Xs each, concentric with the first circle, were displayed; also to increase the dynamic visual movement effect, the 4 Xs in movement in the three concentric circles were displayed to have clockwise movement in the middle circle and counterclockwise movement in the inner and outer circles.

First, it is important to note that all subjects easily see clockwise and counterclockwise movements, thus ruling out any possibility of eye movements tracking the moving Xs since the eyes could not possibly track in opposite directions simultaneously. Far more important, the subjective color effects are even more startling. Many subjects now reported simultaneously seeing more than one color. For example, a typical protocol would be as follows: "I see an inner circle of bright orange, surrounded by two green bands" or "I see an inner circle of green, with a red band and a blue band, now all three are changing, they are now all purple, now its orange again," etc. Also, with this circular display the subjects often reported seeing, in the inner circle, four colored regions like the blades of a fan, rotating in synchronization with the 4 Xs, with thin black sectors separating these regions.

In sum, the range of visual experiences, with the above and similar type displays is enormous. For example, having found these subjective color effects, we returned to our 192 moving line display and covered various sectors of it with cardboard masks and immediately, when viewed in the dark, the black areas covered by the cardboard masks began undergoing vivid color changes of the type just described.

Dynamic visual movement itself is puzzling enough in its own right, but when this phenomenon, in turn, yields yet another even more baffling effect, the theoretical issues are compounded by several orders of magnitude. We have tentatively ruled out an after image type of explanation because of the enormous range of subjective color experiences produced within and between subjects. After-image mechanisms also appear not to be particularly relevant since the color is seen in regions of the display that are transmitting zero energy. More probably, although certainly not to be taken in any sense as final, is the notion that by some mechanism as yet unknown, the movement receptor subsystem of the visual system is activated in such a way by the spatiotemporal input array that it, in turn, stimulates the color receptor subsystem in some quasi-random fashion, and this in turn "fires" the color receptor mechanisms yielding the intense subjective color experiences reported by our subjects.

PATTERN RECOGNITION MECHANISMS AS FOUND IN OVERPRINTING PARADIGMS

In this series of studies, we are concerned primarily with the interactions found in *overprinting paradigms,* those types of sequential presentation of inputs in which the inputs being displayed partially or totally overlap one another in space—that is, inputs which are displayed one on top of another, on some display surface. Typically, such paradigms have been referred to as backward and forward masking paradigms, but this most generally has been applied to those situations in which only two inputs have been involved. Since some of our studies involve more than two inputs, we introduced the term *overprinting* (Mayzner et al., 1967b) to refer to the more general case of the sequential presentation of an N-input string in which the successive inputs are displayed one on top of another at varying input rates.

Interest in overprinting paradigms with N-input strings has increased since Schlosberg's (1965) germinal paper, as evidenced in a number of recent studies (e.g., Katz, Schoenberg, & Mayzner, 1970; Mayzner, 1972; Mayzner & Greenberg, 1971; Mayzner, Tresselt, Checkes, & Hoenig, 1970; Mayzner, Tresselt, Tabenkin, Didner, & Helfer, 1969). In these previous studies, interest focused primarily on the effects of different input rates on performance, and various theoretical issues concerning visual informa-

TABLE 1
Three Sample Letters and the
Noise Field Employed in the Studies

Sample letters	Noise field
. . . .	. . . . .
. . . .	. . . . .
. . .	. . . . .
. . .	. . . . .
. . .	. . . . .
. . .	. . . . .
. . . .	. . . . .

tion processing mechanisms were examined within the context of such over-printing paradigms. Thus, Sperling (1971) was concerned with the implica-tions of overprinting paradigms for distinguishing between what Kahneman (1968) has labeled "integration and interruption theories" of visual infor-mation processing. It is hoped that these studies will provide additional empirical evidence for resolving some of the issues.

For example, in the paper by Mayzner and Greenberg (1971), we re-ported on some five separate studies employing overprinting paradigms, the last two of which were concerned specifically with pattern recognition mechanisms in such overprinting paradigms. More recently (Mayzner, 1972) we have begun to examine very systematically the pattern recogni-tion mechanisms involved in processing alphabetic inputs with such over-printing paradigms. We should now like to review briefly some of the find-ings of this earlier study (Mayzner, 1972), along with some very recent follow-up studies, which are beginning to show very clearly the enormous complexity of pattern recognition mechanisms of simple alphabetic inputs.

As our basic overprinting paradigm, we presented an alphabetic input from 2 to 20 msec in two msec increments, on our CRT, followed by a 500-msec uniform noise field, as shown in Table 1. All letters except Q, were paired with all display on times, yielding a total of 250 discrete dis-plays. Subject WA received these 250 displays 50 times, each time in a different random order, yielding a total of 12,500 responses. In Table 2, the percentage of correct letter recognition responses for display on times from 12 to 20 msec is given, as well as the mean recognition performance for all display on times. The overall results shown in Table 2 demonstrate clearly the very marked differences in recognition performance between letters. This finding raises a very fundamental question: "If letters vary

TABLE 2
Percent Correct Letter Recognitions for Subject
WA for All Letters for Display On Times
from 12 to 20 msec and Mean Recognition Performance
for All 10 Display on Times

Letters	Display on time (msec)					
	12	14	16	18	20	Mean
A	4	28	46	72	84	24.6
B	6	24	30	42	60	17.8
C	4	10	14	14	18	7.4
D	16	24	24	56	76	20.4
E	18	16	26	48	58	20.0
F	18	24	38	52	74	24.8
G	2	6	20	24	30	9.6
H	30	24	32	68	76	28.2
I	30	46	52	50	60	28.8
J	26	54	70	74	86	32.6
K	46	40	72	76	94	37.6
L	44	58	76	92	96	39.8
M	10	16	20	50	58	18.8
N	2	16	24	32	50	13.6
O	12	22	28	36	58	18.8
P	10	14	34	74	62	21.6
R	24	22	24	72	92	25.8
S	18	28	46	72	84	29.2
T	72	90	92	90	88	64.2
U	10	38	54	72	78	26.2
V	6	50	34	64	86	26.2
W	2	12	30	70	78	19.4
X	30	52	66	76	90	34.4
Y	14	20	26	54	60	23.0
Z	18	18	42	76	76	27.8

in their recognition scores would this variation be different from subject to subject, or would different subjects show similar orderings in recognition performance, thus implying perhaps that the underlying processing subroutines of feature analysis are similar from subject to subject?" Correlations between the orderings now obtained on some ten different subjects yield

ρ's ranging from .67 to .94. Thus, as a first approximation it seems reasonable to conclude that some degree of similarity most probably exists in the feature processing subroutines of alphabetic inputs between different subjects.

Confusion matrix data on subject WA's letter recognition performance is given in Table 3 in an attempt to further clarify our preceding results. Examination of the cells of this confusion matrix clearly indicate that even though the subject had the option of hitting the space bar of the Teletype when he believed he saw no letter on the display, he infrequently employed this option (i.e., about 5% of all responses), but rather made errors by typing in an incorrect letter. If we examine these errors, we find that they show certain systematic patterns. For example, the most frequent error when E was displayed was the response F, whereas the most frequent error when F was displayed was the response E. Similarly, when C, which had the poorest correct recognition score of only 7.4%, was displayed, a number of different responses were made, for example, O, G, and D. In sharp contrast, T, which had the highest correct recognition score of 64.2%, showed only one letter with which it was confused, I, and then only to a small degree. It would appear from an analysis of these confusion matrix data that, when the subject failed to make a correct response he often failed because he confused its shape with a highly similar shape.

If the above analysis is correct, it should prove possible to select, on the basis of the confusion matrix scores, subsets of letters that would show high or low confusion scores within a given subset. Having selected high-(HC) and low-confusion (LC) matrix score subsets (i.e., HC and LC letter groups), we would predict that correct letter recognition performance should be better in the LC letter group than in the HC letter group.

The HC letter group consisted of the following 10 letters: B, C, D, G, J, L, O, S, U, and Z. The LC letter group consisted of the letters: A, B, C, J, R, T, V, W, X, and Z. These two letter groups were selected from subject WA's confusion matrix scores in the following way. The 10 letters of the HC letter group were selected such that for a given letter in this group, if we summed the cell scores of the confusion matrix for this given letter with the other 9 letters of the subset, relatively high values were obtained, as follows: B-86, C-166, D-103, G-138, J-48, L-35, O-132, S-60, U-60, and Z-50. In contrast, the same procedure followed with the letters of the LC letter group yielded the following relatively low values: A-48, B-36, C-41, J-22, R-45, T-3, V-50, W-54, X-26, and Z-37.

Two subjects, WA and JG, were presented with 10 trials each of the HC and LC letter groups randomly, with each trial consisting of the 10 letters of a given letter group displayed once at one of 10 display on times, that is, 2, 4, 6, 8, 10, 12, 14, 16, 18, or 20 msec, followed immediately

TABLE 3

Empirical Alphabetic Confusion Matrix
Previously Unpublished Alphabetic Confusion Matrix[a]

									STIMULUS																
RESPONSE	**A**	**B**	**C**	**D**	**E**	**F**	**G**	**H**	**I**	**J**	**K**	**L**	**M**	**N**	**O**	**P**	**R**	**S**	**T**	**U**	**V**	**W**	**X**	**Y**	**Z**
A		2	4	7	1	4	2	26	0	0	0	1	10	3	0	7	7	3	0	0	1	4	2	2	2
B	10		8	7	2	7	31	6	0	8	1	0	6	6	9	4	6	15	0	4	4	2	1	0	5
C	3	9		3	16	1	8	0	0	0	16	0	3	2	6	5	4	2	1	4	4	1	6	0	8
D	6	10	18		14	2	12	0	0	1	13	0	0	2	57	13	3	5	1	4	1	3	1	0	9
E	7	7	6	1		20	3	4	0	1	1	3	4	2	3	8	9	4	1	2	1	3	2	0	7
F	5	11	6	2	39		10	7	0	5	2	4	2	0	0	13	1	4	0	1	1	5	1	0	7
G	12	1	29	6	14	8		7	0	3	0	7	14	6	4	5	9	17	1	4	9	4	2	3	10
H	0	4	6	5	4	2	8		0	5	5	0	9	16	2	7	2	8	1	4	5	15	7	0	7
I	7	11	0	0	3	5	5	1		5	2	3	4	3	2	0	0	4	22	3	1	5	5	3	0
J	4	1	12	12	1	2	1	2	1		1	0	1	7	13	1	2	5	0	3	1	3	2	3	2
K	0	4	4	9	6	1	5	5	0	5		3	16	12	5	9	20	4	0	32	3	3	7	0	4
L	6	11	26	8	10	5	1	1	4	2	0		7	5	11	1	0	4	2	4	1	6	5	2	5
M	1	2	1	2	3	4	3	20	1	2	2	2		56	3	6	2	3	1	8	3	12	4	1	1
N	0	5	42	4	0	3	4	10	0	7	0	0	11		3	6	8	4	0	7	6	7	3	2	3
O	15	5	3	44	1	2	19	0	0	2	1	1	6	2		2	4	4	2	2	4	6	1	0	1
P	8	14	2	5	5	17	6	8	0	4	0	0	5	5	3		3	6	0	3	8	15	2	0	3
R	8	9	13	2	9	12	12	12	1	2	9	0	9	8	8	29		5	0	3	5	7	3	0	8
S	8	27	4	4	4	13	7	3	1	5	3	3	4	2	2	3	8		0	4	4	10	1	0	9
T	3	6	14	1	3	8	11	1	96	4	7	2	24	10	8	9	12	9		3	7	9	13	0	11
U	3	8	4	17	4	0	0	2	0	19	0	2	12	10	16	1	2	2	0		27	3	1	0	2
V	3	3	3	3	3	1	7	0	0	3	1	1	1	3	7	2	0	1	0	23		3	6	50	2
W	3	2	0	1	4	2	6	2	0	3	2	0	3	3	0	2	11	2	1	2	6		3	0	2
X	2	2	3	2	0	4	7	2	12	0	12	6	6	7	0	6	2	2	0	3	5	7		0	1
Y	6	1	0	2	4	4	4	4	13	3	5	3	1	1	1	6	5	3	1	1	3	12	21		4
Z	4	4	4	2	29	12	5	2	0	3	2	1	0	3	3	9	3	10	0	2	2	4	3	1	

[a] Obtained from study 1 (Mayzner, 1972). Each cell in the matrix shows the number of incorrect responses for 250 presentations of each letter (50 presentations at each of 5 display on times; 12, 14, 16, 18, 20 msec).

TABLE 4
Percent Correct Letter Recognitions for HC and LC
Letter Groups for Subjects WA and JG Summed
Across All Letters as a Function of Display on Time

Letter group	Ss	Display on time (msec)										Mean
		2	4	6	8	10	12	14	16	18	20	
HC	WA	3	3	3	8	10	18	10	25	39	50	16.9
	JG	1	1	2	2	6	5	10	22	26	66	15.1
LC	WA	7	11	6	14	20	30	43	48	73	78	33.0
	JG	0	1	0	4	9	23	38	51	67	86	27.9

by the noise field for 500 msec, for a total of 100 display presentations per trial (i.e., 10 "on" times × 10 letters). Again, responses were entered via the computer Teletype, and a computer printout provided the percentage of correct letter recognition scores for each subject for each letter for each display on time.

The results for subjects WA and JG are given in Table 4, and show clearly that the percentage of correct letter recognition scores average out to about 2 to 1 in favor of the LC over the HC letter group. Although only two subjects have been tested, each received a total of 1000 display presentations, and we believe these results would obtain with other subjects.

Since four letters, B, C, J, and Z, were common to both the HC and LC letter groups, a comparison was made between these specific letters. For subject WA, percent correct recognitions for B, C, J, and Z in the HC letter group were 12, 3, 18, and 26%, respectively, whereas in the LC letter group the values were 26, 18, 36, and 31% respectively. For subject JG, percent correct recognitions for B, C, J, and Z in the HC letter group were 11, 2, 12, and 32%, respectively; in the LC letter group the values were 14, 20, 24, and 24% respectively. Thus, percent correct letter recognitions on identical letters are greater in seven out of eight cases, when these letters are embedded in the LC letter group as opposed to the HC letter group.

In an attempt to further specify the parameters involved in letter recognition performances, consider our finding for the letter C. As given in Table 2 its recognition score when embedded with 24 other letters, is 7.4% correct recognition; when embedded with HC letters, it drops to 3% correct recognitions, and rises to 18% correct recognitions when embedded among

9 LC letters. This rapid fluctuation in recognition scores, as a function of context, raises an extremely crucial question. For example, can context alone raise and lower letter recognition scores without constraints?

We are just beginning an extensive research effort into this issue and the very early findings, a few of which I shall mention briefly, are beginning to reveal a picture of truly enormous complexity, if one attempts to unravel contextual parameters from inherent geometric properties of the input or stimulus characters. Thus, in a recently completed study the subjects were presented with a series of trials (display on times ranged from 4 to 20 msec in 4-msec increments) on which they were informed that only one of two letters, followed by a 5 $\times$ 7 noise field, would appear; if they were not sure, they were to guess which letter had appeared. The letter pairs were: HC, YC, WC, NC, LC, DC, OC, GC, HG, YG, WG, NG, LG, DG, and OG. The percentage of correct recognition scores for C in this study, ranged from 30% correct recognitions, when C was paired with G, to 64% correct recognitions when C was paired with Y. In contrast, G ranged from 53% correct recognitions when paired with C to 67% correct recognitions when paired with W. Thus, C and G, which, in Table 2, show percentage of correct recognition scores of 7.4 and 9.6% when embedded with all 24 letters, can range as high as 64 and 67% correct recognitions, in two-letter studies.

In a like manner, the percentage of correct recognition scores for H, Y, W, N, L, D, and O, in Table 2, are 28.2, 23.0, 19.4, 13.6, 39.8, 20.4, and 18.8%, respectively; the equivalent values in this study are 68, 75, 62, 66, 63, 46, and 51%, respectively. It appears from the preceding results that percentage of correct letter recognitions can vary over a very wide range of values, merely as contextual parameters are varied.

In order to explore this phenomena further, we have just begun an intensive study that will systematically vary set size and the letters in the set. Already, very preliminary results present a picture that becomes more and more puzzling. Specifically, three test chains have been examined to date with forced-choice responding, that is, T and C; C and G; and T, C, and G, with display on times ranging from 4 to 80 msec in 4-msec increments. As Table 2 shows, T yielded the highest percentage of correct recognitions, 64.2%; C and G yielded the lowest percent correct recognitions, 7.4% and 9.6%, respectively. If we pair T and C (an average based on four subjects), the results showed percentage of correct recognitions of 67% for T and 58% for C, with the 9% difference about constant across the entire time range from 4 to 80 msec. Pairing C and G, however, yielded an entirely unexpected and highly perplexing outcome. For the entire time range, from 4 to 80 msec, C and G yielded correct recognition scores of 49 and 59%, respectively; most important, however, in the range from 4 to 40 msec, percentage of correct recognition for G went from an average of 32% to an average of 88% in the range from 40 to 80 msec, while C *dropped* from 76 to 22% over the equivalent time ranges. Thus, we find, for the first time that percentage of correct recognition varies very markedly as a function of display on time in a totally inexplicable fashion, that is, a *drop* in percent correct recognitions as display on time increases, at least up to 80 msec. An obvious next step, which we are currently just beginning, is extending the time range beyond 80 msec, as eventually percentage of correct recognitions for C must again begin to increase. It will be of some considerable interest to fix precisely just how much additional time is required for both C and G to reach an asymptotic value of 100% correct recognitions.

With the test chain T, C, and G, it is as if we had the test chain C and G and merely added to it the results for T from the T and C test chain. However, one might ask why is C's recognition performance so radically different in C and G from that with T, C, and G, whereas G is relatively the same in C and G and T, C, and G. Very obviously, the recognition performance for a given letter must vary significantly as a function of a number of parameters, a situation which we are just beginning to elucidate.

What other factors inherent to the input itself, aside from confusibility, might require more execution time for the processing subroutines to operate? It seems to us that letters like T, L, K, X, and the like, which yield some of our highest correct recognition scores, are relatively simple geometric constructions; T and L, for example, are in their generalized form composed of two joined straight-line segments. In contrast, letters like C, G, B, and O, which yielded some of our lowest correct recognition scores, aside from confusibility, are relatively complex geometric constructions, involving line curvature and mixes of straight-line and curved segments. Thus, it seems plausible to us to assume that, when a letter input enters the visual system, simple processing subroutines operate first and, if the input is composed of simple elements such as two straight-line segments, a correct recognition response may occur within a few milliseconds, that is, prior to the arrival of the noise field, which we assume interferes with the smooth application of these processing subroutines. In this sense then, our analysis is closer to interruption models than to integration models of visual masking. However, we do not believe that the noise field stops processing; we prefer instead the position that the noise field interferes, to a greater or lesser degree, with the application of these processing subroutines to the input, the degree of interference being in part a function of the geometric structure of the input and the geometric structure of the noise field and their relation to one another. This point is crucial for input processing for us occurs "in a totally continuous fashion" to both letter and noise inputs as they pass through the visual system. The visual system, in this view, does not stop or interrupt processing the first ("letter") input when the second ("noise") input arrives, but rather now has two processing tasks to handle, together, with a consequent degradation of both inputs if the first input has not been fully processed when the second input arrives. This analysis can be extended to an N-input string, as we discussed previously (Mayzner & Tresselt, 1970b).

If now a more "complicated" input (more complicated geometrically) enters the visual system, and if processing subroutines are applied in some relatively fixed hierarchic order, straight-line elements being processed before analysis subroutines of curvature features is applied, then we would expect more time for their execution, as they are lower in the processing hierarchy. Thus, results such as those obtained in this research would obtain. The exact number of such processing subroutines of feature analysis, that is, straight-line segment subroutines, curved-line segment subroutines, etc., their precise hierarchic ordering, the range of their execution times across subjects, and the like obviously cannot be fully detailed at this time, or we would already have solved the core problem of pattern recognition. However, the results of our research do suggest a fruitful paradigm to pursue. This paradigm has already disclosed (1) a possible hierarchical ordering of processing subroutines of feature analysis does exist, based on geometric properties of the input and potential confusibility patterns, applied in a relative fixed order by the visual system as each new input enters the system, and further that this set of subroutines is probably highly similar across subjects, and (2) that the execution time for these processing subroutines can vary considerably, from a few milliseconds up to and quite probably well beyond 80 msec, across subjects.

OVERVIEW

I hope that I have imparted here at least some of the aspects of our research program into visual information processing mechanisms in the visual system when it is bombarded with highly complex spatio-temporal input configurations. I have only touched upon some of the highlights of the past several years of our work. I have not discussed at all, for example, our work on simple "overprinting" (Katz, Schoenberg, & Mayzner, 1970; Mayzner & Greenberg, 1971; Mayzner et al., 1970; Mayzner et al., 1969) our work on mapping visual inhibitory fields (Schoenberg, Katz, & Mayzner, 1970), partially replicated by Uttal (1973, pp. 447–448), our work on overprinting and sequential blanking effects combined (Tresselt, Mayzner, Schoenberg, & Waxman, 1970), etc., nor have I elaborated on our provisional model of visual information processing (Mayzner & Tresselt, 1970b; Mayzner et al., 1967b).

I have attempted to describe, however briefly, what I believe are at least five fundamental and novel results of our work — sequential blanking, sequential displacement, dynamic visual movement, subjective color effects associated with dynamic visual movement, and pattern recognition mechanisms as found in overprinting paradigms, which any viable model of visual information processing must eventually be able to accommodate. In closing, I should like to make one prediction, namely, that the type of methodology we have attempted to develop over the past decade employing a computer-based CRT display system to study problems of visual information processing is permanently with us and, most important, we are just beginning to realize its potential, with the years ahead promising to yield more exciting and important discoveries than those already found in the past.

ACKNOWLEDGMENTS

This research was supporttd by Grants GB-8037 and GB-22785 from the National-Science Foundation.

REFERENCES

Cumming, G. LINC-8 presents and controls visual experiments. *Behavior Research Methods and Instrumentation*, 1971, **3**, 24–29.

Cumming, G. Perceptual analysis of letters masked by metacontrast. Unpublished doctoral thesis, Department of Psychology, Oxford University, Oxford, England, 1973.

DeValois, R. L. Neural processing of visual information. In R. W. Russell (Ed.), *Frontiers in physiological psychology*. New York: Academic Press, 1966. Pp. 51–91.

Hubel, D. H., & Wiesel, T. N. Receptive fields and functional architecture of monkey striate cortex. *Journal of Physiology*, 1968, **195**, 215–243.

Kahneman, D. An onset–onset law for one case of apparent motion and metacontrast. *Perception & Psychophysics*, 1967, **2**, 577–584.

Kahneman, D. Method, findings, and theory in studies of visual masking. *Psychological Bulletin*, 1968, **70**, 404–425.

Katz, M., Schoenberg, K. M., & Mayzner, M. S., Visual information processing of sequentially presented inputs: II. Effects of list length and interstimulus interval values on subspan storage and retrieval mechanisms. *Perception & Psychophysics*, 1970, **7**, 149–152.

Kolers, P. *Aspects of motion perception*. New York: Pergamon, 1972.

Mayzner, M. S. The research potential of a computer based cathode-ray tube display system. *Behavior Research Methods and Instrumentation*, 1968, **1**, 41–43.

Mayzner, M. S. Visual information processing of alphabetic inputs, *Psychonomic-Monograph Supplements*, 1972, **4**(13, Whole No. 61), 239–243.

Mayzner, M. S., & Agresti, W. W. Changes in dynamic visual movement as a function of changing spatio-temporal display orderings. unpublished manuscript, 1975, in preparation.

Mayzner, M. S., & Greenberg, J. Studies in the processing of sequentially presented inputs with overprinting paradigms. *Psychonomic Monograph Supplements,* 1971, **4**(4, Whole No. 52), 73–84.

Mayzner, M. S., & Tresselt, M. E. Visual dynamics of a novel apparent movement effect. *Psychonomic Science,* 1970, **18**, 331–332.   (a)

Mayzner, M. S., & Tresselt, M. E. Visual information processing with sequential inputs: A general model for sequential blanking, displacement, and overprinting phenomena. *Annals of the New York Academy of Sciences,* 1970, **169**, 599–618.   (b)

Mayzner, M. S., Tresselt, M. E., Checkes, J., & Hoenig, H. A. Visual information processing of sequentially presented Inputs: III. Further effects of list length and interstimulus interval values on subspan storage and retrieval mechanisms. *Perception & Psychophysics,* 1970, **7**, 294–296.

Mayzner, M. S., Tresselt, M. E., & Helfer, M. S. A research strategy for studying certain effects of very fast sequential input rates on the visual system. *Psychonomic Monograph Supplements,* 1967, **2**(5, Whole No. 21), 73–81.   (a)

Mayzner, M. S., Tresselt, M. E., & Helfer, M. S. A provisional model of visual information processing with sequential inputs. *Psychonomic Monograph Supplements,* 1967, **2**(7, Whole No. 23), 91–108.   (b)

Mayzner, M. S., Tresselt, M. E., Tabenkin, N., Didner, R., & Helfer, M. S. Visual information processing of sequentially presented inputs: I. Effects of input timing on subspan storage and retrieval mechanisms. *Perception & Psychophysics,* 1969, **5**, 297–302.

Pollack, I. Visual discrimination of "unseen objects": Forced-choice testing of Mayzner–Tresselt sequential blanking effects. *Perception & Psychophysics,* 1972, **11**, 121–128.

Ratliff, F. *Mach bands: Quantitative studies on neural networks in the retina.* San Francisco, California: Holden-Day, 1965.

Rosenblith, W. A. (Ed.) *Sensory communication.* Cambridge, Massachusetts: MIT Press, 1961.

Schlosberg, H. Time relations in serial visual perception, *Canadian Psychologist,* 1965, **6a**, 161–172.

Schoenberg, K. M., Katz, M., & Mayzner, M. S. The shape of inhibitory fields in the human visual system. *Perception & Psychophysics,* 1970, **7**, 357–359.

Sperling, G. Temporal and spatial visual masking: I. Masking by impulse flashes. *Journal of the Optical Society of America,* 1965, **55**, 541–559.

Sperling, G. Information retrieval from two rapidly consecutive stimuli: A new analysis. *Perception & Psychophysics,* 1971, **9**, 89–91.

Tresselt, M. E., Mayzner, M. S., Schoenberg, K. M., & Waxman, J. A study of sequential blanking and overprinting combined. *Perception & Psychophysics,* 1970, **8**, 261–264.

Turvey, M. T. On peripheral and central processes in vision: Inferences from an information-processing analysis of masking with patterned stimuli. *Psychological Review,* 1973, **80**, 1–52.

Uttal, W. R. *The psychobiology of sensory coding.* New York: Harper & Row, 1973.

3
ATTENTION AND COGNITIVE CONTROL[1]

Michael I. Posner
Charles R. R. Snyder[2]
University of Oregon

INTRODUCTION

To what extent are our conscious intentions and strategies in control of the way information is processed in our minds? This seems to be a question of importance to us both as psychologists and as human beings. Yet as Shallice (1972) has pointed out, most theorists in psychology have avoided consideration of the relationship between conscious and unconscious mental events. While psychological writers rarely deal with this distinction directly, the reader of psychological publications can hardly avoid it. On the one hand, the pages of journals are full of studies in which the "strategies" or "optional processes" of the subject are used to explain the results obtained; on the other hand, we are told that human memory is an associational machine that operates entirely without control of the subjects' strategies (Anderson & Bower, 1973). Both of these views need to be accommodated. Even the most cognitive of theorists recognizes that people are not always able to adapt their thought processes to the strategies required by the task, and Anderson and Bower (1973) explicitly recognize that their strategy-free memory system must be coupled to other strategy-dependent systems.

[1] This research was supported by the National Science Foundation under Grant GB 40310X. The paper was written while the first author was Visiting Professor of Psychology at Yale University and Haskins Laboratories.
[2] Now at Purdue University.

In this paper we review studies designed to provide some experimental analysis of how conscious strategies interact with automatic activation processes to determine performance.

As a first step toward an understanding of conscious control of cognition (Section II) we examine in detail the characteristics of purely "automatic" processes. We are all introspectively familiar with thoughts, ideas, or feelings that seem to intrude upon us rather than occur as a result of our intentions to produce them. We propose three operational indicants of whether a process is "automatic," as we will use the term: the process occurs without intention, without giving rise to any conscious awareness, and without producing interference with other ongoing mental activity. Even with these stringent requirements it is possible to show that many complex but habitual mental processes can operate automatically and thus, in principle, be strategy independent.

Many theorists have proposed a fixed processing stage at which limited-capacity attentional effects are to be found. Sometimes the stage is early in processing and sometimes late, but the idea is that some types of operations are not capacity limited while others are. Our view is different; we see a specific mechanism of limited capacity. This mechanism can be committed flexibly to different stages, depending upon many factors. Thus, it is necessary for us to develop operational methods for distinguishing whether a given process is being performed in an "automatic" or "conscious" mode (Section III).

Many cognitive tasks may be viewed as combining automatic activation and conscious strategies. By reviewing a number of experimental results we try to see how well our distinction aids in furthering the investigation and understanding of these tasks (Section IV). In particular, we try to illustrate how a number of disparate paradigms demonstrate similar principles.

Perhaps the problems of cognitive control have been discussed in an effort to understand the nature of emotion. Signals with emotional significance seem more intrusive than other signals. Some have used this to argue that emotions have a special status in memory and thereby serve to guide our conscious cognitions. We introduce some experiments aimed at understanding the way emotional information is activated in the memory system and how that activation affects our conscious cognitions (Section V).

AUTOMATIC PATHWAY ACTIVATION

Intention

Stroop effect.   There is excellent evidence that subjects cannot choose to avoid processing aspects of an input item that they desire to ignore.

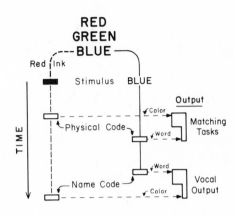

FIG. 1. A schematic explanation of the Stroop effect. Two internal look-up processes produce representations of the ink color name (dashed line) and the word name (solid line) respectively. If the task is one of physical matching, ink colors arrive at output first and interfere with word matching. If the task is one of naming, words arrive at output first and interfere with ink colors. These interference effects result from the time course of the look-up process.

The Stroop effect is based upon this difficulty (Dyer, 1973). When given the task of naming the ink color of the words in Fig. 1, one intends to avoid reading the words, but it is not possible to do so completely.

There is now a great deal of evidence that supports the kind of explanation for this effect which is outlined in Fig. 1 (Dyer, 1973; Hintzman, Carre, Eskridge, Owens, Shaff, & Sparks, 1972; Keele, 1973; Morton & Chambers, 1973; Murray, Mastronadi, & Duncan, 1972). First, the usual Stroop effect arises because of competition between vocal responses to the printed word and the ink color. Keele (1973) demonstrated the importance of output interference by showing that noncolor words, which produce a small interference over a nonword control with a vocal output, produce no such interference when a key press output is used. Second, the direction of interference depends upon the time relations involved. Words are read faster than colors can be named; thus, a color-naming response receives stronger interference from the word than the reverse. Colors can be matched physically faster than can words, so that a matching response results in greater interference from colors on words than the reverse (Murray *et al.,* 1972). Third, words often facilitate the vocal output to colors with which they share a common name (Hintzman *et al.,* 1972).

These three results suggest that color naming and reading go on in parallel and without interference until close to the output. If they result in look-up of the same name, the overall reaction time is speeded; if they produce different names and a vocal output is required, the word tends to compete with the color name and reaction time is increased. One puzzle that remains is this: why does a vocal response to color names interfere so much more than words that are not color names? After all, both have

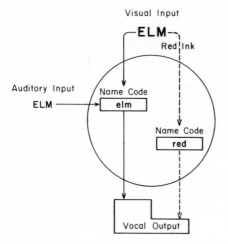

FIG. 2. Amount of interference (milliseconds) with color naming as a function of associative strength: condition: high forward, 95; medium forward, 50; low forward, 20; high backward, 0. An auditory word activates its name code. When the following visual word shares the same pathway it will arrive at output first and produce greater interference with color naming. The lower panel shows supportive data for this theory from Warren (1974).

well-learned names stored in the memory system. The answer lies in the close semantic associations existing between color names and in the fact that prior activation of an item affects the time for look-up of its name, a phenomenon to which we now turn.

Memory activation.   One can use the Stroop effect to investigate the automatic activation pattern of a word in the memory system (Warren, 1972, 1974). Warren presented an auditory item or items, followed after a brief interval by a single visual word printed in colored ink. The only task set for the subject was to name the color of ink as quickly as possible. Warren's results showed clearly that the time for naming the ink color increased with the associative strength between the auditory word and the visual word. As shown in Fig. 2, only associative strength in the forward direction is important; there is no effect of backward associative strength from the visual word to the prior auditory word.

The Warren effect can be explained by a logic quite similar to the one shown in Fig. 1. An auditory word activates a pathway in the nervous system which consists of its auditory representation, its name, and a motor program for its production. When the visual word shares some of the same pathway (e.g., name and motor program) its processing rate is increased. Thus, the word name is delivered more quickly and/or more strongly to the output mechanisms, and thus produces more interference with saying the ink color name. There is no incentive in the task for the subject to activate items related to the auditory word. They are not asked to form associations nor need they be required to recall the auditory items to show the effect. Even when, as sometimes happens, subjects become aware that they are having difficulty in processing related items, they do not seem to be able to shut off the activation process.

The Warren results show why interference in the Stroop effect is greatest for color names, intermediate for associated words, and least for unrelated words. This is due to a general tendency of a word to activate related items. This effect occurs without any apparent intention by the subject. The effect of automatic activation on reaction time drops sharply with delay (Warren, 1972), but the well-known tendency for related words to be reported as "old" on recognition memory tests (Underwood, 1965) suggests that at least on some occasions the effects remain present for a considerable time.

Awareness

Stroop studies. Recently Conrad (1974) showed that the subject may be quite unaware of the activation pattern created by input words. She presented to her subjects sentences that ended with an ambiguous word (e.g., pot). The word was either disambiguated by context or not. Following the oral presentation of the sentence, she showed her subjects a single visual word in colored ink. The subjects' task was to name the color of the ink. In agreement with the Warren effect, she showed that the time to name the color of ink was longer when the word was related to the sentence. This was true both for the ambiguous word itself and for words related to either one of the word's meanings. The size of the interference effect was approximately equal whether the sentence had been disambiguated by context or not. These results are illustrated in Fig. 3. Since the sentences disambiguated by context are consciously perceived in only one way, the finding that both meanings of the ambiguous word are activated is evidence that the activation pattern is not dependent on the subject's conscious percept.

The results of the Conrad experiment seem to us to be striking support for the kind of automatic activation of lexical memory proposed by Anderson and Bower (1973). They postulate that individual items of a proposition look-up related facts in parallel. Context has its effect as the activation patterns of the different lexical items are combined. The importance of context and the fact that we are rarely aware of ambiguity suggest that the equality of activation found by Conrad will change rapidly as one meaning or another comes to dominate. Her findings show that it is possible to develop psychological experiments that reveal memory processes relatively free of context and strategy effects.

Dichotic listening. The Stroop demonstrations all involve the automatic activation of a word meaning when subjects are attending to the

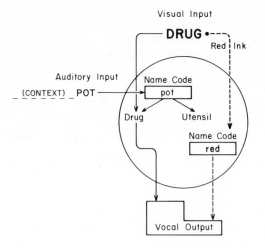

Amount of interference (msec) with color naming as a function of context

Context	Word itself	Appropriate category	Inappropriate category
Ambiguous	73	77	77
Unambiguous	58	61	50

FIG. 3. (Top) The ambiguous word "pot" activates its lexical pathway irrespective of its linguistic context. A following visual word related to either pathway produces greater interference with color naming than a neutral word. Lower panel shows supportive data from Conrad (1974).

channel on which it arrives. One might well argue that form and color are integral dimensions (Garner & Felfoldy, 1970), and thus the inability of the subject to ignore the word while attending to color is a very special phenomenon. Suppose instead that the subject attends to another set of items entirely. Will automatic activation still occur?

Much evidence on this comes from studies of dichotic listening. For example, Lewis (1970) has shown that when subjects are shadowing items to one ear, an item occurring on the unattended channel which has the same semantic meaning as an attended item will slow his rate of shadowing. Mackay (1973) and Lackner and Garrett (1973) have shown than an unattended lexical item may serve to disambiguate the meaning of an attended sentence. In these experiments there is a semantic relationship between the attended and unattended items; thus, the effect could depend upon having an already activated locus in memory related to the unattended item.

Recent work (Corteen & Wood, 1972; von Wright, Anderson, & Stenman, 1975) has eliminated this problem. They first condition subjects to produce a galvanic skin response (GSR) to particular words. They then show that the GSR occurs when these words are presented on an unattended channel during dichotic listening. In the von Wright data, the size of the GSR to semantic associates of the conditioned stimulus was as large when they occurred on the unattended channel as on the attended channel. These results could only occur if semantic classification of the unattended word had taken place. Thus, the dichotic listening studies suggest that very complicated processing, including even stereotyped responses such as the GSR, occur when the subject's attention is focused elsewhere.

In these studies the subjects have relatively little incentive to shift attention to the nonshadowed ear. Attempts to test awareness of unattended information have involved assessing breakdowns in shadowing, obtaining reports of unusual or obscene items, and measuring recognition memory for unattended items. Overall, it seems fair to conclude that a large amount of automatic processing still occurs when the subject's attention is focused on different items.

Parallel Processing

The Stroop method of studying automatic activation requires subjects to attend to a particular position in space, although to the ink color rather than to the word. The dichotic method has subjects attending to a particular modality, though not the channel within that modality to which the unattended item is presented. Is there evidence that unattended items activate semantically related information even when they occur to an unattended modality? The results of several experiments (Greenwald, 1970a, b; Lewis, 1970) indicate that subjects are not successful in filtering out information occurring on a modality that they are instructed to ignore when it has a close semantic relationship to the attended information. Thus, it appears that the intention to ignore a modality will not prevent it from affecting attended processing.

Recent studies have provided another technique for examining the buildup of information on an unattended modality. We know from many reaction time studies that subjects are slow to respond to information occurring on a channel that is not the expected one. This might suggest that the buildup of information about the unexpected stimulus is being delayed because the subject is actively attending elsewhere. A more careful analysis raises doubts about this view, however. Consider the results of the following experiment (Posner & Summers, unpublished). In this experiment, subjects are required to classify a single item as to whether or not it is an animal name. On half the trials the stimulus is an animal name, while on the other half it is not. In pure blocks the stimulus is always auditory or always visual, while in mixed blocks it may be either. In addition, some-

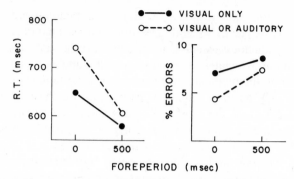

FIG. 4. Reaction time (left) and errors (right) in classifying a visual word as an animal name as a function of amount of warning (foreperiod) and whether or not the words are all visual or mixed visual and auditory. (After unpublished experiments by Posner and Summers.)

times the subject has a warning signal in advance of the stimulus, and at other times he has no warning signal.

When the word is visually presented to the subject, his reaction time is generally fast, provided that he either (1) has a warning signal, or (2) knows the channel of entry. But if neither of these obtain, his reaction time is quite long (see Fig. 4). One might imagine that the subject has his eyes closed or defocussed. However, one feature of the data argues against this interpretation. Although the reaction times under these low attention conditions are long, the accuracy is high. It is as though the buildup of information goes on regardless of whether the subject is attending or not. If he is not attending, the response time is slow, but accurate. We think this is because the quality of information builds up at the same rate with or without attention.

Suppose instead of merely making the subject uncertain about the modality on which the information will arrive, his attention is carefully directed to the wrong modality. LaBerge (1973) reported such a study. The task involved a classification response on the auditory modality (1000-versus 990-Hz tone) or on the visual modality (yellow versus orange light). In pure blocks the subject knew the modality that would be used. In mixed blocks he received the expected modality on .85 of the trials and the signal on the unexpected modality on .15 of the trials. A 1000-Hz tone or an orange light was used as a cue stimulus to rivet the subject's attention on the expected modality prior to the signal stimulus. The results for reaction time show that the method was extremely successful (see Fig. 5). In the pure blocks and when the expected modality was presented in the mixed blocks, the subjects were fast and reaction times were nearly equal. This shows that subjects were attending to the expected modality.

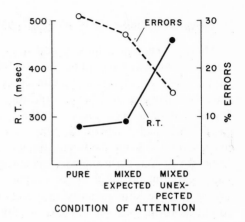

FIG. 5. Reaction time (left ordinate) and errors (right ordinate) as a function of whether signals are all in one modality (pure) or whether they are mixed and subjects are induced to focus on one modality (expected). (After LaBerge, 1973.)

When a stimulus on the unexpected modality occurred, subjects were very slow but showed the most accuracy. In this experiment, which requires fine discriminations, error rates are always high, but they are lowest in just those conditions where the subject's attention is directed to the wrong channel of entry.

One explanation of these cross modality results is that information from the unattended channel is building up in the normal way even though the subject is not attending to it. When he switches attention he is able to execute a response that is more accurate because the information quality is higher. Other interpretations are possible. Since the input remains present until the subject responds, he may take more samples once he has shifted attention. There are studies in the literature where errors occur *more* frequently to unexpected items than to expected ones. Indeed, the increase in accuracy so prominent in Fig. 5 is not found in another condition of the same study in which subjects are involved in a detection rather than a discrimination task. In studies where errors increase when an unexpected event occurs, there are usually many rapid false responses which are made as though an anticipation of the expected event.

Clearly the cross modality data by themselves are not totally convincing. However, coupled with the results of the Stroop and dichotic listening studies, there begins to build a picture of stimulus information automatically activating those internal representations that have been habitually associated with it. Note that this view, which is similar to those presented by LaBerge (1975) and Keele (1973), has the nice feature of making the automaticity of a perceptual pathway closely related to the degree of learning or experience that the subject has had to particular associations. This is the same position that has long been used in the area of motor skills (Fitts & Posner, 1967).

A VIEW OF CONSCIOUS ATTENTION

Many psychologists have identified conscious attention with the limited-capacity processing system discussed by Broadbent (1958, 1971). The idea of the unity of conscious experience compared to the diversity of input stimulation makes such an identification appealing, and we also have followed that basic idea. However, the processing system as Broadbent defined it also had a definite location in the information-processing sequence. Specifically, it stood between stimulation and access to the associative structure of long-term memory. This feature has proven unacceptable because experiments of the type outlined in Section II made it clear that access to long-term memory information is virtually unlimited. This led to efforts to identify the limited-capacity mechanism with other particular mental operations, for example, the view (Keele, 1973) that memory look-up was not limited but that response execution was. These efforts are not entirely successful. Some habitual outputs, such as are involved in the GSR (Corteen & Wood, 1972) or eye movements, may occur without involvement of the limited-capacity system, whereas memory look-up with weak retrieval cues may involve a great deal of conscious capacity.

Limited-Capacity Mechanism

Instead we identify conscious processing with a brain mechanism of limited capacity which may be directed toward different types of activity. For example, it may be directed toward a particular structure in the memory system, a particular input channel or response. If it should be so directed, it will be less available for processing other items. This lack of availability does not prevent automatic activation of the type we discussed in Section II.

Economy.   One major objection to this rather intuitive view of active attention seems to be that it would lack economy. This objection has been raised in response to the idea that emotional words are suppressed from consciousness, but it applies as well to our more general view. In Broadbent's (1973) words,

> It seems to require a biologically unlikely kind of machinery. It seems to mean that the part of the brain which analyzes inputs from the environment, and which is presumably quite complicated, is preceded by another and duplicate part of the brain which carries the same function, deciding what is there in order to reject or accept items for admission to the machinery which decides what is there [p. 67].

If, however, the conscious mechanism is primarily designed not to decide what is there, but to produce integrated actions to often antagonistic habitual responses, its function is not really duplicative. Moreover, the limited-capacity mechanism may serve an important inhibitory function. By giving priority to a particular pathway, it prevents other pathways from having access to any but their habitual response systems (Shallice, 1972). It does not seem worthwhile to debate the general issue, except to suggest that Broadbent's point need not be fatal to the view that we are putting forward.

Pathway inhibition. Another major objection to our view of automatic pathway activation is that it provides for facilitatory but no inhibitory effects within the memory system. This aspect of the theory is very likely in error (Milner, 1957). It is well known that repeated auditory presentation of a word may lead to an alteration of its perceptual quality (Warren, 1970). It is difficult to know the basis of this effect, but it has suggested to some that repetition inhibits input pathways. Eimas and Corbit (1973) have shown that repeated presentation of a phoneme leads to a shift in the phonemic boundary. It is not yet clear that this shift is due to inhibition (fatigue) of the pathway, as they argue. In any case, a successful demonstration of inhibition of a pathway resulting from repeated stimulation would not require great modification of our views, since such inhibition would be pathway specific and differ markedly from the widespread inhibition of all signals resulting from commitment of the central processor.

More serious for our views is the theoretical integration presented by Walley and Weiden (1973). They argue that selective attention results entirely from lateral inhibitory processes in the sensory–memory system. They do not distinguish between automatic pathway effects of the type discussed in Section II and effects of conscious attention. Their views are of importance, but it seems to us that they would have great difficulty in handling the abundant evidence for facilitation due to pathway activation and would also have trouble dealing with the kind of interference found by Warren (1972). Warren has shown that reaction time to name the base word of the Stroop following activation by a related item is facilitated, while the time to name the ink color is retarded. This would not lend itself easily to a lateral inhibition account. The cost benefit experimental results outlined below also seem difficult to accommodate to a lateral inhibition view, at least unaided by additional assumptions.

Cost Benefit Analysis

Theory. The views of automatic and conscious processing we have been setting forth lend themselves to a summary statement (see Fig. 6) that dictates the kind of experimental inquiry we have been following. An input item will automatically activate a specfic pathway in the nervous system. Any item that shares the same pathway will be processed more rapidly and thus be facilitated. This is needed to account for the data obtained by Warren and Conrad. However, as long as the activation pattern is confined to the memory system, there will be no cost or inhibition of the processing of items whose pathways are not activated. This produces a kind of one-way set, in which the nervous system is set to process an item, but is not set against any other item. According to this view, stimulating the memory system in this way produces facilitation but no inhibition.

Once a subject invests his conscious attention in the processing of a stimulus, the benefit obtained from pathway activation is increased, and this benefit is accompanied by a widespread cost or inhibition in the ability of *any* other signals to rise to active attention. This position follows from the limited-capacity nature of the conscious processor. New items still continue to activate input pathways in a purely automatic way, but they are not easily associated to nonhabitual responses. This results in the usual two-sided set familiar in the psychological literature. Subjects do well when the expected stimulus occurs, but are slow in responding to or miss entirely any unexpected item.

Experiments.   In previous papers we have reported in detail the experimental work that has resulted from the cost benefit analysis (Posner & Snyder, 1974). The basic design is to present a single priming item which is either a signal of the same type to which the subject will respond or a neutral warning signal. By manipulating the probabilities that the prime

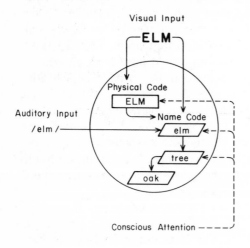

FIG. 6.   A schematic diagram of the role of conscious attention in selecting levels of the automatic activation process upon which to base an output: dashed line, strategic attentional control; solid line, automatic pathway.

——— Automatic Pathway
- - - - Strategic Attentional Control

will be a valid cue to the stimulus item, we hoped to vary the degree of active attention that the subject commits to the prime. According to our theoretical view, when the subject commits little processing capacity to the prime, he should benefit from automatic pathway activation but show no cost. When he actively attends to the prime, he should show benefits from both automatic activation and conscious attention, and these should be accompanied by costs on those trials when the prime is not a valid cue to the target.

To calculate benefit we subtracted the reaction times when the prime matched the array from the reaction times obtained following the neutral warning signal. To calculate cost, we subtracted reaction times obtained following the neutral warning signal from those obtained when the prime mismatched the array. The error data were generally high when the reaction times were long.

The most favorable results are those obtained from "yes" reaction times when the array is a pair of letters that must be matched for physical identity and the prime is either of high validity (prime matches array on .8 of the "yes" trials) or of low validity (prime matches array on .2 of the "yes" trials). Figure 7 provides a cost benefit analysis obtained from these studies as a function of the time by which the prime led the array.

Two features of these data are of primary interest. When the prime is of low validity (upper panel, Fig. 7), there is benefit but no cost. When the prime is of high validity, the benefit begins to accrue more rapidly than does the cost. According to our view, benefit should begin to accrue rapidly after the presentation of the prime as the input pathways are activated. It should be closely time-locked to presentation of the prime. Cost is associated with the commitment of the conscious processor to the prime. This should occur more slowly and depend upon the use the subject intends to make of the prime. The lower panel of Fig. 7 confirms the striking asymmetry of cost and benefit in the condition where the prime is a valid cue. A comparison of the cost function in the upper and lower panels confirms the degree of flexibility that the experimental situation produces in the amount of cost.

The asymmetry in the time course and flexibility of cost and benefit can be demonstrated in data obtained from other studies (Comstock, 1973; Posner & Boies, 1971; Posner & Klein, 1973). In these studies the attention given to a primary letter-matching task is assessed by the degree of interference (cost) in reaction time to a secondary auditory probe. The facilitation in processing the second letter, produced by varying amounts of prior exposure to the first, increases sharply over the first 150 msec of input and levels out after 300 msec. It is very similar in form to those shown in Fig. 7 and illustrates close time-locking to the input signal. Cost func-

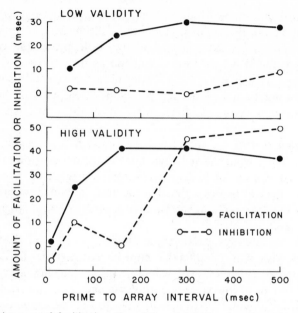

FIG. 7.   Amount of facilitation (benefit) or inhibition (cost) produced by a prime stimulus in relation to a neutral control. The upper panel illustrates a low-validity prime to which subject is not supposed to pay attention; the lower panel illustrates a high-validity prime that is supposed to involve subjects' active attention. (From Posner & Snyder, 1975.)

tions are far more flexible in form. They begin quickly when the subject is given incentive to process the first letter actively. For example, Comstock (1973) turned off the first letter after 15 msec and followed it by a masking field. The cost function for the auditory probe rose sharply within the first 50 msec after first letter presentation. According to our view the subject must have been timing his attention to coincide closely with the letter onset so that he would not miss it. On the other hand, when the first letter is left in the field for two seconds, no cost in processing the probe is found until well after one second (Posner & Klein, 1973).

Strategies

Although these findings provide support for our distinction between pathway activation and conscious attention, other results of our studies (Posner & Synder, 1975) raise problems for it. A complete account of our data requires a knowledge of the strategy the subject used in this task. This task required subjects to perform a match between the two array items. We found clear evidence that subjects also tend to match the prime item against the array. This strategy serves to improve reaction time and reduce error performance on those occasions when the prime and array match, while hurting performance on those occasions when they do not match. Evidence of this strategy appears in the "no" responses. Subjects tend to be faster in rejecting a pair of letters as being identical when they are given a prime that matches neither of them. However, such strategies would not produce the temporal differences in cost and benefit shown in Fig. 7.

We found a task for which there is no evidence of any automatic pathway facilitation at all. In this task subjects are given either a digit or a neutral warning signal (+) as a prime, followed by a row of letters that might or might not contain a single digit. Their task is to indicate if a digit is present in the array. The results show that when subjects are instructed to use the prime to match deliberately against the array, they show both benefit from a matching prime and cost from a mismatch; if they are not so instructed, they show neither cost nor benefit. These results suggest that a more complete model will include an analysis of how strategies imposed by the task affect the way the attentional mechanism interacts with pathway activation. We turn to this question in the next section.

STRATEGIES AND CONSCIOUS CONTROL

A large number of tasks have been studied in recent years which require subjects to make a rapid response to a simple display. The stimuli are familiar ones that come from a particular location and have well-learned semantic associations. The experimenter provides the subject with a specific task the subject is to accomplish with these stimuli. Although subjects usually can carry out the task assigned, they often have to overcome certain automatic tendencies in order to do so. For example, if the display comes from a certain position (e.g., left of the screen) they find it most natural to respond with the key in the same relative position (e.g., left key) (Simon, 1969). If the word used in the display is an unmarked adjective (e.g., good), they find it easier to respond with a key that is also unmarked (e.g., true) (Seymour, 1973). If they are required to say whether a word is a member of a previously memorized list, they are slow to reject a word that has been used in the experimental situation before, even though they correctly rejected it previously (Atkinson & Joula, 1973). These automatic associations tend to speed certain responses and slow others. The subject often appears to overcome these tendencies with practice, but it is doubtful if he does so completely in the usual laboratory experiment. Experimenters usually do one of two things with these tendencies: (1) counterbalance and ignore them, or (2) incorporate them into the model but with a status exactly identical to a component the subject can employ or not employ at will.

In this section we try to examine a few tasks in an effort to see if a distinction between automatic activation and conscious strategies can aid in developing a more consistent account of what often appear to be conflicting results.

Digit Search

Why doesn't the digit search task we discussed at the end of the last section show any evidence of automatic pathway activation? At the time we could only report that this experiment was somehow an exception to our belief that activating a pathway speeded processing of items that shared the pathway. Indeed, we still have no complete explanation, but it seems clear that the strategy of the subject may be rather special in this task. A number of experimental studies are consistent with the view that the human memory system has relatively separate storage areas for letters and digits (Brand, 1971; Jonides & Gleitman, 1972; Posner, 1970; Sanders & Schroots, 1968). There is also some conflicting evidence (Nickerson, 1973), but suppose for the moment that there is a reasonably strong separation between the two types of stimuli in the memory system.

If a subject is asked to determine whether a digit is present in a field of letters, he need simply check to see whether there is activation in that area of memory that represents digits. Notice what happens to this strategy if the subject receives a priming digit. In this case, the priming digit and the digit that is presented in the array will both activate information in the digit area of memory. Thus, the subject will have to make a more careful analysis of the activation in order to determine if the activation pattern is from a priming digit or if it is from one that is in the array. This could very easily slow the subject down, thus counteracting any automatic effect of pathway activation. Experimenters will recognize this hypothesis as entirely *post hoc,* and our data provide no direct confirmation of it.

However, this view provides insight into some interesting discrepancies in the experimental literature. Two studies in which subjects are asked to look for a digit in a field of letters are an experiment by Jonides and Gleitman (1972) and one by Lively and Sanford (1972).

In the Jonides and Gleitman study, when subjects are asked to look for a target item of the opposite class, the array size makes absolutely no difference in the rate of their responses. There is a completely flat function relating the number of items in the array to reaction time. In what appears at first to be a virtually identical condition, Lively and Sanford required subjects to tell whether an array, which consisted of one, two, or four letters, contained a single probe item. On some trials the probe item was a digit; on other trials it was a letter. If one examines those occasions where the probe item was a digit, there is a distinct slope about half that when the probe item is of the same class.

Why the discrepancy between these results? The reason becomes clear when we consider the way in which the subject can use his attentional processes. In the work by Jonides and Gleitman, the subject may ask himself whether there is activation in the area of memory represented by the digits. If there is, he can respond "yes," and if not, "no." In the Lively and Sanford study, activation in the digit area is sufficient basis for a "no" response, but the subject cannot respond "yes" in the absence of such stimulation. Rather, he must shift his attention to the letter area and ask if there is a match in the letter category. If shifts of attention are relatively slow, it is not a very useful strategy to keep one's attention on the digits. Thus, the slope could result from a combination of different strategies adopted to solve this task.

Lexical Decisions

A distinction between automatic activation and conscious attention is also useful in understanding the lexical decision task (Rubenstein, Lewis, & Rubenstein, 1971). These experiments have shown that when subjects are asked to judge whether a string of letters is a word, judgments occur more rapidly following a semantically related item than an unrelated item (Schvaneveldt & Meyer, 1973).

Two mechanisms might produce this effect. The first is based on the concept of automatic activation. According to this view, activation of a particular memory location spreads to nearby locations. The increase in activity in these locations makes it easier to access information stored there. The second model assumes a limited-capacity system that can read out of only one memory location at a time. Time is required to shift from one location to another, and the shifting time increases with the distance between locations. Thus, the association effect occurs because shifting to nearby locations is faster than shifting to more distant locations.

To test these two models, Schvaneveldt and Meyer (1973) presented three words in a simultaneous vertical array. The first and third word were associatively related. They examined whether improvement in the processing of the third word was reduced when the middle word was unrelated. The location-shifting model predicts that an intervening item will abolish the advantage of the association between the first and third items, while the automatic activation model does not. Their initial results conform to the automatic activation model. But the materials were presented simultaneously and there was little real control over the order in which the subject examined them.

Subsequently, work by Meyer, Schvaneveldt, and Ruddy (1973) presents evidence somewhat more favorable to the location-shifting view. In this study they found evidence that the advantage of an association between two words is reduced by an unrelated intervening item, particularly when it is a nonword and thus uses a different output, as well as input, pathway.

The evidence used to choose between automatic activation and location shifting is biased. If both are true, as we believe from our results, one will expect to find facilitation when the items are separated by an unrelated item, and the experimenter will conclude that the effects are due only to automatic activation. In order to separate the automatic from the conscious effects, one may examine what happens to a nonword or unrelated word that occurs following a priming word as compared to one following a neutral condition such as a warning signal. If the facilitation of a word by another word is accompanied by an increase in reaction time to unrelated items, one might argue for an attentional explanation. If the benefit for an associated word is not accompanied by a cost to the unrelated word, a more automatic process seems required. We would expect that attentional mechanisms would be especially important when the frequency of related words is high, and automatic activation when the frequency of related words is low.

Matching Task

A number of years ago one of us reported it was faster to respond "same" to two identical letters than it was when the letters had only their name in common (Posner & Mitchell, 1967). The reason presented for this difference was that with identical letters subjects could respond on the basis of visual information alone and thus emit their response before the letter names were available. In a number of subsequent papers, converging operations were presented that support this position (Posner, 1969, 1973; Posner, Lewis, & Conrad, 1972).

However, an astute reader of this paper will realize that there are now two different explanations for the same phenomenon. One is the levels-of-processing account I have just mentioned. The second is the view that two identical letters will share more of the same pathway than letters that agree only in name. Notice that the first account is a somewhat optional one, since the subject could choose to withhold responding in all cases until he verified the letter name; the second account rests upon an automatic facilitation of the pathway.

The best evidence favoring the second account is an experiment by Eichelman (1970) in which he required subjects to name letters as quickly as possible. Eichelman's subjects, showed an improved reaction time when the letter was repeated on successive trials. This repetition effect was greater for physically identical letters than for those having only their name in common. Eichelman proposed a pathway-activation account of these results. It is also possible to handle these results on the basis of a processing-levels explanation. The idea is that the name of a stimulus presented on a trial is stored along with the visual information. On the next trial the subject first attempts to match the new input to the item presented on the previous trial. If there is a match, he emits the same response without having to identify the new input item. For some time it seemed that this explanation would do. However, subsequently both Warren (1970) and Kirsner (1972)[3] showed that naming was facilitated by presentation of a prior item to which no response was required, and Posner and Boies (1971) reported that physical matches became relatively faster than mismatches as a function of the time by which the first of two items led the second. These results favored a pathway explanation.

The advantage due to pathway activation in the matching and naming experiments is in the range of 30–50 msec. This is about half the general advantage found for physical matches over name matches.

The advantage of physical matches over name matches may consist of two different components. One involves the specific level of information on which the subject may base his response, and the other refers to the general advantage of an activated pathway. In a naming experiment subjects appear to benefit from automatic activation primarily. In simultaneous matching tasks the level-of-processing component seems to dominate. In successive matching, both factors may be involved.

Summary

We feel that subjects can program their conscious attention to (1) receive information from a particular input channel or area of memory and (2) perform particular operations upon received information. These programs, which are under the conscious control of the subject, we have been calling strategies. Strategies cannot prevent the automatic activation processes discussed in Section II. This inability of attention to prevent the build-up of information through automatic activation is in agreement with

---

[3] Unlike Eichelman, Kirsner found no greater facilitation when the new item was physically identical (visual–visual) over when they shared only the name (auditory–visual). This could have resulted from slower decay of name activation with an auditory prime.

ideas that have been advocated by Keele (1973), LaBerge (1975), and Shiffrin (1975).

However, strategies do have a profound effect on what subjects perceive consciously, act upon, and report later. To claim that these effects are not perceptual seems to be a rather peculiar use of the term. Evidence shows clearly that subjects may activate memorial pathways even at the level of representation that underlies physical matching (Posner, 1969) and can thus increase the rate at which information enters the conscious processing system. Increases in the rate of information processing of this type improve both speed and accuracy. Shiffrin (1975) has presented evidence that knowledge of the source of input does not improve d' measures. On the other hand, Smith and Blaha (1969) have shown d' changes when subjects know where in the visual field a signal will occur. Our data do not resolve this conflict, but our feeling is that the main importance of a strategy that turns the subject's attention to an input channel or memory pathway is not so much to facilitate the selected item (benefit) as it is to reduce the likelihood of interruption from outside the selected domain (cost).

The act of maintaining concentration on a pathway requires effort. This is additional evidence that it does not turn off the automatic pathway effects of other stimuli. Rather, concentration serves to reduce the probability that these other stimuli will intrude upon the conscious processor. If such intrusion were completely impossible, it would not be necessary to break off this writing so frequently to respond to various real and imagined stimuli. In the study of emotions and attitudes, psychologists have addressed the question of why stimuli outside of consciousness sometimes intrude upon our thought processes. We turn now to examine this issue in the light of the distinctions discussed in this chapter.

THE PLACE OF VALUE IN A JUDGMENT OF FACT

Perhaps no place is the distinction between automatic and conscious processes more needed than in the study of the role of emotions, affects, and feelings on perception. The "new look" in perception argued that emotional responses to a word influenced our identification of that word (Erdelyi, 1974). How could identification depend on something (emotional response) that cannot arise unless the word is identified? According to our argument this confuses two senses of identification. One involves the activation of the pathway of interest (i.e., the word name and its habitual associates), and the other involves our conscious awareness of that representation. Studies reviewed in Section II (Corteen & Wood, 1972; von Wright et al., 1975) suggest that the former may occur without the latter ever occurring.

If one makes a distinction between automatic and conscious processes, the problem of the role of emotions in perception may be divided into two parts. First, at what level of processing is emotional information accessed in the memory system? Are the emotional attributes of an item stored as an association to the item name, or are they attributes by which names are organized? This latter view, which has been advocated by Osgood, Suci, and Tannenbaum (1955) and more recently by Wickens (1972), holds that emotional connotations are primary semantic attributes that may be contacted prior to word identification. Second, how does the emotional response to a word, however produced, affect our awareness of that word?

The second question has been addressed by recent experimental investigations that suggest that the emotional response to a stimulus may serve to change the rehearsal pattern. Erdelyi and Applebaum (1973) show that an emotional symbol (swastika) captures the subject's attention in a way that reduces the information he is able to report from the rest of a complex display. This suggests that emotional stimuli will often demand attention. Broadbent (1973) has shown that emotional words affect the tachistoscopic recognition of words that follow them in a list. He finds that following the presentation of a nasty word, a subject reduces the range of cues he takes in from the next word. He is less likely to report the first and last letter, but more likely to report adjacent ones. This is similar to the effects found with other stressors (Broadbent, 1958, 1971) and may be related to what one finds with a heightened sense of alertness that commits the central processor to an early stage in the buildup of information (Posner, 1974). Broadbent suggests that the effects of an emotional word upon the report of the next word might also intervene between the emotional classification and the awareness of a given word. Of course, the time between classification and conscious awareness is short in tachistoscopic studies and one might expect weak effects, but the principle that emotional words can affect the conscious processor seems to have been established.

These results do not tell us whether emotion is contacted at a relatively early level in the processing of an item, or whether emotion is treated as a higher level semantic dimension. Since the material treated in this paper seems to show that even higher level semantic dimensions may be contacted rapidly and automatically, the fact that emotions affect the direction of our conscious attention does not give them any special status within the memory system.

Impression Formation

In order to attack this question, we wanted to have a paradigm in which we could vary the strength of the emotional response to an item and see how it affected the factual processing of item information. Many recent investigations of the memorial representation of affect have involved the emotional connotation or evaluation of trait-descriptive adjectives. Asch (1946) investigated the impressions people formed of others, based on a series of adjective traits describing a given person. This has led to a series of experimental investigations (Anderson, 1972) in which people have attempted to form deliberate conscious impressions of others from listening to a set of trait-descriptive adjectives. It is clear from these studies that people can form such impressions. Moreover, Anderson and Hubert (1965) and Anderson and Farkas (1973) have argued that the storage of such information is separate from the specific set of adjectives by which the information is conveyed. They argue that the memory underlying the emotion or evaluation is abstracted from the adjectives and stored separately from the adjectives themselves. The basis for this view is that if asked to recall the adjectives in a given list, the subjects show a relatively strong recency effect, but if asked to rate their overall impression of the person, the primacy effect is stronger.

Our goal was to develop a firmer notion of the memory structures that underlie the emotional classification and to compare them with those that mediate retention of the individual adjectives. In particular we sought to understand the level at which emotional information makes contact with a decision about the presence of a particular trait as a descriptor of a person. The experiments used a memory scanning task developed by Sternberg (1966).

Retrieval of Item and Value Information

In order to observe the relationship between emotion and item information, we provided subjects with three kinds of sentences. The sentences always consisted of a single proper name followed by one to four adjectives. The adjectives might be all positive in emotional tone, all negative in emotional tone, or a mixture of positive and negative emotional tones. Words were selected from norms provided by Anderson. The sequence of events is illustrated in Fig. 8. Following the sentences, subjects were given a single probe word. On half the trials, the probe matched one of the words in the sentence, and on half it did not. Subjects were to respond as rapidly as possible to the question of whether the item in the probe matched an item in the sentence.

The basic results of the experiment are quite simple. For "yes" responses reaction times did not differ for positive, negative, or neutral lists. The "no" responses can be broken down into two types, those in which the emotional tone matched the list and those in which it did not. We compared

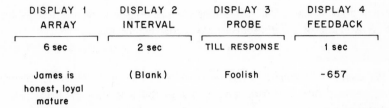

DISPLAY 1 ARRAY	DISPLAY 2 INTERVAL	DISPLAY 3 PROBE	DISPLAY 4 FEEDBACK
6 sec	2 sec	TILL RESPONSE	1 sec
James is honest, loyal mature	(Blank)	Foolish	-657

FIG. 8. Sequence of events in the studies of the role of affect on judgments about the presence of probe adjective.

the two types of "no" responses averaged across conditions where the list was positive and where it was negative (see Fig. 9). This is a particularly sensitive comparison since the probes are the same words in both conditions but follow arrays of differing emotional tone. The results show a small but significantly faster reaction time when the emotional response is opposite to that of the list than when it is identical. This is accompanied by a reduction in error when the emotional response did not match the list. While the difference in reaction times between matching and mismatching "no" responses did not change systematically as a function of size of the list, the error differences changed sharply as a function of size of the list. When the list consisted of four items, there was a much higher probability that the subject would make an error when the emotional response matched

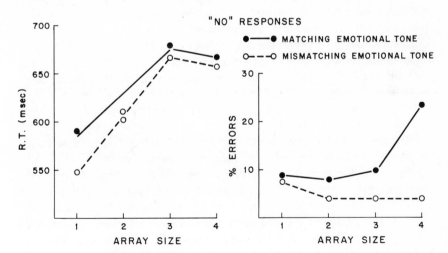

FIG. 9. Reaction time (left) and errors (right) in "no" judgments as a function of array size when the probe word either matches the array items in emotional tone (e.g., both positive) or mismatches them (e.g., array positive and probe negative).

the list than when it did not match. What do these results tell us about the relationship of the item information and the emotion?

Models

There are clear effects of the impression on the task. When the emotional tone of the probe does not match that of the list, subjects are facilitated in responding "no."

There are several possible ways this result might occur. Suppose that the emotional information was present relatively more quickly than the factual information. This might be the case if the subject consciously prepared to match on the basis of emotional tone. One would expect subjects to be able to reject the mismatching emotional tone without any required search of the factual information, and this would produce a flat slope relating mismatching "no" responses to array size. However, there is no tendency for the slope to be reduced when the probe emotion mismatches.

Another view supposes that each word consists of an item and an emotional attribute associated with it. Thus, the adjective "loyal" is associated directly with its denotative and connotative meanings. In this view, a probe word may be rejected as matching any array word more quickly if the mismatch involves both item and emotion than if it involves only item information. Lively and Sanford (1972) have adopted exactly this model for their account of what happens when a subject receives a list consisting of digits and gets a probe that is a consonant. Such a model does not fit our data, since the slope of the "no" reaction time to mismatching emotions is at least as great as for matching emotions.

In their Loyola Symposium paper Atkinson, Herrmann, and Wescourt (1974) suggest that the slope of reaction time versus array size for probes that are outside the category of the list serves as a measure of the degree of semantic analysis required prior to contact with the information representing the category of the probe. They suggest that relatively flat slopes are obtained when the subject has to process little semantic meaning of the probe, and steeper slopes are obtained as the semantic processing required in order to determine the category is increased.

The overall results of the reaction time and error data obtained from our experiment seem most consistent with the following analysis of the relation of emotional information to item information. Suppose there are two independent memory structures. One memory structure consists of the list of trait adjectives that the subject reads in the sentence. The other memory structure consists of an abstracted impression based on an integration of the values presented by the individual adjectives. The time to search the memory structure representing the traits would increase as a function of number of items in the list. On the other hand, the impression would

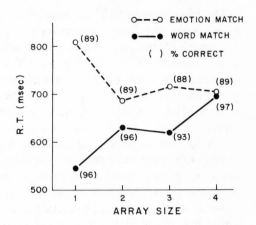

Fig. 10.   Reaction time and percentage correct for "yes" responses when subjects are instructed to match the emotional tone of probe and array deliberately. Word matches are those in which the particular probe adjective was a member of the array; for emotion matches the probe word was not in the array but had the same emotional tone.

tend to get stronger as we increase the number of items on which it is based; thus, one might expect a reduction in reaction time. Since judgments based on the emotional classification alone would only be reliable for mismatching "no" responses, one would expect errors to pile up for matching "no" responses when the output of the emotional structure occurred prior to the output of the list array. This could account for the high error rate obtained with four-item arrays.

To test this idea we performed an experiment in which subjects received the same lists as described previously, but were asked to determine if the probe item had the same emotional content as in the previous list. Two types of "yes" responses are possible: first, those to probe items that were on the list, and second, those that were not identical but shared the same emotional tone. The results (see Fig. 10) support our two-process view of the matching task. The role of the number of items is to increase reaction times for those items that match, but to reduce it for those that mismatch. The two functions come together at about four-item lists.

In brief, what seems to happen is the formation of two memory structures, one consisting of a list of item names, and the other consisting of a generalized emotional response to the items. These separate memory structures appear to be oppositely affected by item length. The data seem most consistent with the view that each memory structure has an output to the binary decision. In cases where the two decisions agree, there seems to be relatively little effect on overall reaction time or errors. In cases where they disagree, however, there appears to be a lengthening of reaction time as if there were some tendency to make the conflicting response. However, the tendency seems slight unless we let the times for the output get very close together. In that case, there seems to be a very difficult decision to be made and a high probability of error.

These data agree with the view of two separate memory systems laid down by the list items (Anderson & Hubert, 1965). However, they do not agree with the view that emotional information concerning the impression is handled in any different way than other semantic dimensions in the memory system. Rather, it appears that evaluations are handled very much like other semantic dimensions. When a number of items have the same emotional content, information is integrated to produce an overall impression against which to evaluate input.

It would be of interest to examine the extent to which the conscious strategy to extract an evaluation is a necessary condition for obtaining the results we have presented. Currently we know only that subjects need no instruction to be influenced by the evaluative components, but we do not know whether they intend to extract such information either because they realize it is useful in the task or simply find it of interest. Manipulations of the probability that the evaluative information will serve as a valid cue to perform the task correctly might help us to deal with this question.

Long-Term Memory

In the psychological literature there are a number of studies that compare the retenton of specific item information with the retention of more abstracted information that stands for a set of items. Much of this literature has used dot patterns to serve as the item instances. If subjects are required to classify a set of patterns into a category, they seem to abstract from that category a prototype or central tendency that comes to stand for that category (Posner, 1969; Reed, 1972). We speculated that the abstraction of emotional information and its storage in terms of an impression would be somewhat the same as found in the previous work with patterns. To study this, we set up an experiment in which the subjects had to learn a list of ten adjectives associated with each of six proper names. Two types of test trials were given: list trials and name trials. On list trials, subjects were shown a name and four adjectives selected from those associated with that name, and they were then probed with a trait that was either from that list or not. On name trials, the subject was merely given the name that was being tested, followed after the same retention interval by a single probe adjective. On the name trials we attempted to assess the long-term memory structure that represented the set of items associated with the person's name, while on the list trials we attempted to replicate the results we obtained in the previous experiment.

The results obtained in the previous experiments were replicated on the list trials. Once again, reaction time to "no" responses that mismatched in emotional tone were faster than for "no" responses that matched in tone. On the name trials we found that the reaction time to mismatching "no" responses was 200–400 msec faster than for matching "no" responses or for "yes" responses. The memory system that came to stand for the emotional response was more available to the subject than that which represented the individual items.

Several alternative explanations of this result are possible. It could be that the subject actively attended to the emotional classification of the list, or it could be that the memory system representing the emotion resisted forgetting more than that of the individual item. Further work will be needed to separate these two accounts.

Summary

Our results, then, taken together with the recent work of Broadbent (1973) and Erdelyi and Applebaum (1973), suggest an overall account of the role of emotion at least when it arises from the evaluative aspect of words. Emotional information is stored as a high level but habitual associate to given words or constellations of words. One would expect that the presentation of an item would automatically activate associated emotional responses. These responses might feed back to affect the conscious mechanism guiding its processing of the various kinds of information associated with the input item. The complexity of this view fits with the rather diverse results that have been obtained in many experiments involving emotional items. Doubtless, what becomes conscious will be a function not only of the level of emotionality raised by the automatic process, but also by strategies used in different experiments. Thus, the presence of emotional information may lead in some contexts to perceptual vigilance, and, in other cases, to perceptual defense. Investigations of the emotional responses to items would seem to profit from the kind of methodology obtainable with trait-descriptive adjectives where a variety of different individual items may be combined to produce a single emotional trace system. Perhaps the most interesting area for study will be how well emotional material transfers from the situation in which it is learned to other tests.

OVERVIEW

Summary

This chapter discussed the distinction between automatic activation processes which are solely the result of past learning and processes which are under current conscious control. Automatic activation processes are those which may occur without intention, without any conscious awareness and without interference with other mental activity. They are distinguished from operations performed by the conscious processing system since the latter system is of limited capacity and thus its commitment to any operation reduces its availability to perform any other operation. Many current cognitive tasks were analyzed in terms of the interaction of automatic activation processes with strategies determined by task instructions. Concentration on a source of signals serves to reduce interference from outside that source. Outside signals still intrude, particularly when they are classified by the memory system as having emotional significance.

Prospects

Where are the views outlined in this paper taking us? I am afraid that it is in two directions, which may well turn out to produce a kind of research schizophrenia. The first direction is toward an understanding of the more detailed mechanisms that subserve the functions of pathway activation, levels of processing, and conscious attention (Posner, 1974). This effort leads to the creation of ever simpler tasks, toward a comparison of behavioral data with evoked potential and single-cell studies, and a closer coordination between human and animal studies. The relative stereotypy of "automatic activation" processes gives hope that a mechanistic and analytic approach may work. In contrast, they will not by themselves allow us to say much about how people will actually perform tasks.

The goal of understanding human performance requires an analysis of strategies useful in particular task environments (Newell & Simon, 1972). In part, this involves an effort to understand how strategies modify and build upon "automatic retrieval" processes. Our studies of the effects of emotion on judgment were addressed to that goal. We hope that further efforts along this line will aid us in understanding how much our prior learning biases the way we can think in a particular task environment.

REFERENCES

Anderson, J. R., & Bower, G. H. *Human associative memory.* Washington, D.C.: Winston, 1973.

Anderson, N. H. Information inflation: A brief survey. Technical Report No. 24. University of California, San Diego: Center for Human Information Processing, 1972.

Anderson, N. H., & Farkas, A. J. New light on order effects in attitude change. *Journal of Social Psychology,* 1973, **28**, 88–93.

Anderson, N. H., & Hubert, S. Effects of concomitant verbal recall on order effects in personality impression formation. *Journal of Verbal Learning and Verbal Behavior,* 1965, **2**, 531–539.

Asch, S. Forming impressions of personality. *Journal of Abnormal and Social Psychology,* 1946, **41**, 258–290.

Atkinson, R. C., Herrmann, D. J., & Wescourt, K. T. Search processes in recognition memory. In R. L. Solso (Ed.), *Theories in cognitive psychology.* Hillsdale, New Jersey: Lawrence Erlbaum Associates, 1974.

Atkinson, R. C., & Joula, J. F. Factors influencing speed and accuracy of word recognition. In S. Kornblum (Ed.), *Attention and performance IV*. New York: Academic Press, 1973.

Brand, J. Classification without identification in visual search. *Quarterly Journal of Experimental Psychology*, 1971, **23**, 178–186.

Broadbent, D. E. *Perception and communication*. London: Pergamon, 1958.

Broadbent, D. E. *Decision and stress*. London and New York: Academic Press, 1971.

Broadbent, D. E. *In defence of empirical psychology*. London: Methuen, 1973.

Comstock, E. M. Processing capacity in a letter-matching task. *Journal of Experimental Psychology*, 1973, **100**, 63–72.

Conrad, C. Context effects in sentence comprehension: A study of the subjective lexicon. *Memory & Cognition*, 1974, **2**, 130–138.

Corteen, R. S., & Wood, B. Autonomic responses to shock associated words in an unattended channel. *Journal of Experimental Psychology*, 1972, **97**, 308–313.

Dyer, F. N. The Stroop phenomenon and its use in the study of perceptual, cognitive and response processes. *Memory & Cognition*, 1973, **1**, 106–120.

Eichelman, W. H. Stimulus and response repetition effects for naming letters. *Perception & Psychophysics*, 1970, **7**, 94–96.

Eimas, P. D., & Corbit, J. D. Selective adaptation of linguistic feature detectors. *Cognitive Psychology*, 1973, **6**, 99–109.

Erdelyi, M. H. A new look at the new look: Perceptual defense and vigilance. *Psychological Review*, 1974, **81**, 1–25.

Erdelyi, M. H., & Applebaum, G. A. Cognitive masking. *Bulletin of the Psychonomics Society*, 1973, **1**, 59–61.

Fitts, P. M., & Posner, M. I. *Human performance*. Monterey, California: Brooks Cole, 1967.

Garner, W. R., & Felfoldy, G. L. Integrality of stimulus dimensions in various types of information processing. *Cognitive Psychology*, 1970, **1**, 225–241.

Greenwald, A. G. A double stimulation test of ideomotor theory with implications for selective attention. *Journal of Experimental Psychology*, 1970, **84**, 392–398. (a)

Greenwald, A. G. Selective attention as a function of signal rate. *Journal of Experimental Psychology*, 1970, **86**, 48–52. (b)

Hintzman, D. L., Carre, F. A., Eskridge, V. L., Owens, A. M., Shaff, S. S., & Sparks, E. M. "Stroop" effect: Input or output phenomenon. *Journal of Experimental Psychology*, 1972, **95**, 458–459.

Jonides, J., & Gleitman, H. A conceptual category effect in visual search: o as letter or as digit. *Perception & Psychophysics*, 1972, **12**, 457–460.

Keele, S. W. *Attention and human performance*. Pacific Palisades, California: Goodyear, 1973.

Kirsner, K. Naming latency facilitation: An analysis of the encoding component in reaction time. *Journal of Experimental Psychology*, 1972, **95**, 171–176.

LaBerge, D. H. Identification of two components of the time to switch attention. In S. Kornblum (Ed.), *Attention and performance IV*. New York: Academic Press, 1973.

LaBerge, D. H. Attention and automatic information processing. In P. M. A. Rabbitt (Ed.), *Attention and performance V*. London: Academic Press, 1975, in press.

Lackner, J. R., & Garrett, M. F. Resolving ambiguity effects of biasing context in the unattended ear. *Cognition*, 1973, **1**, 359–374.

Lewis, J. Semantic processing of unattended messages using dichotic listening. *Journal of Experimental Psychology*, 1970, **85**, 225–228.

Lively, B. L., & Sanford, B. J. The use of category information in a memory search task. *Journal of Experimental Psychology,* 1972, **93,** 379–385.
Mackay, D. G. Aspects of the theory of comprehension, memory and attention. *Quarterly Journal of Experimental Psychology,* 1973, **25,** 22–40.
Meyer, D. E., Schvaneveldt, R. W., & Ruddy, M. G. Activation of lexical memory. Paper presented at the meeting of the Psychonomic Society, St. Louis, Missouri, 1973.
Milner, P. M. The cell assembly: Mark II. *Psychological Review,* 1957, **64,** 242–252.
Morton, J., & Chambers, S. M. Selective attention to words and colors. *Quarterly Journal of Experimental Psychology,* 1973, **25,** 387–397.
Murray, D. J., Mastronadi, J., & Duncan, S. Selective attention to "physical" versus "verbal" aspects of colored words. *Psychonomic Science,* 1972, **26,** 305–307.
Newell, A., & Simon, H. A. *Human problem solving.* Englewood Cliffs, New Jersey: Prentice-Hall, 1972.
Nickerson, R. S. Can characters be classified directly as digits versus letters or must they be identified first? *Memory & Cognition,* 1973, **1,** 477–484.
Osgood, C. E., Suci, G. H., & Tannenbaum, P. H. *The measurement of meaning.* Urbana, Illinois: The University of Illinois Press, 1955.
Posner, M. I. Abstraction and the process of recognition. In G. Bower (Ed.), *The psychology of learning and motivation.* Vol. 3. New York: Academic Press, 1969.
Posner, M. I. On the relationship between letter names and superordinate categories. *Quarterly Journal of Experimental Psychology,* 1970, **22,** 279–287.
Posner, M. I. Coordination of codes. In W. G. Chase (Ed.), *Visual information processing.* New York: Academic Press, 1973.
Posner, M. I. Psychobiology of attention. In M. S. Gazzaniga & C. Blakemore (Eds.), *Handbook of psychobiology.* New York: Academic Press, 1975, in press.
Posner, M. I., & Boies, S. W. Components of attention. *Psychological Review,* 1971, **78,** 391–408.
Posner, M. I., & Klein, R. M. On the functions of consciousness. In S. Kornblum (Ed.), *Attention and performance IV.* New York: Academic Press, 1973.
Posner, M. I., Lewis, J., & Conrad, C. Component processes in reading: A performance analysis. In J. Kavanaugh & I. Mattingly (Eds.), *Language by ear and by eye.* Boston: MIT Press, 1972.
Posner, M. I., & Mitchell, R. F. Chronometric analysis of classification. *Psychological Review,* 1967, **74,** 392–409.
Posner, M. I., & Snyder, C. R. R. Facilitation and inhibition in the processing of signals. In P. M. A. Rabbit (Ed.), *Attention and performance V.* London: Academic Press, 1975, in press.
Reed, S. K. Pattern recognition and categorization. *Cognitive Psychology,* 1972, **3,** 382–407.
Rubenstein, H., Lewis, S. S., & Rubenstein, M. A. Evidence for phonemic recoding in visual word recognition. *Journal of Verbal Learning and Verbal Behavior,* 1971, **10,** 645–657.
Sanders, G. F., & Schroots, J. J. F. Cognitive categories and memory space II: The effect of temporal versus category recall. *Quarterly Journal of Experimental Psychology,* 1968, **20,** 373–379.
Schvaneveldt, R., & Meyer, D. E. Retrieval and comparison processes in semantic memory. In S. Kornblum (Ed.), *Attention and performance IV.* New York: Academic Press, 1973.

Seymour, P. H. K. Judgment of verticality and response availability. *Bulletin of the Psychonomic Society,* 1973, **1,** 196–198.

Shallice, T. Dual functions of consciousness. *Psychological Review,* 1972, **79,** 383–393.

Shiffrin, R. M. The locus and role of attention in memory systems. In P. M. A. Rabbitt (Ed.), *Attention and performance V.* London: Academic Press, 1975, in press.

Simon, J. R. Reaction toward the source of stimulation. *Journal of Experimental Psychology,* 1969, **81,** 174–176.

Smith, S. W., & Blaha, J. Preliminary report summarizing the result of location uncertainty experiments. Institute for Research in Vision, Ohio State University, 1969.

Sternberg, S. High speed scanning in human memory. *Science,* 1966, **153,** 652–654.

Underwood, B. J. False recognition produced by implicit verbal responses. *Journal of Experimental Psychology,* 1965, **70,** 122–129.

von Wright, J. M., Anderson, K., & Stenman, U. Generalization of conditioned GRSs in dichotic listening. In P. M. A. Rabbitt (Ed.), *Attention and performance V.* London: Academic Press, 1975, in press.

Walley, R. E., & Weiden, T. D. Lateral inhibition and cognitive masking: A neuropsychological theory of attention. *Psychological Review,* 1973, **80,** 284–302.

Warren, R. E. Stimulus encoding in memory. Unpublished doctoral dissertation, University of Oregon, 1970.

Warren, R. E. Stimulus encoding and memory. *Journal of Experimental Psychology,* 1972, **94,** 90–100.

Warren, R. E. Association, directionality and stimulus encoding. *Journal of Experimental Psychology,* 1974, **102,** 151–158.

Wickens, D. D. Characteristics of word encoding. In A. W. Melton & E. Martin (Eds.), *Coding processes in human memory.* Washington, D.C.: Winston, 1972.

4
FORM, FORMATION, AND TRANSFORMATION OF INTERNAL REPRESENTATIONS

Roger N. Shepard
Stanford University

SOME CENTRAL ISSUES

The Problem of Nonverbal Internal Representations

Among the kinds of unobservable internal events that have been explicitly discussed in psychology, it is the purely verbal mediators and, especially, the implicit naming responses that have been most extensively acknowledged, formalized and empirically studied. Since such covert responses could be assumed to have the same form and to obey the same laws as the corresponding overt responses from which they derived, the admission of this kind of internal event entailed the least drastic violation of previously self-imposed behavioristic strictures. Moreover, the problems of the form and the transformation of internal representations, with which we shall be principally concerned here, did not arise in nearly so crucial a way. First, since it is clear that generally the word that is learned for a particular object is associated with it by arbitrary convention, there has never been any temptation to puzzle about the formal or structural relation between a word (or its internal representation) and the external object, say, for which that word stands. Second, since a word is not only arbitrary in this sense but also is a fixed, categorical unit, it is not in general the case that the kinds of transformations to which objects are subject in the external world are in any way paralleled by analogous transformations in the corresponding words.

That the scientific study of inherently nonverbal representations is only just beginning is not surprising, then. These, unlike implicit words, clearly are neither derived from nor of the same form as previously overt and physically measurable responses, nor can they be externalized except perhaps in a very limited sense and degree—by a sufficiently talented artist—and then only in the case of concrete visual images, not in the case of abstract schemata. Furthermore, as the work to be considered here is particularly designed to show, there are significant senses in which it can be said that mental images do have a formal or structural relation to their corresponding external objects, and that mental images can be mentally transformed in ways that are parallel or analogous to the kinds of transformations that occur in the corresponding external objects.

In considering the nature of the formal or structural relation between internal representations and their corresponding external objects a distinction, central to what follows, can be drawn between what I have termed *first-order* and *second-order isomorphism*.

First-Order Isomorphism of Internal Representations

First-order isomorphism, in this sense, pertains to the extent that there is some structural resemblance between an individual internal neurophysiological event and the individual external object that it represents (cf. Köhler, 1959; Smith, 1968, p. 91). Suppose, for example, that the neurophysiological event corresponding to the perceptual registration of an external square has four component parts [e.g., activation of four interrelated cell assemblies, in Hebb's (1949) terminology] that correspond in some way to the corners of the square. Then, if these four parts are necessarily arranged in the geometrical form of a square within the neural tissues of the brain, we should have a very thoroughgoing kind of first-order isomorphism. However, even if these four parts are not themselves arranged in the shape of a square within the brain, the very fact that they have some sort of one-to-one relationship to parts of the external object (e.g., corners) entails a degree of first-order isomorphism. Indeed to an extent the same is true of any representations, including various relatives of the Fourier transform (Pollen, Lee, & Taylor, 1971; Pribram, 1971), that preserve within themselves much of the structural information about the external object—even if in greatly altered form.

On the other hand, it is possible that the internal process that effectively signals the presence of a square in the visual field is some simple or, at least, structurally homogeneous neural activity—such as the firing of a particular neuron or, more likely, such as a sufficient level of firing among the functionally equivalent (i.e., mutually substitutable) neurons in a particular subset that, however, may be quite widely or haphazardly distributed within the neural tissues of the brain (see Konorski, 1967). In this second case, there is no first-order isomorphism whatever, because the relation between the external object and the representational event to which it gives rise within the brain is one merely of causal regularity—not one of any kind of structural resemblance.

On initial consideration, this second alternative may appear incompatible with the most undeniable sort of introspective evidence. For, whether the square we experience is perceived, remembered, or merely imagined, the experience itself clearly seems to have internal structure, to be four cornered or, in short, to be square. How, one is tempted to ask, can the firing of a single neuron or even of an undifferentiated population of neurons account for this highly structured, seemingly four-cornered experience that we call our mental picture of the square?

Second-Order Isomorphism of Internal Representations

A partial answer to this question is provided by the principle of second-order isomorphism (Shepard & Chipman, 1970). According to this principle there must indeed be a kind of isomorphism between internal representations and their external objects, but this isomorphism need not be a concrete, first-order one between each individual representation and its corresponding object. Instead, it may be a more abstract, second-order one between the functional relations among the alternative internal representations, on the one hand, and the structural relations among the corresponding external objects, on the other.

Thus, when I say that I am experiencing (perceiving, remembering, imagining, or even hallucinating) a square, or when I say that the square that I am mentally picturing has four corners, I am not claiming that there is something that is literally square or four-cornered going on in my physical brain. (Even if such a thing were in fact going on, how would I know?) Instead, what I am in effect saying is that, whatever it is that is going on in my brain, it has something in common with what was going on in the past when (to greatly simplify the matter) other, generally older persons have said things like "This is a square" and, to a lesser extent, with what was going on when they have informed me that "This is a rectangle," "This has corners," "This has four parts," and so on (cf. Place, 1956; Smart, 1959).

In second-order isomorphism, our knowledge of the world is embodied—not in the structure of each individual internal representation considered by itself—but, rather, in the extent to which different internal representations are functionally equivalent or have something functional in common with each other at the neurophysiological level. This, of course implies, that we can determine that two things have much in common without being able to say what either of the two things is in any absolute sense

(Smart, 1959). There is not necessarily anything mysterious about this. A machine can arrive at an index of similarity between two pictures (e.g., by measuring the amount of light transmitted through a positive transparency of one suitably overlaid on a negative transparency of the other) without at any point having anything that could be considered a description of what is in either picture itself.

We have undertaken several studies in which comparisons can be made between judgments of similarity among the same objects under two different conditions: one in which those objects are actually presented to the subject, and one in which they are only named. The basic idea behind these studies is as follows: To the extent (a) that the same similarity judgments are made under the two conditions and (b) that these judgments are clearly related to identifiable properties of the actual physical objects, one has evidence consistent with the notion that in both conditions subjects are basing their judgments on similar sorts of internal representations—presumably *images* (generated, in the one condition, on the basis of external stimulation and, in the other, on the basis of information stored internally in association with the names). However, to the extent (a) that the similarity judgments are different when only the names are presented or (b) that these latter judgments are related to the names, to associations, or to verbal descriptions more than to the objects themselves, one has evidence that the internal representations elicited by the names were not mental images of those objects but other, perhaps more verbal representations.

In contrast to internal representations that are more or less image-like, internal representations, such as names, that have come to represent the external object through the learning of an arbitrary convention will not, in general, conform even to the second-order principle of isomorphism. Thus, when we merely think the words, "square" obviously has more in common with "spare" (which corresponds to a very different sort of external object, e.g., an extra tire) than with "rectangle" (which corresponds to a very similar sort of external object).

Stimulus Analyzability, Mental Transformations, and Isomorphism

Although the existence of a first-order isomorphism necessarily entails the presence of a second-order isomorphism, the reverse does not hold. Hence, empirical demonstrations of second-order isomorphism leave open the question as to whether there is not after all some degree of first-order isomorphism as well—at least, in some cases.

The answer may be that it does, in fact, depend upon the case. In particular, there appears to be an important distinction, here, between what I have termed *analyzable* and *unanalyzable* stimuli (see Shepard, 1964a;

Shepard & Chang, 1963; and see Garner & Felfoldy, 1970; Torgerson, 1958, Chapter 11; where essentially the same distinction is discussed in somewhat different terms). For, an unanalyzable stimulus such as a homogeneous color does seem even introspectively to be without any internal structure. Hence, we can readily believe that it is represented by the firing of some particular but internally undifferentiated or homogeneous set of neurons. An analyzable stimulus such as the square considered earlier, on the other hand, appears by introspection to have a degree of internal structure.

Indeed, although I suggested before that this apparent structure can in part be explained by invoking only the principle of second-order isomorphism, it is unlikely that a completely adequate account of the representation of analyzable stimuli can be framed without some recourse to the principle of first-order isomorphism. The simple fact that we can differentially attend to component parts of an analyzable stimulus (Shepard, Hovland, & Jenkins, 1961)—that we can, for example, focus upon or vividly imagine the upper right-hand corner of the square, almost to the exclusion from awareness of the rest of the square—strongly indicates that our internal representation *is* differentiated, *does* have parts. And these parts, which by some mechanism of selective attention can thus be differentially accentuated or suppressed, clearly do have some kind of a one-to-one relation to parts of the corresponding external object.

In what follows we shall be primarily concerned with the internal representation of external objects that are relatively analyzable in this sense. A noteworthy property of such representations is that they can be mentally operated upon or transformed in various ways—not only by selective accentuation of their various parts (as noted above) but also by a variety of more complex manipulations corresponding, for example, to rotations or reflections of the object in physical space. Any clarification of the way in which the mind carries out such mental transformations should, at the same time, help to clarify the nature of the internal representations that are thus being transformed. In particular, it should provide useful evidence concerning the extent to which and the sense in which there is, in fact, a first-order isomorphism between such an internal representation and its corresponding external object.

How an Internal Process Is Able
to Represent an External Object at All

In order to avoid a philosophical confusion implicit in the writings of the British empiricists and the Gestalt psychologists alike, it should be explicitly stated that, even when a degree of first-order isomorphism can be shown to exist, the isomorphism is not in itself sufficient to explain how an internal process represents or refers to its corresponding external object.

For, at a sufficiently abstract level, a given internal representation might be isomorphic to any number of quite different external objects (cf. Wittgenstein, 1953, p. 54). To give a specific example, one particular internal representation could as well correspond to either of two reciprocal polyhedra—e.g., either the cube or the octahedron—depending upon whether one set of (eight) subelements of the representation is taken to correspond to the vertices of the polyhedron while another set of (six) subelements is taken to correspond to the faces, or vice versa. And, even if the isomorphism were so concrete that there remained no ambiguity of this sort (i.e., even if the internal representation for a cube were itself a cube), this, as we have seen, would not help at all to explain how one is able to *recognize* the cube, to call it "a cube," to group it with prisms in preference to pyramids, and so on. Clearly isomorphism in itself is not enough.

Whether or not any degree of first-order isomorphism in fact exists, what enables a given internal process to represent or to stand for a particular external object is the way that that internal process functions within the organism—particularly in his relation to that object and to other similar objects. The essential things are, in particular, (a) that there be an orderly causal connection between the external objects and the internal process that is to represent it, and (b) that internal representations corresponding to similar external objects be functionally related so that a response learned to one will tend to generalize to another (as required by second-order isomorphism). When, in addition, there is a degree of first-order isomorphism, it is not there to enable the internal representation to refer to its external object. It is there, rather, to provide the mechanism for the realization of the necessary second-order isomorphism and, especially, to provide the structural information needed for more differentiated responses of selective attention, analysis, transformation, and manipulation.

In sum, no amount of knowledge about the neural structure that, when activated, represents a certain external object can itself tell us which external object that may be. We must also know how the activation of that structure functions within the whole system. The internal process that is my perception of an external square represents the square not because it is itself square but, rather, because it occurs, fully, when (and, except in dreams or hallucinations, only when) I am in the presence of an external square—and, partially, when I am in the presence of a related external object such as a rectangle or perhaps even a right-angled corner. And the internal process that is my mental image of a merely imagined or remembered square represents a square not because *it* is square but, because it has much in common with the process that occurs when, as above, I actually perceive a square. In the last connection, incidentally, the fact that we so readily recognize the parallelism between internal representations in perception and their counterparts in memory and imagination while, at the same time, so clearly distinguish between such percepts and such images seems to be an important example of the fundamentally analogical character of human thought in general. (For another example, suggesting the pervasiveness of an analogical basis of thought, see Shepard, 1972, p. 107.)

The Relevance of Time Measurements

The problem of distinguishing between mental images, on the one hand, and covert verbal descriptions (as opposed to the merely arbitrarily associated names considered above), on the other, is made difficult by the fact that both sorts of internal representations must, at some sufficiently abstract level, be at least partially isomorphic to the external objects that they represent. There is, however, another technique for the study of internal representations that can furnish quite decisive evidence bearing on questions of their more concrete form—including, specifically, such related questions as whether they are essentially pictorial or verbal, analog or digital, continuous or discrete. This is the technique of measuring the time that it takes a subject to respond, discriminatively, to an external stimulus that is in some way related to the internal representation in question.

Thus Posner and his students have strikingly demonstrated that one can distinguish whether the representation in short-term memory of a previously presented letter (e.g., the capital letter "A") is retained in an essentially pictorial form (or visual "code") or simply in the form of the name (or verbal "code") for that letter (e.g., see Posner, Boies, Eichelman, & Taylor, 1969). This is done on the basis of how long it takes the subject to respond "same" to a second presentation of the identical stimulus ("A"), depending upon whether he has been set to detect just this reappearance of the visually identical stimulus ("A") or whether he has been set to detect the appearance of a letter that is identical merely in name (viz., either the upper-case letter "A" or its lower-case counterpart "a").

The finding is that the subject's response, "same," is consistently faster (by some 90 msec) when he is looking for strict visual identity. Evidently in this case he is able to generate an appropriate concrete visual code (which *may* be a kind of mental image) that, perhaps in the manner of a template, can be matched by a very rapid, parallel process against the ensuing external stimulus (cf. Sekuler & Abrams, 1968). When the representation retained in memory is in the form merely of the name of the letter, on the other hand, additional time is required to process the subsequently presented stimulus, to generate its name, and only *then* to test for a match of this generated name to the one retained in memory. Following Posner, similar results have also been obtained with more complex visual patterns (e.g., Cohen, 1969; Tversky, 1969).

In a somewhat different type of experiment using reaction times Moyer and Landauer (1967, 1973), Sekuler, Rubin, and Armstrong (1971), and others have found that the time that subjects require to determine whether the second of two presented whole numbers is larger or smaller than the first decreases monotonically with the size of the numerical difference between them. This strongly suggests the interesting possibility that such decisions of relative magnitude are made by reference to analogue (perhaps even "spatial") representations of these numbers.

These experiments illustrate some ways in which measurements of reaction times can provide evidence concerning the form of internal representations. They do not answer all of the questions that we might wish to raise about the nature of such representations, however. The type of experiment introduced by Posner, for example, is designed to distinguish between some sort of visual representation and a simple name—not between a visual representation and any sort of covert verbal *description* of the visual object. And a simple name would not be expected to embody even the abstract sort of isomorphism that is essential in a description. However, this same type of chronometric method can be extended to distinguish between visual representations and at least partially isomorphic descriptions, as in the experiment by Cohen (1969).

Even if this is done, though, the simple fact that subjects are able to respond most rapidly when they are attempting to detect a concrete, physical match does not in itself establish that the "visual code" on the basis of which they do this is a truly internal representation. For, by "internal representation" or, specifically, "mental image," I mean something that is accessible to the subject's introspection and could be used by him in further cognitive processing even in the absence of the external stimulus. A "visual code," by contrast, *might* consist merely in the priming of the relevant feature detectors in the sensory receptors and, so, have cognitive implications for the subject only in the event that the appropriate external stimulus is then actually presented.

The experiments concerning the time it takes to decide which of two numbers is the larger, though quite suggestive, are rather special. To realize that the internal representations for numbers may have a degree of second-order isomorphism to spatial extent does not take us very far toward an understanding of the nature and degree of the first-order isomorphism that presumably holds between other internal representations and the more complex and highly structured objects to which they correspond.

The Relevance of Transformations

In order to obtain information of a different sort about the internal representation of external objects, my students and I have undertaken a program of research in which reaction times are obtained to visual objects that have been transformed or operated upon in various ways. In most cases the transformation has been one of simple rigid rotation of the object in two- or three-dimensional space. But the effects of other, more complex transformations or manipulations of objects have also been explored.

To be able to recognize an object as the same object despite changes in its orientation is, of course, the reflection of a kind of perceptual constancy—namely, constancy of perceived shape under rotations in space. However, there are both theoretical and empirical reasons for considering this particular kind of invariance to be a rather different case from that of the better understood constancies of color, size, and location. From the theoretical standpoint, it is clear that relatively simple mechanisms of feature detection will suffice to identify a given shape regardless of its size or location. Thus, the normal upright letter "F" can be recognized as such simply on the basis of the presence of a vertical line segment to the right of which are attached two equal horizontal line segments, one by an L-shaped junction at the top, and one by a T-shaped junction in the middle of the vertical line segment—and this is true regardless of the location or over-all size of the figure in the visual field. If, however, the task is to determine whether such a figure is the letter "F" (as opposed, say, to the backward or mirror image of that letter, viz., " ꟻ ") even though the letter is presented in a rotated orientation (e.g., " Ⅎ "), the pattern recognition problem becomes less trivial. And if we are to deal with rotations of three-dimensional objects in depth, the theoretical problem becomes another order of magnitude more difficult still. From the empirical standpoint there is also the difference that, whereas the equivalence of objects that differ merely in location or size can often be recognized almost as easily and quickly as if they were identical in location or size, the equivalence of objects that differ in orientation requires appreciable additional mental effort and, as we have found, time.

Two kinds of measured time are of interest: (a) the time required to determine whether or not an object, once it is actually presented, meets a certain specified condition—despite the fact that the object is presented in some rotated or otherwise transformed manner; and (b) the time required to prepare for such a transformed stimulus on the basis of appropriate advance information and so to be able to respond to the ensuing stimulus as rapidly as if it had been presented without transformation (i.e., in its preferred orientation or standard form). In connection with this latter kind of time I shall argue that the act of "preparation" for the transformed stimulus consists in the generation of an appropriate mental image and that the preparation time provides an indication of the time it takes to generate and to transform such a mental image.

The basic motivation behind such experiments derives from the notion that one can learn something about an object (in this case a *mental* object) from an investigation of the way it behaves under transformation. What the time data suggest is that visual objects are mentally manipulated in a manner that is in some degree analogous to the way that corresponding real objects would be operated upon in physical space. This, in turn, provides a further indication of the degree of first-order isomorphism that the internal representations that are thus transformed must themselves have to their corresponding external objects. In addition, the transformational competency that is revealed in some of these experiments suggests that the complex geometrical constraints that govern transformations of physical objects in the external world (and their projections onto the two-dimensional retina of the eye) are to a significant extent incorporated as rules that govern the internal workings of the mind.

SUMMARY OF SOME EXPERIMENTAL FINDINGS

Since many of the experimental studies that I had originally intended to report in this section have now been published in relatively complete form elsewhere, there is no need to go over them in any detail here. I need merely list the principal findings together with references to the relevant published sources, where available. The intention is to furnish, in as succinct a form as possible, an adequate empirical basis for a consideration, in the following, final section, of what I believe to be some important theoretical issues concerning the form, formation, and transformation of internal representations of external objects. Though numbered consecutively throughout for ease of later reference, the ensuing experimental findings are grouped into those obtained from the quite different paradigms of second-order isomorphism and reaction time, respectively.

Paradigm of Second-Order Isomorphism

Beyond the original study by Shepard and Chipman (1970), the only published studies from which the following results derive are those of Gordon and Hayward (1973) and Shepard, Kilpatric, and Cunningham (1975). In addition, as yet unpublished findings (obtained by David Wessel and in collaboration with Castro, Cooper, and Scowcroft) will also be briefly mentioned.

1. *Judgments of similarity among objects are essentially the same whether the objects are actually presented or only named.* This has now been demonstrated for sets of stimuli of such varied forms and modalities

as the visual shapes of 15 of the states of the U.S. (Shepard & Chipman, 1970), photographs of well-known faces of political figures (Gordon & Hayward, 1973) and of motion-picture actors (Shepard & Castro, in preparation), distinctive odors (Shepard & Scrowcroft, in preparation), spectral colors (Cooper & Shepard, in preparation), letters of the alphabet and sounds of orchestral instruments (Wessel, in preparation), and numbers and numerals presented in such symbolic forms as Arabic numerals, Roman numerals, printed names, and spoken names and in such more concrete forms as rows of dots, tally marks, and finger counts (Shepard, Kilpatric, & Cunningham, 1975).

2. *The form of the names or symbols used in lieu of the objects themselves has, in fact, no effect on the judged similarities among those subjects.* This has now been demonstrated in a rather strong, quantitative way in the extensive study of Shepard *et al.* (1975).

3. *Judgments of similarity are explainable in terms of identifiable properties of the objects judged (whether or not those objects were actually presented).* This has been demonstrated most clearly, by techniques of multidimensional scaling, in the studies by Shepard and Chipman (1970), by Shepard *et al.* (1975), and by Cooper and Shepard (in preparation); but supportive evidence obtained by a different technique can be found in the report of Gordon and Hayward (1973).

4. *The equivalence of the similarity judgments under the actual-objects and name-only conditions is greatest for subjects who report the greatest use of imagery (in the name-only condition).* This result, although thus far based on just one study (Shepard & Castro, in preparation), points to the potential bearing of individual differences on the study of (e.g., verbal versus visual) forms of internal representation. (The following finding resulted from a more extreme exploitation of this possibility.)

5. *In the absence of appropriate imagery, judgments of similarity tend to lose their second-order isomorphic structure.* In the study by Cooper and Shepard (in preparation) it was found that multidimensional scaling of the similarities among spectral colors as judged by normally sighted subjects yielded a highly regular "color circle" (whether the colors were actually presented or only named). However, multidimensional scaling of the similarities among the names of those same colors as judged by congenitally blind subjects exhibited little more structure than a rough grouping into the "warm" and the "cool" colors. Apparently the knowledge about the relations among the colors that subjects without color perception and, presumably, imagery assimilate merely from exposure through language is very incomplete compared with that readily picked up by subjects with some color imagery—whether they are normally sighted or, as we found, partially color blind (viz. protonopic or deuteronopic dichromats).

Paradigms of Reaction Time

Starting with the initial experiment of Shepard and Metzler (1971), we have now amassed a considerable body of results based on objective measures of the time required to carry out various types of mental operations on objects in space. The paradigms, though all of a basically similar chronometric type, differ depending upon whether the presentations are simultaneous or successive and upon whether the measured time is that required (a) to respond to an object that is suddenly presented following the application of an unexpected spatial transformation, (b) to prepare for the presentation of an object following a pre-indicated transformation, and/or (c) to respond to such a transformed object after having already attained a state of preparation for it. I now extend the list of empirical findings by adding some of the principal results obtained by means of these various reaction-time paradigms.

6. *The time to determine that a spatially transformed object is of inherently the same shape as some comparison or standard object increases monotonically with the extent of the transformational difference between the two objects.* This has now been demonstrated with both simultaneous and sequential presentations, and with a variety of novel and familiar two- and three-dimensional objects some of which do and some of which do not possess a conventionally well-established untransformed or canonical form. In the most extensively investigated case, in which the transformation is one of rigid rotation, a marked monotone increase in reaction time with angular difference has been consistently obtained with alpha-numeric characters by Shepard and Klun and, following them, by Cooper and Shepard (see Cooper & Shepard, 1973a, b); with two-dimensional random polygons (Cooper, 1975); with three-dimensional nonsense shapes composed of cubical blocks (Metzler & Shepard, 1974; Shepard & Metzler, 1971); and with pictures of left and right human hands in various positions (Cooper & Shepard, 1975). Consonant results have also been obtained with other types of transformations, including reflections (see below) and sequences of bends or folds (Shepard & Feng, 1972).

7. *Under appropriate conditions, the monotone increase in reaction time with extent of transformation is uniformly linear.* The principal evidence here comes, again, from those studies in which the transformation was one of rigid rotation. The "appropriate conditions" in this case apparently require that the reference orientation be experimentally defined—either by explicitly presenting a comparison object in a particular orientation (Cooper & Shepard, 1973b, Experiment II; Metzler & Shepard, 1974) or by providing pretraining on an arbitrarily selected, but precisely defined

orientation for each object (Cooper, 1975), as opposed to using a pre-experimental, conventionally defined orientation that may encompass an appreciable range of more or less upright positions (as in the case of letters, numerals, or hands; cf. Cooper & Shepard, 1973a, b, Experiment I; 1975). In addition, the linear increase in reaction time has been obtained as a function of the extent of other, more complex spatial transformation, including, again, sequences of folds (Shepard & Feng, 1972).

8. *When the subject is set to carry out the mental rotation in a particular* (*clockwise or counterclockwise*) *direction, reaction time continues its linear increase beyond 180° through the full 360° circle.* This finding, which shows that the time is not a fixed function of the (angular) difference between the two objects to be compared but, rather, is determined by the particular mental *trajectory* used to pass from the one to the other, arises principally from the doctoral dissertations recently completed by Cooper (1973) and by Metzler (1973) (see Cooper, 1975; Metzler & Shepard, 1974.) Once again, further support for the notion that it is the mental trajectory rather than the relation between the end states that is the determining factor can also be found in other studies, including that of Shepard and Feng (1972; and further work, mentioned below).

9. *The linear increase in reaction time with angle of rotation of a three-dimensional object has essentially the same slope whether the axis of rotation coincides with the line of sight, so that the transformation corresponds to a rigid rotation of the two-dimensional retinal image, or is orthogonal to the line of sight, so that the transformation corresponds to a much more complex, topologically discontinuous deformation of the retinal image.* The essential equivalence between such "picture-plane" and "depth" rotations is reported in Shepard and Metzler (1971) and, most completely, in Metzler and Shepard (1974). (It is not strictly correct to conclude that the axis of rotation has no effect at all, however. The results of Metzler and Shepard do indicate that mental rotation is more rapid when the axis of rotation does than when it does not coincide with a natural axis of the three-dimensional object itself.)

10. *For a given axis of rotation, the reaction time has a strong dependence only upon the angle of rotation in three-dimensional space; it is influenced relatively slightly by whether or not such a rotation entails topological discontinuities in the two-dimensional retinal image.* Thus, Metzler and Shepard (1974) noted that, for a fixed angle of rotation (of either 40 or 60°) the additional time attributable to the occurrence of such a discontinuity in the retinal image (less than .1 sec on the average) was equivalent to the increase expected for a rotation of only about five degrees.

11. *When the subject is given sufficient advance information concerning both the object to be presented and the orientation in which it is to appear,*

the reaction time becomes uniformly fast (on the order of 400 msec) and independent of that orientation. This evidence for the subject's ability to ready a kind of visual template may be found in the reports of Cooper (1975), of Cooper and Shepard (1973a, 1975), and of Metzler and Shepard (1974). Indeed, Cooper and Shepard (1973b, Experiment II) showed that, when an alphanumeric character was expected in a predesignated orientation, discriminative reactions were faster to such a rotated character than to that same character in its normal, upright orientation.

12. *The dependence of reaction time on the angle of rotation is approximately the same both for the time needed to prepare for such a rotated object and for the time needed to respond to such a rotated object in the absence of advance preparation.* Evidence that similar sorts of mental processes thus occur in responding to a presented stimulus and in preparing for one that has not yet been presented is reported, in sharpest form, by Cooper (1975) and also by Cooper and Shepard (1973b) and by Metzler and Shepard (1974).

13. *During mental preparation for a rotated object, the orientation of the object for which the subject is most prepared from moment-to-moment is actually rotating in physical space.* Cooper and Shepard (1973b, Experiment II) showed that, during a paced preparatory mental rotation, the orientation for which a presented test stimulus would yield the shortest reaction time was progressively changing in rotational orientation, and that reaction times to test stimuli departing from that rotating optimum orientation increased linearly with that departure. Likewise, Metzler (1974; see Metzler & Shepard, 1974) found incidental evidence that reaction time to a test stimulus increased when the time at which it was presented departed somewhat from what should have been the optimum time for that subject according to the rate of mental rotation previously estimated for that subject.

14. *Advance information giving merely the orientation of a to-be-presented object is not sufficient to enable subjects to prepare for it in this way; subjects must also have information as to which concrete object is to be presented in that orientation.* The results of Shepard and Klun and of Cooper and Shepard (see Cooper & Shepard, 1973b) have provided rather clear evidence of this sort that subjects are able to prepare for a rotated stimulus by "mentally rotating" what apparently must be a concrete mental image and not merely some abstract frame of reference.

15. *The internal representations that are mentally transformed in these ways preserve rather complete structural information about the external objects to which they correspond.* One indication of this is the speed and accuracy with which subjects were able to determine whether a test probe that was one of two isomeric (mirror image) configurations of seven cubi-

cal blocks did or did not match their mentally-rotating representation of such a three-dimensional object in the experiment by Metzler (1973; see Metzler & Shepard, 1974). More recent and much more direct evidence will be forthcoming from an as yet unpublished study by Cooper and Podgorny, in which the objects were the random polygons previously used by Cooper (1975) but in which the test probes included, in addition to reflected or mirror image versions of the stimulus object, other polygons that differed from those objects by various, perceptually scaled degrees of random perturbation.

16. *The structural information contained in a mentally transformed internal representation does not come into play solely upon the external presentation of a corresponding stimulus; it is accessible to the subject for further cognitive processing in the absence of such an external stimulus.* This is of course suggested by the fact that subjects in these experiments report that, in preparing for the presentation of a rotated object, they have a mental picture of the designated object rotating into the designated orientation. It is also suggested by the fact that the subjects in Cooper's experiments were able to draw remarkably accurate approximations to the random polygons that they had been mentally rotating (Cooper, 1973). A different kind of evidence comes from an unpublished pilot experiment by Shepard and Feng which will now be briefly described, despite the very limited and preliminary character of the data, in order to provide further concrete illustration in connection with the present point as well as with a few of the preceding points.

Subjects were asked to report, as quickly as possible, the results of performing a pre-specified operation on a particular letter—which was then only named and not visually presented. Thus, on a particular trial the subject might be instructed to state "what results when you rotate 90° to the left the following capital letter—'N'?" The time would then be recorded from the naming of the letter ("N") by the experimenter to the reporting of the result ("Z") by the subject. The following five operations were explored: reflection about the vertical axis, reflection about the horizontal axis, rotation of 90° to the left (counterclockwise), rotation of 180° (in the picture plane), and the double operation of reflection about the vertical axis followed by reflection about the horizontal axis. The letters used and the effects of the operations on these are shown in Fig. 1. In some cases the letter turns into itself, in some cases it turns into another letter (or symbol), and in some cases it turns into a nameless design (in which case the subject reported "nothing"). Since the instructions were all presented in the auditory modality and no visual stimuli were presented, most subjects could and, indeed, preferred to keep their eyes closed during this visualization task.

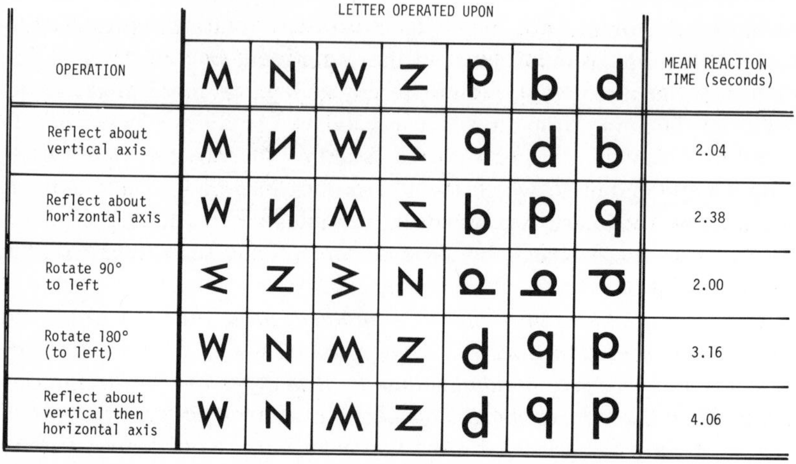

Fig. 1. Results of applying each of five spatial operations on each of seven letters. For each operation, the numbers at the right give the mean times that subjects required, altogether, (a) to imagine the (orally) designated letter, (b) to imagine the designated operation performed on that letter, and (c) to identify and name the result of that operation.

The mean reaction times obtained in this pilot experiment are shown for the five different operations in the right-most column of the figure. These times all include, in addition to the time required to perform the operation itself, the times required to form the visual image and to "recognize" and then report the result of the operation on that image. Notice that these overall reaction times are shortest for the two reflections and the 90° rotation (about 2 sec each), that the 180° rotation takes appreciably longer (about 3 sec), and finally that the double reflection takes the longest time of all (about 4 sec). The difference between these last two times is particularly interesting since, as can be seen in the table, both kinds of operations (the 180° rotation and the double reflection) yield identical images. The consistently longer reaction times for the double reflection indicates, then, that the subjects *were* following directions and coming to their answers by carrying out the particular operations specified. It also indicates, again, that reaction time depends upon the particular trajectory of the subject's internal process, and not just on the relation between the initial and terminal states. On the basis of these data and further data that are still being collected, we hope to determine whether the times for the hypothetical component operations are properly additive within the task and, also, suitably constant from one task to another.

Finally, with respect to the last of the empirical findings listed above (viz. 16), the fact that subjects are able to give an accurate report of the result of such operations on purely imagined objects supports the notion that the internal representations that they initially generated were to some extent structurally isomorphic to the objects represented. Furthermore, it establishes that the structural information in these representations could be used by them as a basis for further cognitive processes, including imagined reflections or rotations and, especially, "perceptual" identification of the products of such transformations. And, of course, the fact that the reports can be given after no more than two or three seconds is consonant with the subjects' claim that the representation is more of the nature of an image than of the nature of a verbal description.

THEORETICAL DISCUSSION

Implications of the Experimental Findings for Internal Representations and Their Transformations

No single one of the 16 experimental findings listed above can by itself determine the exact nature of the kind of internal representations or "mental images" with which we have been concerned. However, each finding can help to rule out certain possibilities. Thus, together, they indicate that the internal representation for an external object is:

1. *Not just a subvocal or mental pronunciation of the name of the object*—because judgments of the similarities among objects that are not physically present but only named nevertheless correspond closely to relations among the objects themselves and not to relations among their names (Findings 1, 2, 3, and 4); and because a name does not by itself contain the information that would be required to anticipate the outcome of various transformations on an object in space (Findings 6, 11, 12, 15, and 16).

2. *Not just an implicit verbal description of the object*—because the decision as to whether an external stimulus corresponds to that internal representation can be made within a period (200–400 msec) that is too brief for the generation and testing for agreement of a verbal description (Finding 11); and (tentatively) because subjects who claim to have used visual images, more than subjects who claim to have used verbal descriptions, evidently produce judgments of similarity among named objects that agree more closely with relations of similarity among the objects themselves (Finding 4 and 5).

3. *Not just the priming of certain feature detectors at the sensory input*—because the internal representation can be transformed, identified, and named internally without the presentation of any related external ob-

ject (Findings 15 and 16); because the internal representation has a closer correspondence to the external three-dimensional object than to the two-dimensional retinal projection (Findings 9 and 10); and because, in order to explain how the relevant set of sensory feature detectors is selected in the case of preparation for rotated objects, one must postulate complex cognitive processes that necessarily go far beyond the level of such sensory feature detectors themselves (Findings 7, 8, 12, and 13).

4. *Not just a structureless internal event* (such as the firing of a particular neuron or a sufficient subset of a particular set of functionally equivalent neurons) that has a relation to the external object that is one of regular causality only—because the functional relations among the internal representations parallel the significant relations among the corresponding external objects (Findings 1 and 3); and because the ability to grasp, to manipulate, or to anticipate the results of spatial transformations on an external object requires that some structural information about the external object and hence the way it behaves under transformation is encoded within the internal representation itself (Findings 9, 10, 14, 15, and 16).

5. *Not a concrete, spatially isomorphic model* such, for example, that a cube is represented by a precisely cubical pattern of activity in the physical brain—because such a purely spatial isomorphism makes no provision for the representation of nonspatial attributes such as color (Findings 1 and 5); because it is neuroanatomically implausible that three-dimensional shapes are thus isometrically replicated within the thin and convoluted layers of the cerebral cortex; because the passive importation of such a spatially isomorphic replica merely puts off the whole problem of how a cubical pattern (whether external or internal) comes to be categorized as a cube to be connected with the word "cube," or to control the grasping or drawing of the cube (Findings 15 and 16); and, finally, because the marked dependence of reaction time on spatial orientation of an external object shows that the internal representation is not of the three-dimensional object as it is in itself but of the three-dimensional object *as seen from a particular point of view* (Findings 6, 7, 8).

Tentatively, it appears that the internal representation for an external object is some sort of neural process that, first, has in part a regular causal relation to its external object (unique causal connection); second, bears to other internal representations functional relations of mutual substitutability or excitability that closely mirror significant relations among the corresponding external objects (second-order isomorphism); and third, has within itself some inner structure that although not concretely isomorphic to that of the corresponding external object nevertheless encodes, in some more abstract way, structural information about that object-in-its-relation-to-the-observer sufficient to guide highly differentiated manipulatory acts and to anticipate the consequences of certain basic spatial transformations (abstract first-order isomorphism).

Thus, the representation of a square need not itself be square, but it presumably does need to contain parts (perhaps associated subsets of neurons) that abstractly signalize, in addition to the presence of the square itself, the presence of four equal straight lines, the presence of four right-angled corners, the topological connectivity among these, and something about the overall orientation of the figure with respect to the observer. In addition to this internal representation itself, there must also be general machinery that can "read" any such representation in order to guide precise motor acts of grasping or manipulation, and that can carry out the internal analogues of basic external operations and, so, anticipate the results of such external operations as rigid rotation in space.

Moreover, the linearity and, hence, additivity of the times required to carry out such operations (Findings 7, 8, and 12) as well as the demonstrated one-to-one correspondence between a mental and a physical rotation (Finding 13) suggest that these operations are carried out as analog processes in the sense that, in some perhaps abstract way, they simulate the physical processes to which they correspond in the external world. Thus, in order to modify an internal representation corresponding to a particular three-dimensional object viewed in a particular orientation so that the representation then corresponds to that object as it would appear in a very different orientation, there may be no way to proceed but to impose small successive adjustments on the internal representation and, so, to pass through a "trajectory" of internal representations that corresponds to the actual rotation of the external object. To extend the formulation of "second-order isomorphism" so that it applies to transformations as well as to internal representations, one could say that, whatever the neurophysiological processes are that take place during an imagined rotation, they at least have something in common with the processes that take place when the rotation of an external physical object is actually being perceived.

Precisely how the spatial structure of external objects is represented and precisely how spatial transformations of such representations are performed at the neurophysiological level is not yet clear. It does however appear that something about the abstract formal structure of these internal representations and their transformations can perhaps be discerned through converging experimental operations without having, necessarily, to presuppose any particular type of neurophysiological embodiment. In a final speculative section, I shall go further and suggest that, with respect to richness and potential interest, this abstract formal structure may not fall greatly short of that which has been deemed necessary to account for man's linguistic competence by recent transformational grammarians.

First, however, something should perhaps be said about the relationship of the sort of concrete, semipictorial representations that we have been primarily concerned with here to other sorts of internal representations (a) that appear to be more closely tied to sensory modalities other than vision, (b) that are more verbal than pictorial, or (c) that, even though essentially nonverbal, are too abstract or schematic to correspond to any particular external object.

Isomorphism and Modality of Internal Representations

I have already noted explicitly, if briefly, that the principle of second-order isomorphism should apply to concrete internal representations in all modalities including, for example, the auditory and olfactory. I have also implied that, regardless of the modality of the internal representation, a degree of first-order isomorphism is to be expected whenever the representations are of sufficiently "analyzable" stimuli and, especially, whenever they are subject to mental transformations that preserve some of the structural information concerning those analyzable stimuli. Stimuli in the olfactory domain may always be essentially unanalyzable in this sense and, as in the case of single musical tones (in the auditory domain) or homogeneous colors (in the visual), there may be little or no first-order isomorphism between such stimuli and their internal representations. On the other hand, complex temporal patterns in the auditory, tactual, or kinesthetic modalities may well have analyzable structures. And perhaps these can even be subjected to purely mental manipulation or transformation in ways that are closely analogous to the kinds of mental rotation, reflection, or folding of visual objects discussed above.

Consider, for example, the question of what properties of a melody can still be recognized after it has been transformed, for example, by transposition, inversion, or retrogression (Dowling, 1971). Under transposition, quite small departures from the previous note-to-note intervals will generally be detected, though any new melody in which the directions and approximate sizes of the intervals are preserved will be recognized as having a temporal "pitch contour" of a similar general form. Under inversion, however, only the general shape of this contour may still be recognized and precise information concerning intervals may be lost—just as a face, when visually inverted, is still seen as a face but may lose much of its unique identity or expression (Yin, 1969).

The considerations that led us to confine our initial investigations to visual images and their transformations were chiefly two. First, there was the fact that the principal experimental technique that we have employed—viz. the measurement of reaction times—is much freer of diffi-culties when the structural information in the stimulus is conveyed by a pattern spread out in space than by one spread out in time. Second, there seems to be less likelihood in the visual domain that the status of the inter-nal representation as a genuine mental image would be questioned. For, in the case of a melodic or kinesthetic pattern, say, it could easily be argued that the internal representation is merely the covert execution of a previ-ously learned and potentially externalizable motor act (of singing or gestur-ing). In contrast, a visual image seems to be inherently different from any sort of motor act; part of the challenge here is to devise techniques that will enable us to infer something about the nature of such relatively unex-ternalizable internal representations.

The concept of second-order isomorphism provides a way of defining, to a certain extent, what we mean by the "primary modality" of a particular set of internal representations. Thus the findings of Conrad (1964) and Sperling (1963) that the letters most often confused in short-term memory were those (such as D and T, or F and S) that are similar in sound rather than those (such as P and R, or M and W) that are similar in visual ap-pearance was legitimately taken as evidence that, even though the letters were initially presented via the visual modality, their internal representa-tions in memory were primarily tied to the auditory modality.

However, the principle of second-order isomorphism has really to do with the relationship between the internal representations and the objects to which they correspond in the external world—regardless of the modality through which those objects may have been perceived. From this stand-point, the principal thrust of Conrad's experiment is not to determine whether the internal representations are tied to this or that sensory modal-ity, as such. Rather, it is to determine whether the structure of the internal representations corresponds to the structure of the alphabetic characters (which, after all, might be perceived through such different modalities as vision and touch) or to the very different structure of their arbitrarily asso-ciated names (which, again, might be experienced as heard or as covertly articulated by oneself). When the structures are very nearly the same (as when we contrast an alphabetic character as seen or as felt, or contrast a sound as heard or as subvocally pronounced) it becomes difficult to de-termine modality by a principle, such as isomorphism, that is concerned only with structure (cf. Wickelgren, 1969).

One can still investigate the interaction between internal representations of a particular type and the particular modality used to test these represen-tations, to introduce distracting stimulation, or to test the efficiency of con-current sensory processing (cf. Attwood, 1971; Brooks, 1967; Chase & Calfee, 1969; Segal & Fusella, 1970; Sternberg, 1967). However, in many experiments in which the effects of different sensory modalities are explored, it may be that the variable having the principal effect is not the modality as such but the structural similarity between the interfering input and the internal representations in question. Such a possibility is consonant, anyway, with the suggestion that internal representations should be regarded from a cognitive rather than from a sensory point of view.

In any case, the internal representations with which we have been concerned in the experiments reviewed in this paper are probably less modality-specific, more "amodal" (Michotte, Thinès, & Crabbé, 1962) than my use of such terms as "visual image" probably suggests. As I have emphasized, to perceive an external object (e.g., a letter or a three-dimensional form) is not just to classify or to label it. It is also to be ready to grasp, to trace, and to manipulate it in a variety of highly differentiated ways (cf., Festinger, Ono, Burnham, & Bamber, 1967). And to have a mental image of a cube is perhaps to be prepared for the tactual sensations of having a cubical block placed in one's hand as well as for the visual sensations of having the outline of a cube projected on one's retina.

Externalizability and Abstract
versus Concrete Internal Representations

I have suggested that the study of nonverbal internal representations such as mental images is more difficult and has been slower to get underway because, in part, an image cannot be externalized in the sense that a covert verbal process can be turned into an overt, observable process. There is nevertheless a sense in which even a mental image can in principle be externalized. An artist, for example, may be able to produce a sketch or painting that satisfies him as a reproduction of a visual image that has arisen in his memory, imagination, hypnagogic reverie, dream, or hallucination. And memory images even in people of little or no artistic talent have sometimes been reconstructed with remarkable accuracy by means of a technique used in so-called "police art." Basically this is the technique in which a witness selects pictures of various parts of a face (hair, eyebrows, eyes, nose, mouth, etc.) from large arrays that systematically vary in all degrees of shape, size, and color, and then arranges these parts within an appropriately selected facial outline until he "recognizes" the whole configuration as similar to the face that he remembers but could not describe (cf. Shepard, 1968).

Of course when we speak of "externalizing" a mental image in these ways we do not mean to imply that the internal representation that is thus "externalized" was itself anything like the picture finally produced. Even the first-order isomorphism, if any, must be much more abstract than this.

What we mean, rather, is that the reconstructed external picture reexcites within its creator's brain a neural event, state, or process that has a sufficient degree of functional equivalence to the neural event, state, or process that was to be "externalized."

The crucial precondition for this sort of externalization, then, is that there be a roughly one-to-one correspondence between each internal representation and an external stimulus that corresponds to it in the sense that that stimulus (and generally only it or one very similar to it) fully elicits the internal representation in question (or one sufficiently substitutable with it). It is for just such internal representations—because each roughly corresponds to some definite external scene or picture—that we reserve the term "image."

There are, however, other internal representations that are much more abstract than these concrete mental images precisely in that they can not be set into adequate correspondence with any one external thing. To recur to an historic example, we can perhaps go along with Berkeley (1710) when he claimed that he could not think of a triangle without thinking of some particular, concrete triangle—at least if by "think" we understand him to mean "form a mental image or picture." However, when he uses this to attack the "doctrine of abstract ideas" we must conclude that he has been led into fundamental error by his empiricistic predilection for supposing that any mental content must be a copy of some particular thing that has been experienced through the senses. For it has since become clear, from developments in psychology, physiology, and artificial intelligence (e.g., see Shepard, 1964b) as well as from purely philosophical considerations, that there must be internal representations that are neither concrete visual images of particular external objects nor arbitrarily associated names for these. There must, in short, also be representations or schemata that are abstract in the sense that they can be fully elicited—not just by a particular external object—but by a wide and often quite heterogeneous class of external objects, situations, or events (cf. Konorski, 1967).

Thus there must in fact be *some* internal event that occurs in an individual when and only when he is presented with a triangle, whatever its particular shape may be. (How else are we to explain his ability as a child to extend the use of the word "triangle" to the whole class after having learned it in connection with just a very few examples?) But, if so, this internal representation will be even more difficult to externalize than a mental image. The best we can do is to assemble the entire set of objects to which such an internal representation in a sense refers. And even this is, for many of the more abstract representations, obviously not really feasible. It is understandable, then, that the study of abstract schemata is even less advanced than the study of the more concrete sort of internal representations or mental images with which we have been concerned here. There are nevertheless indications that even highly abstract internal representations possess some degree of second-order (and perhaps even first-order) isomorphism (see, e.g., Johnson, Cox, & Curran, 1970).

Symbolic Reference
and Verbal versus Nonverbal Internal Representations

Of course there are, in addition to nonverbal internal representations (whether abstract schemata or concrete images), verbal or symbolic internal representations of the sort that occur when we think of the name or when we think of a description of an external object. When I am presented with an external triangle (whether visually, tactually, or even kinesthetically), an internal event will occur in my brain that is rather concrete in the sense that it occurs only when something very like that particular triangle is presented. This is what we refer to as my perceptual image of that particular triangle. (And, as we have noted, this internal event will probably include subevents that correspond to analyzable parts of the triangle such as corners and edges.) At the same time, events will also occur that are more abstract in the sense that they may occur whenever I am presented with *any* triangle, or even any polyhedron, or any geometrical figure, and so on in increasing degrees of abstraction. These we refer to as my general schema or concept of triangle, polyhedron, etc. Finally, however, an event may also occur that corresponds to my thinking the word "triangle" or, very rarely, to my thinking of some descriptive phrase such as "three vertices connected by straight lines."

Just what is the nature of these latter, purely verbal internal representations? Here, I think, we must distinguish two quite different aspects of the internal representation: the structural form of the internal representation as such, and the way that the internal representation may function to symbolize or to refer to something entirely different—something to which it is related by a purely learned, conventional association and not by any inherent structural isomorphism.

Thus, whether I internally generate the (visual–kinesthetic) form of the written word "triangle" or, much more commonly, the (auditory–articulatory) form of the spoken word "triangle," the resulting internal representation as such will be isomorphic only to the structure of the word "triangle" (as written or as pronounced). It will have no structural resemblance or isomorphism whatever to the three-cornered spatial object to which that word by convention refers. Indeed under special circumstances (as when, for example, I keep repeating the word over and over until "semantic satiation" sets in and the word seems, subjectively, to lose all meaning) this may be all that occurs.

Usually, however the meaning psychologically accompanies the word. When I hear the word "triangle" I don't just hear a pattern of sound (as I might if the word were spoken in a language completely unknown to me); the concept of a triangle is given to me right along with the pattern of sound. Indeed, it is the meaning that I primarily attend to and remember (so that, soon after, I may know that I learned a certain fact about triangles without being able to say whether I learned it from reading a book or from listening to a lecture). What, then, is this meaning? It surely is not the visual image of a particular triangle. For, although such an image may accompany my hearing, reading, or thinking the word "triangle," it need not do so. And, even if it did, it could not be the meaning of "triangle" because that word refers to triangles in general—not to the particular triangle that corresponds to some one mental image. In terms of the present framework, the obvious answer is that the "meaning event" that accompanies the word is neither the internal representation of the word itself nor a concrete mental image; it is, rather, the abstract internal event that corresponds to the whole class of objects that we call triangles.

It is perfectly evident, from studies of cognitive processes in animals (e.g., Herrnstein & Loveland, 1964; Köhler, 1925; Premack, 1971; Tinklepaugh, 1932), in the young child (Piaget, 1954, e.g., p. 67; Sinclair-de-Zwart, 1969), in the congenitally deaf (Furth, 1966), in cases in which certain parts of the brain have been damaged (Barbizet, 1970, p. 68; Geschwind, 1965) or surgically cut (Gazzaniga, Bogen, & Sperry, 1965; Sperry, 1968; Sperry & Levy, 1970), and in cases in which temporary aphasia has been induced by direct electrical stimulation of the cerebral cortex (Penfield & Roberts, 1959, p. 117), that one can have a concept without having access to the word that is conventionally associated with that concept. Owing to severely limited externalizability, this may be a considerable impediment to communication. It does not, however, exclude the possibility of thought. Indeed, the "imageless thought" of the Würzburg school (Mandler & Mandler, 1964) may amount to the formation and transformation of internal representations of this more abstract, though nonverbal type. From this standpoint, the attempt to classify people into those who think in pictures and those who think in words appears to overlook the fundamental and ubiquitous role of more abstract, schematic and, hence, inherently unexternalizable internal representations in all processes of thought.

This is not to deny that the advent of language has decisively changed the character of thought processes and, hence, of what can be accomplished by such processes. It has, first of all, made these processes relatively externalizable—that is, communicable—and, thereby, susceptible to intersubjective correction, cumulative refinement, and permanent record. Moreover, by permitting the separation of the syntactic or logical form of deductive, inductive, and analogical processes of reasoning from the affectively laden and structurally encumbered contents reasoned about, language makes possible the greater order, objectivity, freedom from distortion or error, and (possibly) swiftness of thinking upon which present highly developed society, technology, and science undoubtedly depends.

I merely wish to suggest, first, that the nonlinguistic aspects of thought seem to have been relatively overlooked—probably owing to their inherently less externalizable nature. And, second, that it may be oversimplified and misleading to imply, as is often done, that it is the advent of language as such that accounts for the great and perhaps unique power of human thought. In the next and final section, I shall point (along with Gregory, 1970, p. 180; Lenneberg, 1969, p. 642; and others) toward an alternative that I think is worthy of further exploration. It is, rather, that the full development of man's present linguistic competency has been made possible by structural changes in the human brain that have at the same time made possible other, nonlinguistic, competencies that—though little studied—may not be of appreciably less interest or importance.

Some Possible Parallels
between Spatial and Linguistic Competencies

In his discussion of the relation between language and mind, Chomsky (1968) has written: "Are there other areas of human competence where one might hope to develop a fruitful theory, analogous to generative grammar? Although this is a very important question, there is very little that can be said about it today. One might, for example, consider the problem of how a person comes to acquire a certain concept of three-dimensional space . . . [p. 64]." But, later in the same work (p. 77) he adds:

. . . there seems to be little useful analogy between the theory of grammar that provides the basis for this normal, creative use of language, and any other cognitive system that has so far been isolated and described; similarly, there is little useful analogy between the schema of universal grammar that we must, I believe, assign to the mind as an innate character, and any other known system of mental organization. It is quite possible that the lack of analogy testifies to our ignorance of other aspects of mental function, rather than to the absolute uniqueness of linguistic structure; but the fact is that we have, for the moment, no objective reason for supposing this to be true [Chomsky, 1968, p. 64].

Undaunted by Chomsky's own assessment of the situation, a number of those in the field of artificial intelligence who have been working towards the explicit mechanization of perceptual processes have continued to make significant use of ideas deriving from linguistics in general and from transformational grammar in particular (e.g., Clowes, 1969, 1971; Miller & Shaw, 1968). Whatever the current status of such efforts, there do appear to be a number of rather suggestive parallels between linguistic and perceptual–spatial competencies:

1. *Deep versus surface structure.* Fundamental to transformational grammar is a distinction between the surface structure of a sentence, which is just the string of words as they are actually uttered, and the deep structure, which contains information about such things as how those words are (implicitly) grouped into larger coherent units and how those words, their order, and that (implicit) grouping must behave under various transformations. However, this distinction between deep and surface structure appears to be quite analogous to the distinction, long recognized as crucial in perception, according to which the internal representation of a three-dimensional object is fundamentally different from the two-dimensional pattern that is its projection upon a sensory surface. And, just as the deep structure underlying a sentence is presumed to be more closely related than the surface string of words to what we ordinarily refer to as the "meaning" of that sentence, the internal representation in perception is evidently more closely related than the pattern on the sensory surface to the external object represented.

2. *Ambiguity, synonymy, and anomaly.* Strong indicators of the existence of deep structures in language are the facts of ambiguity (in which the same surface structure is consistent with two or more deep structures), synonymy (in which two different surface structures have essentially equivalent deep structures), and anomaly (in which different segments of the surface structure are not simultaneously consistent with any one deep structure). But exactly these same phenomena have long been known in visual perception. In ambiguous figures such as the reversible cube (Necker, 1832), duct–rabbit (Jastrow, 1900, p. 295), or young woman–old hag (Boring, 1930), we have examples in which the same retinal stimulus leads, at any moment, to one of two incompatible perceptual interpretations. An analogue of synonymy can be found in the recognition of identity in three-dimensional shape of two different perspective views of the same object, which has been so central to our considerations here. And an analogue of anomaly is obviously provided by the drawings of so-called "impossible objects" by Penrose and Penrose (1958), and others (cf. Huffman, 1970).

3. *Hierarchical organization in deep structure.* According to phrase-structure grammar, behind the surface structure of each sentence there is an underlying or deeper hierarchical organization so that, for example, the

linear string of words "The man hit the ball" is interpreted as arranged into nested subunits as indicated by the parentheses in "(The man) ((hit) (the ball))." But there are strong indications that perceptual processes are very hierarchical in the case of nonlinguistic stimuli also—as has been pointed out above (in the discussions of representational events and subevents in first-order isomorphism, and of simultaneously occurring concrete and abstract representational events), and also by Konorski (1967), Neisser (1967, p. 254), and those concerned with the automation of scene analysis and object recognition (e.g., Clowes, 1971; Guzman, 1968; Huffman, 1971; Selfridge, 1959; Waltz, 1972; Winston, 1970).

4. *Transformations on deep structure.* A central tenet of transformational grammar is of course that, in order to account for otherwise inexplicable features of grammar as well, perhaps, as for its creative power, we must assume that we generate and interpret sentences by applying various obligatory and optional transformations that mediate between deep and surface structures and that carry deep structures into other deep structures of different forms. But in a possibly analogous way, the identification of an external object may require the application of internal transformations relating such a three-dimensional object to its two-dimensional retinal projection and relating the internal representation of one such object to that of another, for example, rotated object.

5. *The sequential character of transformation.* A number of studies of sentence comprehension have indicated that overall reaction times are additive combinations of reaction times for component processes that presumably are performed in a sequential manner. (See, for example, Chase & Clark, 1972; Clark & Chase, 1972; and, for some earlier approaches, Gough, 1965; McMahon, 1963; Miller & McKean, 1964). Introspective reports concerning the kinds of spatial operations imagined in the experiments reviewed in the preceding section, as well as the linearity and additivity of the reaction times, appear to have similar implications for transformations imagined on objects in space.

6. *Complexity and power of the transformational rules.* Chomsky has argued that the unique richness and creative power of the implicit rules of transformational grammar are revealed in the ability of any normal human adult to recognize whether a never-before-heard string of words in his own language is or is not a well-formed sentence, or to recognize whether two very different strings of words are or are not synonymous. However, a similar if not exactly equivalent richness and power may be implied by a subject's ability to recognize, with great precision, whether a never-before-seen line drawing is or is not a cube, whether the swarming motion of a set of random points in a two-dimensional plane is or is not the projection of a rigidly rotating three-dimensional cluster (see Gibson

& Gibson, 1957; Green, 1961; White & Mueser, 1960), or, as in the work reviewed here, whether two perspective views are or are not of the same three-dimensional object.

7. *Underlying, possibly innate, schematisms.* The most controversial aspect of Chomsky's position is perhaps his insistence that the ability of a child to master the complex and powerful grammar of any natural language on the basis of the relatively small sample of sentences actually heard implies the inborn existence of some underlying mental schematism to which all natural languages conform. Whether or not this has rigorously been shown to be true with respect to language, the dependence of perception upon some internally applied constraints appears to be an unavoidable implication of behavioral experiments (Bower, 1966, 1967; Fantz, 1965; Ganz & Wilson, 1967; Hebb, 1937), physiological evidence (Hubel & Wiesel, 1963, 1968), and logical considerations (Minsky, 1961; Shepard, 1964b, pp. 63–64). As just one example, whether it is innate or not, some underlying schematism or principle is evidently reflected in our tendency to see the two-dimensional projection of a cube as a cube and not as one of the infinite variety of other hexahedral shapes that would also yield that very same projection (Attneave & Frost, 1969; Ittleson, 1968). And, to this, we might add the recent indications of rather direct connections between perception and semantics pointed out, for example, by Clark, Carpenter, and Just (1973), and the anthropological arguments of Lévi-Strauss (1967) which at least suggest that certain general schematisms may underlie *all* human cognitive processes.

8. *Role of neuroanatomical structure.* Extensive evidence is now available on humans (from clinical studies of the effects of brain lesions, from experimental investigations of so-called split-brain patients and, recently, from studies of lateralization of function using reaction times or evoked cortical potentials in normal subjects) to show that linguistic and spatial competencies are primarily dependent upon the intactness of corresponding portions of the left and right hemispheres of the cerebral cortex, respectively. Thus, with respect to spatial abilities in patients who have undergone commissurotomy, Gazzaniga, Bogen, and Sperry (1965) presented the drawings of a patient who could produce a recognizable perspective view of a cube only by using his nonpreferred left hand (which is controlled by his right hemisphere), and Levy (Sperry & Levy, 1970) has shown that the right hemisphere is markedly better in tasks resembling the mental paper-folding task studied by Shepard and Feng (1972). In normal subjects, moreover, Gibson, Filbey, and Gazzaniga (1970) have found reaction-time evidence suggesting that what we have called mental rotation is also performed in the right hemisphere. Since it is known that the language functions can shift to the right hemisphere if severe damage occurs to the

left before the age of about 12 years (Lenneberg, 1969), it may be presumed that the very same structures of the brain can subserve the two types of functions considered here, viz. those of language and those of spatial intuition. Possibly these particular structures are especially adapted to dealing with certain very general types of hierarchical deep structures and with certain very general kinds of transformations on these. If so, the "innate schematisms" of which Chomsky speaks, though possibly quite restrictive in their effects within either the linguistic or spatial domain, may nevertheless be so much more general than his remarks suggest as to apply to *both* of these seemingly very disparate domains.

Of course, there also are salient differences between the specific forms of the deep structures and transformations that develop in the cases of these two kinds of human competence. First, transformations appear to be of a discrete, digital, and often binary nature in the linguistic case, whereas they appear to be of a more continuous, analogue, and quantitative variety in the spatial case. Second, although spatial intuition appears to be inherently confined to dealing with representations and transformations corresponding to objects and operations in a space no greater than three dimensions, it is not obvious that there is any analogous restriction in the case of linguistic competence. Finally, the isomorphism between the deep structure and the possible external state of affairs that it represents seems to be relatively more abstract in the case of language and relatively more concrete in the case of spatial perception.

However, these apparent differences may be more superficial than fundamental. The fact that binary spatial gestures (such as a flipping of the hands from palms up to palms down, or a motion of the hand from one side to the other side) often accompany linguistic shifts (such as a switch from the affirmative to the negative, or from an "either" phase to an "or" phase) hints that there may just be, at the deepest level of representation, a rather direct correspondence between grammatical and spatial intuition. Possibly, too, it may not be entirely fortuitous that highly developed manual dexterity and use of tools (which require powerful spatial abilities) appeared at about the same time in the same species as did language and grammar. Such speculations suggest various possibilities for other eventual inquiries: Is it the case, for example, that the ability to imagine complex spatial transformations is, as language, largely unique to man? And, even: Is it possible that a deeper investigation into linguistic competence will reveal that it, also, is constrained by something analogous to the seemingly inherent limitation of spatial intuition to three-dimensional space?

Whether or not there is any merit in these last, highly speculative queries, it does appear that a clarification of the fundamental nature of internal representations and their transformations may be necessary in order to gain a significantly deeper insight into that most intriguing of all subjects of scientific study—the human mind.

ACKNOWLEDGMENTS AND HISTORICAL NOTE

The preparation of this paper was largely completed during my 1971–1972 tenure as a John Simon Guggenheim Fellow at the Center for Advanced Study in the Behavioral Sciences, Stanford, California. Much of the work has been supported by my National Science Foundation research grant No. GB-31971X. I am greatly indebted to my former students and co-workers including particularly Lynn Cooper, Christine Feng, Joseph Klun, and Jacqueline Metzler for their invaluable contributions to this work; to Sherry Huntsberger and Robert Nozick for their very helpful suggestions concerning the manuscript; and to Robert Solso for making possible, at long last, the publication of this earliest and most extensive exposition of the theoretical notions behind my current line of work.

The original basis of this paper was a December 1969 invited presentation in a series of talks by cognitive psychologists at the Salk Institute, La Jolla, California, organized by Eugene Galanter. An expanded version was circulated by December 1971 in essentially the present form—with the exception of the middle section on "experimental findings," which has been both shortened and brought up to date for the purposes of this volume. That earlier version, under the slightly longer title "Studies of the form, formation, and transformation of internal representations," was to have appeared, along with the other papers presented at the Salk Institute, in a volume *Cognitive mechanisms,* edited by Galanter. However, publication of that volume was finally abandoned in the absence of completed manuscripts from some of the speakers.

During the several years that have elapsed since I first drafted the theoretical sections of this paper, I have had no reason to change my theoretical viewpoint in any significant way. At this point I would perhaps want to shift the discussion in the last, most speculative subsection of the paper to reflect certain neo-Chomskian developments in linguistics such, particularly, as those of generative semantics. Nevertheless, I still believe that the "possible parallels" tentatively considered in that section, even if not formulated in the most satisfactory way, point to an issue of great and, I feel, undiminished interest.

REFERENCES

Attneave, F., & Frost, R. The determination of perceived tridimensional orientation by minimum criteria. *Perception & Psychophysics,* 1969, **6**, 391–396.

Attwood, G. An experimental study of visual imagination and memory. *Cognitive Psychology,* 1971, **2**, 290–299.

Barbizet, J. *Human memory and its pathology.* San Francisco, California: Freeman, 1970.

Berkeley, G. *A treatise concerning the principles of human knowledge.* Dublin, 1710.

Boring, E. G. A new ambiguous figure. *American Journal of Psychology,* 1930, **42,** 444–445.

Bower, T. G. R. The visual world of infants. *Scientific American,* 1966, **215,** No. 6, 80–92.

Bower, T. G. R. Phenomenal identity and form perception in an infant. *Perception & Psychophysics,* 1967, **2,** 74–76.

Brooks, L. R. The suppression of visualization by reading. *Quarterly Journal of Experimental Psychology,* 1967, **19,** 289–299.

Chase, W. G., & Calfee, R. C. Modality and similarity effects in short-term recognition memory. *Journal of Experimental Psychology,* 1969, **81,** 510–514.

Chase, W. G., & Clark, H. H. Mental operations in the comparison of sentences and pictures. In L. Gregg (Ed.), *Cognition in learning and memory.* New York: Wiley, 1972.

Chomsky, N. *Language and mind.* New York: Harcourt, Brace & World, 1968.

Clark, H. H., Carpenter, P. A., & Just, M. A. On the meeting of semantics and perception. In W. G. Chase (Ed.), *Visual information processing.* New York: Academic Press, 1973.

Clark, H. H., & Chase, W. G. On the process of comparing sentences against pictures. *Cognitive Psychology,* 1972, **3,** 472–577.

Clowes, M. B. Pictorial relationships—A syntactic approach. In B. Meltzer & D. Michie (Eds.), *Machine intelligence 4.* New York: American Elsevier, 1969. Pp. 361–383.

Clowes, M. On seeing things. *Artificial Intelligence,* 1971, **2,** 79–116.

Cohen, G. Pattern recognition: Differences between matching patterns to patterns and matching descriptions to patterns. *Journal of Experimental Psychology,* 1969, **82,** 427–434.

Conrad, R. Acoustic confusions in immediate memory. *British Journal of Psychology,* 1964, **55,** 75–84.

Cooper, L. A. Internal representation and transformation of random shapes: A chronometric analysis. Unpublished doctoral dissertation, Stanford University, 1973.

Cooper, L. A. Mental rotation of random two-dimensional forms. *Cognitive Psychology,* 1975 (in press).

Cooper, L. A., & Shepard, R. N. The time required to prepare for a rotated stimulus. *Memory & Cognition,* 1973, **1,** 246–250.   (a)

Cooper, L. A., & Shepard, R. N. Chronometric studies of the rotation of mental images. In W. G. Chase (Ed.), *Visual information processing.* New York: Academic Press, 1973.   (b)

Cooper, L. A., & Shepard, R. N. Mental transformations in the discrimination of left and right hands. *Perception and Performance,* 1975 (in press).

Dowling, W. J. Recognition of inversions of melodies and melodic contours. *Perception and Psychophysics,* 1971, **9,** 348–349.

Fantz, R. L. Visual perception from birth as shown by pattern selectivity. *Annals of the New York Academy of Sciences,* 1965, **118,** 793–814.

Festinger, L., Ono, H., Burnham, C. A., & Bamber, D. Efference and the conscious experience of perception. *Journal of Experimental Psychology Monographs,* 1967, **74** (4, Whole No. 637).

Furth, H. G. *Thinking without language: Psychological implications of deafness.* New York: Free Press, 1966.

Ganz, L., & Wilson, P. D. Innate generalization of a form discrimination without contouring eye movements. *Journal of Comparative and Physiological Psychology,* 1967, **63,** 258–269.

Garner, W. R., & Felfoldy, G. L. Integrality of stimulus dimensions in various types of information processing. *Cognitive Psychology,* 1970, **1,** 225–241.

Gazzaniga, M. S., Bogen, J. E., & Sperry, R. W. Observations on visual perception after disconnexion of the cerebral hemispheres in man. *Brain,* 1965, **88,** 221–236.

Geschwind, N. Disconnexion syndromes in animals and man. *Brain,* 1965, **88,** Part I: 273–294, Part II: 585–644.

Gibson, A. R., Filbey, R., & Gazzaniga, M. S. Hemispheric differences as reflected by reaction time. *Proceedings: Federation of American Societies for Experimental Biology,* 1970, **29,** 658. (Abstract)

Gibson, J. J., & Gibson, E. J. Continuous perspective transformations and the perception of rigid motion. *Journal of Experimental Psychology,* 1957, **54,** 129–138.

Gordon, E. E., & Hayward, S. Second-order isomorphism of internal representations of familiar faces. *Perception and Psychophysics,* 1973, **14,** 334–336.

Gough, P. B. Grammatical transformations and speed of understanding. *Journal of Verbal Learning and Verbal Behavior,* 1965, **4,** 107–111.

Gregory, R. L. *The intelligent eye.* London: Weidenseld & Nicolson, 1970.

Green, B. F., Jr. Figure coherence in the kinetic depth effect. *Journal of Experimental Psychology,* 1961, **62,** 272–282.

Guzman, A. Computer recognition of three-dimensional objects in a visual scene. MAC Technical Report 59, Project MAC, M.I.T., Cambridge, Massachusetts, 1968.

Hebb, D. O. The innate organization of visual activity: I. Perception of figures by rats reared in total darkness. *Journal of Genetic Psychology,* 1937, **51,** 101–126.

Hebb, D. O. *The organization of behavior.* New York: Wiley, 1949.

Herrnstein, R. J., & Loveland, D. H. A complex visual concept in the pigeon. *Science,* 1964, **146,** 549–551.

Hubel, D. H., & Wiesel, T. N. Receptive fields of cells in striate cortex of very young, visually inexperienced kittens. *Journal of Neurophysiology,* 1963, **26,** 994–1002.

Hubel, D. H., & Wiesel, T. N. Receptive fields and functional architecture of monkey striate cortex. *Journal of Physiology,* 1968, **195,** 215–243.

Huffman, D. A. Impossible objects as nonsense sentences. In J. Doran (Ed.), *Machine intelligence.* Edinburgh, Scotland: University of Edinburgh Press, 1970.

Ittleson, W. H. *The Ames demonstrations in perception.* Darien, Connecticut: Hafner, 1968.

Jastrow, J. *Fact and fable in psychology.* New York: Houghton Mifflin, 1900.

Johnson, P. E., Cox, D. L., & Curran, T. E. Psychological reality of physical concepts. *Psychonomic Science,* 1970, **19,** 245–247.

Köhler, W. The mentality of apes. New York: Harcourt, Brace, 1925.

Köhler, W. *Gestalt psychology.* New York: New American Library, 1959.

Konorski, J. *Interpretive activity of the brain.* Chicago, Illinois: University of Chicago Press, 1967.

Lenneberg, E. H. On explaining language. *Science,* 1969, **164,** 635–643.

Lévi-Strauss, C. *The savage mind.* Chicago, Illinois: University of Chicago Press, 1967.

Mandler, J. M., & Mandler, G. *Thinking: From association to Gestalt.* New York: Wiley, 1964.

McMahon, L. E. Grammatical analysis as a part of understanding a sentence. Unpublished doctoral dissertation, Harvard University, 1963.

Metzler, J. Cognitive analogues of the rotation of three-dimensional objects. Unpublished doctoral dissertation, Stanford University, 1973.

Metzler, J., & Shepard, R. N. Transformational studies of the internal representation of three-dimensional objects. In R. Solso (Ed.), *Theories of Cognitive Psychology: The Loyola Symposium.* Hillsdale, New Jersey: Lawrence Erlbaum Assoc., 1974.

Michotte, A., Thinès, G., & Crabbé, G. Causalité, permanence et réalité phénoménales. In A. Michotte & J. Nuttin (Eds.), *Studia psychologica.* Louvain: Publications Universitaires de Louvain, 1962. Pp. 374–406.

Miller, G. A., & McKean, K. A chronometric study of some relations between sentences. *Quarterly Journal of Experimental Psychology,* 1964, **16,** 297–308.

Miller, W. F., & Shaw, A. C. Linguistic methods in picture processing—A survey. *Proceedings Fall Joint Computer Conference,* December, 1968, 279–290.

Minsky, M. Steps toward artificial intelligence. *Proceedings of the Institute of Radio Engineers,* 1961, **49,** 8–30.

Moyer, R. S., & Landauer, T. K. Time required for judgments of numerical inequality. *Nature,* 1967, **215,** 1519–1520.

Moyer, R. S., & Landauer, T. K. Determinants of reaction time for digit inequality judgments. *The Bulletin of the Psychonomic Society,* 1973, **1,** 167–168.

Necker, L. A. Observations on some remarkable phenomena seen in Switzerland; and an optical phenomenon which occurs on viewing of a crystal or geometrical solid. *Philosophical Magazine,* 1832, **1,** 329–337.

Neisser, U. *Cognitive psychology.* New York: Appleton-Century-Crofts, 1967.

Penfield, W., & Roberts, L. *Speech and brain-mechanisms.* Princeton, New Jersey: Princeton University Press, 1959.

Penrose, L. S., & Penrose, R. Impossible objects: A special type of visual illusion. *British Journal of Psychology,* 1958, **49,** 31–33.

Piaget, J. *The construction of reality in the child.* New York: Basic Books, 1954.

Place, U. T. Is consciousness a brain process? *British Journal of Psychology,* 1956, **47,** 44–50.

Pollen, D. H., Lee, J. R., & Taylor, J. H. How does the striate cortex begin the reconstruction of the visual world. *Science,* 1971, **173,** 74–77.

Posner, M. I., Boies, S. J., Eichelman, W. H., & Taylor, R. L. Retention of visual and name codes of single letters. *Journal of Experimental Psychology Monographs,* 1969, **79,** No. 1, Part 2.

Premack, D. Language in chimpanzee? *Science,* 1971, **172,** 808–822.

Pribram, K. *Languages of the brain.* Englewood Cliffs, New Jersey: Prentice-Hall, 1971.

Segal, S. J., & Fusella, V. Influence of imaged pictures and sounds on detection of auditory and visual signals. *Journal of Experimental Psychology,* 1970, **83,** 458–464.

Sekuler, R. W., & Abrams, M. Visual sameness: A choice time analysis of pattern recognition processes. *Journal of Experimental Psychology,* 1968, **77,** 232–238.

Sekuler, R., Rubin, E., & Armstrong, R. Processing numerical information: A choice time analysis. *Journal of Experimental Psychology,* 1971, **90,** 75–80.

Selfridge, O. G. Pandemonium: A paradigm for learning. In *The mechanisation of thought processes* (Proceedings of a symposium, National Physical Laboratory, Teddington, England). London: Her Majesty's Stationery Office, 1959.

Shepard, R. N. Attention and the metric structure of the stimulus space. *Journal of Mathematical Psychology*, 1964, **1**, 54–87. (a)

Shepard, R. N. Computers and thought: A review of the book edited by E. Feigenbaum & J. Feldman. *Behavioral Science*, 1964, **9**, 57–65. (b)

Shepard, R. N. Some psychologically oriented techniques for the scientific investigation of unidentified aerial phenomena. In Symposium on unidentified flying objects. *Hearings before the Committee on Science and Astronautics, U.S. House of Representatives*, July 29, 1968, 223–235.

Shepard, R. N. Psychological representation of speech sounds. In E. E. David, & P. B. Denes (Eds.), *Human communication: A unified view*. New York: McGraw-Hill, 1972.

Shepard, R. N., & Chang, J.-J. Stimulus generalization in the learning of classifications. *Journal of Experimental Psychology*, 1963, **65**, 94–102.

Shepard, R. N., & Chipman, S. Second-order isomorphism of internal representations: Shapes of states. *Cognitive Psychology*, 1970, **1**, 1–17.

Shepard, R. N., & Feng, C. A chronometric study of mental paper folding. *Cognitive Psychology*, 1972, **3**, 228–243.

Shepard, R. N., Hovland, C. I., & Jenkins, H. M. Learning and memorization of classifications. *Psychological Monographs*, 1961, **75** (13, Whole No. 517).

Shepard, R. N., Kilpatric, D. W., & Cunningham, J. P. The internal representation of numbers. *Cognitive Psychology*, 1975 (in press).

Shepard, R. N., & Metzler, J. Mental rotation of three-dimensional objects. *Science*, 1971, **171**, 701–703.

Sinclair-de-Zwart, H. Developmental psycholinguistics. In D. Elkind & J. H. Flavell (Eds.), *Studies in cognitive development: Essays in honor of Jean Piaget*. London and New York: Oxford University Press, 1969.

Smart, J. J. C. Sensations and brain processes. *Philosophical Review*, 1959, **68**, 141–156.

Smith, E. E. Choice reaction time: An analysis of the major theoretical positions. *Psychological Bulletin*, 1968, **69**, 77–110.

Sperling, G. A. A model for visual memory tasks. *Human Factors*, 1963, **5**, 19–31.

Sperry, R. W. Hemisphere deconnection and unity in conscious awareness. *American Psychologist*, 1968, **23**, 723–733.

Sperry, R. W., & Levy, J. Mental capacities of the disconnected minor hemisphere. Paper presented at the American Psychological Association meetings, Miami, September 4, 1970.

Sternberg, S. Two operations in character-recognition: Some evidence from reaction-time measurements. *Perception & Psychophysics*, 1967, **2**, 45–53.

Tinklepaugh, O. L. Multiple delayed reactions with chimpanzees and monkeys. *Journal of Comparative Psychology*, 1932, **13**, 207–243.

Torgerson, W. S. *Theory and methods of scaling*. New York: Wiley, 1958.

Tversky, B. Pictorial and verbal encoding in a short-term memory task. *Perception & Psychophysics*, 1969, **6**, 225–233.

Waltz, D. Shedding light on shadows. *Vision Flash 29*, Artificial Intelligence Laboratory, Massachusetts Institute of Technology, Cambridge, Massachusetts, 1972.

White, B. J., & Mueser, G. E. Accuracy in reconstructing the arrangements of elements generating kinetic depth displays. *Journal of Experimental Psychology,* 1960, **60,** 1–11.

Wickelgren, W. A. Auditory or articulatory coding in verbal short-term memory. *Psychological Review,* 1969, **76,** 232–235.

Winston, P. H. Learning structural descriptions from examples. A. I. Report 231. Artificial Intelligence Laboratory, Massachusetts Institute of Technology, Cambridge, Mass., 1970.

Wittgenstein, L. *Philosophical investigations.* New York: Macmillan, 1953.

Yin, R. K. Looking at upside-down faces. *Journal of Experimental Psychology,* 1969, **81,** 141–145.

SECTION II

5

RETRIEVAL AS A MEMORY MODIFIER: AN INTERPRETATION OF NEGATIVE RECENCY AND RELATED PHENOMENA

Robert A. Bjork[1]
University of Michigan

Although it is commonplace to assume that the type or level of processing during the input of a verbal item determines the representation of that item in memory, which in turn influences later attempts to store, recognize, or recall that item or similar items, it is much less common to assume that the way in which an item is retrieved from memory is also a potent determiner of that item's subsequent representation in memory. Retrieval from memory is often assumed, implicitly or explicitly, as a process analogous to the way in which the contents of a memory location in a computer are read out, that is, as a process that does not, by itself, modify the state of the retrieved item in memory. In my opinion, however, there is ample evidence for a kind of Heisenberg principle with respect to retrieval processes: an item can seldom, if ever, be retrieved from memory without modifying the representation of that item in memory in significant ways.

It is both appropriate and productive, I think, to analyze retrieval processes within the same kind of levels-of-processing framework formulated by Craik and Lockhart (1972) with respect to input processes; this chapter is an attempt to do so. In the first of the two main sections below, I explore the extent to which negative-recency phenomena in the long-term recall of a list of items is attributable to differences in levels of retrieval during initial recall. In the second section I present some recent results from ex-

---

[1] Now at the University of California, Los Angeles.

periments designed to assess the differential long-term effects of certain direct manipulations of the way in which an item is initially retrieved.

NEGATIVE RECENCY

In the last six or seven years, there have been a great number of experimental demonstrations that the items at the end of a list, although better recalled initially than any other list items, are the worst-recalled items on tests of final recall administered after substantial delays. The term *negative recency* (Craik, 1970) has come to denote this phenomenon, and I will follow that usage even though I consider the choice of that term to be somewhat unfortunate ("negative recency" has an earlier, different, and generally well-known meaning).

Several Illustrative Experiments

Bjork (1968), Experiment I. In the first of two experiments, Bjork demonstrated negative recency across learning trials in the acquisition of the items in a single free-recall list. Sixty subjects were each presented a list of 40 words three times. The words in the list were presented at a 2-sec rate, and there was a test of immediate free recall following each presentation of the list. The words in the list were scrambled from presentation to presentation, except for eight critical words, two of which were assigned to each of the following four serial-position sequences: MMM, RRM, MMR, and RRR (where M denotes the middle 12 input serial positions in a list presentation, and R denotes the last six input serial positions).

The results of Bjork's first experiment are shown in Fig. 1, in which are two comparisons of particular interest: performance on MMM words versus performance on RRM words, and performance on MMR words versus performance on RRR words. In both comparisons, the words differ in their input positions during the first and second presentations, but they were in the same input portion of the list during the third presentation of the list. Not only were RRM and RRR words not learned better than MMM and MMR words, respectively, as measured by performance following the third presentation, but also they appear to have been learned less well in spite of their greater likelihood of recall following the first and second presentations of the list.

Bjork (1968), Experiment II. In a second experiment, Bjork obtained a similar result. Each of 24 subjects was shown each of five 24-word lists twice. The words in any one list were presented at a 2-sec rate, and an immediate free-recall test followed each presentation of a list. The 24 words in any one list were randomized from the first to the second presen-

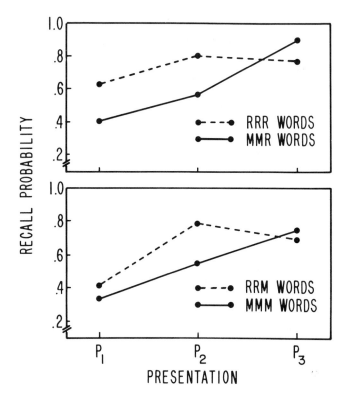

Fig. 1.   Learning curves as a function of certain critical sequences of successive input regions across three presentations of a list; R and M denote the recency and middle portions of a list, respectively. (After Bjork, 1968, Experiment I.)

tation, except for eight critical words, two of which were Primacy words (presented in one of the first four input positions on both presentations), four of which were Middle words (presented in one of the middle eight input serial positions on both presentations), and two of which were Recency words (presented in one of the last four input positions on both presentations). After the second presentation and recall of the fifth and final list, and after a phony debriefing period lasting several minutes, there was a final free-recall test of subject's memory for all words from all lists.

In Table 1 the recall proportions for Primacy, Middle, and Recency words are shown as a function of time of test. Once again, the striking feature of the results in Table 1 is that Recency words, in spite of their higher level of immediate recall following each of the two list presentations, are recalled less frequently on the final test than are Middle words.

TABLE 1
Proportions of Critical Words
Recalled Initially and Finally[a]

| | Initial tests | | |
Item type	First	Second	Final test
Primacy items	.50	.70	.54
Middle items	.33	.52	.42
Recency items	.60	.68	.35

[a] After Bjork (1968, Experiment II).

Craik (*1970*).   In an experiment similar to but simpler than the one just reported, Craik obtained a very marked contrast between the initial and final recall of the end items in a list. Each of 80 subjects was presented 10 15-word lists. After each list there was an immediate recall, and after all ten lists there was a final-recall test for all items from all lists.

Craik's results are shown in Fig. 2. The initial-recall curve exhibits the typical strong positive effect of recency, with the recall probability for the very last item in the list approaching one, but the final-recall curve in Fig. 2 decreases systematically across the recency portion of the list.

Madigan and McCabe (*1971*).   With a paired-associate probe procedure, Madigan and McCabe obtained an even more stunning contrast between the initial and final recall of recency items. Each of 30 subjects was presented 50 five-pair lists of paired associates. After each list, the stimulus member of one of the pairs was presented as an immediate probe test of the subject's memory for the paired response. At the end of the experiment there was a final probe retest of all 50 tested pairs.

The results obtained by Madigan and McCabe are shown in Fig. 3. Recall of the response member of the fifth pair in a list was all but perfect initially, but those same response members were never recalled on the final test.

A Depth-of-Retrieval Interpretation of Negative Recency

One reason that negative-recency phenomena have aroused considerable interest is that they are unintuitive. If one simply views retrieval as an important learning event, the conditions that maximize initial recall should, in turn, maximize final recall. From that standpoint, the last item in a list should be the best-recalled item in final recall rather than the worst-recalled item.

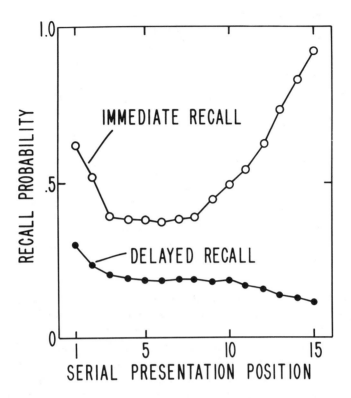

FIG. 2. Immediate and final recall proportions as a function of input serial position. (After Craik, 1970.)

It is unrealistic, however, to assume that retrieval from memory is a singular event that has uniform consequences on the state of the retrieved item. One interpretation of negative recency (Bjork, 1970; Craik, 1970) is based on the assumption that the long-term benefits of an initial retrieval are an increasing function of the depth or difficulty of the initial retrieval. In particular, retrieval from short-term memory (STM) is assumed to consist of a kind of rapid dumping, which has little, if any, effect on later efforts to retrieve those items from long-term memory (LTM), whereas an initial retrieval that itself constitutes a retrieval from LTM does facilitate later efforts to retrieve from long-term memory. Thus, negative recency comes about because of differential effects of the initial retrieval: long-term recall of items in the beginning and middle of a list is enhanced by an initial retrieval, whereas long-term retrieval of items at the end of a list does not profit from their initial retrieval from STM.

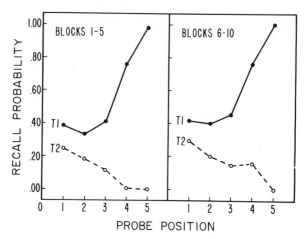

Fig. 3.   Immediate (T1) and final (T2) paired-associate recall probabilities as a function of input position. (After Madigan & McCabe, 1971.)

In order to test the depth-of-retrieval interpretation of negative recency, I designed an experiment (Bjork, 1970, Experiment I) similar to Craik's (1970) experiment reported above, except that the initial presentation of a list either was or was not followed by an initial test. Each of 32 subjects was presented eight 16-word lists. After each list there was a 30-sec period during which subjects either recalled the list or shadowed nine-digit numbers presented at a 2-sec rate. Four of the lists were followed by an initial recall, and the other four lists were followed by digit shadowing. Subjects could not anticipate whether a given list would be followed by an initial recall or digit shadowing because that activity was cued by a postinput cue (a row of question marks or a nine-digit number presented after the last word in a list), and the cuing was haphazard across the eight lists. At the end of the experiment there was a final free-recall test for all items from all lists.

The obtained results (shown in Fig. 4) are quite consistent with the depth-of-retrieval interpretation of negative recency. Overall, final recall was enhanced by the initial recall, but the item that profited least from the initial recall was that item recalled most frequently during the initial recall—the last item in the list.

An Amount-of-Rehearsal Interpretation of Negative Recency

Negative recency also may be interpreted as reflecting differences in amount of rehearsal prior to an initial retrieval. In this view, recency items

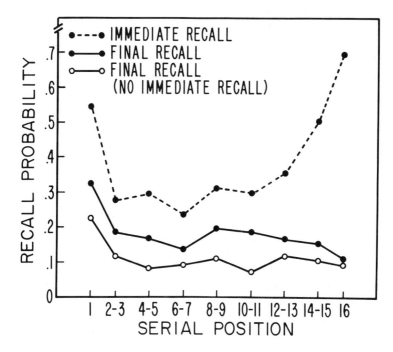

F<small>IG</small>. 4.   Immediate and final free recall as a function of input serial position. (After Bjork, 1970, Experiment I.)

receive less rehearsal prior to initial recall that do earlier items in the list. The near-perfect initial recall of recency items is attributable to the strong likelihood that those items remain available in STM at the time of the initial recall. In terms of their strength of representation in LTM, however, recency items are weaker than any other items, and that weakness results in their inferior long-term recall. Thus, no appeal to differential effects at the time of retrieval is necessary to account for negative-recency phenomena.

One problem with the amount-of-rehearsal interpretation is that it is inconsistent with the results shown in Fig. 4. If initial retrieval were assumed to have no effect on later retrieval, then the two final-recall curves should fall on top of each other. If initial retrieval were assumed to have a uniform positive effect on later retrieval, then the two final-recall curves in Fig. 4 should diverge rather than converge across the recency portion of the list, since those items are recalled more frequently than are any other items in the initial-recall lists.

That problem notwithstanding, Rundus and Atkinson (1970) obtained what seemed to be strong evidence in favor of the amount-of-rehearsal interpretation of negative recency. Subjects were presented a series of 20-word lists after each of which there was a test of immediate free recall, and after all of which there was a test of final free recall. The words in any one list were presented at a relatively slow rate (5 sec per word). Subjects were required to rehearse aloud, and their overt rehearsal of the words in a list was recorded. Rundus and Atkinson obtained the typical positive and negative effects of recency in the initial and final tests of free recall, respectively. The result of particular interest, however, was that there was a negative-recency effect in the number of overt rehearsals devoted to an item as a function of its input serial position. That is, the last item or two in a list did, in fact, receive fewer overt rehearsals prior to immediate recall than did earlier items in the list.

Although the Rundus and Atkinson results appear to provide strong support for an amount-of-rehearsal interpretation of negative recency, other considerations and evidence render the amount-of-rehearsal interpretation altogether untenable. One problem is that the words actually recalled initially should, from the standpoint of the final recall, profit at least as much from their overt recall as they do from any one within-list overt rehearsal. When the observed likelihood of initial recall as a function of input position is added to the overt-rehearsals function, the resulting function exhibits little if any negative recency. Any argument about the extent to which that problem is a serious problem becomes academic, however, in view of results obtained by Craik and Watkins (1973, Experiment II) and by Light (1974).

In the Craik and Watkins experiment, 16 subjects were each presented 12 lists with 12 words in each list. The words in any one list were presented at a 3-sec rate, subjects were required to rehearse aloud, and each subject's overt rehearsals were recorded. The last four words in each list were printed in capital letters, and the subjects were instructed to recall those four items first during the initial recall that followed each list. For six of the 12 lists the initial recall was immediate, and for the other six lists the initial recall was delayed by a 20-sec unfilled period, during which subjects were free to continue their overt rehearsal of the words in that list. At the end of the experiment, there was a test of final free recall.

The results of the Craik and Watkins experiment are shown in Fig. 5. Even though the last four list items receive a great deal more rehearsal prior to the delayed initial free recall than they do prior to the immediate initial free recall, the level of final free recall is essentially the same in both cases, and there is negative recency in the final-recall curve in both cases.

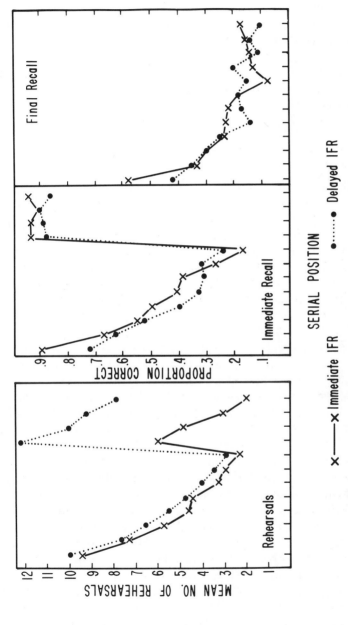

FIG. 5. Number of (a) overt rehearsals and probabilities of (b) initial and (c) final free recall as a function of input serial position and delay of initial recall: (×) immediate IFR; (●) delayed IFR. (After Craik & Watkins, 1973.)

By themselves, the Craik and Watkins results indicate quite dramatically that negative recency is not attributable to a deficiency in the *amount* of rehearsal given recency items prior to initial recall, but the results of two recent experiments by Light (1974) snuff out any lingering hope one might have for the amount-of-rehearsal interpretation of negative recency. Using a paired-associate probe paradigm similar to that employed by Madigan and McCabe (1971), Light increased both the incentive and the time available for subjects to rehearse the terminal items in a list. In spite of the additional rehearsal of terminal pairs effected by those manipulations, there remained sizable negative-recency effects in final probed recall.

A Levels-of-Processing Interpretation of Negative Recency

Although there is little or no evidence for the amount-of-rehearsal interpretation of negative recency, there is substantial evidence that differences in the *type* or *level* of processing of list items prior to an initial recall are at least as important as differences in the depth of initial retrieval in producing negative recency in long-term recall. As has been demonstrated by a number of recent studies (Bjork & Jongeward, 1974; Craik & Watkins, 1973; Jacoby, 1973; Jacoby & Bartz, 1972; Mazuryk, 1974; Mazuryk & Lockhart, 1974; Meunier, Ritz, & Meunier, 1972; Woodward, Bjork, & Jongeward, 1973), it is necessary to distinguish between rehearsal as a rote, cyclic activity and rehearsal as a constructive associative activity. The former type of rehearsal, referred to as *primary* rehearsal (Woodward *et al.,* 1973) or *maintenance* rehearsal (Craik & Watkins, 1973), does not facilitate long-term recall, whereas the latter type of rehearsal, referred to as *secondary* rehearsal (Woodward *et al.,* 1973) or *elaborative* rehearsal (Craik & Watkins, 1973), does facilitate long-term recall. The position I would like to argue in this section is that the terminal items in a list receive less secondary rehearsal or processing prior to initial recall than do earlier items, and that deficiency, together with their more superficial retrieval during initial recall, results in their inferior long-term retention.

Before I cite some supporting evidence for the levels-of-processing interpretation of negative recency, I want to specify the position in more detail. As a prototypical situation, consider the processing devoted to a single word in a typical free-recall list. During the time a word is presented, a subject may engage in some mixture of primary and secondary processing activities. Those activities may vary substantially from one word to the next, but the nature of such processing should not vary systematically with a word's input serial position. The initial few words in a list might receive more processing during their presentations because of the minimal competition for processing time from earlier items in the list, and that greater processing might in fact produce the positive primacy observed in both initial and final recall, but after the first few items, the processing during an item's presentation should be relatively uniform across input serial position. A similar pattern should hold for the processing of an item during the brief period just subsequent to its presentation, and any such rehearsal will tend to be of the primary or maintenance type, which means that it will have little consequence for long-term recall in any case. As the interval from the presentation of a particular item lengthens, however, and as more subsequent items are presented, any within-list retrievals (rehearsals) of that item will be increasingly of the secondary or elaborative type. The likelihood that a given item will be retrieved or rehearsed will decrease, of course, as the interval from its presentation increases, but any within-list retrievals that do occur will be increasingly potent in terms of their effect on long-term recall. According to the present characterization, then, the inferior long-term recall of recency items is attributable to two consequences of their being last presented and first recalled: (a) their immediate superficial readout from STM does not facilitate their later retrieval from LTM, and (b) compared to earlier list items, the opportunities for within-list retrievals or rehearsal of the secondary type are severely restricted. I do not, of course, mean to imply that these assumed differences in processing during input and output are independent of each other; clearly, any assumed differences in retrieval processes during output must be in large part determined by differences in encoding, rehearsal, and forgetting processes during input.

No additional support for the first of the two assumed components of negative recency will be cited here. Some evidence that depth-of-retrieval during initial recall is a factor in negative recency has already been cited, and the phenomena discussed in the next section constitute stronger if less direct evidence for such an assumption.

Evidence for the contribution of within-list processing to negative recency derives from several sources. First, Mazuryk (1974) has shown that it is possible to produce positive rather than negative recency in final free recall if subjects are cued to rehearse the recency items in a list in an associative (or secondary) fashion. In Mazuryk's experiment, subjects were presented 12 14-word lists and immediate recall was required after each list. During the presentation of the tenth word in each list, subjects were instructed, by means of prearranged cues, how to process the last four words in the list. They were cued either to rehearse each of the last four items in turn in a rote (primary) fashion—either overtly or covertly—or they were cued to generate as many verbal associates to each of the last four words as they could. The two rote-rehearsal conditions (covert and overt) produced marked positive recency in immediate recall (recall of the four recency items was near-perfect), but those conditions also resulted in negative recency in final recall. The associate-processing condition, in contrast, resulted in positive recency in both immediate and final recall (the levels of initial and final recall of the four recency items were lower and much higher, respectively, than were the levels of initial and final recall of those items in the rote-rehearsal conditions).

Mazuryk's results are consistent with the notion that recency items are typically processed in a superficial fashion and that their early recall tends to truncate the opportunity for deeper postpresentation processing of those items. That interpretation is also supported in a quite different way by the results of an experiment by Glenberg and Melton (1974). In Glenberg and Melton's experiment, subjects were required to rehearse aloud during the presentation of several free-recall lists, each of which was followed by an immediate free recall. Of the various analyses of subjects' rehearsal processes carried out by Glenberg and Melton, the analysis of particular interest involves items in the middle rather than at the end of a given list. For items whose free recall was not influenced by primacy or recency, Glenberg and Melton were clever enough to look at recall probability as a function of not only the number of overt rehearsals but also as a function of the spacing of those rehearsals. That is, if an item was given a certain fixed number of overt rehearsals, recall was plotted as a function of the average spacing between successive rehearsals.

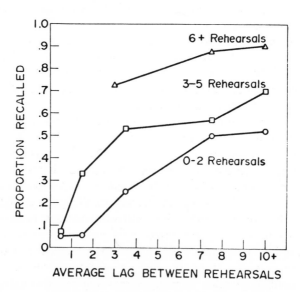

Fig. 6.   Free-recall probabilities as a function of the average spacing of a word's within-list overt rehearsals. (After Glenberg & Melton, 1974.)

Glenberg and Melton's results are shown in Fig. 6. Given a fixed number of rehearsals, there were quite remarkable increases in recall as a function of the spacing of those rehearsals.

The Glenberg and Melton results are correlational in nature, which means that there are at least two different ways of looking at those results. The least interesting and least plausible interpretation, from my standpoint, is the possibility that the increase in recall as a function of spacing has nothing to do with spacing per se, but that, rather, both spacing of overt rehearsals and initial free recall increase as a function of the degree to which items are well learned when they are initially presented. Thus, if items are not reasonably well learned when they are presented initially, they become unavailable for rehearsal quickly, which means that they will not survive long interrehearsal intervals, whereas well-learned items will survive such intervals. Although the results in Fig. 6 might reflect nothing more than such a selection effect, it seems more plausible to me that they reflect primarily the increased long-term benefits of a within-list retrieval as a function of the delay of that retrieval from the preceding retrieval or input of that item.

The level-of-processing interpretation of negative recency put forward in this section views negative recency phenomena as the natural consequences of a subject's rehearsal and retrieval processes during the input and output, respectively, of a list of items. Götz and Jacoby (1974) and Mazuryk and Lockhart (1974) have also interpreted negative recency phenomena in terms of a kind of level of processing framework, but their interpretations differ somewhat from the present view. In both the Götz and Jacoby (1974) and Mazuryk and Lockhart (1974) interpretations, retrieval processes during initial recall are not, by themselves, assumed to play a major role in producing negative recency during final recall. Rather, the explanatory burden is put on differences as a function of serial position in the level of processing (or type of retrieval cues established) during the input of a list. Such differences are not assumed to reflect natural or typical processing activities as much as they are assumed to reflect a subject's efforts to maximize the level of initial recall. The subject is assumed, in anticipation of the end of a list and the subsequent test of immediate recall, to intentionally encode the last few list items in a low-level fashion that makes them readily available for initial recall but impairs their long-term recall. Such a view requires, of course, that subjects be able to anticipate the end of a list. One testable implication of the Götz and Jacoby (1974) and Mazuryk and Lockhart (1974) interpretations is that list-length uncertainty (that is, introducing substantial variation in the number of items presented in each of a series of lists presented for initial recall) should reduce greatly or abolish negative-recency effects in final recall.

RELATED PHENOMENA

There is little doubt, at least in my own mind, that negative-recency phenomena reflect some very important differences in the extent to which different types of retrieval processes modify the long-term state of an item in memory. From a procedural standpoint, however, the negative-recency paradigm constitutes a somewhat indirect means of manipulating retrieval processes. In the present section, the long-term consequences of some more direct manipulations of the delay, difficulty, and type of initial retrieval are reviewed.

Delay of Retrieval

In order to examine more directly the extent to which the delay of an initial retrieval influences the effectiveness of that retrieval as a memory modifier, Whitten and Bjork (1972) devised a paradigm that is a kind of hybrid combination of the standard free-recall and Brown–Peterson paradigms. Subjects were each shown several lists of words to free recall, but the lists differed from typical free-recall lists in several important ways: (a) the 24 words in a list were presented as 12 word doubles rather than as single words; (b) the presentation of any two successive word doubles was separated by 22-sec of intervening distractor activity; (c) embedded at one of three different points within the distractor activity following a given word double (after retention intervals of 4, 8, or 14 sec), there was a 3-sec interval during which the word double was either presented again or was tested for recall; and (d) the free-recall test following any one list was delayed by a period of distractor activity long enough to nullify the influence of short-term memory.

The results of Whitten and Bjork's (1972) experiment are shown in Fig. 7. The proportions of words correctly recalled on the embedded within-list tests and on the free-recall test following a given list are plotted as a function of the delay from the initial presentation of a word double until the within-list test or second presentation of that word double. The top two curves in Fig. 7 are simply what one might expect: The fact that performance on the within-list test decreases with the delay of that test is hardly surprising, and the increase in the free recall of words in the present–present condition as a function of spacing is a result that has also become altogether commonplace.

It is the bottom curve in Fig. 7 that is of particular interest. The fact that performance in the present-test condition increases with the delay of the initial test is by no means an obvious result. If one simply views correct initial retrieval as a learning event, then one would expect the probability

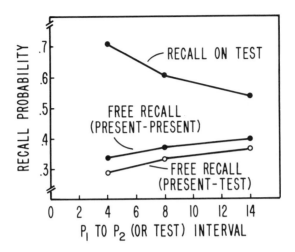

Fig. 7. Within-list recall and subsequent free recall as a function of presentation–presentation or presentation–test interval. (After Whitten & Bjork, 1972.)

of subsequent retrieval to decrease rather than increase with the delay of the initial retrieval. If, however, one assumes that the extent to which an act of retrieval serves as a learning event is a function of the depth, difficulty, or complexity of that act, then the results of the present-test condition are not surprising. Landauer and Eldridge (1967) obtained a somewhat similar result using a paired-associate paradigm, although the increase in performance as a function of presentation–test interval in their situation seemed restricted to very short intervals.

Difficulty of Retrieval

In order to interpret Whitten and Bjork's (1972) results as supporting the notion that the effectiveness of a retrieval act is an increasing function of the difficulty of that act, it is necessary to assume retrieval difficulty increases with retrieval delay. Although such an assumption seems altogether reasonable, the results of an experiment by Gardiner, Craik, and Bleasdale (1973), and the results of several unpublished experiments carried out by Eva Bradford, illustrate in a more direct fashion that the difficulty or complexity of an initial retrieval influences its effect on subsequent retrieval.

In the Gardiner *et al.* (1973) experiment, the definition and first letter of each of 50 words (frequency less than one per million) were presented to subjects who were instructed to retrieve that word as quickly as possible.

The retrieval latency for each word that was, in fact, retrieved was recorded, and, at the end of the experiment, subjects were asked to write down as many of the 50 words as they could remember. In general, final-recall probability increased with initial-retrieval latency: only 27% of those words retrieved within 15 sec were recalled on the final test, whereas 48% of those words retrieved between 15 and 60 sec were recalled.

One problem with the Gardiner *et al.* (1973) results is that the differences in final-recall probability as a function of initial-retrieval latency might be attributable to the amount of time a subject is exposed to the definition and first letter of a given word, rather than to the difficulty of the initial retrieval. That is, during the test of final recall, subjects' memory for definitions and first letters presented earlier might mediate their recall of the corresponding words.

Such mediation problems are avoided somewhat, but not entirely, by the design employed by Eva Bradford in several unpublished experiments. On each of a series of trials in Bradford's experiments, subjects were instructed to give an associate of a certain type in response to the presentation of a word. In the simplest of her experiments, one of two prearranged cues was presented prior to the presentation of a given word. One cue instructed subjects to give their first associate to the subsequent word, whereas the other cue instructed them to give a novel associate, that is, an associate that they thought other people would be very unlikely to give in response to that word. At the end of the experiment, subjects were asked, without forewarning, to recall as many as possible of the associates they had generated during the experimental session.

Bradford's results are consistent with the notion that the extent to which a later recall profits from an initial recall is a function of the difficulty or complexity of the retrieval processes during the initial recall. In the simple experiment described above, 45% of the novel associates were recalled on the final test, whereas only 31% of the first associates were recalled. In a more complex experiment in which subjects were cued to give second associates, superordinates, coordinates, and so forth, as well as first associates and novel associates, there was also a general positive correlation between the level of final recall and the difficulty of initial retrieval.

Although it seems likely in Bradford's experiments that the recall of associates during final recall was mediated, in part, by subjects' memory for the presented words that gave rise to those associates during the experimental session, it seems unlikely that the direction of the differences in final recall could be attributable to such processes. One would expect, for example, that it would be easier to regenerate and recognize having given a first associate to a given word than it would be to regenerate and recognize a second or novel associate.

Levels and Stages of Retrieval

A recent dissertation by Whitten (1974) constitutes what is probably the most tightly controlled and analytical investigation of test events as learning trials. In each of several experiments, Whitten employed postinput cues to subjects as a means of manipulating the nature of an initial retrieval without also influencing the nature of the encoding processes during the initial presentation of an item. It is beyond the scope of this chapter to present either the method or the results of Whitten's several experiments in full detail, but the following incomplete descriptions of two of his experiments should clarify the general methodology and some of the principal results of his research.

The structure of a typical trial in the first of Whitten's experiments is diagrammed in Fig. 8. After a READY signal and a 1-sec blank period, each of four common words was presented for .75 sec in the window of a high-speed memory drum. A .50-sec search-mode signal followed the fourth word on a trial and preceded the presentation of a probe (test) word. The search-mode signal (RRRRRR or MMMMMM) served as a postinput cue to subjects to recall aloud the list word that either rhymed with (RRRRRR) or meant the same as (MMMMMM) the probe word. In the particular illustration shown in Fig. 8, the correct response on an RRRRRR trial would be the list word rhyming with STATION ("NATION"), and the correct response on an MMMMMM trial would be the list word that meant the same as COUNTRY (also "NATION"). The lists were constructed such that, across subjects, the same pool of words was recalled on both acoustic-search and semantic-search trials. At the end of the ex-

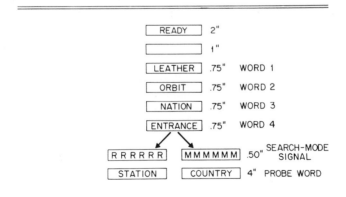

FIG. 8.   Sequences of events on a typical acoustic-search (left arrow) or semantic-search (right arrow) trial in Whitten's (1974) Experiment I.

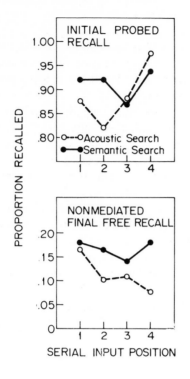

Fig. 9. Initial and final recall as a function of input serial position and initial-test search mode. (After Whitten, 1974.)

periment, subjects were asked to recall as many of the words presented during the experiment as they could.

The proportion of tested words recalled initially on acoustic-search and semantic-search trials is shown as a function of serial input position in Fig. 9, together with the nonmediated final-recall proportions for those words. "Nonmediated final free recall" denotes a scoring procedure in which cases where the recall of a probed list word was preceded and possibly mediated by the just prior recall of its corresponding probe word were excluded from the analysis. Whether such cases were or were not excluded did not, in fact, change the basic pattern of results on the final recall.

Several aspects of Whitten's results in Fig. 9 merit comment:

1. The initial test of a word, whether based on an acoustic search or semantic search, contributed greatly to its final recall. The final-recall proportions for list words that were not tested initially fell between .02 and .04 in all conditions.

2. The initial-recall curve in the acoustic-search condition exhibits positive recency, whereas the final-recall curve exhibits negative recency. If one assumes that the acoustic code of a word is lost rapidly enough that

only the fourth word in a list was reliably retrieved on the basis of its acoustic trace, and that the earlier words in a list—the first word in particular—tended to be retrieved on the basis of a deeper-level encoding of some type, then the final-recall curve can be interpreted as demonstrating that initial retrieval on the basis of an acoustic trace does relatively little to facilitate later recall.

3. Initial retrieval on the basis of a semantic search, however, appears both to be less sensitive to input recency and to have much more substantial effects on final recall.

In his research on tests as learning trials, Whitten was concerned not only with "depth" of retrieval as a factor, but also with the relative contributions of the search and recovery components of a retrieval process. Thus, if a set of items is presented and there is an initial effort to retrieve one of those items based on some cue, any later attempt to retrieve those items will reflect encoding processes during their presentation plus whatever modifications in the state of those items are attributable to searching through the set and recovering (recalling) a given item at the time of the initial retrieval.

In order to gain some information about the relative contributions of initial search and initial recovery to final recall, and in order to gain information on several other questions as well, Whitten devised a very clever and very complex experiment. The procedure was much the same as that outlined in Fig. 8 except that (a) two words rather than four words were presented on a given trial; (b) on some trials neither of the two list words matched the probe word in terms of the cued relation, although in some of such cases there was a match between one of the list words and the probe word in terms of the uncued relation (the correct response on such trials, whether the uncued relation existed or not, was "no match"); (c) on some trials there was no test at all (on such trials, NO TEST replaced the search-mode signal and a simple arithmetic problem replaced the probe word); and (d) on trials where the cued relation did exist between one of the list words and the probe word, the uncued relation might or might not exist between the probe and the other list word. In addition to obtaining the probabilities of initial probed recall and final free recall, Whitten also obtained the latencies of initial recall and the probabilities of final recognition. The final-free-recall proportions shown in Fig. 10 constitute a small subset of the results from Whitten's experiment (for the full details, see Whitten, 1974).

In the condition designations at the bottom of Fig. 10, the first two letters indicate the relation between each of the two list words and the probe word (A = acoustic, S = semantic, and X = unrelated), and the letters

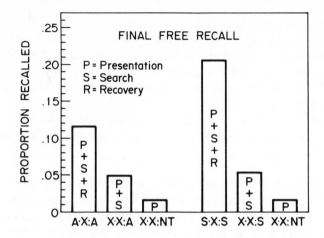

Fig. 10.   Final free recall as a function of initial list type, where P is presentation, S is search, and R is recovery. (After Whitten, 1974, Experiment III.)

after the colons indicate the cued search mode (A = acoustic, S = semantic, and NT = no test). Several aspects of the results in Fig. 10 merit comment:

1. Words that are presented and initially recalled are much better recalled finally than are words not initially recalled.

2. Initial retrieval of a list word based on its semantic properties produces substantially better final recall of that word than does initial retrieval of a word based on its acoustic properties.

3. Finally, searching through a set of items in memory to see whether any of those items have a particular acoustic or semantic property appears to facilitate the later recall of those items, although the extent of such facilitation is small compared to cases where an item is actually recovered (recalled) as an outcome of an initial search.

CONCLUSION

The phenomena reviewed in this chapter constitute compelling evidence that an item's state in memory is modified by its retrieval and, more importantly, that the extent of such modification is a function of the depth or level of the retrieval processes involved. There are several thoretical and practical implications of this general result that merit comment:

1. There is one sense in which there is nothing surprising in the present results. Given that level of processing during the input of a verbal item has been shown to be a potent factor in determining one's retention of

that item, and that the degree to which rehearsal facilitates later recall is also a function of the level of processing involved, there seems little reason not to expect a similar relationship in the case of retrieval processes.

2. Although the present results seem consistent with other recent results, it remains a nontrivial matter to say why the effectiveness of test trials as learning events should depend on the level or depth of the retrieval processes involved. My own guess is that deeper, more difficult, more complex retrieval processes have two distinct long-term advantages over shallower, less difficult, and less complex retrieval processes: (a) they reactivate or strengthen encodings of an item that are more durable, less susceptible to interference, and, therefore, more supportive of long-term retention, and (b) because they involve taking a slower and more complex route to an item in memory, they multiply or elaborate the routes available for subsequent retrieval. The fact that long-term recognition seems to profit less from an initial retrieval than does long-term recall (see, e.g., Hogan & Kintsch, 1971; Whitten, 1974) might reflect the relative unimportance of the second factor mentioned above when long-term recognition rather than long-term recall is tested.

3. Whatever the mechanisms involved, the present results have some obvious practical implications. Tests have long been appreciated as important learning events in educational contexts, but there has been some tendency to structure the tests embodied in a learning program in such a way that the typical student will seldom if ever fail to come up with the correct answer. In part, such trivial tests are apparently motivated by the notion that the production of a correct response optimizes the learning on a test. The present results, to the extent that they can be generalized to an educational context, suggest that efforts in programmed texts and elsewhere to optimize the learning process by means of frequent superficial tests designed to produce near-perfect reponding are misguided.

ACKNOWLEDGMENTS

The preparation of this chapter and the author's research reported herein were supported by the Advanced Research Projects Agency, monitored by the Air Force Office of Scientific Research under Contracts F44620-72-C-0019 and AF49(638)-1235, respectively, with the Human Performance Center, Department of Psychology, University of Michigan.

REFERENCES

Bjork, R. A. The short-term and long-term effects of recency in free recall. Paper presented at the Meeting of the Psychonomic Society, St. Louis, Missouri, 1968.
Bjork, R. A. Control processes and serial position effects in free recall. Paper presented at the Mathematical Psychology Meetings, Miami, Florida, 1970.

Bjork, R. A., & Jongeward, R. H., Jr. Rehearsal and mere rehearsal. Unpublished manuscript, 1974.

Craik, F. I. M. Fate of primary memory items in free recall. *Journal of Verbal Learning & Verbal Behavior,* 1970, **9,** 143–148.

Craik, F. I. M., & Lockhart, R. S. Levels of processing: A framework for memory research. *Journal of Verbal Learning & Verbal Behavior,* 1972, **11,** 671–684.

Craik, F. I. M., & Watkins, M. J. The role of rehearsal in short-term memory. *Journal of Verbal Learning & Verbal Behavior,* 1973, **12,** 599–607.

Gardiner, J. M., Craik, F. I. M., & Bleasdale, F. A. Retrieval difficulty and subsequent recall. *Memory & Cognition,* 1973, **1,** 213–216.

Glenberg, A. M., & Melton, A. W. Rehearsal processes associated with degree of spacing of repeated items in free recall learning. Unpublished manuscript, 1974.

Götz, A., & Jacoby, L. Encoding and retrieval processes in long-term retention. *Journal of Experimental Psychology,* 1974, **102,** 291–297.

Hogan, R. M., & Kintsch, W. Differential effects of study and test trials on long-term recognition and recall. *Journal of Verbal Learning & Verbal Behavior,* 1971, **10,** 562–567.

Jacoby, L. L. Encoding processes, rehearsal, and recall requirements. *Journal of Verbal Learning & Verbal Behavior,* 1973, **12,** 302-310.

Jacoby, L. L., & Bartz, W. A. Rehearsal and transfer to LTM. *Journal of Verbal Learning & Verbal Behavior,* 1972, **11,** 561–565.

Landauer, T. K., & Eldridge, L. Effect of tests without feedback and presentation-test interval in paired-associate learning. *Journal of Experimental Psychology,* 1967, **75,** 290–298.

Light, L. L. Incentives, information, rehearsal, and the negative recency effect. *Memory & Cognition,* 1974, **2,** 295–300.

Madigan, S. A., & McCabe, L. Perfect recall and total forgetting: A problem for models of short-term forgetting. *Journal of Verbal Learning & Verbal Behavior,* 1971, **10,** 101–106.

Mazuryk, G. F. Positive recency in final free recall. *Journal of Experimental Psychology,* 1974, **103,** 812–814.

Mazuryk, G. F., & Lockhart, R. S. Negative recency and levels of processing in free recall. *Canadian Journal of Psychology,* 1974, **28,** 114–123.

Meunier, G. F., Ritz, D., & Meunier, J. A. Rehearsal of individual items in short-term memory. *Journal of Experimental Psychology,* 1972, **95,** 465–467.

Rundus, D., & Atkinson, R. C. Rehearsal processes in free recall: A Procedure for direct observation. *Journal of Verbal Learning & Verbal Behavior,* 1970, **9,** 99–105.

Whitten, W. B. Retrieval "depth" and retrieval component processes: A levels-of-processing interpretation of learning during retrieval. Technical Report No. 54, Human Performance Center, University of Michigan, Ann Arbor, Michigan 1974.

Whitten, W. B., & Bjork, R. A. Test events as learning trials: The importance of being imperfect. Paper presented at the Midwestern Mathematical Psychology Meetings, Bloomington, Indiana, 1972.

Woodward, A. E., Jr., Bjork, R. A., & Jongeward, R. H., Jr. Recall and recognition as a function of primary rehearsal. *Journal of Verbal Learning & Verbal Behavior,* 1973, **12,** 608–617.

6

ENCODING, STORAGE, AND RETRIEVAL OF ITEM INFORMATION

Bennet B. Murdock, Jr. and Rita E. Anderson
University of Toronto

In thinking about the broad topic of cognition, it is probably necessary to distinguish between memory and the cognitive processes. The cognitive processes are the operations; the information stored in memory is the data base for these operations. In a way, the distinction is similar to the distinction between program and data in computer programming. The information used can be relatively permanent information in long-term memory, as in problem solving, thinking, and reasoning or it can be relatively transient information of the immediate past, as in reading, comprehending speech, or listening to music. Although much of the emphasis in these Loyola symposia has been on the cognitive processes, our research interest has been more directly concerned with memory. However, as the two are interrelated, perhaps work on the memory system will be relevant to the cognitive processes.

In this paper we would like to consider the encoding, storage, and retrieval of item information. By item information is meant the information about the occurrence of some event. More specifically, item information is that which allows us to recognize some particular object, event, or experience as familiar. The object or event could be a bar of music, the face of a childhood friend, a particular landscape, a certain taste or odor, even a déjà vu experience. Here, however, the focus is rather more prosaic; we shall concentrate on the recognition of once-presented words.

Other types of information are also stored in memory. Associative information is one that provides information about relationships between events or objects. It could be a temporal relationship, a semantic relationship, a logical relationship, categorical relationships, and probably many more. Serial-order information is another, and is the information relating a series of objects or events. Serial-order information allows us to preserve in memory the order information in the letters of the alphabet, the days of the week, the months of the year, or the spelling of words. Justification and elaboration of these distinctions may be found elsewhere (Murdock, 1974). Associative information and serial-order information will not be discussed further here; the rest of this paper will concentrate exclusively on item information.

In order to understand item information (or, more specifically, in order to use data to test hypotheses about memory for item information), it is necessary to consider the three phases of memory: encoding, storage, and retrieval. These are sequential and interdependent processes. The changes over time that characterize the storage of information depends upon what was initially encoded, so storage depends upon encoding. Retrieval depends upon the current state of the memory trace; thus, retrieval depends both on encoding and on storage. Also, what is encoded may even depend upon the expected form of the retrieval. Without a rather specific characterization of all three processes, it is difficult to draw conclusions from data. Most of the data to be discussed in this paper pertains primarily to retrieval, but to interpret them it is necessary to make assumptions about the prior encoding and storage of the retrieved information.

We have recently been conducting a series of studies on recognition memory, and the picture that seems to be emerging is a very simple but very old-fashioned view of human memory. Let us outline it briefly, then consider certain aspects in more detail. Suppose a list of items is sequentially presented, and we represent these items by the letters of the alphabet. First A is presented, and it is the most recent. Then B is presented, so B is now most recent and A is one step removed. Then C is presented, so now A is two steps removed and B is one step removed. Suppose this continues, item by item, until say 13 items have been presented. Successive memory frames could be represented as follows:

$$\text{``Now''}$$

$$A$$

$$A \quad B$$

$$A \quad B \quad C$$

$$A \quad B \quad C \quad D$$

$$\cdot$$

$$\cdot$$

$$\cdot$$

$$A \quad B \quad C \quad D \quad E \quad F \quad G \quad H \quad I \quad J \quad K \quad L \quad M$$

After each item is presented, the contents of memory change. The new item is the most recent, all older items move back one space, but the relative position in the queue stays constant.

What do these letters represent? They are intended to represent information stored in memory, not the stimulus items presented to the subject. It is a poor picture indeed of what is going on inside the nervous system, but it is the best one can do at present. As Milner (1961) has noted, the brain must perform some temporal to spatial transformation on the data it receives, and he suggested several possibilities. Unfortunately, our understanding of these processes has not materially advanced in the interim. One point, however, should be emphasized. The contents of memory do not persist unchanged as they age. Their traces become progressively degraded as new items are presented. It could be considered as a fall in the signal-to-noise ratio, as Brown (1959) has suggested, or it could be a loss of features or attributes, as Bower (1967) has suggested. Whatever the exact characterization of the memory trace, there is clearly loss of information, or forgetting, over time.

How does recognition occur? Basically, recognition means that the difference ϵ between a test item or probe and a stored memory trace is less than some critical value. Conversely, failure to recognize means that the difference between a probe and all examined stored memory traces is greater than another critical value, where these two critical values are not necessarily the same. Therefore, there must be a difference detector to compare a probe stimulus with stored memory traces. It is more convenient to work with $1/\epsilon$, the reciprocal of ϵ. In this way, small differences give rise to large values, and large differences give rise to small values. Over a large number of trials there will be a distribution of $1/\epsilon$, and the characteristics of this distribution will depend upon the testing situation. A hypothetical distribution is shown in Fig. 1. It may also be a representation of the outcome of "pattern completion" as discussed by Kintsch (1975).

In Fig. 1, the lower criterion is a and the upper criterion is b. The outcome of a recognition test depends upon where the observation falls relative to a and b. If it exceeds b, the subject will give a "yes" response (i.e., report that the probe is an old item); if it falls below a, he will give a "no" response (i.e., report that the probe is a new item); and intermediate observations give rise to uncertainty depicted by the question mark in Fig. 1. The shaded areas denote the proportion of "yes" and "no" responses that should occur. This decision aspect is similar to a model proposed by Atkinson and his colleagues (e.g., Atkinson, Herrmann, & Wescourt, 1974). They too suggest that there are upper and lower cutoffs for "yes" and "no" responses. However, they suggest that fast "yes" and "no" re-

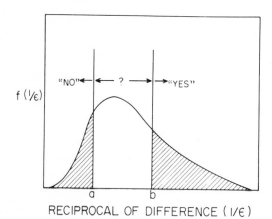

Fig. 1. Hypothetical distribution of $1/\epsilon$, the reciprocal of the output of the difference detector involved in recognition. The two cutoff points a and b are thresholds: observations below a give rise to "no" responses; observations above b give rise to "yes" responses; intermediate outcomes are uncertain.

RECIPROCAL OF DIFFERENCE ($1/\epsilon$)

sponses indicate direct access, and the data we shall present seem inconsistent with a direct-access view.

How does retrieval occur? We define *retrieval* as the utilization of stored information, the standard definition of this term (e.g., Melton, 1963). How is memory interrogated to obtain the necessary information to feed into the difference detector to assess the familiarity of a probe item? A flow chart to describe the process is shown in Fig. 2. First, the probe is encoded, then the criteria are set. Next, the comparison process starts where the encoded version of the probe is compared with the stored memory traces. The most recent item is examined first. If the output from the difference detector is greater than b, than a "yes" response is given. If not, the next most recent item is examined, with again the possibility of a "yes" response. This process continues, item by item, until a match is found or the processor comes to the end of the list. If there is clearly nothing like it [i.e., the maximum value of $1/\epsilon < a$] then the subject gives a "no" response; otherwise, he must decide whether to look again. If he does, he may move a or b closer to the middle of the distribution in order to reduce his uncertainty.

Provision for a "no" response is not adequately represented in the flow chart of Fig. 2. For this scheme to work, a "match register" as suggested by Sternberg (1969) would be necessary to keep a record of the best match obtained to date. If a series of comparisons were made, then this match register would have to be updated whenever some match was found that, although below b, was still better than any previous match. (Again, if the match was better, the difference ϵ would be smaller, but the reciprocal of the difference $1/\epsilon$ would be larger than the previous contents of this match register.) A "no" response would occur only if the contents of this match register was less than a after all list items had been scanned. The

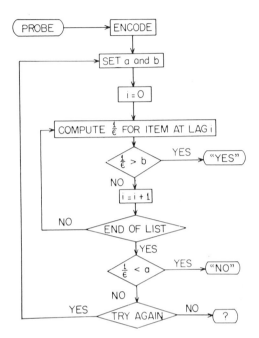

FIG. 2. Flow chart to illustrate the processes involved in the retrieval of item information from recent memory.

reason for specifying this aspect of the decision system is that we have some data showing that the upper and lower criteria are separately manipulable. When the subjects were instructed to be especially careful about high-confident "yes" responses or high-confident "no" responses (but not both), then the frequencies of these responses were lower and their latencies were longer.

Some of the data which suggested this model are given in Tables 1 and 2, which show the results of a recognition-memory study using a confidence-judgment procedure. The summary tables are shown in Table 1 separately for each of the eight subjects, in all cases pooled over Sessions 2–7, lists within session, and test position. In Table 2 mean latency and standard deviations are shown as a function of confidence judgments, pooled over old and new items. The outer loop (interrogate memory again) is suggested by the increase in latency from high-confident to low-confident judgments for both "no" and "yes" responses. Variability should increase in the same way, and in general it does. Symmetrical results should obtain for judgments of comparable certainty (e.g., $+ + +$ and $- - -$), which is also approximately correct. On the average, the outer loop requires about 250 msec for practiced subjects. Criterion changes would be reflected in the fact that the a posteriori probability decreases from $+ + +$ through $+ +$ to $+$ but increases from $- - -$ through $- -$ to $-$. Thus, on some pro-

TABLE 1
**Frequencies of Confidence Judgments
to Old and New Test Items**[a]

S	Item type	Confidence judgments					
		− − −	− −	−	+	+ +	+ + +
RO	Old items	42	111	472	701	465	1089
	New items	1137	925	628	161	18	11
JM	Old items	59	281	262	472	472	1334
	New items	1168	1005	408	200	68	31
XC	Old items	846	126	41	103	297	1465
	New items	2435	127	33	41	107	237
RC	Old items	163	495	293	458	383	1088
	New items	1649	893	201	102	25	9
DB	Old items	63	450	31	118	766	1452
	New items	809	1515	57	88	353	58
EW	Old items	99	180	340	564	671	1026
	New items	796	896	739	338	87	24
LB	Old items	325	206	111	186	129	1853
	New items	2254	378	116	74	19	39
CM	Old items	205	119	5	97	544	1906
	New items	2428	263	3	28	118	39

[a] Data of the eight Ss of Experiment I from Murdock and Dufty (1972).

portion of the tests subjects get clear and unambiguous information from memory; they make a fast and accurate (high-confident) response (yes or no) forthwith. If they look again, they are slower and less accurate, that is, their a posteriori probability is less extreme. If they require yet a third interrogation, they are even slower and a and b have moved even further in. However, they are not at the chance level even at the lowest confidence judgment; 2×2 tables of old and new items by − and +

TABLE 2
Mean Latency and Standard Deviations (msec) for Each Confidence Judgment[a]

S		Confidence judgments					
		− − −	− −	−	+	+ +	+ + +
RO	Mean	706	1015	1563	1362	991	653
	SD	140	233	299	289	208	148
JM	Mean	862	1107	1271	1253	1122	699
	SD	268	377	428	373	315	212
XC	Mean	1016	1624	1794	1726	1517	936
	SD	603	698	675	635	557	374
RC	Mean	989	1261	1547	1459	1373	1036
	SD	296	457	494	460	371	296
DB	Mean	865	970	1200	1230	987	701
	SD	149	201	244	194	200	174
EW	Mean	872	921	1028	1023	957	801
	SD	237	230	285	248	230	209
LB	Mean	917	1366	1607	1728	1608	808
	SD	309	442	508	387	383	296
CM	Mean	774	1364	1844	1535	1267	718
	SD	251	396	305	305	349	227

[a] Data of the eight Ss of Experiment I from Murdock and Dufty (1972).

confidence judgments show that they are still discriminating with above-chance accuracy.

It will be recognized that this view of memory for item information is essentially a "tape recorder" model of memory. Incoming items are directly encoded; temporal information is preserved in the format of store; deterioration in the record increases over time; and retrieval occurs by means of a backward serial self-terminating scan. The "conveyor-belt" analogy

(Murdock, 1974) is probably a more accurate analogy then a tape-recorder analogy, since the latter requires repositioning information for retrieval which seems not to happen in human memory. In any case, whatever the analogy, this general point of view is not a novel characterization of human memory, but it is not too popular today.

Why is it unpopular? First, it presents too impoverished a view of initial perception (Neisser, 1967). However, perceptual processes are not thoroughly understood, and perhaps it will turn out that such a view is really not inconsistent with what we know about the initial perceptual processing mechanisms. Second, it goes against the current cognitive Zeitgeist. However, to take a very simple view of the cognitive processes, it can be argued that they would be impossible to perform in the absence of some "experiental record." How could we read, understand speech, appreciate music, or even talk if we did not have some relatively raw and unprocessed record of recent experience? These cognitive processes would seem to require the constant interpretation and reinterpretation of information recently presented, and if we did not have at least a spotty record of what had recently transpired, these particular cognitive processes probably would be impossible.

Another reason for the unpopularity of a tape-recorder type of model is that, intuitively, it seems like a very poor system for retrieving information from long-term memory. If you are asked where you lived when you were 10 years old, it seems rather unlikely that you look back through all the intervening years to find the answer much as you have to look through a deck of IBM cards to find one particular card. Even though the work of Penfield (e.g., Penfield & Perot, 1963) has presented evidence consonant with this view, and even though there is some very recent evidence suggesting that age of acquisition is an important variable in retrieving information from long-term memory (Carroll & White, 1973; Lachman, 1973; Loftus & Suppes, 1972), the retrieval argument is still a very cogent criticism (e.g., Broadbent, 1966).

A mistake made by the critics is, perhaps, to assume that a serial scan as implied by this model is the only way one can retrieve information in memory. Instead, this may in fact be one method, but we have other methods as well. To think that the human brain has only one retrieval mechanism is surely false. As a biological organism, the human nervous system is characterized by variety and diversity, not by rigid and restricted stereotyped patterns. For instance, photobiologists tell us about all the many different mechanisms the body has to protect itself against the damages done by light. There may be more than 50 such mechanisms that have been positively identified. If that kind of diversity exists for information processing at the cellular level, surely we cannot expect a single mechanism or process to cope with all the diverse demands of retrieving information from memory. Thus, an experiental record for storage and a serial scan for retrieval is one way the nervous system stores and retrieves information, but there are surely many others as well.

Here then is the general point of view about the encoding, storage, and retrieval of item information. Let us now consider each of these three phases in somewhat more detail, along with some relevant experimental evidence.

ENCODING

The view of the encoding of item information that seems currently favored is an attribute model of memory. No representation of an item per se is stored; rather, certain features are selected or abstracted, and these features, or attributes, represent the stored information. Such a view of memory was clearly formulated by Bower (1967) and has been modified or elaborated by Anderson and Bower (1972), Bower (1972), Kintsch (1970), Norman and Rumelhart (1970), Underwood (1969), and Wickens (1972). There is also an unpublished attribute model by Lockhart, presented and discussed in Murdock (1974). In addition to the models, there is the now considerable experimental evidence to demonstrate that memory, like perception, is selective. Instructions to concentrate on, or attend to, certain dimensions of the presented items will have a demonstrable effect, often quite large, both on accuracy of later recognition or recall and the type of errors that might be made. Although such results are not necessarily inconsistent with other interpretations of encoding, they are certainly consistent with an attribute view and in some cases seem to be taken as definitive evidence for such a view.

However, certain criticisms of an attribute view may be advanced. First, they do not provide any property list. If only certain features or attributes are encoded, one would like to know what they might be. No such list of potential attributes has been suggested. The difficulty of establishing an adequate property list has been a major stumbling block to the acceptance of this approach in the area of pattern recognition, and it is no less a problem in the area of memory. Second, attribute models are sometimes circular. When errors of a certain kind occur, then one infers what kind of encoding must have occurred. If such errors do not occur, however, then the encoding did not occur either—hardly a satisfactory method of analysis. Third, direct tests of attribute information seem to show that almost any feature of the stimulus, however improbable, has some later representation in memory. This point has been discussed and documented in Murdock (1974). Fourth, one implication of a strict attribute view should be remembered. If only a few features are abstracted and encoded, then the original stimulus information must be as fleeting as iconic or echoic memory. Were this the case, then delayed reinterpretations of the initial stimulus event based on different features would seem to be precluded. Yet there is at least anecdotal evidence that delayed reinterpretations do occur—the writing–righting example of Lashley (1951) or the double entendres of slapstick comedy. More generally, interpretation of written or spoken speech would seem to demand some persistence in unanalyzed form of the original incoming stream of information.

An attribute model presupposes that the pattern-recognition system works on the basis of feature testing. If this were so, that would be a strong argument for this view. That is, it is generally assumed that the output from the pattern-recognition system is the input to the memory system. If pattern recognition used a feature-testing method, then a natural representation of mnemonic information in these terms would follow. However, it now seems unlikely that pattern recognition does work in this fashion. No exhaustive property list has yet been suggested, and the human perceptual system does not seem bothered by the ambiguities that current property lists predict. Also, current workers in artificial intelligence seem to have given up this viewpoint and are investigating quite different types of perceptual processing (e.g., Clowes, 1971).

An alternative hypothesis worth considering is that both the pattern-recognition system and the memory system work in parallel on the same stored trace. Rather than postulate two successive stages—first, a pattern recognition system that operates on the iconic or echoic image, then a memory system that receives as input the output from the perception system—perhaps the two work more nearly in parallel. They simply may be different aspects of the activities which the central processing mechanism can use when operating on the stored trace. Thus, the stimulus is more holistic; the analytic features of memory are the outcome of processing (e.g., Craik & Lockhart, 1972).

All of this is simply another way of saying that the initial information stored in memory is representational. When a stimulus is presented, be it a word, a picture, a few bars of music, even written or spoken prose, the radiant energy striking the receptors (eye or ear, as the case may be) is transduced into some neural pattern of activity, and that neural pattern of activity forms the initial basis of memory. (Where the storage takes place and what its nature is are questions for those investigating the nature of the engram.) Within limits, all physical features represented in the stimulus are initially present in the stored memory trace. It is this initial memory trace on which the central processor works, and we use the terms *per-*

ceive and *remember* to describe the subjective counterpart of the activity of the central processing mechanism. Of course, the processing is selective, and what we remember is a joint function of what we have selected at the time of encoding and what we retrieve at the time of testing (Tulving & Thomson, 1973).

Although the initial encoding is representational, it is also quite transient. Some features drop out quickly; others drop out more slowly. Imagine an unfixed (or inadequately fixed) photographic print exposed to light. Gradually the features fade; the details become progressively less clear; and in many ways the quality of the print becomes degraded. (The basic subject matter of the print may hold up for a while despite the loss of detail.) Another analogy that might be given is the recognition of computer-generated pictures of faces (Harmon, 1973). They can be degraded selectively in a random or systematic fashion. This happens to memory traces, by decay or interference.

What evidence is there for this view? One of the most direct bits of evidence comes from a study by Bregman (1968), who showed that semantic, phonetic, graphic, and contiguity cues all decayed (decreased in effectiveness) at about the same rate. Additional evidence comes from recognition-memory tests. When one asks, for instance, whether a word was spoken in a male or female voice, whether it was shown in upper-case or lower-case letters, or indeed whether it was presented in an auditory or visual mode, the recognition accuracy is at above-chance levels for a period of at least several minutes. (Many such studies are cited in Murdock, 1974, so the interested reader could pursue this topic there.) Iconic memory in the sense of Sperling (1960) does exist, but it is a special case. When one overloads the store with a brief burst of information (12–25 letters in a 50-msec display), one can indeed get decay curves with time constants well below 1 sec. Such presentation conditions are not typical, and we should not be misled into thinking that stimulus information about single items such as words or nonsense syllables decays in such a rapid fashion. Also, even iconic memory as first studied by Sperling may display at least some of the capacity limitations characteristic of short-term memory (Chow & Murdock, 1974).

The false-recognition effect is commonly taken as evidence for the attribute view. In studies of recognition memory, subjects frequently respond "yes" to new items which are similar on some dimension to a specific word on the list. This effect was first noted by Underwood (1965), and since then it has been given ample documentation and extension. The attribute interpretation is that the word is initially encoded as a bundle of features, and the odd feature gets forgotten. Thus, in some number of cases the lure (a new item similar but not identical to the old item) matches an old item as the subject has lost the discriminating feature(s). The "yes" response reflects this fact. There is an intuitive appeal about this interpretation, and it fits nicely with a distinctive-feature analysis of phonemes, letters, or even words. Despite the popularity of this interpretation, it may not be completely correct.

An alternative that may be preferable is to suggest that the feature contribution is operative at the time of test rather than at the time of presentation. Thus, the initial item (word, sentence, or whatever) is encoded and stored in a relatively veridical fashion. At the time of test, the probe is encoded and the memory comparison ensues. However, the comparison is not a template-matching process; it might possibly work on a feature-testing basis. That is, a few key features of the probe are selected and they are compared with the stored traces. A false-positive response indicates that the discriminating features have not entered into the comparison process. It is clearly more likely when the lure is similar to an old list item, as long as the experimenter's definition of similarity agrees with that of the subject.

Call these two views an encoding and a retrieval view, respectively. According to an encoding view, the false-recognition effect arises from selectivity at the time of encoding. This effect, in the retrieval view, arises from selectivity at the time of retrieval. The sheer existence of the effect does not discriminate between these two views, because false alarms to similar lures would be expected in either case. Perhaps a more critical test is how the false-recognition effect varies with lag, where lag is the number of items intervening between presentation of the target item and presentation of the related lure. Current evidence (Donald Thomson, 1973, personal communication) suggests there is perhaps a slight rise followed by a slight fall. In any event, there seems to be no very precipitous changes over a considerable lag range. Whether either an encoding or a retrieval view could accommodate such a lag effect (or noneffect) would depend upon the explicit assumptions about the initial encoding and the changes in the stored trace. We have been told by Robert Lockhart (1973, personal communication) that he thinks his model would not handle it, but the predictions from other models have not been worked out.

Recently, evidence has become available that how information is initially processed has important memorial consequences. Comparing incidental and intentional learning paradigms, Jenkins and his colleagues (e.g., Hyde & Jenkins, 1973) have shown that processing words in a semantic fashion leads to much more effective recall than initial processing which lacks a semantic (or associative) focus. With both recognition and recall, Craik (1973) has shown a hierarchy of results with the highest level of accuracy following the initial semantic processing of words. Performance deteriorates as more attention is paid to such features as how the words sound or what spelling patterns exist. In fact, in a "poor man's" levels-of-processing study, Endel Tulving (1974, personal communication) has obtained very large differences in recognition accuracy even when subjects are completely informed about the tasks, given ample time to examine each word, but are merely instructed how first to respond to each word presented to them by the experimenter.

The data suggest, then, that the mere presentation of stimulus information is not sufficient to make predictions about subsequent memory performance. What the subject does to the item, or what dimensions he responds to, has important consequences as well. We are reluctant to say "how he encodes it" for the initial encoding can be representational. It would be more accurate to say "those features of the initial encoding he initially emphasizes" gives a more adequate characterization of the processes involved. Unfortunately, to note the existence of this phenomenon is not to explain it. It is difficult to be explicit here because the variation of interest is qualitative not quantitative. We have no very adequate way of conceptualizing the separate dimensions involved, let alone trying to understand similarities and differences among them. Also, the analytic problem is considerable as well. Encoding, storage, and retrieval are successive and interdependent processes. Is the difference in initial encoding restricted to that stage, or does it carry over to storage or retrieval as well? It could be that small differences in encoding are magnified by large differences in forgetting, or large differences in encoding could persist unchanged in amplitude over an appreciable retention interval.

A recent result that would seem to support the encoding view of the false-recognition effect was reported by Elias and Perfetti (1973). They found that, when encoding instructions were manipulated, mean confidence judgments were higher for appropriate lures. That is, if subjects were given associative or learning instructions, they were more willing to accept semantically related words as old, whereas, if they were given rhyming instructions, they were more willing to accept acoustically related words as old. This result, however, would not be incompatible with the retrieval view if subjects generated a few associations (of the appropriate kind) before they made their recognition judgment. (Encoding conditions was a between-subjects variable.) That is, the associations generated at the time of test would be more likely to match one or more of the associations generated at the time of presentation if the lure was similar to the initial item when the similarity was defined by the encoding condition. More generally, performance on a recognition–memory task is the output from the difference detector, and since the value of $1/\epsilon$ varies continuously over some range similarity manipulations are bound to change the number of observations that fall outside of the upper and lower bounds.

STORAGE

How does stored information change over time? Two aspects of this question will be considered here: first, the temporal format of item information and how it changes, and second, forgetting, the decrease in accuracy that occurs over time.

Temporal Format of the Store

The view presented here suggests that the time of arrival of incoming information is somehow directly represented in the memory trace. Also, it is preserved (though with decreasing accuracy) as additional information follows. What evidence is there for this view? Some evidence was reviewed in Murdock (1972), in particular, the existence of recency effects in short-term memory experiments, order-of-recall effects, intrusion data, and transpositions. Although none of these are instances of recognition memory, it is hard to imagine how they would come about were the format of storage not temporally organized. More pertinent to item information are judgments of frequency and recency. Subjects can report with reasonable accuracy when and how often specific items had been presented. They are not perfect at this, but they are clearly far better than chance.

A counter to some of these arguments would be a strength-theory position. As suggested, for instance, by Peterson (1967) and by Hinrichs (1970), perhaps a subject infers the age of an event from its strength. If one postulates trace decay then, given a string of items, the more interference the more decay. When tested, a subject could perhaps simply assess the current *strength* of an item and translate that into the required temporal judgment. This position has been very thoroughly reviewed recently by Wells (1974), and her conclusion is negative. Citing some of her own data as well as some frequency and recency data by Hintzman and Block (1971), she feels that a strength theory is simply contraindicated by the available data. As the arguments are too lengthy and detailed to cover here, the interested reader is referred to her paper.

Since judgments of recency are a critical test for our model, it is reassuring to know that the model can give acceptable fits to data at a quantitative level. If one assumes a temporally ordered memory with exponential trace decay, imagine that the subject scans this array when asked to make a judgment of recency. He either finds the item or he does not. If he finds the item, he counts the number of later items and gives that as his judgment of recency. Otherwise he guesses in a rational fashion. Such a model not only can predict the characteristic overshoot–undershoot function of judgment-of-recency studies but also the experimental data points are fit well by the model. Further details and documentation are presented elsewhere (Murdock, 1974, pp. 278–279).

A model quite different from strength theory has been suggested by Anderson (1968). Information is stored in a large storage array which can be represented as an $m \times n$ matrix. A large number of neural elements is presumed to enter into this array, and each new item presented is simply added to the array. There is no storage of independent items; instead, it is an interactive storage. For recognition, retrieval can be effected by computing spatial cross correlation and autocorrelation functions. Old items can be recognized, new items can be rejected, and similarity effects can be demonstrated.

In some ways this is a very attractive model, since much of the knowledge we have of the nervous system would seem to argue against discrete, localized storage of specific items. However, the main objection to this model is that there seems to be no way it could represent the temporal format of store. In particular, how could the subjects in the experiments by Hintzman and Block possibly have made veridical judgments of frequency and recency if the human memory system really functioned according to this scheme? Here we would seem to have a discrepancy between what is known or suspected about brain function and what is indicated by the behavioral data. Perhaps one should believe the latter, and assume that the relevant principles of brain functioning simply are not yet known.

However, it must be admitted that the discrepancy between how behavioral data suggest the brain must store information and what informed opinion thinks about how the brain does store information is a bit disquieting. Thus, John (1967) argues that we should think of memory not as small local changes but rather as the spatiotemporal patterning of neural activity among large aggregates of neurons. From the work of Lashley on, the trend seems to have been to think large rather than to think small. Although we are not too familiar with all the neurophysiological or biochemical literature on memory, we do not know of any specific suggestions as to how the temporal format of store might be arranged. Therefore, this section must end on the pious opinion that it must manage somehow, though we do not know how.

Forgetting

It will come as no surprise to say that item information undergoes forgetting over time. Recognition accuracy decreases with lag, the number of items intervening between the presentation of an item and its test. The general effect is common knowledge, but some of the detailed aspects of the forgetting may be less well known. Consequently, it may be worthwhile to document just what these effects are.

Here we shall be referring to some data we have collected over the past several years using a fairly standard recognition–memory paradigm. We use a discrete-trials procedure where a list of study items is first presented, then a test list follows. The test list is twice as long as the study list since it contains half old and half new items. The experiments are run on a laboratory computer (PDP-12A), which constructs the lists, presents the items on the CRT display, and records the responses. The presentation time is typically about 1 sec per item. Test trials are self-paced; the items are presented one by one, and each stays in view until the subject responds. We have augmented the standard procedure by recording confidence judgments and latencies. Confidence judgments run on a six-point scale from "sure it's a new item" to "sure it's an old item." The subject communicates this information to the computer by depressing one of six telegraph keys in a row in front of him, and the latency of this response is recorded.

The stimulus items are words randomly selected from the Toronto word pool, a list of about 1040 two-syllable common English words not more than eight letters long, with homophones, contractions, and proper nouns excluded. Each trial consists of a random selection from the word pool; in some experiments, repetitions are prohibited until two successive lists have intervened. The order of presentation in the study and test phases are randomized, though in some experiments there is a lower bound (seven) on lag. Each subject is given many lists per session and tested over a number of sessions; the data-collection process is a fairly massive enterprise. For each item tested we record its lag (with new items coded uniquely), confidence judgment (the telegraph key pressed, on a 1–6 scale), and the latency of this response. The latency is the time elapsing between the presentation (onset) of the test item and the depression of the telegraph key selected. We use a 25-msec time base, and all latencies over 6.40 sec are truncated to 255.

The first two experiments were reported in Murdock and Dufty (1972), and they are referred to as Experiments I and II. The data of Tables 1 and 2 came from Experiment I. Two more experiments were reported by Murdock (1974), and they are referred to here as Experiments III and IV. [Descriptions and some data will be found in Murdock (1974, pp. 271–274 and on pp. 274–275)]. Two more experiments are reported here, and they are referred to as Experiments V and VI. The casual reader need not worry about keeping clear the details of these separate experiments. An appreciation of the general paradigm described above will be sufficient, and necessary details will be repeated when they are important. The detailed indexing is provided for the benefit of any readers who wish to track down any particular experiment, either to look for alternative explanations of the data or to pursue further investigation of these problems on their own.

Forgetting is the change in stored information over time. One way of showing the forgetting of item information is to compute the change in d', the standard signal-detection or strength theory measure of recognition memory. Illustrative data are shown in Fig. 3, where d' measures were computed for each of four subjects at each of six output blocks (Test Positions 1–5, 6–10, 11–15, 16–20, 21–25, 26–30). The d' values were computed from the confidence-judgment matrices using the EPCROC program of Ogilvie and Creelman (1968), and the slope values (a measure of the variance ratio of the two underlying distributions) was generally unity for the first two or three output blocks and slightly less than unity for the remaining output blocks. All four subjects show the same effect, a gradual decrease in d' over the course of testing, and as a first approximation the contention of the strength theory of Wickelgren and Norman (1966) is clearly borne out by the data. That is, as predicted, the decrease in d' does seem to be roughly exponential, for each of the subjects individually. Comparable results have also been reported by Schulman (1974).

The EPCROC program provides an estimate of the goodness of fit for each solution. A maximum-likelihood estimation procedure is used, and the goodness of fit is simply a standard χ^2 value (the sum of the squared deviations between observed and expected entries in the 2×6 cells in the confidence-judgment matrix divided by the expected values). The values of χ^2 summed over the six output blocks were 24.95, 54.77, 17.87, and 49.16 for RO, JM, XC, and RC, with 20, 21, 19, and 18 df, respectively. In all, these fits are very good indeed. For RO and XC, the observed χ^2 value is close to the expected χ^2 value (its df) and, although JM and

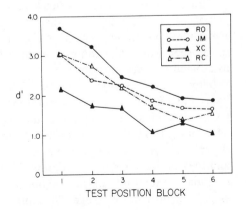

FIG. 3. The effect of test position (six blocks of five trials each) on d' for each of four subjects. (Data from Experiment I.)

RC are clearly worse, the deviations come only in the later test positions. Also, the large numbers result from small absolute departures observed from expected frequencies, where the χ^2 statistic heavily penalizes deviations (e.g., an observed frequency of 4 given an expected frequency of 1).

We have, then, a very powerful tool to represent the forgetting of item information over time, at least in this experimental paradigm. We can accurately summarize a vast quantity of data with an exceedingly simple statement; namely, it is more or less the case (and more rather than less) that d' decreases exponentially over the course of testing. This statement summarizes the combined data for old and new items with the d' statistic obtained by a powerful estimation program from data obtained in a confidence-judgment procedure. Is this all there is to say, and can we now sally forth, armed with this technique, to conquer such diverse and sundry problems as word-frequency effects, repetition and lag effects, and even recall and recognition comparisons? Unfortunately, no—the conclusion given above is a bit too pat. Basically, there is one major problem that is overlooked by this analysis. The critical variable for old items seems to be lag, not test or output position.

Relevant data are shown in Fig. 4. This figure includes both hits and false alarms. For hits, the upper curve shows how the proportion of "yes" responses to old items declines with lag, where lag is the number of items intervening between presentation and test. The next curve shows how the proportion of "sure yes" responses decline with lag. Qualitatively, these two curves are much the same, so the criterion level selected affects the absolute performance level but not so much the relative changes over lag. For false alarms, the basis of classification must be test position, since they have no lag. The lower "yes" curve shows how the false-alarm rate (the proportion of new items that are incorrectly called old) changes with test position. The bottom (unlabeled) curve shows how the proportion of all responses that were not "sure no" changes with test position. Again, these two curves are rather similar. Also, the changes in hit rate as a function of lag seem somewhat more pronounced than the changes in false alarms as a function of test position.

Why is lag the critical variable? The reason is that the curves for old items fall off smoothly and monotonically over almost the whole range. [A primacy effect in recognition memory has been found before; see, e.g., Murdock (1968, Fig. 3, p. 84).] If one takes output or test postition as the critical variable, one is of necessity averaging over different lag values, and they are demonstrably different. Therefore, we are not saying that test position is irrelevant; we are saying that lag is the more sensitive variable since it spans a wider range. Of course, it is quite true that lag obliterates

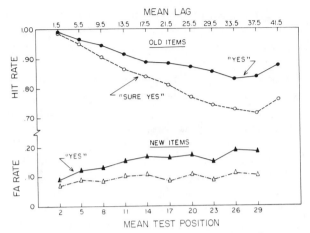

FIG. 4.   The upper two curves show the proportion of "yes" responses and "sure yes" responses to old items as a function of lag. The lower two curves show the proportion of "yes" responses and all responses except "sure no" to new items as a function of test position. (Data from Experiment III.)

the distinction between input and output interference. Thus, to take an example, Lag 4 is a mixture of 4 study and 0 test items, 3 study and 1 test, 2 and 2, 3 and 1, and 0 study and 4 test items. Norman and Waugh (1968) report that there is both study and test interference, though it was not clear whether their effects were equal. The next step involves using a two-way classification of input position by test position and see if the diagonals (lag) overlap. If they do not, then we may have to modify our current stress on lag. In any event, even if lag is not the final answer, it is a better measure than output position.

Assuming that lag is the critical variable for old items, this raises a rather fundamental point about the commensurability of old and new items and summarizing the data with a single integrative statistic such as d'. If one simply pools over the entire test phase and looks at the resulting yes–no or confidence-judgment data, then one is obscuring temporal changes that certainly exist and which might be of interest. If one partitions the data on output or test position, one has a way of aligning old and new items so one can observe how d', say, changes over test position; the problem is that test position is not the critical variable for old items. If one analyzes the hit rate for old items as a function of lag and the false-alarm data for new items as a function of test position, then one is selecting the proper bases for analyses. However, they cannot be directly compared to yield an overall summary statistic like d'. No solution is proposed here, but at least the problem should be recognized.

To summarize the conclusions about forgetting, the situation seems to be as follows. First, a strength-theory analysis fits the data rather well; furthermore, it is extremely efficient from a data-reduction point of view. It is possible to summarize a vast quantity of data (namely, how the distributions of confidence judgments to old and new items change over the course of testing) with the parameters of an exponential decay d' function. If all one wishes is a summary statistic so one can compare effects of experimental manipulations such as presentation rate, list length, word frequency, instructional strategies or whatever, one could not ask for much more. However, the main criticism is this: it obliterates the distinction between two separate changes, those for old items and those for new items. One must use the test position as a basis for classification, and it is quite clear that the more relevant variable for old items is lag. Once this fact is acknowledged, one is led to ask how one can compare performance on old items as a function of lag to new items as a function of test position, and strength theory gives no answer. (One could perhaps align them on the basis of total number of items scanned but, since strength theory postulates direct access, one is no longer working within the same theoretical framework.) Finally, it is not yet completely certain that even lag is the variable. It, in turn, can be broken down into study and test position, and the final decision on the relative importance of each is still in question.

RETRIEVAL

Retrieval is the utilization of stored information at the time of test. We would like to discuss three aspects of retrieval: first, the possibility that retrieval occurs by means of a backward serial scan through the contents of recent memory; second, the retrieval processes that seem to be involved in forced-choice recognition; third, how the retrieval processes may differ, depending upon whether the amount of material to be examined is below or above the memory span.

Backward Serial Scanning

Given that some faded copy of the stimulus information exists in a temporally ordered memory array, how is this information retrieved? That is, when a probe is presented and the subject must decide whether it is new or old, how does he do it? One possibility is direct access or a dictionary lookup. Given the probe, perhaps the subject is able to go directly to the appropriate memory representation and report what he finds. If, for instance, some lexical representation in semantic memory shows signs of recent activation (in another terminology, has a list marker or a time tag), then the subject would give a "yes" response. Otherwise, he would respond "no." Intermediate cases are also possible, and a decision system would probably be added as an intervening stage of processing between memory and the overt response.

The data seem to show that direct access does not occur. Instead, as shown in the flow chart of Fig. 2, retrieval seems to occur by means of a backward serial self-terminating scan. In a study–test procedure, test items are examined as well as study items. Suppose the situation is as follows:

$$A \ \ B \ \ C \cdots K \ \ L \ \ M \ \ * \ \ d \ \ r \ \ x \ \ k?$$

where A through M denote the study items, $d, r,$ and x are the first three test items and k is the current probe. (The asterisk denotes the break between the study phase of the procedure and the test phase of the procedure.) The lag of k is 5 items (2 study items plus 3 test items) and the data seem to show that, in retrieval, the test items (i.e., $x, r,$ and d in that order) are examined as well as study items ($M, L,$ and K in that order). Whether examination time is the same for study and for test items will be considered later. What is important here is that the scan does not skip back to the asterisk and start from there. Instead, study and test items are both examined.

The data that originally suggested a scanning model are shown in Figs. 5 and 6. Figure 5 shows the lag-latency function for high-confident "yes" responses to old items for the data of Experiment III. These data are pooled over the four subjects and the three different presentation rates

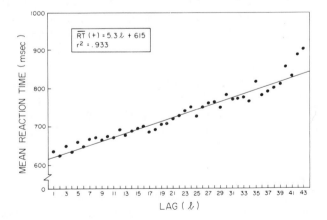

FIG. 5. Lag-latency function for high-confident "yes" responses to old items. (Data from Experiment III.)

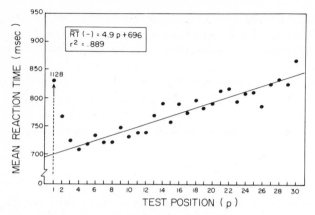

FIG. 6.   Test position-latency function for high-confident "no" responses to new items. (Data from Experiment III.)

used. Figure 6 shows the test position–latency function for high-confident "no" responses to new items for the data of the same experiment. The data are pooled in the same way. These same data were shown in blocked form in Fig. 10.3 and 10.4 of Murdock (1974, p. 272); here each separate lag and each separate test position is shown. The straight lines drawn through the data points are the least-squares regression lines; slopes, intercepts, and r^2 (as a measure of goodness of fit) are shown in each figure.

The main points to note about these two figures are that the functions are linear, the lag-latency and the test-position latency functions have about the same slope, and the numerical value of the slope is about 5 msec per item. Thus, if we take the slope as a measure of scanning time, the interpretation would be that the scan goes on at the rate of something in the order of 5 msec per item. Unlike the paradigm of Sternberg (1966), a self-terminating process is supported by the equality of positive and negative slopes. Different independent variables from Sternberg are used here. For old items, the independent variable is lag, since the critical variable seems to be the number of items intervening between presentation and test. For new items, the independent variable is test position. When the probe is a new item, the total number of items scanned is, of course, the sum of an item's test position and the list length. Although not represented in Fig. 6, the scan is then presumed to go back to the beginning of the study list, as illustrated in the flow chart of Fig. 2.

A small problem about these data should be noted. The first one or two test positions consistently give abnormally high latencies. For the data in Fig. 6, the mean latency was 1128 msec for the first position (which is off scale) and 768 msec for the second position. The reason may be that it takes subjects one or two responses to switch over from "record" mode to "reproduce" mode, that is, to change from studying the list items to giving responses. (In Experiment III, due to a programming oversight, the first item tested was always new. Consequently, Lag 0 was never tested. One subject became aware of this feature part way through the experiment. The others were asked, but had not noticed it.) Because other processes are involved, these aberrant values would bias the estimate of scanning time. To know how many data points should be excluded, we ran linear regression analyses on the data of Fig. 6 with the first 0, 1, 2, 3, or 4 data points excluded. The resulting slopes were 1.72, 4.42, 4.85, 4.97, and 4.93 msec per item, respectively. The values of r^2 were .039, .819, .889, .887, and .874, respectively. As a result, the decision was made to exclude Test Positions 1 and 2 from the regression analysis, and the values shown in Fig. 6 were determined accordingly.

It should be noted that all the data presented in Fig. 5 and 6 are conditionalized on high-confident judgments. For the lag-latency function, the response must be not only "yes" but "sure yes," otherwise it is excluded from the tabulation. Similarly, for the test position-latency function, the response must be not only "no" but "sure no." According to the model, these cases illustrate the situation where there is only a single interrogation of memory. Were lower confidence–judgment cases included as well, the result would then be a mixture of single and multiple observations. (In Experiment III, the high-confident category was used 81% of the time for old items and 85% of the time for new items.) One consequence of conditionalizing in this way is that the number of observations entering into the latency functions will vary from subject to subject, depending upon his criterion. (It is abundantly clear that subjects show considerable individual differences in the placement of their criteria; this point can be appreciated by examining the data shown in Table 1.) However, we are not concerned here with the frequency of high-confident responses; rather, we are concerned with their latencies, given that they have occurred.

The next experiment to be discussed, Experiment V, was an attempt to test the limits of scanning. Longer lists were used; specifically, the study lists were 64 words long and, since the test phase contained 128 words, the maximum lag was 190. (At the shorter end, no lags less than 7 were tested.) Eight subjects were tested. There was one practice session, six test sessions, and eight lists per session. Presentation rate was 1.2 sec per word, but in all other respects the procedure was like that of Experiment III. Stimulus lists were always constructed by sampling without replacement from the Toronto word pool. (In this experiment and Experiment III, two buffer lists were used. That is, no word could be resampled until at least two additional lists intervened.)

If the results of Experiment III were surprising, the results of Experiment V are even more so. The lag-latency and test position-latency functions (for high-confident "yes" and "no" responses to old and new items) are shown in Figs. 7 and 8. Over the full range, both functions seem to be linear. Although the fit is better for old than for new items, in neither case is it all that bad; the values of r^2 are .966 and .856 for old and new

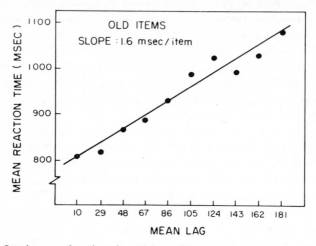

FIG. 7.   Lag-latency function for high-confident "yes" responses to old items. (Data from Experiment V.)

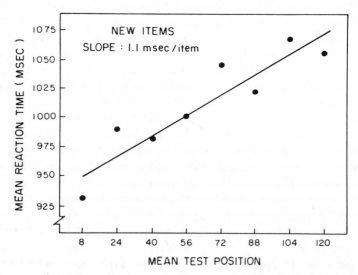

FIG. 8.   Test position-latency function for high-confident "no" responses to new items. (Data from Experiment V.)

items, respectively. Thus, the same pattern of results that we found in Experiment III emerges again from Experiment V, and it suggests that the same processes are operative for 15-item study lists and for 64-item study lists.

However, we now seem to have scan rates that are almost preposterous. With slopes of 1.0 and 1.6 msec per item, we are approaching the temporal resolving power of the central nervous system (e.g., the minimum interresponse time of single neurons at their maximum firing rate). Of course, if we scan that rapidly, the individual elements need not operate at this speed. The volley principle of hearing (Wever, 1970) is an example, and conceivably a similar principle could apply to memory scanning. The fact that the slope of the lag-latency function is 1 msec per item could mean that items are scanned in groups of 2 at 2 msec per item, in groups of 3 at 3 msec per item, etc. However, even 2, or 3, or 5 msec per item still seems rather improbable, so perhaps we should consider other possibilities.

One possibility is that the data are just "noise"—spurious not genuine results. However, both experiments (Experiments III and V) have been repeated, and the results are replicable. Also, the results hold for individual subjects. The lag-latency functions for the four subjects of Experiment III is shown in Fig. 9. Clearly the slope shows some variation from subject to subject, but the linearity seems to hold in each of the four cases separately.

Another possibility is the direct-access view already mentioned. When presented with the probe, perhaps the subject uses some direct look-up

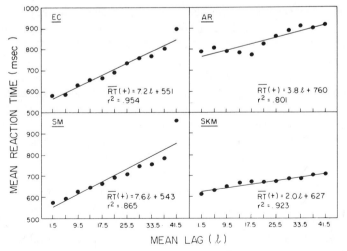

Fig. 9.   Lag-latency functions for the four subjects of Experiment III.

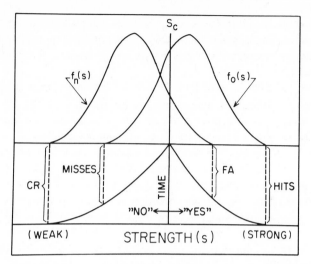

Fig. 10.   Direct-access or strength-theory model to show the relationship between the memory-trace strengths (s) of old and new items, the yes–no criterion (s_c), the transfer function to map strength into latency, and the resultant latency ranges expected by the model for hits, false alarms (FA), misses, and correct rejections (CR). (From Murdock, 1974, Fig. 3.3.)

procedure to determine whether it is an old or new item. One version of such a model is shown in Fig. 10. There are separate strength distributions for old and new items, the separation between the means determines d', the yes–no criterion is given in the figure by s_c, and the transfer function mapping strength into latency decreases exponentially on both sides of the criterion. There are several problems with this model, and they have been discussed elsewhere (Murdock, 1974, pp. 282–283). Basically, it does not explain the fact that the slopes for new and old items are the same, nor can it come close to predicting both the accuracy and the latency data with the same parameter values. Perhaps a direct-access or strength-theory view could be patched up by modifying the assumptions about strength, latency, or their relationship. However, such modifications would have to be made and tested before they could be evaluated.

Another possibility is that there are criterion changes over the course of testing. Relevant data to answer this question are shown in Fig. 11, where the change over output position of three criterion cuts is shown. These are the data of the four subjects of Experiment III, whose d' values are shown in Fig. 3. The values for Fig. 11 were obtained from the EPCROC program, and the criterion is given as a standard score relative to the mean of the new-item distribution. As can be seen, there is a slight upward tendency for the highest criterion (the cut between $+ +$ and

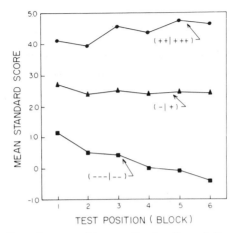

F<small>IG</small>. 11.   The effect of test position on the location of three criteria, measured as a standard score relative to the new item distribution. (Mean values of the four subjects of Experiment I.)

$+ + +$), no change at all in the yes–no cut (between $-$ and $+$), but a rather clear downward trend for the lowest criterion cut (between $- - -$ and $- -$). If latencies are thought to decrease as the distance from the yes–no criterion increases, then the fact that the middle curve is level indicates that the "sure old" and "sure no" responses are on the average farther and farther from the yes–no cut as the number of tested items increases. By this line of reasoning, one would expect that the latency of those items extreme enough to lie outside the upper or lower criterion should actually decrease as test position increases. Since they increase, a criterion interpretation seems to be ruled out.

A different interpretation might suggest the locus of the lag-latency effect to be in the encoding stage. Perhaps there is some residual facilitation in the perceptual recognition of a repeated item but this facilitation decreases (linearly, say) with lag. Were such the case, the linear lag-latency effect would be expected, but its existence would tell us nothing whatever about scanning. The main problem with this interpretation is the test position–latency function for new items. It too is a linear function and the slope is essentially the same as the lag-latency function for old items. New items are not by definition list members so no encoding facilitation would be expected. Thus, the encoding interpretation would seem to be unable to account for the fact that the linear functions for old and new items have essentially the same slope.

A final possibility is simply that retrieval gradually slows down over the course of testing, and this is a general not a specific effect. Old and

TABLE 3

**Accuracy (Proportion of "Yes" Responses) and
Latency (of High-Confident "Yes" Responses to Old Items)
(msec) as a Joint Function of Study and Test Position**[a]

	Test position									
Study	2	5	8	11	14	17	20	23	26	29
	Accuracy									
2	.889	.903	.900	.930	.889	.895	.887	.840	.888	.867
5	.887	.894	.868	.887	.872	.849	.875	.811	.833	.799
8	.917	.928	.898	.894	.859	.858	.817	.829	.786	.840
11	.954	.938	.948	.918	.902	.901	.881	.840	.824	.842
14	.979	.989	.979	.964	.942	.942	.897	.897	.909	.866
	Latency									
2	723	671	664	675	727	728	721	769	787	866
5	733	668	693	704	748	730	756	792	798	817
8	714	685	683	673	704	754	766	764	807	790
11	668	646	657	693	703	739	763	745	768	800
14	637	634	657	674	678	715	730	768	785	797

[a] Data from 4 Ss in Experiment III.

new items have the same slope because they are both subject to this slow-down, and the fact that the function is linear is simply how it works out. The problem here is that, for old items, lag not test position is the critical variable. A given lag can be achieved variously: items presented early in the study and test list, items presented in the middle of both, or items presented late in both. Were the latency change a function of habituation over the course of testing, then the reaction times should differ systemati-cally. In general they do not; latency is about the same for any given lag. Relevant data are shown in Table 3, which gives the proportion of correct responses (to old items) as a joint function of study and test position (each in blocks of three), also the mean latency of high-confident "yes" responses to old items in the same way. There is, of course, some variation within a given lag (e.g., for Lag 14 the mean latencies are 723, 668, 683, 693, and 678 msec for study-test positions of 2, 5, 8, 11, and 14, respectively). However, by and large the variation seems more random than systematic.

Since these alternative possibilities seem inconsistent with the data, what further evidence is there for a backward serial self-terminating scan? We have not as yet conducted any experiments designed to test directly for this kind of process. Instead, our efforts thus far have been directed toward internal analyses of the data we have already collected, partly to be certain that the linear functions are genuine and partly to see what further light, if any, can be cast on the scanning process by the available data. As concerns the first point, these linear reaction-time functions seem to be genuine; we have obtained them in five different experiments. However, all these results are paradigm specific; whether they hold under other conditions remains to be seen.

One comparison which supports the scanning model is the fact that high-confident "no" responses to old items seem to have about the same reaction time as high-confident "no" responses to new items. The interpretation would be that the former illustrated those cases where the target item had either been missed on the scan or had been forgotten so was no longer available. In either case, then, the scan should go back to the beginning of the list, and no difference between old and new items would be expected. Data supporting this claim are shown in Table 4. Mean latencies are shown for old and new items by confidence judgments for Sessions 8–13 of each of the four subjects in Experiment I who had been given this extended testing. Although there is a tendency for slower reactions to old items,

TABLE 4
Mean Latency (msec) by Confidence Judgment
for Old and New Items[a]

S	Item type	Confidence judgments					
		− − −	− −	−	+	+ +	+ + +
RO	Old items	715	1225	1700	1510	1075	662
	New items	695	1068	1595	1632	1165	638
JM	Old items	775	815	988	968	880	640
	New items	765	842	985	1028	965	772
XC	Old items	890	1465	1582	1580	1368	792
	New items	832	1658	1980	1732	1318	915
RC	Old items	1082	1238	1638	1460	1370	1028
	New items	950	1202	1558	1558	1538	1162

[a] Data from Four Ss in Experiment I from Murdock and Dufty (1972)

TABLE 5

Standard Deviations (msec) and Frequencies of
High-Confident "Yes" Responses to Old Items by Lag

Lag	EC		AR		SM		SKM	
	SD	Freq.	SD	Freq.	SD	Freq.	SD	Freq.
1.5	180	(77)	322	(75)	71	(88)	107	(85)
5.5	117	(267)	394	(261)	91	(288)	107	(269)
9.5	179	(444)	307	(428)	143	(474)	156	(475)
13.5	228	(575)	314	(626)	140	(655)	147	(664)
17.5	196	(584)	288	(684)	175	(668)	208	(744)
21.5	240	(553)	406	(739)	239	(616)	195	(720)
25.5	286	(486)	419	(648)	244	(616)	204	(659)
29.5	265	(399)	386	(581)	271	(541)	190	(664)
33.5	270	(318)	652	(438)	343	(370)	256	(450)
37.5	445	(198)	392	(281)	308	(213)	283	(325)
41.5	402	(69)	431	(118)	622	(83)	262	(113)

[a] Data from 4 Ss in Experiment IV.

this effect is relatively small in comparison to differences that exist across confidence judgments.

A second bit of evidence comes from an analysis of the variability of the "sure yes" responses to old items. By any convolution principle, if each item comparison has some variability, the variance of the obtained reaction-time distributions should increase with lag. Pertinent data are shown in Table 5, which gives the standard deviation for each subject of all "sure yes" responses at the specified lags (1.5, 5.5, 9.5, . . . , 41.5). The number of observations entering into each computation is shown in parentheses after the value for the standard deviation. (The mean latencies for these lags are shown in Fig. 9.) In general, this expectation is supported by the data. By and large, the variability in reaction time does seem to increase over lag for each of the four subjects of the experiment.

Other data suggest that the outer loop is optional, not obligatory. That is, the multiple interrogations seem to be a consequence of the confidence–judgment procedure, not a necessary requirement of the recognition process. The evidence that suggests this conclusion is shown in Table 6. There, mean latencies (and frequencies) are shown for the confidence–judgment and the yes–no procedure of Experiment II. For the confidence–judgment procedure, the data are summed over the three sessions, old and new items, and yes and no responses. For the yes–no procedure, the data are summed

TABLE 6
Mean Latency (msec) and Frequency (in parentheses) for Confidence–Judgment and Yes–No Procedure[a]

	Confidence–judgment procedure						Yes–no procedure			
	Sure		Maybe		Guess		Yes		No	
S	Lat.	Freq.	Lat.	Freq.	Lat.	Freq.	Lat.	Freq.	Lat.	Freq.
1	786	(2013)	1198	(601)	1662	(266)	830	(1417)	927	(1463)
2	868	(1991)	1249	(858)	2067	(21)	704	(1486)	751	(1394)
3	753	(2774)	1890	(29)	1714	(75)	762	(1370)	739	(1507)
4	973	(1788)	1289	(643)	1541	(449)	846	(978)	919	(1901)
5	1429	(2289)	2623	(370)	3206	(213)	1112	(1212)	1066	(1668)
6	1204	(1445)	1439	(794)	1654	(641)	887	(1118)	876	(1762)
7	1098	(2748)	1732	(127)	2200	(2)	1048	(987)	1119	(1883)
8	1029	(1752)	1640	(304)	1358	(818)	914	(965)	869	(1914)
Mean:	1010		1478		1676		876		916	

[a] Data from 8 Ss in Experiment II from Murdock and Dufty (1972).

175

over the three sessions and old and new items. By and large, the mean latencies of yes–no judgments are about the same as the "sure" confidence judgments, and clearly faster than the "maybe" and the "guess" confidence judgments. Were the same processes operative under the two procedures, then the yes–no results would be a probability mixture of the three confidence–judgment conditions, which is clearly not the case. If anything, the yes–no latencies are slightly faster than even the high-confident ("sure") judgments. If this difference is reliable, it would suggest that perhaps even with high-confident responses there is still the occasional second look.

Up to this point, we have simply assumed that lag is the relevant variable for old items. However, as has been noted, lag has two components which can be separated. These are the number of study items and the number of test items intervening between the presentation of an item and its test. The lag-latency function is clearly linear. Does this necessarily mean that study items and test items are scanned at the same rate? As it happens, the answer is no. Let us examine a little more analytically the two components contributing to the lag measure, and see what conclusions do and do not follow.

Assume that the time to access an item in memory is the sum of two components. The first component is the retardation or interference generated by study items, which is

$$t_1(i) = a_1 + b_1(L - i), \tag{1}$$

where i is the subscript for serial position, L is list length, and a_1 and b_1 are the intercept and slope of this linear function. The second component is the interference generated by test items, which is

$$t_2(j) = a_2 + b_2(j - 1), \tag{2}$$

where j is the subscript for test position and a_2 and b_2 are the intercept and slope, not necessarily the same as a_1 and b_1. Then the combined interference is

$$t_1(i) + t_2(j) = a_1 + a_2 + b_1(L - i) + b_2(j - 1) \tag{3}$$

or, more simply,

$$z = cx + dy, \tag{4}$$

where x is the number of subsequent study items $(L - i)$, y is the number of prior test items $(j - 1)$, c and d are their respective scanning times, and the intercepts $(a_1 + a_2)$ plus the times required for other stages are included in z, the "normalized" reaction time (or latency).

If we consider all cases at lag n (where $n = x + y$) and pool, then the mean latency $\bar{z}_n$ at lag n is

$$\bar{z}_n = \frac{1}{n+1} \sum_{k=0}^{n} \{ck + d(n-k)\}$$
$$= \left(\frac{c+d}{2}\right) n. \tag{5}$$

Thus, mean latency will be a linear function of lag with a slope which is the average of the scanning times for study and test items. (The intercept has been absorbed in $\bar{z}_n$, but would clearly be nonzero in the usual lag-latency data plot.) Let us consider some special cases.

CASE 1. $d = 0$. This would mean that the scan skips back to the study list without examining any of the test items. Further, whatever the time to skip back to the study items, it would not vary systematically over the course of testing. When the probe is a new item, $x = L$. Consequently, for any value of c, the test position–latency function would be flat (i.e., have a slope of 0). Since the data consistently reject this, $d > 0$. That is, test items are scanned, and the central processor does not skip over them and go directly back to the study items in the list.

CASE 2. $c = 0$. Since $z = cx + dy$, if $c = 0$, then the lag-latency and the test-position latency functions would have the same slope but possibly a different intercept. Since this is exactly what the data show, it could be that the linear functions reflect output interference only, and there is no scanning of study items. (This point was made less formally several pages back.) Therefore, the linear data functions are not in themselves adequate to exclude this possibility; further analyses are necessary. We shall return to this point shortly.

CASE 3. $c = d$. This is a possible but not necessary condition. Were this the case, then the data would be as they are. However, it could well be that $c \neq d$, and the data would still be as they are. Thus, when equations (2) and (3) are considered together, it is quite clear that the linear lag-latency and test position-latency functions are really not very informative at all about the relative scanning rates for study and test items. Further data analyses are necessary.

To this end, we reanalyzed the confidence-judgment data of Experiment III, where 15-item study lists had been used. The two-way classification of Table 3 (position in the study list and position in the test list) was used, and each item was classified accordingly. Then, to get the input function we summed across output positions, and to get the output function we summed across input positions. The mean reaction times are shown in Fig. 12, where the mean reaction time for high-confident "yes" responses to old items is plotted as a function of number of intervening study or test items. With two exceptions, the functions are clearly linear, and the slope for test items is somewhat greater (6.5 msec per item) than the slope for study items (4.2 msec per item). This would suggest that the rate at which test items are scanned is slightly slower than the rate at which study items are scanned. However, it is clearly the case that both c and d are greater than zero; also, their average (5.3 msec per item) is of necessity close to the slope of the lag-latency function of Fig. 5.

What about the two bad points? The point for 1 intervening test item is clearly too high, and the point for 13 intervening study items is clearly too low. A plausible (though ad hoc) reason for the former is the inertia of shifting from study to test. The first few responses may be too low because the shift from record mode to reproduce mode takes time. For the latter, a plausible (though again ad hoc) reason is the primacy effect. We consistently find a primacy effect wherein the first few items have an elevated hit rate. Why this primacy effect should also manifest itself in the latency data is surely not clear (though perhaps somewhat comforting to a strength theorist); for the time being we can only acknowledge its existence and hope that it is no more than a second-order effect.

Of course, we are taking some liberties with the data of Fig. 12. We are emphasizing the uniformities and disregarding the inconsistencies. Others may prefer a different interpretation. In any case, these data seem

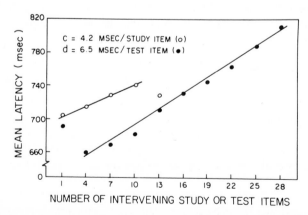

Fig. 12. Mean latency for high-confident "yes" responses to old items, in one case (open circles) as a function of number of intervening study items (pooled over all test positions) and in the other case (closed circles) as a function of number of intervening test items (pooled over all input serial positions). (Data from Experiment III.)

to shed some further light on the scanning process. There seem to be two components, one for study items and one for test items. Together, they determine the lag-latency function already displayed. The slopes of Fig. 12 may differ; test items take half again as long to scan as study items. Whether this is a reliable difference under these particular conditions, and whether it will be generally true in other sets of data, remains to be seen.

Forced-Choice Recognition

In a forced-choice recognition-memory procedure, each test consists of the simultaneous presentation of m alternatives of which one is an old item, or target, and $m - 1$ are new items, or lures. The task of the subject is to select the one old item from the m alternatives. In our experiments, the latency of this response (the time from onset of the display to depression of the button indicating the subject's choice) is recorded, no confidence judgments are requested, all items are tested so there are as many tests as there are items in the list, and, as in the confidence-judgment procedure, the test trials are self paced. As described elsewhere (Murdock, 1974, p. 271), in what is here called Experiment III the same four subjects who were given 12 sessions on a confidence-judgment procedure were also given 12 sessions on a forced-choice procedure. On each session there were 32 lists, each list was 15 items long, and they were blocked into four subsets of eight. In each subset, the values of m were either 2, 3, 4, or 6. For each subject, the order of these four subsets was counterbalanced over the 12 forced-choice sessions. As in the confidence-judgment procedure, there were four sessions at a fast rate, four sessions at a medium rate, and four sessions at a slow rate. (The particular presentation rates used differed across subjects, but they can be determined from Fig. 10.5 in Murdock, 1974, p. 273.) As in the confidence–judgment procedure, presentation rate was also counterbalanced across subjects. In other respects, the forced-choice procedure was like the confidence–judgment procedure of this experiment.

What happens in a forced-choice procedure? There are a number of possibilities. For instance, the subject could select the first alternative from the m alternatives in the test, scan the entire list for that; then, if not found, the subject could scan the entire list for the second alternative, and so on, until a match was found or he was obliged to guess. Another possibility is that all m alternatives in the probe could be compared first to the last memory item, then to the next to last, and so on until a match was found or a guess was necessary. These two possibilities simply reverse the inner and outer scanning loops. In the latter possibility, the scan rate could be independent of the value of m (the number of alternatives in the probe) or it could vary systematically with m. What is the effect of output interference in the discrete-trials procedure we use? Will the scanning rate for the kth test position vary as a function of the value of m in the $k - 1$ test positions? That is, what is the proper unit of output interference; is it simply a function of k, the number of prior tests given regardless of m, or is it a function of k and m, where it would reflect the total number of items involved in scanning rather than simply the total number of prior tests? If it is the latter, does it make any difference what position in the m alternatives the target item occupies?

Faced with this bewildering array of possibilities, we started with the simplest one. Suppose the basic unit of output interference is simply the number of tests given, and it is independent of the position of the target among the lures. Then, one can meaningfully compute a lag-latency function where, as before, the lag is simply the number of study items plus the number of test units (regardless of m) between presentation and test of each item. It is necessary to conditionalize on correct responses for this lag-latency function. Otherwise, there is no way to know how many items were scanned. Incorrect responses could occur because one of the lures was indiscriminable from a list item, or they could occur because the subject scanned the entire list, did not find a match, and guessed. Consequently, as computed here, the lag-latency function for a forced-choice procedure is based only on correct responses.

The lag-latency functions for the forced-choice procedure of Experiment III are shown here in Fig. 13. As can be seen, each function is reasonably linear, and both the slope and the intercept vary systematically with m. The least-square values of the regression analysis are included in Fig. 13. Consider the relation between the slope and m. It is approximately the case that the slope divided by m is a constant, namely, 6 msec per alternative. It seems unlikely that this value differs from the slope of the confidence–judgment procedure of this same experiment, which was approximately 5 msec per item (see Fig. 5). Consider the relation between the intercept and m. It is approximately the case that the intercept divided by m is a constant, namely, 500 msec per alternative. The intercept of the lag-latency function for the confidence-judgment procedure of this same experiment was 627 msec (see Fig. 5). Again there is not too much discrepancy among these values.

What do these results mean? Here is a very simple explanation. When a probe is presented, all the alternatives in the probe are encoded. Each alternative requires 500 msec to encode. In a confidence–judgment procedure, there is only a single alternative; in a forced-choice procedure, there are m alternatives. Then, the backward serial scan starts. All alternatives (one in the confidence–judgment procedure, m in the forced-choice procedure) are compared to the memory items, but the rate is a function of m.

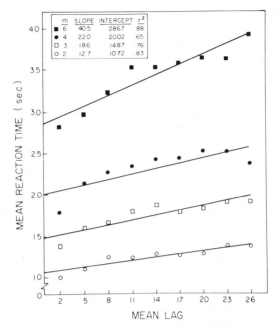

m	SLOPE	INTERCEPT	r^2
■ 6	40.5	28.67	.88
● 4	22.0	20.02	.65
□ 3	18.6	14.87	.76
○ 2	12.7	10.72	.83

FIG. 13. Mean reaction time for correct responses as a function of lag for the four conditions (2, 3, 4, and 6 alternatives) of the forced-choice procedure of Experiment III.

It is about 6 msec per alternative, which means a slope of 12 msec per item in the two-alternative forced-choice condition, 18 msec per item in the three-alternative forced choice condition, etc. In the confidence–judgment procedure, since there is only a single item to compare, the rate is about 5 or 6 msec per item. Thus, the retrieval processes for forced-choice recognition are basically the same as the retrieval processes for a confidence–judgment or yes–no procedure. More specifically, the encoding time and the scanning rate are linear functions of m, and the yes–no case is simply the limiting case of forced-choice recognition, namely, when $m = 1$.

This analysis has several problems. However, before considering these problems, think what it would mean if this analysis were correct. It would mean that the two main types of recognition memory, yes–no and forced-choice, could be subsumed under common principles. The former would be just a special case of the latter. The time to access information in memory would depend upon the amount of material to compare, but the principles underlying each would be the same. Although this analysis applies only to latency, it should be possible to extend it to accuracy as well. Quantitative predictions should be possible, and one could use either procedure interchangeably. Theoretically, considerable unification would have been achieved.

One problem is the possibility of multiple observations. That is, it is assumed in this analysis that there is only one execution of the outer loop. If there were more, then the estimates of scanning times would be seriously in error. However, perhaps the assumption of a single observation is tenable. It has already been suggested that the multiple observations may be a consequence of the confidence–judgment procedure. The evidence for this possibility was shown in Table 5, where latencies for the yes–no procedure were given. Since the forced-choice procedure of Experiment III did not require confidence judgments, perhaps the result was like that of a yes–no procedure, where the mean latencies are more consistent with single rather than multiple observations.

Another problem is that it seems less defensible to use lag as the independent variable in a forced-choice procedure than in a confidence–judgment procedure. One would think that the amount of output interference would vary systematically with m, and the lag measure pools over study items and test units indiscriminately. The best way to resolve this issue is to analyze study and test positions separately for each value of m. The results of this analysis are shown in Tables 7 and 8. Table 7 shows mean accuracy as a joint function of study and test position for each value of m, where the results are pooled over the four subjects and the three different presentation rates of Experiment III. Table 8 shows mean latency in the same way.

For accuracy (Table 7), it is roughly the case that accuracy decreases with test position and the intercept is an increasing function of study position. What is more critical is the latency. If lag really were the critical variable for scanning, then all entries along a given diagonal should be equal. For instance, in Table 8, for $m = 2$ the mean latencies were 1303, 1204, and 1225 msec for the three cases of Lag 8 (8–2, 11–5, and 14–8). There are nine diagonals for each value of m, or 36 in all. The question is whether the variation along these diagonals is random or systematic. By inspection it seems fairly nonsystematic, but some quantitative test is desirable. However, such a test by itself would not be too meaningful. What is really needed is some alternative model, and then some comparative tests would be possible.

The other main problem is guessing. If the target item had been forgotten, or if it was missed on the scan, the subject would have to choose at random from the m alternatives after he looked through the entire list. On some proportion of the trials he would be correct by chance. All correct responses enter into the lag-latency function, and guessing would introduce a bias into the estimated scanning times. Further, since the chance prob-

TABLE 7
Proportion of Correct Responses in Forced Choice as a Joint Function of Study and Test Position[a]

Study	Test position 2	5	8	11	14	Test position 2	5	8	11	14
			$m = 2$					$m = 3$		
2	.937	.925	.930	.893	.915	.870	.885	.845	.770	.820
5	.911	.885	.874	.862	.875	.859	.786	.784	.863	.838
8	.934	.905	.943	.879	.894	.893	.873	.839	.830	.815
11	.958	.943	.901	.892	.924	.930	.846	.840	.854	.844
14	.974	.949	.932	.938	.928	.971	.917	.881	.883	.897
			$m = 4$					$m = 6$		
2	.817	.831	.824	.812	.689	.774	.755	.739	.668	.681
5	.836	.814	.749	.770	.740	.720	.712	.706	.677	.667
8	.785	.776	.757	.796	.779	.744	.771	.717	.662	.671
11	.879	.837	.843	.766	.763	.843	.758	.670	.684	.645
14	.948	.882	.864	.810	.769	.906	.831	.827	.726	.727

[a] Data from 4 Ss in Experiment III.

TABLE 8
Mean Latency (msec) of Correct Responses in Forced Choice as a Joint Function of Study and Test Position[a]

Study	Test position 2	5	8	11	14	Test position 2	5	8	11	14
			$m = 2$					$m = 3$		
2	1387	1201	1228	1436	1366	1915	1622	1778	1869	1905
5	1340	1203	1258	1339	1326	1770	1708	1800	1826	1963
8	1303	1224	1194	1419	1317	1702	1751	1800	1851	1854
11	1123	1204	1242	1329	1233	1671	1659	1771	1951	1982
14	1016	1134	1225	1160	1262	1368	1507	1648	1899	1972
			$m = 4$					$m = 6$		
2	2450	2239	2463	2472	2368	3269	3438	3193	3583	3920
5	2346	2252	2234	2601	2572	3503	3435	3736	3937	3704
8	2251	2253	2301	2760	2473	3016	3509	3946	3509	4019
11	2158	2193	2330	2652	2553	2929	3434	3603	3638	3765
14	1805	2116	2367	2348	2510	2813	3040	3358	3533	3536

[a] Data from 4 Ss in Experiment III.

ability varies with m, the effect of this bias would vary across conditions (number of alternatives). In particular, one could argue as follows: the longer the lag, the more the forgetting. Since forgotten items have a longer latency (errors are indeed slower than correct responses), reaction times increase with lag because there are more forgotten items which are correct by chance (and so enter into the calculations of Fig. 13). The slope of these lag-latency functions increases with m because there is proportionately more forgetting. The reason for this is output interference; for any test position past the first, the greater the value of m the more total items intervene between study and test. The more forgotten items the greater the bias. Therefore, the lag-latency functions of Fig. 13 have nothing to do with different scanning rates; they only reflect the greater contribution of guessing as lag and m increase.

The exact effects of guessing depends upon the detailed assumptions one wishes to entertain. Suppose that the probability that an item will be remembered decreases linearly with lag at a rate (slope) proportional to m. Then assume that the lag-latency function is composed of two components, remembered items having a fast reaction time that increases linearly with lag and forgotten items having a slow reaction time that is independent of lag. Then assume that the obtained reaction-time functions are simply a probability mixture of these two cases. It is easy to show that the lag-latency function would be a polynomial (quadratic) function of lag with a maximum value that decreases with lag. However, the data suggest the lag-latency function is linear, not curvilinear. If the remembered items have a fast reaction time that is independent of lag, then the lag-latency function would be linear but the slope would *decrease* with m. Since the data show that the slope increases with m, this alternative does not seem very promising either. Finally, the forgotten items could increase or decrease proportionately to lag and that would not affect the slope values, since the contribution of guessing is to affect the intercept but not the slope. Therefore, on closer examination, the guessing interpretation of Fig. 13 does not hold.

Perhaps other assumptions would result in better predictions. One cannot be sure until the matter has been explored systematically. However, we can say that one particular guessing model is quite inconsistent with the data. To conclude this section, let us reiterate the main finding about the forced-choice results. The lag-latency function is linear; its slope is a multiplicative function of m, the number of alternatives in the probe, and so is its intercept. One possible interpretation is that the intercept reflects the time to encode the probe, the slope reflects the scanning rate, and the time to scan each memory trace is a linear function of the number of alternatives in the probe which enter into the comparison. By this interpretation, the confidence–judgment (or yes–no) procedure would simply be a special case of forced choice, namely, $m = 1$.

RETRIEVAL AT SHORT AND LONG LAGS

One of the more surprising results from the present series of experiments is the consistent discrepancy between the scan rate found here and the scan rate typically reported for very short lists of items. Sternberg (1966) and many others find values more like 35 msec per item than 5 msec per item. If the Sternberg paradigm has revealed the existence of high-speed scanning, perhaps the study–test paradigm used here has revealed the existence of very high-speed scanning. Further, the comparison between short lists and long lists give results that are exactly opposite to what one might expect. It is commonly believed (e.g., Theios, 1973) that scanning is relatively fast for short lists of items. Ergo, it must be slower for long lists of items. In fact, our data suggest exactly the opposite. The scanning rate seems to be faster for long lists of items than for short lists of items. This possibility has also been suggested by Mohs, Wescourt, and Atkinson (1973). This finding is not really counterintuitive, once you think about it, but it is contrary to the theoretical assumptions entertained by most current workers in the field. Consequently, this finding should be examined with some care before it is accepted.

The reliability of the data is probably not open to question. For subspan lists, there are by now many studies which give scan rates of 35 ± say 15 msec. We have found scan rates in the low (1–5) msec range in four or five different experiments, and 3 ± 2 is clearly different from 35 ± 15. However, the experimental paradigms are quite different. In the Sternberg paradigm, subspan lists are used, and accuracy is high (error-free performance is the ideal). Only a single item is probed on each trial, and it is a yes–no procedure; confidence judgments are not employed. Reaction time is plotted as a function of set size, and lag is not considered. (More accurately, serial position effects are the subspan counterpart of lag effects and, while they are not ignored, they are not looked upon with any great favor by those sympathetic to a serial exhaustive scanning model.) By contrast, in our procedure, list length is well in excess of memory span; accuracy is far from perfect; many items are tested on each trial; confidence judgments are employed; we conditionalize on high-confident correct responses; and latency is plotted as a function of lag or test position. Finally, although both paradigms make separate plots for old and new items, in the subspan case parallel slopes suggest an exhaustive search, whereas in the supraspan case parallel slopes suggest a self-terminating search. (More correctly, in the supraspan case parallel functions for old and new items are consistent with either a self-terminating or an exhaustive process. The distinction between them must rest on comparison of selected study and test positions.)

There are, however, several sets of data which suggest there may be different processes used in retrieving information from short and long lists. Atkinson and his colleagues (e.g., Atkinson, Herrmann, & Wescourt, 1974; Atkinson & Juola, 1973) have used prememorized lists and, in one experiment, find a slope of 4 msec per item for the function plotting mean latency of positive responses as a function of list length (left panel of Fig. 2, p. 588, Atkinson *et al.*, 1974). Using the same technique, Burrows and Okada found a slope of approximatey 60 msec per item for subspan lists and 15 msec per item for supraspan lists. Their data is plotted in Murdock (1974, p. 284, Fig. 10.11). This same effect has also been found with pictures by Banks and Fariello (1974), at least in their first experiment. Although other experiments (e.g., Corballis & Miller, 1973; Wingfield & Branca, 1970) have not found such discontinuities, presumably there are procedural differences. The positive results quite clearly support the view that there can be different retrieval processes for long and short lists.

However, different experimental paradigms are involved in these comparisons. The most direct and satisfactory way to compare retrieval at short and long lags is to use the same experimental paradigm to study both. One cannot extend the Sternberg paradigm to long lags since that would inevitably violate one of its basic preconditions; namely, error-free performance. However, one could easily vary list length in our study–test paradigm so the lag range would cover any desired span. That is exactly what we have done in Experiment VI, the last experiment reported here. The list length was either 4, 8, 16, 32, or 64 words. Given the general accuracy level of recognition memory, with 4-item lists we expect to have essentially perfect accuracy; with 64-item lists there are many mistakes, and the intermediate conditions should portray the effect of the transition from subspan lengths to supraspan lengths.

In this experiment, after a practice session 5 subjects were given 20 experimental sessions, 4 on each of the 5 list lengths. The number of lists per session varied inversely with list length; it was 128, 64, 32, 16, and 8 for list lengths of 4, 8, 16, 32, and 64 words, respectively. In all cases, the same study–test paradigm was used, and twice as many items were tested as studied. The presentation rate was 1.2 sec per item, and the order of conditions across sessions was counterbalanced over the subjects. All lags were sampled, but a minimum of two lists had to intervene before any word could reappear. In other respects, the procedure was the same as in previous experiments.

TABLE 9

Slope (msec per item) and r^2 for Lag-Latency and
Test Position-Latency Functions for Each List Length[a]

Length	Old items		New items	
	Slope	r^2	Slope	r^2
4	−17.7	.949	−27.2	.947
8	5.3	.948	0.7	.038
16	2.8	.516	3.7	.911
32	2.5	.861	2.4	.907
64	1.1	.899	0.9	.727

[a] Data from 5 Ss in Experiment VI.

The main results of this experiment are shown in Table 9. With one exception (new items at List Length 8) the goodness of fit as measured by r^2 is quite acceptable. Therefore, the usual lag-latency and test position-latency functions were obtained. Examination of slope changes suggests two effects: (a) there is a discrepancy between subspan lists, which have a negative slope, and supraspan lists, which have a positive slope, and (b) for supraspan lists, the slope seems to decrease with list length. These two effects, and their implications, will be discussed in turn.

To discuss the second finding first, the scan rate for supraspan lists seems to become faster as list length increases. This seems clearly the case for lists from 16 to 64, and probably is true over the range 8–64 if one disregards the new-item result for List Length 8. (Admittedly, it is always rather risky to single out one particular discrepant result and dismiss it as untrustworthy. We have no reason as to why it should be unreliable nor any proof that it is. Further experimentation is currently in progress to try to clarify this problem.) In any event, what could this effect mean? Perhaps there is a speed–accuracy tradeoff: the greater the range the faster the scanning, but the more errors that result as a consequence. Such a mechanism is not unreasonable; it seems to occur in skilled performance, and retrieval of information from memory is not an unpracticed art. Notice, incidentally, that the scan rate must be preset before testing begins. The maximum possible lag steadily increases over the course of testing. Were the scan rate to change systematically as a consequence, then the linear latency functions would not occur.

If there is a speed–accuracy tradeoff, then accuracy should decline. Evidence that in fact accuracy does decrease with list length is shown in Table

TABLE 10
Hits and Correct Rejections for Each Subject
at Each List Length[a]

S	Item type	List length				
		4	8	16	32	64
1	Old items	.993	.922	.849	.760	.689
	New items	.996	.983	.970	.961	.844
2	Old items	.986	.913	.830	.749	.676
	New items	.997	.977	.955	.911	.880
3	Old items	.997	.971	.907	.848	.789
	New items	.999	.992	.958	.900	.786
4	Old items	.990	.935	.842	.772	.738
	New items	.997	.960	.903	.836	.737
5	Old items	1.000	.991	.979	.940	.912
	New items	.999	1.000	.996	.985	.947

[a] Data from Experiment V.

10. For each subject, the hit rate and the correct rejection rate is given as a function of list length. As can be seen, without exception there is a monotonic decrease in accuracy as list length increases from 4 to 64. The amount of decrease varies from subject to subject, and in general correct rejections seem to hold up better than hits. However, the main trend is unambiguous. These data do not, of course, establish that the speed–accuracy interpretation is correct. All one can say is that, for supraspan lists, there are these separate tendencies: scan rate increases and accuracy decreases as list length increases. This evidence is only correlational, and more convincing proof is needed. It would be nice if one could somehow control the scan rate and show that, when it was made faster or slower, accuracy changed accordingly. However, we are not quite ready yet to try this *tour de force*.

Before leaving the topic of scanning rate, a possible ambiguity should be clarified. To say that the scan rate "is faster" could mean several things. One possibility is that the basic process, whatever it is, simply speeds up as there is more to scan. Another possibility is that fewer features enter into the comparison process, but the comparison time per feature is invariant over list length. As a simple example, perhaps 5 features entered into the comparison process with lists of 15 items but only a single feature entered into the comparison process with a list of 64 items. If the basic unit of analysis was the feature test, if each feature test required 1 msec, and if this was a serial process, then the slopes of the lag-latency functions would be 5 and 1 msec per item for lists of 15 and 64 items, respectively. Consequently, it is not that the base rate speeds up but that the number of steps decrease. We have as yet made no attempt to separate these two alternatives, so our statements that the scanning rate "is faster" must remain ambiguous until further clarification is possible.

The other main finding from Experiment VI is that the slope is *negative* for subspan lists but *positive* for supraspan lists. One could not ask for much clearer confirmation of the original hypothesis. That is, it was initially suggested that there might be different processes involved in retrieving information from short lists and from long lists, and that contention has clearly been supported by the results shown in Table 9. But beyond that, what do these results mean? A lag-latency function with a positive slope is one thing, but a lag-latency function with a negative slope is quite another matter. Descriptively, it means that latencies were becoming *shorter* the *longer* the lag. Clearly a backward serial self-terminating scan just will not do when the list length is less than the memory span.

One possibility is forward scanning for short lists. This possibility is unlikely, as the lag-latency function should then be flat in the middle, which it is not. A more promising alternative is the following. With a very short list, subjects can keep all members of the set of old items in "active memory" (Sternberg, 1969). It is perhaps advantageous to do so, for then they are continually being refreshed and perhaps reaction times are faster. However, given the experimental procedure we use, after each old item is tested, the size of this set of old items decreases by one. It is initially four; after the first old item is tested (whether first, second, or whatever) it drops to three. When the second old item is tested, the size of the active set drops to two. This depletion process continues until all old items have been tested, at which point all remaining items must be new. (Each old item was tested exactly once in each list and, although this feature of the experiment was not explicitly pointed out to the subjects initially, they certainly had enough practice to realize it.)

Lag is inversely related to set size, where by set size is meant the size of the active set or the number of old items remaining to be tested. This confounding is presumably inconsequential with long lists, because with a list of a dozen or more words keeping them all in active memory is clearly impossible. However, a list of four items is clearly another matter, and perhaps set size rather than lag is the critical variable. That is, the linear regression analysis reported in Table 9 used lag for old items and test position for new items, but other analyses are clearly possible. In particular, the data could be reanalyzed in such a way that set size was the independent variable. That is, all old and all new items tested when there are four items in the active set provides one point; all old and all new items tested when there are three items in the active set provides the next point; all old and all new items tested when there are two items in the active set provides the next point; and finally there is the case where only one old item remains. (One could even have a set size of zero, but then it is not a memory comparison task.)

Fortunately, the data were recorded and saved in such a way that this analysis could be done. It was, and the results are shown in Fig. 14. Here the independent variable is set size. To the left, all test positions are included. To the right, the first test position is excluded. The reason for this dual analysis goes back to a point mentioned earlier. In general, the first test position generally gives abnormally long latencies. For longer list lengths it is always excluded from the analysis. This effect has been attributed to the inertia involved in shifting from "record mode" to "reproduce mode," and seems not unreasonable given the task. This inertia may be less and less of a factor as list length decreases. Therefore, we analyzed the results both ways just as a precaution. As the two panels show, the results are somewhat different.

When the first test position is included, mean reaction time is a linear function of set size; the functions for old and new items are parallel; the intercept for new items is greater than that for old items; and the slopes of the two functions are slightly more than 60 msec per item. All these are typical Sternberg-type effects, though the slopes are somewhat greater than the typical 35 msec-per-item values generally reported. When the first

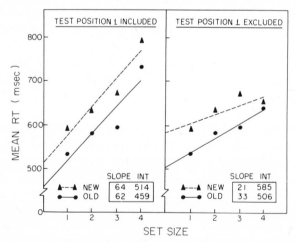

FIG. 14. Mean reaction time as a function of set size for correct responses to old and new items. In the left panel, the first test position was included; in the right panel, it was not. (Data from Experiment VI.)

test position is excluded, both functions are reasonably linear, but now the slopes are less. The slope is 21 msec per item for new items but 33 msec per item for old items.

We are not going to speculate on what the differences between the left- and the right-hand panel mean. Further analysis, both analytically and experimentally, is necessary to sort out the possibilities. Instead, we prefer to close by emphasizing the general import of these results. The main point of Fig. 14 is to demonstrate that we now have made contact with the standard results obtained from the Sternberg paradigm. When one analyzes the data of subspan lists with set size as the basis of classification, linear functions for old and new items appear that have slopes quite consistent with those found in the Sternberg paradigm. Thus, there is no basic discrepancy between the recognition–memory paradigm used for long lists of words and the Sternberg paradigm used for short lists of words. In fact, it would seem that the Sternberg paradigm could be considered to be a special case of the study–test paradigm that has long been used in research on recognition memory.

Finally, what do these results tell us about the retrieval processes for subspan and supraspan lists? In general, they are certainly consistent with the suggestion made by Murdock (1974, pp. 283–285) that retrieval at short lags involves parallel processing while retrieval at long lags involves serial processing. However, Experiment VI was not directly addressed to the serial–parallel distinction. It focused on the possibility of separate processes, whatever their nature, in the two cases. The outcome seems quite clear. To reiterate, the main conclusion emerging is that different processes are involved in the two cases. With subspan lists, the number of items in active memory seems to be the critical variable, and this information is not accessed by a backward serial self-terminating scan. For superspan lists, lag is the critical variable and a backward serial self-terminating scan is used. These processes are faster when long lags are involved than when short lags are involved. Although all the results obtained with long lists of items are consistent with the notion of a backward serial scan, whether this is the correct interpretation remains to be seen; probably alternative explanations can be found. However, some unification of results from short and long lists has been achieved, and perhaps we now know a bit more about the encoding, storage, and retrieval of item information in relatively simple and well-structured experimental situations.

ACKNOWLEDGMENTS

The research on which this paper is based was supported by Research Grants APA 146 from the National Research Council of Canada and OMHF 164 from the Ontario Mental Health Foundation. We would like to thank Philip Dufty, Khalid

El-Ayat, and Howard Kaplan for invaluable programming assistance during various phases of this project.

REFERENCES

Anderson, J. A. A memory storage model utilizing spatial correlation functions. *Kybernetik*, 1968, **5**, 113–119.

Anderson, J. R., & Bower, G. H. Recognition and retrieval processes in free recall. *Psychological Review*, 1972, **79**, 97–123.

Atkinson, R. C., Herrmann, D. J., & Wescourt, K. T. Search processes in recognition memory. In R. L. Solso (Ed.), *Theories in cognitive psychology: The Loyola Symposium*. Hillsdale, New Jersey: Lawrence Erlbaum Associates, 1974. Pp. 101–146.

Atkinson, R. C., & Juola, J. F., Factors influencing speed and accuracy of word recognition. In S. Kornblum (Ed.), *Attention and performance IV*. New York: Academic Press, 1973. Pp. 583–612.

Banks, W. P., & Fariello, G. R. Memory load and latency in recognition of pictures. *Memory & Cognition*, 1974, **2**, 144–148.

Bower, G. H. A multicomponent theory of the memory trace. In K. W. Spence & J. T. Spence (Eds.), *The psychology of learning and motivation: Advances in research and theory*. Vol. 1. New York: Academic Press, 1967. Pp. 229–325.

Bower, G. H. Stimulus-sampling theory of encoding variability. In A. W. Melton & E. Martin (Eds.), *Coding processes in human memory*. Washington, D.C.: Winston, 1972. Pp. 85–123.

Bregman, A. S. Forgetting curves with semantic, phonetic, graphic, and contiguity cues. *Journal of Experimental Psychology*, 1968, **78**, 539–546.

Broadbent, D. E. The well ordered mind. *American Educational Research Journal*, 1966, **3**, 281–295.

Brown, J. Information, redundancy and decay of the memory trace. In *The mechanisation of thought processes*. National Physical Laboratory Symposium No. 10, Her Majesty's Stationery Office, 1959.

Carroll, J. B., & White, M. N. Word frequency and age of acquisition as determiners of picture-naming latency. *Quarterly Journal of Experimental Psychology*, 1973, **25**, 85–95.

Chow, S. L., & Murdock, B. B., Jr. Iconic memory and the central information processor. Unpublished manuscript, 1974.

Clowes, M. B. On seeing things. *Artificial Intelligence*, 1971, **2**, 79–116.

Corballis, M. C., & Miller, A. Scanning and decision processes in recognition memory. *Journal of Experimental Psychology*, 1973, **98**, 379–386.

Craik, F. I. M. A "levels of analysis" view of memory. In P. Pliner, L. Krames, & T. M. Alloway (Eds.), *Communication and affect: Language and thought*. New York: Academic Press, 1973. Pp. 45–65.

Craik, F. I. M., & Lockhart, R. S. Levels of processing: A framework for memory research. *Journal of Verbal Learning and Verbal Behavior*, 1972, **11**, 671–684.

Elias, C. S., & Perfetti, C. A. Encoding task and recognition memory: The importance of semantic encoding. *Journal of Experimental Psychology*, 1973, **99**, 151–156.

Harmon, L. D. The recognition of faces. *Scientific American*, November, 1973, 70–82.

Hinrichs, J. V. A two-process memory-strength theory for judgment of recency. *Psychological Review*, 1970, **77**, 223–233.

Hintzman, D. L., & Block, R. A. Repetition and memory: Evidence for a multiple-trace hypothesis. *Journal of Experimental Psychology,* 1971, **88**, 297–306.

Hyde, T. S., & Jenkins, J. J. Recall for words as a function of semantic, graphic, and syntactic orienting tasks. *Journal of Verbal Learning and Verbal Behavior,* 1973, **12**, 471–480.

John, E. R. *Mechanisms of memory.* New York: Academic Press, 1967.

Kintsch, W. Models for free recall and recognition. In D. A. Norman (Ed.), *Models of human memory.* New York: Academic Press, 1970. Pp. 334–374.

Kintsch, W. Memory representations of text. In R. L. Solso (Ed.), *Information Processing and cognition: The Loyola Symposium.* Hillsdale, New Jersey: Lawrence Erlbaum Associates, 1975. Pp. 269–294.

Lachman, R. Uncertainty effects on time to access the internal lexicon. *Journal of Experimental Psychology,* 1973, **99**, 199–208.

Lashley, K. S. The problem of serial order in behavior. In L. A. Jeffress (Ed.), *Cerebral mechanisms in behavior.* New York: Wiley, 1951. Pp. 112–136.

Loftus, E. F., & Suppes, P. Structural variables that determine the speed of retrieving words from long-term memory. *Journal of Verbal Learning and Verbal Behavior,* 1972, **11**, 770–777.

Melton, A. W. Implications of short-term memory for a general theory of memory. *Journal of Verbal Learning and Verbal Behavior,* 1963, **2**, 1–21.

Milner, P. M. A neural mechanism for the immediate recall of sequences. *Kybernetik,* 1961, **1**, 76–81.

Mohs, R. C., Wescourt, K. T., & Atkinson, R. C. Effects of short-term memory contents on short- and long-term memory searches. *Memory & Cognition,* 1973, **1**, 443–448.

Murdock, B. B., Jr. Modality effects in short-term memory: Storage or retrieval? *Journal of Experimental Psychology,* 1968, **77**, 79–86.

Murdock, B. B., Jr. Short-term memory. In G. H. Bower (Ed.), *The psychology of learning and motivation: Advances in research and theory.* Vol. 5. New York: Academic Press, 1972. Pp. 67–127.

Murdock, B. B., Jr. *Human memory: Theory and data.* Hillsdale, New Jersey: Lawrence Erlbaum Associates, 1974.

Murdock, B. B., Jr., & Dufty, P. O. Strength theory and recognition memory. *Journal of Experimental Psychology,* 1972, **94**, 284–290.

Neisser, U. *Cognitive Psychology.* New York: Appleton-Century-Crofts, 1967.

Norman, D. A., & Rumelhart, D. E. A system for perception and memory. In D. A. Norman (Ed.), *Models of human memory.* New York: Academic Press, 1970. Pp. 19–64.

Norman, D. A., & Waugh, N. C. Stimulus and response interference in recognition-memory experiments. *Journal of Experimental Psychology,* 1968, **78**, 551–559.

Ogilvie, J. C., & Creelman, C. D. Maximum likelihood estimations of receiver operating characteristic curve parameters. *Journal of Mathematical Psychology,* 1968, **5**, 377–391.

Penfield, W., & Perot, P. The brain's record of auditory and visual experience: A final summary and discussion. *Brain,* 1963, **86**, 595–696.

Peterson, L. R. Search and judgment in memory. In B. Kleinmuntz (Ed.), *Concepts and the structure of memory.* New York: Wiley, 1967. Pp. 153–180.

Schulman, A. I. The declining course of recognition memory. *Memory & Cognition,* 1974, **2**, 14–18.

Sperling, G. The information available in brief visual presentations. *Psychological Monographs*, 1960, **74** (11, Whole No. 498).

Sternberg, S. High-speed scanning in human memory. *Science*, 1966, **153**, 652–654.

Sternberg, S. Memory-scanning: Mental processes revealed by reaction-time experiments. *American Scientist*, 1969, **57**, 421–457.

Theios, J. Reaction time measurements in the study of memory processes: Theory and data. In G. H. Bower (Ed.), *The psychology of learning and motivation: Advances in research and theory*. Vol. 7. New York: Academic Press, 1973. Pp. 43–85.

Tulving, E., & Thomson, D. M. Encoding specificity and retrieval processes in episodic memory. *Psychological Review*, 1973, **80**, 352–373.

Underwood, B. J. False recognition produced by implicit verbal responses. *Journal of Experimental Psychology*, 1965, **70**, 122–129.

Underwood, B. J. Attributes of memory. *Psychological Review*, 1969, **76**, 559–573.

Wells, J. E. Strength theory and judgments of recency and frequency. *Journal of Verbal Learning and Verbal Behavior*, 1974, **13**, 378–392.

Wever, E. G. *Theory of hearing*. New York: Dover, 1970.

Wickelgren, W. A., & Norman, D. A. Strength models and serial position in short-term recognition memory. *Journal of Mathematical Psychology*, 1966, **3**, 316–347.

Wickens, D. D. Characteristics of word encoding. In A. W. Melton and E. Martin (Eds.), *Coding processes in human memory*. Washington, D.C.: Winston, 1972. Pp. 191–215.

Wingfield, A., and Branca, A. A. Strategy in high-speed memory scanning. *Journal of Experimental Psychology*, 1970, **83**, 63–67.

7

WITHIN-INDIVIDUAL DIFFERENCES IN "COGNITIVE" PROCESSES

William F. Battig
University of Colorado

"Cognition" and/or "information processing" clearly have become far and away the most impressive sounding and popular labels denoting the research interests and activities of present-day psychologists and other behavioral scientists concerned with the understanding of virtually any aspect of human performance. Moreover, the recent ascent of "cognitive psychology" to its present exalted status undoubtedly constitutes one of the most sudden and remarkable turnabouts in the entire history of a discipline characterized by its strong resistance to major changes in its vocabularies and/or modes of thinking.

What makes the current high popularity of cognition especially astounding is that even its most dedicated advocates seem unable to provide us with a clear or consistent definition of exactly what is meant by or encompassed under the cognitive label, or how it is to be distinguished from the allegedly "noncognitive" character of whatever is (or was) not described as cognitive psychology. Especially to those not directly involved in this so-called cognitive revolution, "cognition" may understandably be interpreted as just another general label that is broad and ambiguous enough to encompass almost everything (whether old or new) that attempts either directly or indirectly to go beyond actually observable behavior into the workings or processes of the mind. Certainly such an interpretation could readily follow, for example, from Solso's (1973) attempt to specify what is meant by "cognition" in his preface to the report of the first of these Loyola Symposia on this topic.

My reasons for raising the question of what is conveyed by the terms

195

"cognition" or "information processing" (which I will make no distinction between for present purposes) are not because I have anything useful to offer by way of definition, nor even because I think it necessary to establish a clear-cut definition of these terms. Rather my concern derives from the currently strong "band-wagon" effect, whereby researchers adapt the cognitive label to their work primarily because by doing so it seems to become more acceptable, up-to-date, popular, and/or attention demanding. As an inevitable result, much of the new cognitive terminology has already achieved sufficient ambiguity to be a serious detriment to effective communication, as indicated, for example, by Restle's (1973) analysis of the varied "encodings" used by cognitive researchers for the key cognitive concept of encoding. An even more extreme example is the cognitive resurrection of the term "structuralism" to the point where a 1974 Eastern Psychological Association symposium uses this label (referring to the Wundt–Titchener "school"?) as synonymous with cognitive psychology.

In my own case, the looseness and ambiguity of cognitive terminology mean that although I do make use of it, I find little therein that goes substantially beyond what can be conveyed by older more traditional concepts commonly employed by researchers in verbal learning and memory who are often characterized as noncognitive. Perhaps this reflects my primary concern with the analysis of what now are called cognitive processes in verbal learning and memory for so long (over 15 years), that I had little choice but to adopt allegedly noncognitive "stimulus–response" terminologies which then were predominant. Nonetheless, my limited enthusiasm for cognitive terminological contributions certainly does not obscure my positive interest in some of the more substantive contributions emerging under the cognitive banner, which at the very least have made the underlying processes of primary concern to me consistent with the principal foci of a vastly expanding area of impressive theoretical and empirical research activity.

More important than any terminological confusions, however, cognitive psychologists also appear to be developing some more unfortunate aspects that, if continued, could well lead to a premature disenchantment if not dissolution with respect to present cognitive approaches. I consider some of these potentially serious enough to convince me to begin this chapter with some brief discussion thereof, with the purpose of calling attention to the dangers that could result from continuance or expansion of such counterproductive practices. This will be followed by a more detailed presentation of some recent research in our laboratory concerned with what seems to us to be a very basic and fundamental question with particular relevance to cognitive and/or information-processing research, which has to date received little if any attention from researchers in this or any other area. This research seems to us to demonstrate quite convincingly the importance of differences *within* individuals in the processes (cognitive or otherwise) that are employed in perceiving, learning, and/or memorizing different items or units constituting typical verbal-learning lists or tasks.

SOME QUESTIONS ABOUT
CURRENT COGNITIVE RESEARCH PRACTICES

As one who has spent most of his research career battling against the excessive simplicity and restrictiveness of traditional theoretical and methodological approaches, particularly to verbal learning and memory, I have been particularly unhappy to see some of what I found most objectionable therein being extended to much of the newer cognitive research. Such commonalities of shortcomings seem inconsistent with the special emphasis typically placed upon the major conceptual and/or methodological differences between cognitive and older stimulus–response associationistic research approaches. Yet I find at least the following three not uncommon features of cognitive research, which had also contributed to the dissatisfaction with earlier noncognitive research that helped to produce the revolution leading to the current development of cognitive psychology.

Premature Limitations on Scope of Inquiry

Perhaps most dangerous to the future of cognitive psychology is the increasingly widespread intolerance displayed by a substantial number of cognitive researchers and theorists toward those research problems or methods that fail to fit in with their sometimes very narrow ideas about what the "important" and/or "interesting" problems are and what cognitive psychologists should be doing. It seems almost axiomatic that particularly during the early stages of development where cognitive psychology unquestionably is at present, we can ill afford to become prematurely restrictive and thus should be providing maximal encouragement and support for the creation and development of new types of problem areas, theories, and methodological approaches. Surely those who were involved in the pioneering stages of modern cognitive research need not be reminded of how difficult it was to get their new ideas and research approaches accepted, particularly when these ran counter to the prevailing views of the older "establishment."

Nonetheless, my own recent experiences have indicated present-day cognitivists to be *less* receptive to new or different research methods or ideas, and far more willing to make premature intuitive value judgments about what is or is not interesting or worthwhile research, than what characterized the earlier stimulus–response associationistic establishment that once predominated much as do cognitive information-processing researchers today. Hopefully it would be superfluous here to cite specific instances where research initially judged as uninteresting or irrelevant subsequently became hot topics of central importance (which would include some of today's most exciting areas of cognitive research), or cases where seemingly very important and interesting research topics or controversies soon disappeared from the scene without contributing much of anything.

Rather than wasting further space belaboring what should be an obvious point, however, I shall simply reiterate my very strong impression that maximum progress in cognitive (or any other) research areas is most likely to be achieved if exploration of new and different research approaches is strongly encouraged and their evaluation based upon the empirical and/or theoretical contributions emerging from their usage rather than premature value judgments about their potential interest or importance. I fear that we may already have bypassed some potentially very significant new directions in cognitive research because they have been discouraged if not precluded by opposition from influential cognitivists, especially those significantly involved in editorial and/or grant evaluation capacities.

Failure to Benefit from Other Research Experiences

Another unfortunate characteristic pervading much (but by no means all) cognitive research seems to be a lack of knowledge about either previous or current research labeled noncognitive, and/or a failure to relate appropriately new research findings to those deriving from earlier research concerned with similar problems. In my own contacts with what is being done, particularly by neophyte cognitive researchers in what I identify as verbal-learning or memory research areas, I often have been impressed by the substantial overlap with other research known to me that is either unknown to or being ignored by these cognitivists.

Such failures to relate appropriately to other relevant research regrettably are not limited to the unfamiliarity of the investigator(s) with a particular article or two (something that inevitably plagues all of us owing to the virtual explosion in numbers of laboratories working on a particular problem, the consequent increases in numbers of published and unpublished articles, and the proliferation of journals or other sources where they are to be found). Even more detrimentally, this insularity has extended to more general conceptual and methodological levels such that even very thoroughly developed ways of unconfounding and/or controlling basic variables or processes importantly involved in cognitive research fail to be taken into account by such researchers.

As support for the latter contention, two examples brought to focus in some recent research in our laboratory can be cited. One concerns the

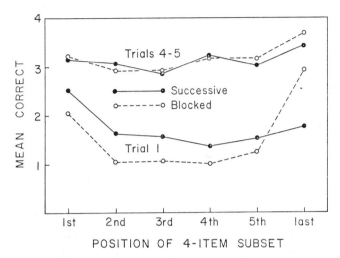

FIG. 1.   Mean number of words correctly recalled as a function of serial position of four-item subsets under conditions of successive presentation of each word individually and blocked presentation of four-word subsets, separately for the first trial and Trials 4–5 (Chapman, Pellegrino, & Battig, 1974).

"serial position curve" in free recall, and particularly the allegedly general finding of much better and earlier recall of the last items to be presented (known as the "recency effect"). This serial-position function has become so important, particularly to theoretical formulations involving a basic distinction between short-term and long-term stages of memory, that Norman's 1970 *Models of Human Memory* included a separate appendix describing such serial-position data in a form appropriate to their usage for testing of memory models.

What is typically overlooked about this free-recall serial-position function is that its shape changes dramatically with practice, and thus represents an acquisition and/or transfer phenomenon rather than a direct manifestation of distinct short-term and long-term memory components. More specifically, as shown in Fig. 1 from Chapman, Pellegrino, and Battig (1974) and elsewhere (e.g., Hasher, 1973), the large recency component that has become so basic to memory models can either be reduced or eliminated completely with unpracticed subjects. Evidence of its heavy dependence upon practice dates back at least to Wing and Thomson (1965). Even earlier, Murdock (1963) had acknowledged this as a possible explanation for "proactive inhibition" effects in short-term memory for paired associates and footnoted its possible generalization to free recall. More recently, he has explicitly described and discussed this phenomenon (Murdock, 1974, p. 237). Nonetheless, Murdock's (1962) data have been widely accepted as providing the classical serial-position curve for free recall (e.g., Norman, 1970), although each subject received 80 lists (20 in each of four sessions), and changes over practice were disregarded because of minimal differences between complete sessions.

The point is that highly misleading results and interpretations can result when one ignores, as cognitive researchers frequently do, such major changes resulting from practice on the same or related tasks as that described above. This example clearly indicates some serious difficulties in explaining the free-recall serial-position curve according to extant models based on separate short-term (recency) and long-term (primacy) memory stores. Returning to Fig. 1, its first-trial serial-position curve corresponds closely to the classical Murdock (1962) curves only when presentation is simultaneous in four-item blocks, whereas the recency component disappears under the typical successive presentation of individual items. This discrepancy clearly must be accounted for by cognitive memory models, so that continued usage of methodologies based upon numerous repeated measures without appropriate analysis and evaluation of simple practice effects can only interfere with development of adequate models.

More recently we have been forced into an explicit reacknowledgement of another important point that has received little attention from modern cognitivists, despite its longstanding documentation to the extent that Underwood's (1964) *Scientific American* article stated without qualification that "when it comes to forgetting, or remembering, what counts is not the nature of the material but the degree of original learning [p. 92]." Nonetheless, recent cognitive approaches to long-term memory typically attach little importance to controlling for differences in original learning (which may not even be distinguished from memory), as well as using shorter retention intervals than had characterized earlier allegedly noncognitive research on long-term memory and forgetting.

Thanks to the strong influence of my colleague Bruce Ekstrand, several recent studies at Colorado have included one-week delayed retention tests. As a result, we now have an impressive variety of experiments showing that factors that have important facilitative effects during original learning have little if any effect on amount of long-term retention. To date, only Pellegrino's (1974) dissertation has been published, showing at best small differences in delayed retention despite large acquisition effects due to number and type of attributes involved in a hierarchically organized free-recall list. Two subsequent free-recall experiments by Terry Barrett, in collaboration with Pellegrino, Ekstrand, and William Maier, have shown no delayed recall differences whatever, despite large acquisition differences produced by various types of experimenter-imposed organization. Another by Patricia Lauer and William Streby shows if anything poorer delayed recall under alphabetical organizational conditions that significantly facilitate acquisition. Finally, a thesis still in progress by Gilles Einstein shows absolutely no decrement in one-week delayed retention for subjects forced to process a related visually-presented list during presentation of the aurally-presented list they were instructed to learn.[1]

Although none of the foregoing experiments showed any differences in level of retention, all of them showed substantial retention differences in amount and/or type of output organization during the delayed retention test(s), which faithfully reflected the organizational differences produced during acquisition. Thus, it would appear that modes of organization and/or processing are themselves retained quite well after a week's delay, but that these have no overall facilitative effect on amount retained. This of course would have important implications for current cognitive theorizing about memory, much of which is based on the questionable assumption that the same type of long-term memory store functions at any interval longer than a few minutes. For present purposes, however, it is cited as further documentation of the problems created for those cognitive researchers who do not familiarize themselves adequately with what has been learned from earlier "noncognitive" research.

Contradictory Cognizance of Complexity

If there is one thing we should all be able to agree upon from accomplishments thus far in cognitive research, it is that even the seemingly simplest cognitive phenomena have turned out to be far from simple in terms of the processes involved and the models required to account for them. This is particularly true of theoretical developments in more complex cognitive phenomena, most notably in "semantic memory" where recent theories (e.g., Kintsch, Anderson-Bower, and Norman and associates) have reached a level of complexity probably unsurpassed anywhere in psychological research.

Having taken a general position against parsimony before having any cognizance of cognitive psychology as presently conceived (Battig, 1962), I of course am very favorably disposed toward the high levels of complexity

---

[1] Also of interest in Einstein's experiment is a second retention test a month after his one-week delayed test (administered by telephone with no advance notice to his subjects). On this second test, subjects who had processed a related visual list during original learning of the aural list showed significantly better recall of the latter than did his control subjects who received no interfering visual task (and therefore had shown faster original learning). Rather than being inexplicable, this reversal between original learning and retention is entirely consistent with previous findings that increased intratask intereference during original learning serves to facilitate later retention and/or transfer of this learned material (Battig, 1972).

involved in recent cognitive theoretical developments. I find it absolutely incredible, however, that one of the most influential cognitive theorists, who is dealing at an exceedingly complex level with semantic memory and the structure of general knowledge, could simultaneously "plead for simplicity of experimental design" and "shudder at the thought that the power of the computer will come to rule our experimental design, so that experiments become so complex that only elaborate statistical analyses can ferret out the conclusions [Norman, 1973, p. 87]."

Much of the discussion in the first Loyola Symposium (Solso, 1973, pp. 175–187) revolved around Norman's objections to current experimentation on the grounds that much more thought and theoretical development are needed before it makes any sense to try to answer the questions raised thereby through experimental work. In this discussion, Norman also argues for the great difficulty in doing experiments to test and confirm that the ideas of cognitive theorists actually describe human processes, claiming that at present neither he nor anyone else knows how to do such experiments.

Much of the difficulty in Norman's position, it seems to me, derives from his apparent assumption that with more advanced thinking and theoretical development concerning the complex cognitive processes and questions of concern to him, there will somehow emerge ways of doing simple kinds of experiments adequate to test these ideas. Even a superficial examination of such complex cognitive theories as have been developed to date should be sufficient to demonstrate the unlikelihood that such simple experiments can be found even in principle. This might be possible if the multiple factors and processes encompassed by these theories operated independently of one another, so that each could be examined separately. With the complex interactive networks characterizing most current cognitive theories, however, multivariate experiments and analytic procedures seem to offer the only feasible means of evaluating such theories experimentally.

In this connection, it may be worth noting that Clark's (1973) criticisms of statistical analyses that fail to treat linguistic materials as random variables become important only to the extent that these variables characterizing linguistic materials interact substantially with the "treatment" variable(s) central to the experiment. Put another way, if those linguistic and other factors incorporated into cognitive theories were amenable to simple single-factor kinds of experiments, it would make little difference whether or not these were evaluated as random variables.

In a similar vein, the numerous and/or substantial interactive effects characterizing complex cognitive theories also indicate the fruitlessness of focusing research attention only upon those variables which produce very large and generalizable effects upon performance, rather than being concerned also with smaller and presumably less important factors. It seems highly likely that at least some of these allegedly minor variables can be principal determinants of the magnitude (and even the direction) of the effects of major variables. Moreover, a host of minor variables which are of little importance individually may well combine to become more important than any single major variable, especially when their effects remain uninvestigated and either unknown or ignored.

Consequently, contrary to Norman (1973), I would argue strongly that the major problem with cognitive experiments is that the simple experiments we all would like to be able to do may turn out to be grossly inadequate to the task of evaluating complex interactive types of cognitive theories. Thus, instead of the more complex experiments induced by advanced computer technology serving to "simply make the understanding of the experiments that much more difficult" (Norman, 1973, p. 86), hopefully this may contribute importantly toward raising our experimental designs and analyses to a level of complexity appropriate if not essential to the evaluation of current and future cognitive theories. Advances in computer technology would seem at least as applicable to facilitating the analysis and interpretation of experimental results, as they have been to the development and simulation of complex cognitive theoretical models.

As will become apparent in the following section, the foregoing comments concerning insufficient complexity of cognitive experiments derive mainly from what we have learned through our experimental efforts to identify and unravel the several and complicated processes involved in verbal learning and memory of what once were conceived to be relatively simple kinds of verbal lists or tasks.

PROCESSING DIFFERENCES WITHIN INDIVIDUALS

By 1970, our research on the analysis of basic processes primarily in paired-associate and serial verbal learning tasks had "progressed" to the point where our efforts to extend the precision and refinement of these analyses were virtually stalemated, because of the substantial "error variance" involved in the tasks and procedures we were using. We clearly had gotten ourselves boxed into a corner where in order to make further progress in these lines of research, we could no longer afford to continue the usual treatment accorded by experimental researchers to the individual difference factors generally assumed to represent the major sources of this unwanted error variance. That is, we clearly could no longer get by with ignoring individual differences as an unfortunate nuisance factor.

As we began to consider what to do about individual difference variables, and what existed in the way of previous research thereupon that might profitably be applied within our research paradigms, we soon realized that we would have to start almost from scratch with respect to the questions with which we were directly concerned. In particular, we were impressed by the disappointingly small relationships generally found between performance on the tasks of concern to us and classical types of psychometric tests or measures, even those which should have been measuring essentially the same types of processes that supposedly were centrally involved in the verbal learning and memory tasks we were using in our research. Consequently, we quickly decided that we could best begin by focusing on variables and measures in which individuals might be expected to differ that were derived directly from the tasks with which we were working, rather than trying to adapt individual difference measures that had been developed for other purposes.

Having decided upon the latter approach, it also seemed desirable not only to disassociate ourselves from previous research approaches to individual differences, but, more important, to try to find some new ways of approaching the problems with which we were concerned. At least partially owing to the influence of developments in information-processing research, one of my first thoughts was that the most promising locus of individual differences might well be at the level of these underlying cognitive processes, an idea that has since been explicated quite convincingly by Hunt and his associates (e.g., Hunt, Frost, & Lunneborg, 1973). Our research, however, has yet to reach this level of analysis, because I decided that a more elementary question required our prior attention, as described below.

This question is one that apparently has been at least as completely ignored by researchers directly concerned with individual differences, as have the latter by experimental psychologists. That is, we could find nobody who had seriously considered the possibility that the variance assumed to reflect individual differences might be due to differences *within,* rather than between, individuals. More specifically, given two processes or strategies, both of which could potentially be used in performing on some given experimental task, those concerned with individual differences would begin by assuming that these reflected the consistent usage of one of these alternative processes by some individuals and/or under some conditions, with the other process being employed by other individuals and/or under other conditions. At least as likely, it seemed to me, is that any given individual would be quite capable of using *both* processes or strategies. Moreover, both might well be employed in processing different individual units or items contained in the same task. Or to complicate things further, both processes could be used either simultaneously or at different stages or levels of processing the same individual item.

In trying to investigate this problem, we first had to discover some not totally unproductive way to begin, and of course found little if anything in previous research that was of any help. In my initial 1970 grant proposal, I suggested three possible approaches involving (1) development of new tasks and methodologies for assessment of the range and consistency of learning processes within and between individual learners, (2) longitudinal study of a few subjects in a large number of learning situations, and (3) addition of measures of between- and within-individual differences within experimental learning and transfer paradigms used in our ongoing research on other substantive problems.

To date, we have yet to try anything involving the second approach (although we hope to begin this type of research in the near future), and our efforts along the lines of the first approach have been largely ineffectual. The latter reflects primarily our inability to get subjects to use the various multiple rules or strategies that we were trying to build into and obtain direct measures of within these tasks, and our subjects' apparent insistence on using their own processing techniques, which our techniques were inappropriate for assessing. These difficulties in forcing subjects to use the rules and strategies we were trying to impose upon them not only impressed us with the wide range and adaptability of their available processing strategies, but, more important, convinced us that a necessary prerequisite for getting anywhere with this research would be to develop techniques for assessing the processes that our subjects preferred to employ.

Thus, such progress as we have made to date has come entirely from the third approach listed above, involving primarily the assessment of processes actually used by subjects for different individual items contained in the same tasks, in experiments directly concerned with more general processing analyses. Such an approach, of course, necessarily sublimates the "individual-differences" problems to at best secondary concerns within these experiments. As a result, we have had difficulty in convincing journal editors that our efforts to analyze and describe differences between and within individuals are important enough to merit inclusion in journal articles reporting these experiments, which in some cases have been totally unsuccessful (e.g., Pellegrino & Battig, 1974[2]).

There are several compensating advantages of this third approach, however, that have increasingly convinced us that it deserves more general usage by other investigators as well as ourselves. Perhaps most important, it focuses our research efforts upon processing analyses of phenomena of

[2] Also missing from this article due primarily to editorial pressures is any mention of the missing recency effect in the serial-position curve for naive subjects on the first trial displayed in Fig. 1, although it was through these data that we first took note of this phenomenon.

more general interest, and where we at least have some clues as to the processes actually used by subjects. At a more practical level, few if any constraints are imposed as to the types of phenomena and problems that can be investigated, with the result that these tend to be limited only by what we find interesting enough to be worth investigating. Parenthetically, it perhaps should be noted that our laboratory seems to operate most productively when I encourage students to work on problems of primary interest to them, rather than limiting them to what happens to be of major concern to me, even when my preliminary (and frequently erroneous) intuitions suggest that students' choices are unlikely to pay off. It is primarily because of such experiences that I began this chapter by objecting to premature limitations on the scope of inquiry that seem to characterize too many cognitive researchers.

In any event, the descriptions to follow of what we have learned primarily about "within-individual differences" in processing strategies or techniques cover a wide enough range of different tasks and types of processes to defy presentation under a single heading. For want of a better system, what is to follow will be divided into separate sections representing the four major types of verbal-learning tasks used in our research as well as that of many other investigators. We will begin with serial learning, wherein our evidence concerning within-individual differences at present seems most advanced, impressive, and relevant to a general understanding of the processes involved. This will be followed by a section on paired-associate learning, wherein substantial progress can also be reported, and then by a brief discussion of a recent experiment in verbal-discrimination learning. The final section will be concerned with free-recall learning and organization, wherein substantially more research has been done than with the other three tasks, but where the level and type of analyses concerned with within-individual differences have been quite different.

SERIAL LEARNING

The preceding emphases of this chapter are especially well supported by our recent research on serial learning, thus offering another reason for describing it first. Probably no problem area has been as strongly rejected by cognitive researchers as outmoded and irrelevant to their interests, despite the critical importance ascribed to sequential processing and ordering in recent cognitive conceptualizations (as illustrated by Trabasso's chapter in this volume). This undoubtedly reflects the historical role of serial learning as the research topic most strongly dominated by stimulus–response associationistic vocabularies and interpretations, to the extent that we tend to forget that it was also one of the earliest topics (e.g., Lashley, 1951) wherein the antiassociationistic views were influentially applied that since have come to typify cognitive psychology.

To minimize the likelihood that potential readers will stop at this point if we use the customary appellation of this research as concerned with variations in the "functional stimuli" used in serial learning, these instead will be referred to herein as types of processing. Although this terminological shift is not intended to convey anything substantively different from what I would mean if I labeled these "functional stimuli," it should at least reduce those extreme antibehavioristic misconceptions that seem to accompany any reference to "stimuli" (or responses) in certain quarters.

However we choose to label it, the primary purposes of the research to be described in this section were to develop and apply a more satisfactory methodology to the investigation of how serial learning takes place. The relevance of this research effort to the present concern with processing differences within individuals derives from the following rather fortuitous set of coincidences surrounding the initiation of this serial learning research, at a time when our initial attempts to develop new methods adequate for the assessment of within-individual differences were getting nowhere, and we were desperately searching for another more promising approach. Perhaps most important was James Voss' expressed interest in the summer of 1970 in doing some collaborative research, and his suggestion of applying a "probe" technique for the direct assessment of serial learning at the time each individual item was first produced correctly. Immediately thereafter, Carla Posnansky began her graduate work at Colorado, and became involved in this line of research. As will become apparent, any success in this research effort is due primarily to Posnansky's extensive accomplishments in developing and effectively using this serial probe technique experimentally.

Since detailed descriptions of this probe methodology have been provided in several places (Posnansky, Battig, & Voss, 1972; Posnansky, 1972, 1974), only a brief description focusing on the features of the technique relevant to the assessment of individual differences within and between subjects will be necessary here. The serial probe technique, similar in some respects to one used previously by Woodward and Murdock (1968; Woodward, 1970), involves presentation of a sequence of probes separately for each individual item in the list (except for the first three items) immediately following the trial on which the item was first recalled (or anticipated) correctly. By presenting probes representing the item's numerical and spatial position in the list, as well as the one or three items preceding this item in the serial order, in appropriate sequences that terminate as soon as the subject produces the correct item, it becomes possible to infer whether item recall was based upon its serial position, its preceding

TABLE 1
Mean Percentages of Items for Each Serial Probe Type
(and Probe Failure)
for Different Subjects and Conditions[a]

Subjects and conditions	Type of probe			
	Prior item	Position	3 prior item	Probe failure
College Students				
First list	41.0	25.7	10.3	23.0
Second list	45.8	27.4	11.1	15.7
Recall method	44.3	27.3	7.8	20.6
Anticipation	37.9	24.1	12.5	25.5
Children				
Experiment 1	54.2	21.9	10.2	13.8
Experiment 2	59.0	23.7	12.0	5.3
Grade 2	48.0	23.0	20.0	9.0
Grade 4	60.5	22.5	11.7	5.3
Grade 6	68.5	25.5	4.2	1.7

[a] From Posnansky (1972, 1974).

item, or its three preceding items. It must be noted, however, that this inference is based entirely upon which probe cue produces correct recall when it is first presented in the probe sequence, and thus does not preclude the possibility that an alternative probe type not yet presented might also have led to correct recall. In other words, if an item has already been recalled correctly upon introduction of one probe, the present technique offers no way to determine whether another as yet unpresented probe type would also have been sufficient to produce correct recall, a possibility enhanced by the multiple effectiveness of more than one probe type indicated by Posnansky's results.

Table 1 summarizes some of the more relevant findings concerning relative importance of the three basic probe types from Posnansky's (1972, 1974) major experiments, one using college students and two others with elementary school children as subjects. These data clearly demonstrate substantial variability in processing across the prior-item, position, and three-prior-item probe types, as well as indicating (especially in adults) that some items are processed in a manner different from any of the present three probe types.

This suggested multiple usage of positional along with single- and multiple-item sequential processing in serial learning is clearly indicative of substantial differences either or both between and within individual subjects. That it is primarily the latter is clearly indicated by another type of analysis evaluating how consistently a given subject's most frequently used strategy (which in most cases was sequential processing represented by the prior-item probe) was used across the several probed items. These analyses showed that percentage of items on which a given subject employed his most common strategy was only slightly above the percentage of usage of the most common prior-item probe (45.0 as compared with 41.0 with college students, whereas with children these consistency percentages were 56.5 and 69.1 as compared respectively with 54.2 and 59.0 for prior-item cues in the two experiments).

Clearly the variations in cue usage shown in Table 1 reflect primarily usage of different cues across individual list items within the same individual, rather than differences across individuals. Because several recent serial-learning theorists have proposed differential usage of sequential and positional processing as a function of serial position of the items, Posnansky's (1972, 1974) reports include detailed analyses of relative probe usage as a function of serial position. Although these showed some indication that positional probes were more effective particularly for items at the end but also near the beginning of the list, the present probe types each received relatively consistent usage across all serial positions. Thus, these probe results clearly indicate marked within-individual variations as to how different individual items in the same serial list are processed, which are not closely related to the serial positions of the items within the list.

Table 1 also shows generally unimpressive differences in relative effectiveness of these probe types as a function of age, first versus second lists, or recall versus anticipation methods. Most noteworthy is the marked reduction in instances where subjects could respond correctly to none of the three probe types in children as compared with adults, especially with the older children. This appears indicative that these "probe failures" reflect primarily greater usage by adults of more complicated processing not adequately represented by any of the present probe types, rather than to inherent inadequacies in the present probe techniques. Other differences worth noting in Table 1 are the greater relative usage of the three-prior-item probe (and corresponding reduced correct responding to the single prior-item probe) by younger than older children, and under the anticipation than the recall procedure with adults.

Although Posnansky's (1974) dissertation research does suggest some processing differences between children and adults, as noted above and in Table 1, the communalities appear far more impressive than do any differences. Even her second graders had no difficulty in learning 9-word lists to a one-errorless trial criterion in about six trials, while fourth and sixth graders learned 12-word lists in even fewer trials. As indicated in the "probe failures" column of Table 1, children actually were more successful in coping with and responding correctly to the probe task than were adults.

This impressive performance by children, although perhaps unexpected on the basis of the problems commonly encountered by verbal learning researchers attempting to study young children, should come as no surprise to those a decade ago who remember Mary Poppins and "supercalifragilisticexpialidocious" (a serial list of 14 primarily nonsense units). In any event, that children were successful in serial learning and showed probe performance quite similar to that of adults would seem to indicate that the present within-individual differences in and multiple-process nature of serial learning represent something far more basic than just belatedly acquired complications and/or flexibilities in processing shown by adult subjects.

Because of recent indications that some cognitive theorists (such as Anderson & Bower, 1973) are being inappropriately seduced by the alleged primacy of positional processing in serial-learning tasks in much the same manner as were several of us who were involved in the earlier serial-learning "functional stimulus" controversy, another important feature of the data in Table 1 may also merit explicit discussion here. This concerns the consistently far greater effectiveness of prior-item than position probes, to the extent that if one- and three-prior-item probes are pooled together as representative of sequential processing, the latter becomes more than twice as effective as positional processing.

This prevalence of sequential over positional processing is of course not inconsistent with a substantial body of recent research, as summarized, for example, by Bewley (1972). It is therefore to be hoped that cognitive researchers will not follow the Anderson and Bower (1973) precedent of relying upon such as Ebenholtz' (1972) very one-sided evaluation favoring positional processing as the primary factor in serial learning, which fails even to acknowledge the existence of most of the strong evidence contrary to his position.

These analyses and conclusions, however, should not be interpreted as arguing against the importance of positional processing in serial learning, merely because this appears not to be as widely used as sequential processing. Clearly positional processing accounts for 20–25% of the present probed recalls (which probably is an underestimate because it excludes the first three items wherein positional processing may well be most predominant). Nonetheless, as indicated by Table 1, percentages of correct responses to positional probes remained far more consistent across those major variables evaluated in Posnansky's (1972, 1974) experiments. Thus, there is little reason to expect that positional processing would ever become the predominant mode of processing in serial learning.

In concluding this section, it seems clear that processing of materials to be learned in serial order is a complex multiprocess affair, such that a given individual subject makes use of both single- and multiple-item sequential processing as well as positional processing, and probably also more complex types of processing such as subjectively determined groupings and hierarchical structures. It therefore seems essential that future theoretical attempts to account for serial learning and ordering phenomena take full cognizance of the evidence summarized herein. Among other things, this argues strongly that past unsuccessful efforts to account for serial learning in terms of simple sequential and/or positional "functional stimuli" or processes (see, e.g., Bewley, 1972) have to be inadequate and inconclusive. To quote Posnansky (1972), "Since individual subjects use more than one (and often all) of the three types of functional stimuli when learning a serial list, previous research attempts to determine the functional stimulus could hardly have produced anything other than contradictory findings [p. 192]." For present purposes, however, the important point is that several types of processing (at least, at the level analyzed herein and presumably at any other level as well) clearly play significant roles in serial learning, and that the typical individual subject will make multiple use of most if not all of these during the course of learning a single serial list or task.

PAIRED-ASSOCIATE LEARNING

Some of our recent research concerned with the analysis of processes in paired-associate learning and memory has also yielded some useful information concerning differences between and within individuals. Although these findings have generally been quite consistent with those emerging from our research on serial learning, as described in the preceding section, the levels and types of process analyses have been completely different in the paired-associate research. Consequently, it is appropriate to begin with a brief description of the principal bases and purposes of this research, and of the processes of primary concern therein.

Both for conceptual and pragmatic reasons, this paired-associate research has been primarily concerned with processing at the relatively molar level of how the two members of a given individual paired-associate pair are connected or associated together. Our approach has followed very closely that advocated so effectively by Paivio (1971), emphasizing imagery as distinguished from (as well as related to) the verbal types of processing which had been the traditional emphasis of most previous researchers and/or theorists concerned with learning and memory of verbal materials.

Paivio's approach seemed to us to offer a particularly promising frame-work within which to evaluate the existence and magnitude of within-individual differences for the following reasons. Perhaps most important is that his "dual coding hypothesis" is relatively unique among influential theories in this general area in its heavy emphasis upon the existence of entirely different ways in which subjects can process any given item or pair. That is, a fundamental part of Paivio's conceptualization involves the applicability of either or both imaginal and verbal types of processing particularly for high-imagery paired-associate materials. In addition, Paivio's research program on imagery has actually included a direct concern with individual differences. In common with other verbal learning researchers showing any interest in individual differences, however, Paivio limits himself entirely to consistent between-individual differences, and does not consider the possible significance of the within-individual variations in how a given type of pair may be processed that are of particular interest to us.

Although imaginal and verbal types of processing thus seemed a natural and obvious direction for our research to explore, the extent to which this has become focal in our laboratory during the past few years reflects primarily its substantial interest particularly as a thesis topic to some of our students. In particular, Michele Mondani is primarily responsible not only for our first experiment in this area (Mondani & Battig, 1973), but also for a doctoral dissertation representing far and away our most extensive investigation of individual-difference factors (Mondani, 1973). More recently, Shu-in Huang and Kay Barrow have also done Master's theses concerned with imagery, with another just completed experiment by Huang also providing some corroborative information on within-individual differences described in this section.

Except for Mondani's (1973) dissertation, however, none of the aforementioned experiments included a primary concern with within-individual differences, and all of these experiments to date have focused upon more general substantive questions concerning possible differences between imaginal and verbal types of processing. Moreover, with the exception of Barrow's demonstration that pleasantness is an effective variable totally independent of imagery in paired-associate learning and memory, all these imagery experiments have been at least partially concerned with a single general issue. This is Paivio's (1971) suggested compromise resolution to the old "associative-symmetry" controversy, such that imaginal processing is in parallel and thus produces equivalent "symmetrical" associations in both directions, while verbal processing takes place sequentially and thus can be unidirectional or asymmetrical. Even our efforts to evaluate directly this hypothesis, however, got us into an issue primarily at the level of how to measure associative directionality which can be interpreted as arguing for substantial within-individual variations, and thus will be described briefly before getting into data and analyses more directly concerned with this latter point.

As reported elsewhere (Mondani & Battig, 1973), we found that the customary comparisons used to evaluate associative symmetry between correct responses in forward (stimulus–response) and backward (response–stimulus) recall tests produced significant although not impressively large differences in support of Paivio's (1971) hypothesis. Since we had obtained both forward and backward recall measures from each subject for each pair, however, we were also able to evaluate associative directionality in terms of numbers of instances where correct responses were given in either the forward or backward direction but not both, which we have labeled *unidirectional* (as contrasted with bidirectional) recall or responses. Such an evaluation of asymmetrical or directional processing seems entirely consistent with Paivio's actual statement of this hypothesis (1971, p. 278), which makes no explicit mention of its limitation to instances where associations are in the forward but not backward direction (although his discussion clearly implies the predominance of the former in cases of verbal or auditory–motor sequential processing).

Irrespective of its consistency with Paivio's hypothesis, however, the important point for present purposes is that the Mondani and Battig (1973) evidence for greater symmetry with concrete than abstract word pairs was far more impressive for differences in unidirectional than in relative forward–backward recall. This indicates that despite the forward directional requirement of the present paired-associate task, at least some abstract pairs nonetheless were processed more in the backward than the forward direction. Even stronger support for this contention has subsequently emerged from Huang's experiments, especially her thesis, which included bidirectional (presentation of all pairs in both directions) as well as the typical unidirectional learning conditions, wherein she obtained significant concrete–abstract differences only for the unidirectional response measure. Thus, we appear to have stumbled upon another potentially important type of within-individual difference in paired-associate tasks, such that a given individual subject may process some pairs in a given list in a backward rather than the required forward direction (especially if these are abstract pairs).

Unfortunately, it was not until after we had found the Mondani-Battig results with this unidirectional recall measure to be replicated even more strongly in Huang's data, that we realized the importance of analyzing the consistency across individual items in the strategies reported postexperimentally by subjects, as had been done in Posnansky's (1972, 1974) serial-probe experiments described in the previous section. Consequently, such analyses came only after the Mondani and Battig (1973) article had been published, and thus are reported herein for the first time.

As described previously (Mondani & Battig, 1973), all subjects learned three nonoverlapping 20-pair lists, respectively representing concrete, abstract, and mixed (10 concrete and 10 abstract) types of pairs. Subsequently they were asked to provide written descriptions individually for each pair of what they had thought of while learning that pair. These reports were classified into six classes or types of strategies labelled as imagery, sentences, associations or meanings, repetition, other (sound, phonetic), and nothing (with other and nothing being combined for purposes of the present analyses). Following Posnansky (1972, 1974), the number of pairs for which a given subject's most frequently reported strategy had been used was tabulated separately for each subject and list (with separate tabulations also for the concrete and abstract pairs in the mixed list).

In support of the consistency results reported in the previous section, this analysis also revealed that even under conditions where only pairs of the same type (concrete or abstract) are included, subjects typically report using different strategies for different individual pairs within the same list. This was particularly true of the concrete pairs, wherein Paivio has contended that either imaginal or verbal processing can be used, and our results showed closely comparable overall frequencies of reported usage of imaginal as compared with verbal (combined sentence and association or meaning) types of processing. More specifically, with the unmixed concrete list the mean percentage of the 20 pairs for which subjects reported using their preferred strategy was only 57.35%, increasing to 63.96% for the concrete pairs in the mixed list. Even for abstract pairs, the corresponding percentages of preferred strategy usage were only 67.70% within the abstract list, with a more substantial increase to 82.08% within the mixed list. These increased consistencies within the mixed list containing pairs of both types could be due to practice effects, since the mixed list was always the last to be learned. Nonetheless, the present results offer no support whatever for an explanation of these inconsistencies as reflecting the heterogeneity of the types of pairs included in the same list.

Even stronger evidence for the importance of within-individual differences as to types of processes or strategies employed in learning different individual pairs in the same list is provided by the fact that only one of the 48 subjects in this experiment reported the same strategy for all pairs of the same type (concrete or abstract) across both unmixed and mixed lists. Moreover, a maximum of only five of these 48 subjects even showed complete consistency across all pairs of the same type within any single list. At least under the conditions of this experiment, consistent use of a single processing strategy for an entire list of items was clearly the exception rather than the rule.

In addition to the foregoing evidence for within-individual differences, this experiment also showed substantial between-individual differences, such that all types or classes of strategies were reported as predominant by at least one subject, with the single unsurprising exception that nobody reported most frequent usage of imagery with abstract pairs. Moreover, the most commonly reported strategy (imagery and sentences for concrete and abstract pairs, respectively) occurred for only about half of the 48 subjects, with a maximum of 25 reporting imagery as predominant for concrete pairs in the mixed list.

Since the previous Mondani and Battig (1973) report covers the largely ineffectual analytic efforts directed toward the assessment of relationships of actual performance to type(s) of learning strategies reported, no effort will be made to review these findings again here. Worth noting, however, are the significant positive correlations found between recall performance on abstract pairs and reported usage of sentence strategies. Since this relationship was most impressive within the final mixed list, it was interpreted as suggesting that "a major characteristic of efficient 'verbal learners' may be their greater ability to shift appropriately from an old less efficient to a new more appropriate strategy during the course of learning" (Mondani & Battig, 1973, p. 407).

The latter suggestion that flexibility or adaptability to requirements of the learning tasks may be the individual-difference variable most importantly related to performance has come also from others of our recent paired-associate experiments (e.g., Rogers & Battig, 1972). However, this not only constitutes little beyond a restatement of the obvious, but was also the major conclusion emerging from my little-known foray into problem-solving research using a "word-formation" task (Battig, 1957) years before I published my first verbal-learning paper. Thus, it can hardly be cited as an important advance in our understanding of individual differences in verbal learning and/or memory abilities, although it perhaps may merit more serious consideration by others concerned with this general problem. It does, however, offer a possible rationale as to why subjects in verbal learning and memory experiments display so much variability in processes or strategies used for different items within the same task, as clearly demonstrated by the analyses reported herein.

Similar analyses to those reported above have also been conducted within Huang's recently completed experiment, wherein postexperimental verbal reports of type(s) of strategies used for each of the 24 pairs in the list were also obtained. This experiment differed from Mondani and Battig (1973) in several ways, most notably its inclusion of (1) mixed concrete–abstract and abstract–concrete word pairs in addition to the previously used concrete–concrete and abstract–abstract pairs; (2) equal subsets of pairs within each list representing high intrapair compatibility rela-

TABLE 2

Mean Percentage Consistencies of Use of Most Frequent
Strategy for Types of Paris Varying in
Imagery and Intrapair Compatibility

Intrapair compatibility	Imagery condition				
	Concrete–concrete	Concrete–abstract	Abstract–concrete	Abstract–abstract	Total
High	56.94	47.92	46.53	68.06	54.86
Low	24.31	27.78	34.03	33.33	29.86
Total	44.06	37.85	40.28	50.70	42.36

tionships (e.g., army–soldier, power–wealth) and minimal relationships between the words constituting a given pair (e.g., money–body, first–dense);
(3) a higher learning criterion of 20/24 correct pairs in a single trial
(which was the same for all imagery conditions); and (4) only one of
the four combinations of the concrete and/or abstract word pairs constituting the single list learned by each subject.

Presented in Table 2 are the mean percentages of reported usage of
subjects' predominant strategies separately for each of the four combinations of concrete and/or abstract word pairs, and for high and low intrapair
compatibility. These results show even less within-individual consistency
than did the Mondani-Battig comparisons, with only the concrete–concrete
and abstract–abstract high-compatibility pairs showing as much as 50%
usage of the predominant strategy (these figures being virtually identical
to the 57.35 and 67.70% for unmixed concrete and abstract pairs of low
compatibility used by Mondani and Battig). These consistencies, however,
are lowered to less than 35% for low-compatibility pairs included in the
same list with an equivalent number of high-compatibility pairs. Moreover,
the high-compatibility pairs show significantly reduced strategy consistencies for pairs constituted of one concrete and one abstract word (concrete–abstract and abstract–concrete). Thus, the large within-individual
variations found in the Mondani–Battig data are shown to be if anything
underestimated, as compared with what is found with low-compatibility
pairs contained in lists also including high-compatibility pairs, or even with
highly compatible concrete–abstract or abstract–concrete word pairs.

This section will be concluded by a preliminary report of some of the
more relevant results from Mondani's (1973) dissertation, a full report
of which is presently being written up for publication. This differed from

the previously described research in that mediational strategies for each pair were actually produced in writing during each pair presentation for study, using the production technique of Paivio and Foth (1970). Moreover, direct comparisons were made between *Free* conditions where subjects were completely free to choose between imaginal (picture) and verbal (sentence) types of strategies, as compared with being forced by the experimenter to use a specified type of strategy for each individual pair on the first two study trials. Half of the subjects under forced conditions were required to use the same type of mediator on both trials for each pair, whereas the remaining subjects were required to use a different type of strategy on the two trials for each pair, designated respectively as *Stay* and *Shift* conditions. Each of these forced subjects was required to use pictures for half of the pairs on each trial, and sentences for the other half. After these two study trials under Free, Stay, and Shift conditions, all subjects were given first a paired-associate recall and then a pair recognition test, followed by another study trial always under Free conditions and then a second series of recall and recognition tests.

Other variables in this experiment besides the Free, Stay, and Shift mediational strategy conditions included incidental and intentional learning instructions on the first two trials (with the third free trial necessarily being under intentional conditions), and lists constituted entirely from either concrete or abstract word pairs. To make an imaginal strategy feasible with abstract pairs, all pairs were always constructed from related words which could potentially be imaged together (e.g., HISTORY–EVENT, LAW–HEARING) and pretested to insure that subjects could in fact produce both images and sentences for each pair. Finally, because the original lists of 20 pairs proved to be far too easy to be sensitive to any differences between the foregoing variables, these were modified so that equal halves of the 20 pairs represented double-function (each word appearing as a stimulus in one pair and a response term in another pair) and single-function pair types. Despite its belated addition for practical reasons, this latter variable nonetheless produced particularly interesting results (another bit of support for my previous argument herein against premature limitations on the scope of inquiry).

Although only picture and sentence types of strategies were possible under the present conditions, and all pairs were of the high compatibility shown in Table 2 to produce more consistent strategy usage, Mondani's Free subjects nonetheless showed substantial inconsistencies in their usage of these strategies, with only one out of 40 subjects showing complete consistency over all pairs across all three trials. The percentage of pairs on which a given subject's favored strategy was used under Free conditions was only 76.3% on the first trial, increasing to 81.8% and 85.9% on the second and third trials. These consistency measures were virtually identical for single-function (82.75%) and double-function pairs (81.25%), and only slightly higher for abstract (83.4%) than concrete pair lists (79.2%). However, the greater consistency under incidental (85.9%) than intentional learning instructions (76.7%) nearly reached statistical significance at $p < .05$.

Also of interest in Mondani's results was the prevalence of sentences over pictures as the preferred strategy even with concrete pairs, for which only five of the 20 subjects used more pictures than sentences. Moreover, final-trial consistencies were significantly less for the forced (79.4%) than the free group (85.9%). On this third trial, the forced Stay and Shift groups additionally showed significantly greater consistencies on double-function (81.63%) than single-function pairs (77.13%), as well as following the preliminary intentional (82.75%) than incidental instructional conditions (76%), in sharp contrast with the greater Free-group incidental consistencies noted above. Clearly, giving subjects the freedom to choose their own strategies after two forced trials reduces their consistency of usage of any particular type of strategy, particularly with single- rather than double-function pairs and when instructions to learn the pairs were not given until just before the final study trial.

In addition to the foregoing analyses concerned with consistencies in usage of picture and sentence types of strategies, Mondani's data also showed substantial changes across trials in the particular mediator of a given type that was used for a particular pair. Under Free conditions, such within-type shifts across the first two trials were actually slightly more common (43.25%) than were repetitions of the same mediator (36.6%), and the latter were only slightly more frequent (46.1%) than were shifts (42.4%) under Stay conditions. On the third trial after the first recall and recognition test, however, Stay conditions produced substantially fewer within-type shifts (23.1%) than repetitions (35.9%), but still more shifts between picture and sentence types (41%). Shift conditions, however, yielded a preponderance of within-type shifts (56.1%) as contrasted with strategy repetitions (39.6%), and Free conditions resulted in nearly as many within-type shifts (44.6%) as repetitions (49.6%). Such within-type shifts were especially frequent within abstract lists, wherein the third-trial percentage was 45.4% as compared with 37.1% repetitions. Thus, there clearly were substantial changes within subjects from trial to trial in the particular mediational strategies that were produced under the present experimental conditions.

Such correlational analyses as have been completed to date on Mondani's data provide at best very little evidence of any sizeable or consistent relationships between type(s) and variations in mediational strategies used by subjects, and their actual recall or recognition performance. This appears partially attributable to the frequency with which subjects employed less effective strategies, instead of alternative strategies which were demonstrably more effective for learning a given type of pair. In particular, the present double-function abstract pairs (which proved to be most difficult to learn) yielded fewer errors attributable to their double functionality if picture rather than sentence strategies were employed. Despite this, subjects learning such pairs predominantly rejected picture mediators, and shifted to the use instead of sentence mediators.

In conclusion, the paired-associate analyses reported herein extend the findings of substantial within-individual variations in processes employed for different items in the same list to encompass paired-associate as well as serial learning, and more global cognitive types of pairwise processing strategies (imaginal as compared with verbal). They also demonstrate that evidence of within-individual differences of comparable magnitudes emerges from diverse methodologies involving (1) assessment of processes through probes given immediately after an item has been learned, (2) postexperimental reports of strategies used for individual items, and (3) actual production of mediators during the time that the materials are being studied and/or processed. Thus, it should be redundant to reiterate that the differences within individuals in type(s) of processing strategies used for different individual items within the same list are sufficiently general and pervasive that they can continue to be ignored by present-day theorists and researchers only at great risk.

VERBAL-DISCRIMINATION LEARNING

Within-subject variations of comparable types and magnitudes to those described in the two previous sections on serial and paired-associate learning also have emerged from a single recently completed experiment in verbal-discrimination learning. This experiment respresents a follow-up to one Carla Posnansky and I had run previously to evaluate and compare the effects of differences in imagery and intrapair association value of the words constituting verbal-discrimination pairs in mixed as compared with unmixed lists. Because of the unexpected results of this initial experiment, we were forced into an attempted differential processing interpretation that was weakened by our failure to obtain direct measures of how the various types of pairs had actually been processed.

Consequently, we decided to replicate the basic conditions of the first experiment, but with a postexperimental assessment procedure similar to that introduced by Rowe and Paivio (1971). This required each subject to indicate separately for each of the 24 individual pairs which of six types of methods or strategies had been used in learning that pair (single imagery, compound imagery, verbal association, compound sentence, repetition, or "other").

The results showed an overall average of only 57.4% consistency of reported usage of whatever was the most common strategy used by each subject for pairs representing any one of the four pair types (all possible combinations of high and low imagery with high and low intrapair associations). These percentage consistency measures were relatively unaffected by whether or not pairs differing in imagery and/or association value were included in the same list, but were somewhat higher (64.3%) for pairs that were low both in imagery and association value than for any of the other three pair types (57.2% or below).

Repetition was the predominantly reported strategy for all types of pairs except for those high both in imagery and association value (where compound imagery was most common), and for high-imagery, low-association-value pairs in lists containing also pairs low in both imagery and association value (where single imagery was most frequent). However, in lists consisting entirely of one pair type only two out of 40 subjects reported the same strategy for all 24 pairs. Even in lists mixed as to pair type, there were only 6 instances out of a total of 120 where a subject was 100% consistent across all 6 or 12 pairs of a particular type, and only one of 50 subjects in these mixed-list conditions reported the same strategy for all pairs within this list. So once again we find that substantial variations in reported strategies for different pairs of exactly the same type are predominant in verbal-discrimination learning under the present conditions, just as was the case for serial and paired-associate learning as described in the preceding sections.

FREE-RECALL LEARNING

We have not applied the types of analyses described in the preceding three sections in any of our substantial number of experiments using free-recall tasks for a very simple reason. This is the difficulty of specifying within such tasks what the "functional" units are that are learned or processed by subjects. Unlike serial, paired-associate, and/or verbal-discrimination tasks, there has been general agreement among free-recall researchers that the individual item or word often does not represent the subjective unit wherein processing takes place. Moreover, we have substantial evidence to indicate that the number, type(s), and composition of these functional units may change systematically across trials as well as depending upon types of items and presentation conditions (e.g., Pellegrino & Battig, 1974; Chapman et al., 1974).

Consequently, our free-recall research efforts in which particularly James Pellegrino as well as Patricia Lauer and Gilles Einstein have been the primary student contributors, have been focused primarily on the analysis and understanding of the organizational processes presumably responsible for this high diversity in the functional units that are actually processed by subjects in free-recall tasks. We hope soon to be in a position to begin to probe more directly the processes actually used by subjects at the level of these functional units, but our knowledge about the latter still falls short of enabling us to embark productively upon such an endeavor.

Probably our major accomplishment to date has been to develop techniques adequate for the direct specification and comparison of the roles played by the several principal bases for organization as reflected in free-recall output sequences. The first and most basic contribution here has been Pellegrino's (1971) development of general techniques for assessing output consistencies in units containing more than two items which are not necessarily recalled in the same order on successive trials. Such types of measures have subsequently been extended to provide similar indices of category clustering, input–output order consistencies (including organization based on primacy and recency of item presentation), organization based upon prior recall of newly learned items, and consistencies between recall and overt-rehearsal sequences. Detailed reports of these analyses are published elsewhere (Pellegrino & Battig, 1972, 1974; Einstein, Pellegrino, Mondani, & Battig, 1974; Chapman et al., 1974). Thus, only a few highlights of this research especially relevant to the existence and significance of between- and within-individual differences will be described here.

Probably the most important finding that has been consistent throughout this research, and is presented most completely and convincingly in Pellegrino and Battig (1974), is the evidence for systematic shifts in the relative importance of the several aforementioned bases for organization across successive trials on the same list within the same subjects (which is also illustrated in Fig. 1). More specifically, subjects typically begin by recalling items primarily in their serial presentation order on the first trial, followed by the increasing predominance of recency and priority (prior recall of newly learned items) strategies on middle trials, with substantial development of higher-order "subjective organization" only on later trials after most items had been learned. With categorized lists and/or a fixed serial order across trials, the latter develops earlier and the recency and priority strategies on intermediate trials are correspondingly less extensive. Moreover, under the typical free-recall conditions with unrelated words and unsystematically varied serial orders across trials, recency and priority are extended to later trials whereas subjective organization is reduced.

Although the organizational changes across trials described above were sufficiently consistent across subjects to override any individual differences, the latter were nonetheless present in considerable magnitude in the Pellegrino and Battig (1974) data. Across the several conditions of this experiment, different individual subjects could be found who showed either high primacy or recency either with or without substantial input–output or output–output recall consistencies. For example, with a categorized list in a completely constant serial order, there was one subject who consistently recalled the list in its serial order (totally ignoring category-based organization) but another whose recall was totally unrelated to input order and until the final trials showed only moderate output–output consistencies. As another example, with unrelated lists in a constant serial order, there were two subjects who were closely comparable in all respects except that one consistently recalled the last recency items first (except for the first trial) while another always recalled the initial items first.

A number of correlational analyses were carried out within these free-recall experiments, which typically produced substantially stronger relationships between amount and type of organization and recall performance than have typified our research using other types of verbal learning tasks. Since these are complex and inconsistent enough to defy a meaningful brief description, and they are included in the published reports of these experiments, no effort will be made to repeat this information here.

Instead, this section will be concluded with a description of our limited and relatively unsuccessful attempts to apply another type of technique for the assessment of individual difference variables, which thus far has been employed only in two major free-recall experiments. This involves preceding the actual experimental task by a "pretest" designed to assess the extent to which each individual subject makes use of some particular process(es) potentially relevant to performance on the task. Our first effort in this direction dates back to 1970, when we were just starting to investigate individual-difference factors, in Lauer's thesis concerned with the relative importance of categorical and first-letter communalities within subsets of words upon free-recall performance and organization (Lauer & Battig, 1972).

All subjects in this experiment first were given a pretest list of 25 words representing all possible combinations of five taxonomic categories (professions, dwellings, weapons, fruits, and metals) with five initial letters (A, C, M, P, and S). They were asked to try to discover two ways in which these words could be grouped, and to list their two sets of groupings separately on the work sheet, which contained these 25 words in an order that maximally separated words from the same conceptual and first-letter categories. Subsequently, subjects were asked to recall these words, before performing on the nonoverlapping free-recall task that constituted the basic part of this experiment.

Information from this pretest about individual differences was severely limited because taxonomic organization was so much more powerful than first-letter organization, with the result that subjects rarely used the latter at all unless forced to do so by their experimental conditions. In any event, those few subjects who made substantial use of alphabetical organization during pretest recall did show significantly reduced recall performance as compared with subjects who did not, and the subsequent major free recall list likewise showed recall performance to be negatively related to first-letter organization but positively related to taxonomic organization. So although this pretest offered little if any useful new information about individual differences, it still seemed to be worth exploring further.

Consequently, we decided to try a different pretest designed explicitly to assess taxonomic organization in the Pellegrino and Battig (1974) experiment. This pretest was adapted from the Loftus and Scheff (1971) categorization technique, whereby subjects were initially presented each of the individual words included in their subsequent free-recall list, and given 10 sec to write as many category labels appropriate to that word as they could. Because this pretest familiarization with the list words could well influence subjects' subsequent free-recall learning and organization thereof, we made pretesting one of the manipulated variables in the experiment, such that equal halves of the subjects in each group did and did not first undergo this categorization pretest.

This experimental manipulation of pretesting conditions indicated that pretesting on the list words significantly facilitated free-recall performance only on the first two trials, and only on the middle and final items in the presentation order such that serial-position differences were markedly reduced. Pretesting affected organization only in that smaller-size organizational units were reduced as compared with no pretest, primarily on the first two trials and for input–output organization. Moreover, pretesting produced greater priority of recall of newly learned items. Thus, the effects of the pretest were clearly large enough to indicate that it cannot be used without materially affecting performance on the subsequent free-recall task, although this may be primarily or entirely because the same words were used on both tasks.

External pressures to eliminate most of the foregoing information about the pretest variable from the published report of this experiment (Pellegrino & Battig, 1974) caused me to agree with considerable reluctance to do so. Thus, that article omitted completely any mention of the correlational analyses of numbers (and repetitions across words) of different category labels on the pretest as related to subsequent recall performance and organization. These findings therefore will be described briefly here, wherein they are more relevant to the major emphases of this chapter, and particularly to the point made in the earlier section on paired-associate learning indicating flexibility or adaptability to the requirements of the particular task to be a particularly important individual-difference variable in verbal tasks.

Although total numbers of category responses produced during the pretest appeared almost totally unrelated to subsequent free-recall organization of these words, repetitions of the same category responses across unrelated (but not categorized) words proved to be significantly negatively correlated with subjective or output–output organization. With fixed presentation orders, such negative relationships were consistent across all trials, whereas with varied presentation orders they reached significance only on the final two trials. Categorized word lists, however, yielded quite different correlational results, showing pretest category repetitions to be positively correlated with categorical clustering across all trials with fixed but not with varied presentation orders.

If we interpret category repetitions as an index of lack of flexibility in a subject's cognitive structure(s), the foregoing rather complicated set of correlational findings may simply be telling us that such flexibility is a positive determinant of subjective organization of unrelated words, but is negatively related to organization of categorized word lists which contain a built-in strong categorical structure. Again reverting to our much earlier verbal problem-solving research, this appears entirely consistent with my conclusion therein that "the ability to vary one's approach according to the requirements of the problem may be associated with problem-solving efficiency" (Battig, 1957, p. 104). Thus, little if anything new concerning individual differences has emerged from our use of pretest measures in free-recall experiments, and the potential for bias and contamination as a consequence of pretesting appears sufficient so that at present we have no plans for further usage of this type of methodology.

In concluding this section, it appears that despite the usage of quite different approaches to the evaluation of between- and within-individual differences in our free-recall experiments, the results thereof seem most indicative of the centrality of variations in the usage of multiple processing techniques within a given individual subject as a function of trials as well as learning materials and procedures. Thus, our case is further strengthened for within-individual variations in type(s) of processing strategies as being important enough to require serious consideration in most if not all areas of current cognitive information-processing research.

GENERAL CONCLUSIONS

The most consistent finding throughout the research reported herein on within-individual differences is that whenever we have looked for them, we have never failed to find them in considerable magnitude. They occur irrespective of the type of verbal learning task employed, or the types and levels of processes examined therein. We find them whether we try to assess them at the time the individual is actually studying the materials, immediately after these have first been responded to correctly, or through some type of postexperimental inquiry. Variations within individuals appear across different types of learning materials, different items of the same general type, and different trials on the same individual item or pair. In short, whatever the complications they may present for the cognitive researcher or theorist, we have to date been able to identify no task or conditions whatever where the typical individual subject will use only one type of processing consistently for different items of a particular type either within or across successive trials.

So what does this mean for the future of cognitive research? Most importantly it clearly tells us that any successful theoretical efforts must necessarily be multiprocess in nature. Most present models of cognitive process and structure are fundamentally insufficient because they offer only a single type of theoretical account presumed to be applicable to all of the phenomena encompassed by the theory. With only occasional exceptions, even the possibility that basically different types of processing may be used for exactly the same type(s) of materials under identical conditions appears not to have been considered explicitly by cognitive (or any other) researchers.

The clear implication for cognitive theorizing, that follows from the widespread evidence for substantial within-individual processing differences described in this chapter, can be characterized as follows. No matter what the theory, it is likely that there will be some individuals who will behave in such a way as to offer convincing support for it, but other individuals who will not. Likewise there will be some experimental procedures and conditions wherein substantial support for the theory will be forthcoming, but others that will be contradictory to any theory under consideration. More important, any given individual will provide evidence consistent with the theory for some items or instances of a given type, but not for other items of this type. It even appears that a given individual may process a given item as predicted by the theory at one point in time, but not at some other time. Or put another way, no matter where or how it is evaluated, any theory or model may well be both entirely correct and totally wrong, depending upon what type(s) of processing the particular subject happens to be using for a given item within a particular task.

The foregoing should not be taken to imply that there is no hope for the future of cognitive research. Models already exist that contain the necessary machinery to cope with within-individual process variations (e.g.,

Anderson & Bower, 1973), but these remain to be developed in a manner appropriate to the evaluation of within-individual differences. Clearly we must face up to the task of determining to what extent these within-individual differences are lawfully related to identifiable variables, and thus can be accounted for in some systematic fashion. This certainly will not be easy, but we already have made substantial progress in the development of methodologies appropriate to this task, and there appears to be no feasible alternative except to get to work on it. Of course, we could decide to give up on cognitive research as too complicated, as has been not uncommon throughout the history of psychological research on other complex problems, but that would be diametrically opposed to our intent in investigating within-individual process variations. All we are trying to do is to find out whether such phenomena are important enough to require our serious consideration, and the answer to that question is clearly a resounding yes!

One final point for speculation concerns why the human organism should predominantly use multiple processes, rather than sticking with a particular mode of processing consistently? Our research suggests one possible line of explanation, although it falls far short of convincingly demonstrating the validity thereof. This is in terms of the potential role played by multiple types of processing in extending the capacity and reducing overload on the system, in much the same manner as has been attributed to, for example, "chunking" of individual items into larger functional units. One common characteristic of our experimental tasks, and of most others used in cognitive research, is that the subject is forced to process quite a large number of items, enough so that usage of different types of processing on different individual items or subsets thereof could well be useful as a means of encoding, which serves to reduce interference between these items and thereby enhances the functional capacity of memory. Consistent with this speculation is our repeated finding that it is those subjects who are most flexible or adaptable to changing their processing strategies to fit the requirements of the particular task or individual items contained therein that perform best on these tasks. Thus, whatever the complications they may produce for the researcher trying to understand cognitive processes, within-individual variations therein may well serve to increase substantially the efficiency and capacity of the cognitive systems and/or structures used by individuals in performing on the tasks required of them.

ACKNOWLEDGMENTS

This is publication No. 48 of the Institute for the Study of Intellectual Behavior, University of Colorado, and is based primarily upon research supported by Research Grants GB-25433 and GB-34077X from the National Science Foundation. Major contributions to the research described herein were made particularly by three of the author's former students, Drs. Michele S. Mondani, James W. Pellegrino, and Carla J. Posnansky, as well as by present students Terry R. Barrett, N. Kay Barrow, Gilles O. Einstein, Shu-in Huang, and Patricia A. Lauer.

REFERENCES

Anderson, J. R., & Bower, G. H. *Human associative memory*. Washington, D.C.: Winston, 1973.

Battig, W. F. Some factors affecting performance on a word-formation problem. *Journal of Experimental Psychology*, 1957, **54**, 96–104.

Battig, W. F. Parsimony in psychology. *Psychological Reports*, 1962, **11**, 555–572.

Battig, W. F. Intratask interference as a source of facilitation in transfer and retention. In R. F. Thompson & J. F. Voss (Eds.), *Topics in learning and performance*. New York: Academic Press, 1972. Pp. 131–159.

Bewley, W. L. The functional stimulus in serial learning. In R. F. Thompson & J. F. Voss (Eds.), *Topics in learning and performance*. New York: Academic Press, 1972. Pp. 187–214.

Chapman, C., Pellegrino, J. W., & Battig, W. F. Input sequence and grouping in free recall learning and organization. *American Journal of Psychology*, 1974, **87**, in press.

Clark, H. H. The language-as-fixed-effect fallacy: A critique of language statistics in psychological research. *Journal of Verbal Learning and Verbal Behavior*, 1973, **12**, 335–359.

Ebenholtz, S. M. Serial learning and dimensional organization. In G. H. Bower (Ed.), *The psychology of learning and motivation*. Vol. 5. New York: Academic Press, 1972. Pp. 267–314.

Einstein, G. O., Pellegrino, J. W., Mondani, M. S., & Battig, W. F. Free recall performance as a function of overt rehearsal frequency. *Journal of Experimental Psychology*, 1974, **103**, 440–449.

Hasher, L. Position effects in free recall. *American Journal of Psychology*, 1973, **86**, 389–397.

Hunt, E., Frost, N., & Lunneborg, C. Individual differences in cognition: A new approach to intelligence. In G. H. Bower (Ed.), *The psychology of learning and motivation*. Vol. 7. New York: Academic Press, 1973.

Lashley, K. S. The problem of serial order in behavior. In L. A. Jeffress (Ed.), *Cerebral mechanisms in behavior*. New York: Wiley, 1951. Pp. 112–136.

Lauer, P. A., & Battig, W. F. Free recall of taxonomically and alphabetically organized word lists as a function of storage and retrieval cues. *Journal of Verbal Learning and Verbal Behavior*, 1972, **11**, 333–342.

Loftus, E. F., & Scheff, R. W. Categorization norms for fifty representative instances. *Journal of Experimental Psychology*, 1971, **91**, 355–364. (Monograph)

Mondani, M. S. Changes in use and effectiveness of imaginal and verbal mediators as a function of learning materials and instructions. Unpublished doctoral dissertation, University of Colorado, 1973.

Mondani, M. S., & Battig, W. F. Imaginal and verbal mnemonics as related to paired-associate learning and directionality of associations. *Journal of Verbal Learning and Verbal Behavior*, 1973, **12**, 401–408.

Murdock, B. B., Jr. The serial-position effect of free recall. *Journal of Experimental Psychology*, 1962, **64**, 482–488.

Murdock, B. B., Jr. Short-term retention of single paired associates. *Journal of Experimental Psychology*, 1963, **65**, 433–443.

Murdock, B. B., Jr. *Human memory: Theory and data.* Hillsdale, New Jersey: Lawrence Erlbaum Associates, 1974.

Norman, D. A. *Models of human memory.* New York: Academic Press, 1970.

Norman, D. A. The computer in your briefcase. *Behavior Research Methods and Instrumentation*, 1973, **5**, 83–87.

Paivio, A. *Imagery and verbal processes.* New York: Holt, Rinehart & Winston, 1971.

Paivio, A., & Foth, D. Imaginal and verbal mediators and noun concreteness in paired-associate learning: The elusive interaction. *Journal of Verbal Learning and Verbal Behavior*, 1970, **9**, 384–390.

Pellegrino, J. W. A general measure of organization in free recall for variable unit size and internal sequential consistency. *Behavior Research Methods and Instrumentation*, 1971, **3**, 241–246.

Pellegrino, J. W. Organizational attributes in list acquisition and retention. *Journal of Experimental Psychology*, 1974, **103**, 230–239.

Pellegrino, J. W., & Battig, W. F. Effects of semantic list structure differences in free recall. *Psychonomic Science*, 1972, **29**, 65–67.

Pellegrino, J. W., & Battig, W. F. Relationships among higher order organizaitonal measures and free recall. *Journal of Experimental Psychology*, 1974, **102**, 463–472.

Posnansky, C. J. Probing for the functional stimuli in serial learning. *Journal of Experimental Psychology*, 1972, **96**, 184–193.

Posnansky, C. J. An investigation of serial learning and retention processes in children. *Journal of Experimental Child Psychology*, 1974, **18**, 127–148.

Posnansky, C. J., Battig, W. F., & Voss, J. F. A new probe technique for the identification of serial learning processes. *Behavior Research Methods and Instrumentation*, 1972, **4**, 129–132.

Restle, F. Coding of nonsense vs. the detection of patterns. *Memory & Cognition*, 1973, **1**, 499–502.

Rogers, J. L., & Battig, W. F. Effect of amount of prior free-recall learning on paired-associate transfer. *Journal of Experimental Psychology*, 1972, **92**, 373–377.

Rowe, E. J., & Paivio, A. Word frequency and imagery effects in verbal discrimination learning. *Journal of Experimental Psychology*, 1971, **88**, 319–326.

Solso, R. L. (Ed.) *Contemporary issues in cognitive psychology: The Loyola symposium.* Washington, D.C.: Winston, 1973.

Underwood, B. J. Forgetting. *Scientific American*, 1964, **210**, 91–99.

Wing, J. F., & Thomson, B. P. Primacy-recency effects in free recall. *Proceedings of the 73rd Annual Convention of the American Psychological Association*, 1965, 57–58.

Woodward, A. E. Continuity between serial memory and serial learning. *Journal of Experimental Psychology*, 1970, **85**, 90–94.

Woodward, A. E., & Murdock, B. B., Jr. Positional and sequential probes in serial learning. *Canadian Journal of Psychology*, 1968, **22**, 131–138.

8

CONSCIOUSNESS: RESPECTABLE, USEFUL, AND PROBABLY NECESSARY

George Mandler
University of California, San Diego

I welcome this opportunity to act as *amicus curiae* on behalf of one of the central concepts of cognitive theory—consciousness. Another statement, however imperfect, may be useful to undo the harm that consciousness suffered during fifty years (approximately 1910 to 1960) in the oubliettes of behaviorism. It is additionally needed because so many of us have a history of collaboration with the keepers of the jail and to speak freely of the need for a concept of consciousness still ties the tongues of not a few cognitive psychologists.

I hope to show that consciousness is respectable in the sense that it has become the object of serious and impressive experimental research; it is useful because it avoids circumlocutions as well as constructions, such as short-term memory and focal attention, that are more easily addressed by an appeal to consciousness as part of the apparatus of cognition; and it is probably necessary because it serves to tie together many disparate but obviously related mental concepts, including attention, perceptual elaboration, and limited capacity notions.

THE REVIVAL OF CONSCIOUSNESS

The history of consciousness is strewn with philosophical, theological, and pedestrian semantic debris; the history of unconscious concepts has, by inherited contrast, suffered similarly. Having made the decision to recall the concept of consciousness to service, it is useful to start baldly with the distinction between conscious and unconscious processes. I do so with some sense of embarrassment vis-à-vis the contributions of others. Freud, in particular, has contributed much to the finer distinctions among shadings of the unconscious. However, if we are to make a fresh start within the experimental investigation of consciousness, we shall probably also have to rediscover these distinctions within the new realm of discourse. For present purposes the distinction among preconscious, preattentitive, primary processes, and unconscious are premature. It suffices to distinguish those processes that are accessible to consciousness and those that are not. We shall note that Neisser, for example, assumes that the product of preattentitive (preconscious) processes are holistic, vague, and unelaborated. It is not at all certain that current research on reading and language production and comprehension will bear out this assumption. Miller (1962), following Freud, set a distinct boundary between preconscious and unconscious processes, implying that the latter are inaccessible. The evidence suggests that accessibility of unconscious processes shades from the readily accessible to the inaccessible. In what follows I shall have repeated occasions to use the various different terms of consciousness as they occur in context. However, the intent, from my vantage point, is—at this time—to distinguish only between the contents of consciousness and unconscious processes. The latter include these that are not available to conscious experience, be they feature analyzers, deep syntactic structures, affective appraisals, computational processes, language production systems, action system of many kinds, or whatever.

Much of what we know and say today about consciousness has been known and said by others before us, in the past hundred years by Wundt, the Würzburgers, Lashley, and many others. I only want to summarize here the high points of a modern view of consciousness as it has developed, or rather revived, during the development of a disciplined and highly structured new view of cognitive psychology.

The development of this viewpoint was tentative, as one would expect it to be against the background of the established dogma of behaviorism in the United States. In 1962, George A. Miller, one of the prophets of the new mentalism of the 1970s, started off his discussion of consciousness by suggesting that we "ban the word [consciousness] for a decade or two until we can develop more precise terms for the several uses which 'consciousness' now obscures [p. 25]." More than a decade has passed and we seem to be doing as prescribed without any intervening banishment. Most current thought on the topic was, as a matter of fact, well summarized by Miller.

Following William James, Miller stressed the selective functions of consciousness—the notion that only some part of all the possible experiences that are available at any point in time and space is selected for conscious expression. Miller also noted what we will stress again later, namely that "the selective function of consciousness and the limited span of attention are complementary ways of talking about the same thing [p. 49]." And, with Lashley, he reminds us that "[it] is the *result* of thinking, not the process of thinking that appears spontaneously in consciousness [p. 56]."

It is well to keep that last statement in mind, because it is an important part of the new mentalism, of modern cognitive psychology, of the human information processing approach. "Thinking" or cognition or information processing for the psychologist is a term that refers to theoretical processes, complex transformations on internal and external objects, events, and relations. These processes are not conscious; they are, in the first instance, constructions generated by the psychological theorist. By definition the conscious individual cannot be conscious—in any acceptable sense of the term—of theoretical processes involved to explain his actions. In the same sense, the term *mind* refers to the totality of theoretical processes that are ascribed to the individual. To accept this point of view avoids the solipsisms and sophisms of philosophies of mind.

The important advances in our excursions into consciousness must come through the usual interplay of empirical investigation and imaginative theory. The functions of consciousness are slowly being investigated and the beginnings of theoretical integrations of the concept of consciousness into cognitive models are emerging.

As a prolegomena to theory and better understanding of private knowledge, Natsoulas (1970) has examined the content of "introspective awareness." Although he does not present us with any conclusions, Natsoulas has provided a partial list of the problems that psychologists and philosophers encounter when they want to deal directly with these contents. We have, in general, not gone far beyond such a listing since it is obviously too early to argue for a specific model of private experience or consciousness—it does not exist, not even in the broadest outline. However, some of the necessary first steps have been taken to build some of the components that such a theory must accommodate. At the same time, psychologists are becoming sensitive to the need for a critical evaluation of common sense and philosophical notions about consciousness. Many phenomenologically oriented philosophers and psychologists are still wedded to a Wundtian idea that psychology should be the study of conscious mental events, whereas unconscious (mental) mechanisms are to be left to some other world such as physiology.

In modern theory, one of the most influential books, Neisser's *Cognitive psychology* (1967), is strangely circumspect about the problem of consciousness. Was it too early then to talk openly about the Imperial Psychology's clothes? Not that Neisser avoids the subject—he clearly talks about consciousness though one comes upon it in circuitous ways. In his final chapter Neisser tackles the relationship between iconic memory and consciousness; he comes to consciousness via the attentive processes in visual perception and thence to memory. He notes that the constructive processes in memory "themselves never appear in consciousness, their products do" (Neisser, 1967, p. 301). And in rational problem solving the executive processes "share many of the properties of focal attention in vision and of analysis-by-synthesis in hearing [p. 302]." Noting the distinction between primary and secondary processes (see also Garner, 1974), he asserts that rational and therefore presumably conscious thought operates as a secondary process—elaborating often unconscious, probably unlearned primary process operations in the Freudian sense. The products of the primary process alone, preceding consciousness and attention, are only "fleetingly" conscious unless elaborated by secondary processes. By implication the elaboration by secondary processes is what produces fully conscious events. By tentative implication primary processes are "like" preattentive processes in vision and hearing, the conscious processes are "like" focal attention. The secondary processes elaborate and select. We shall hear similar arguments from Posner and Shallice shortly. However, Neisser's contribution to the study of consciousness is in his discussion of preattentive processes and focal attention. When we turn to these processes, the clues from the final chapter open up a major contribution to the theory of consciousness. I apologize for the talmudic exegesis before coming to this point, but it does, I believe, illustrate the gingerly and skitterish way in which psychologists, up until very recently, have permitted themselves to talk about consciousness.

In Chapter 4, Neisser starts by taking the term "focal attention" straight from Schachtel (1959), a psychoanalyst whose history has not prevented a frank discussion of these forbidden topics. If you will, in what follows, permit the free translation of "attention" into consciousness, you will note why Neisser's contribution is important.

First, "attention . . . is an allotment of analysing mechanisms to a limited region of the field [p. 88]." In other words, consciousness is a limited capacity mechanism. On the other hand, preattentive processes, that is, processes that are not in attention but precede it, have the function of forming the objects of attention. Some of these preattentive processes (the primary processes of the final chapter) are innate. Many actions are under such preattentive control. Walking, driving and many others are "made without the use of focal attention [p. 92]." There are processes that run off outside of consciousness (unconsciously) while others do not: "More permanent storage of information requires an act of attention [p.

93]." Transfer to permanent storage requires consciousness. As apparently do some decisional processes. Harking back to another era, "the processes of attentive synthesis often lead to an internal verbalization [p. 103]." We often talk about the contents of consciousness.

In brief summary, then, Neisser's interpretation is in concord with much modern speculation about the role of consciousness. It is a limited-capacity mechanism, often synonymous with the notion of attention. The processes that make up consciousness are secondary processes, secondary in elaboration and time to primary, preattentive processes that are unconscious, sometimes innate and often the result of automatization. Consciousness is an area that permits decision processes of some types to operate, where the outputs from different systems may be integrated, and where transfers to long term storage systems take place.[1]

Among the important attempts specifically to incorporate awareness notions into contemporary cognitive theory, Shallice (1972) has argued for the necessity of studying phenomena of consciousness if for no other reasons than that there exist a number of concepts in current psychological theory that require the implicit or explicit postulation of some consciousness mechanisms. Among these are the postulation of conscious rehearsal in primary memory and the frequent equation of attention and consciousness (see, e.g., Mandler, 1974); others are methodological, as in experiments which require subjects to monitor private experiences (e.g., Sperling, 1967). In his theoretical development Shallice argues for an isomorphism between phenomenal experience and information-processing concepts. Specifically he develops in some detail the notion that the content of consciousness can be identified with a selector input that determines first what particular action system will become dominant, and, second, sets the goal for the action system.

Another approach, derived from problems of attention, has been mounted by Posner and his associates. They have focused on those mental operations which are characterized by interference effects or in other words, by a limited capacity mechanism which may be related to the "subjective experience of the unity of consciousness" (Posner & Keele, 1970). By studying the processes that interfere one with another and showing how limited capacity is assigned to different functions, one can "connect the operations of this limited capacity mechanism to intention, awareness, storage and other traditional functions of consciousness" (Posner & Keele, 1970).

Both Shallice and Posner deny any attempt to specify a mechanism of

---

[1] In a personal communication Neisser has indicated that he does *not* believe that consciousness is a useful concept for a stage of mental processing and that his avoidance of the concept has been deliberate rather than unconscious.

consciousness or private experience that is coextensive with common language uses of the concept. The attempt is, so to speak, from the bottom up, trying to specify with some rigor some of the mechanisms that may be isomorphic with consciousness and learn more about their operation within theoretical systems.

Posner and Boise (1971) in their ingenious study of the components of attention have noted that "attention in the sense of central processing capacity is related to mental operations of which we are conscious, such as rehearsing or choosing a response . . . [p. 407]." Conversely, they noted that the contact between input and long-term memory is not part of this attentional (conscious) process, and in fact, the conscious component of the processing mechanism occurs, as a result, rather late in the sequence of "attentional" events.

Posner and Klein (1973) have summarized this interpretation of the use of "consciousness" within the context of experimental investigations. They suggest that it refers to operations such as rehearsal or priming that require access to a limited capacity system. Although the conscious processes are usually late in the processing sequence and follow "habitual" or preattentive encoding, they are flexible and may occur early under time pressure. Also, in a bridge to other similar views these processes are seen as setting up required responses "without depending upon the actual release of the motor program" (Posner & Klein, 1973, p. 34).[2]

The recurrent theme of readiness for and choices among actions has also been invoked by Festinger et al. (1967). They have suggested that, in part, the conscious aspect of some perceptual phenomena depends on preprogrammed sets of efferent (action) programs that a particular input puts into a state of readiness for immediate use.

The limited evidence from the experimental studies as well as from informed theory points to extensive preconscious processing which is, under some circumstances, followed by conscious processing. Much of behavior, however, is automatic and does not require conscious attention. Typically such actions are called habitual, automatic, or preprogrammed. Typically also they tend to be ballistic in form and run off with little variation.

It is far beyond the scope of this paper to discuss the problem of automaticity and the kinds of structures that occur automatically in contrast with those that require attentional, conscious work. In reference to response sequences—or actions systems as I prefer to call them now—I have discussed the notion that cognitive structures or symbolic analogues of discrete actions systems develop during overlearning (Mandler, 1962). It is well known in the integration that occurs during skill learning, for example, driving. I allude to the probem here simply to note that much of "learned"

---

[2] Posner has extended these views most instructively in this volume.

behavior and actions can be integrated into new central structures, which then become functional units represented cognitively as single chunks and manipulable consciously in the constructions of new plans and new actions. At the action side of consciousness relatively little work has been done to describe how the limited capacity system is used in integrating representation of overt actions into larger units. Just as consciousness deals with chunks of incoming information, so must it deal with chunks of efferent actions.

In the arena of perceptual events the topic of automatic processing or encoding confronts us repeatedly as the converse of conscious processing. Posner and Warren (1972) have discussed the variety of such automatic processes involved in coding mechanisms. Generally what is automatic is very much like what Neisser calls preattentive, parallel processes. In contrast, Posner and Warren note that conscious processes are more variable and that conscious constructions provide the new mnemonic devices needed to store material in long term representations. It is here that we face the insistence that new encodings for long term storage depend on a functioning conscious system.

LaBerge (1974) has addressed the issue of automatization in a novel way—asking not only about the relation between automatization and attention, but also about the process whereby certain coding systems become automatized. He concludes that during postcriteria performance there occurs a gradual withdrawal of attention from the particular components of a task. Under this process of decreasing attention (consciousness?) the part of the processing involved in coding the particular perceptual material is being made automatic. Eventually much of the perceptual processing can "be carried out automatically, that is prior to the focussing of attention on the processing." LaBerge also implies that this postcriterial, overlearning process produces the integration of new, higher order units or chunks. He is obviously addressing the development of preattentive processes, and also the functional unity and autonomy of these units, particularly when he notes that often "one cannot prevent the processing once it starts." There is a useful similarity between these propositions about the development of automatic encodings and my previous discussion on the representation of overlearned action patterns.

We have here a possible distinction between two kinds of unconscious (preattentive, primary) processes. Those that are innate or preprogrammed or dependent primarily on some structural characteristics of the organism; those that, though initially conscious, become, by some process such as overlearning, automatic and unconscious. Although the latter are easily brought into consciousness it is also intuitively likely that this might be difficult, if not impossible, for the former.

It seems to be agreed that consciousness is a clearing house that enters into the flow of processing under certain specifiable, but at present still not specified, conditions. Certain processes operate on conscious information generaged by nonconscious (preattentive) processes. However, it bears repeating that there are important nonconscious postattentive processes that are operative subsequent to information generated by conscious processes. Many of these involve actions (which my older colleagues in psychology have inadequately called "behavior") that operate often without conscious attention. These actions and their representation systems are as complex and as finely structured as the preattentive perceptual systems. Unfortunately, partly by accidents of history, cognitive psychologists tend to be somewhat careless about specifying how organisms come to act. However, the hierarchic, structural view of action has an honorable and creative history. I would draw your attention to the most recent and important exposition of this view proposed by Gallistel (1974).

In summary, current thought has concentrated on the consciousness of the perceptual or encoding side of information flow. Some attention has been given to its functions in memory storage and retrieval. Much is still to be done at the output side. Current notions have focussed on the functions of consciousness as selecting encoded sensory information and preparing choices among appropriate action or response alternatives. Many other functions of consciousness still await detailed analyses or may be incorrect assignments to this particular system.

CONSCIOUS CONTENTS AND PROCESSES

My own interest in consciousness arose in part out of a long-term project on the relation between mind and emotion, and more immediately out of some recent considerations of the limits of attention and consciousness (Mandler, 1974). In that presentation I argued for a direct translation between focal attention and consciousness. I suggested that some of the so-called short-term memory phenomena are best assigned to the limited capacity mechanism of consciousness and that the limitations of that single conscious system in terms of dimensional analyses may serve as a bridging concept for George A. Miller's puzzle about the similar limitations he noted for both short term memory and absolute judgment.

The limited capacity of "short-term" memory, the immediate memory span, as well as the limitation in absolute judgment task to some seven values or categories, can usefully be assigned to the limited capacity of conscious content. The limitation refers to the limited number of values on any single dimension (be it physical, acoustic, semantic or whatever) that can be kept within the conscious field.

The main points of the argument relevant to the present topic concern certain distinctions among the concepts of attention, consciousness and short-term memory. In the first instance, I want to restrict the concept of consciousness to events and operation within a limited capacity system, with the limitation referring to number of functional units or chunks that can be kept in consciousness at any one point in time. This concept has much in common with what has been called *focal attention*. Attentional processes are those mechanisms that deal with the selection of objects or events that occur in consciousness. Second, I want to assert a distinction between short-term memory and consciousness. The limited reach of consciousness has a respectable history, going back at least 200 years (see Mandler, 1974). However, it is not a memory system—it does not involve any retrieval. What is in the momentary field of consciousness is not remembered, it is psychologically present.

None of the foregoing denies the utility of the conception of different memory systems, whether long term, working, or operational. It is probably most reasonable to consider these different "systems" on a continuum of depth of processing, as proposed by Craik and Lockhart (1972). Different types of analyses require different processing depths and different processing times. But the information that, so to speak, can be "read off" the contents of consciousness is not memorial as such. Depth of processing determines how and what can be remembered. If processing time is short, or encoding "superficial," and if the code decays rapidly, it will be short; if processing is extended or if encoding is "complex," information adequate for long term retrieval or reconstruction will be stored. Within certain limits, the storage processes—at whatever depths—can only take place on conscious material; conversely, retrieval usually implies retrieval into the conscious field. However, the memory *mechanisms* and the contents of consciousness are two very distinct kinds of mental events.

Posner, who has contributed much to recent investigations of the structure of the limited capacity system of conscious events, suggested as early as 1967 that "operational" and "short-term" memories should be considered as different systems. The operating systems may vary à la Craik and Lockhart in their time course and their products, but they should not be confounded with the immediately given content of consciousness. The confounding of these two systems in early investigations and theories is understandable, given the very brief time course of some memory processes and the rapid changes in the focus of consciousness (attention). However, within consciousness many different kinds of operations may be performed—consciousness is not limited in the complexity of the information it draws on, only in the amount. Consciousness is modality independent, and, depending on the task facing the individual, many involve very complex and abstract operations. In general then, I will prefer to use the term *consciousness* to focal attention (although they may have to be interchanged) but differentiate strictly between consciousness and short-term memory processes, which deal with storage and retrieval (cf. Craik & Lockhart, 1972).

I do not intend to invoke a separate processing stage or system to accommodate the concept of consciousness. Consciousness, in the first instance, refers to a state of a structure. Certain operations and processes act on these structures which constitute conscious content. Cognitive structures, or schemas, may, under certain circumstances, become conscious, that is, enter the conscious state; when they do not, they are by definition unconscious. Limited capacity refers to the number of such unitary structures that may be conscious at any one point in time. There is no separate system, however, that contains the conscious contents. Rather conscious structures differ from others in that certain operations, such as storage, retrieval, and choice (see below), may be performed on them.

It is beyond the intent of this chapter to discuss the origins of consciousness. It is a characteristic of the organism that certain structures can become conscious, but it is a function of human interactions with the environment that determines which structures do in fact become conscious. Piaget (1953) has discussed extensively these interactions and stressed the transactions among perceptions of the self, the environment, and the development of consciousness. The development of consciousness is not, from my view, some magical burgeoning of internal awareness but rather dependent on specific organism–environment interactions. These involve, to a large part, the internalizations of actions (see also Mandler, 1962). More important, however, the conditions of personal and social development determine what can and what cannot be represented in consciousness. Depending on these conditions, different individuals, groups, and cultures will have different conscious contents—different social and cultural consciousness, different realities. However, the primary purpose of the present chapter is to discuss how these conscious contents operate, not what they are or how they might be established.

Finally, conscious contents can be spoken about. I shall discuss later the lack of any one-to-one correspondence between consciousness and language, but this should not obscure the important relationship between private conscious events and language. It is by the use of the latter that we primarily communicate our own private view of reality, and it is in turn by the use of language that, in the adult at least, many conscious structures are manipulated and changed.

With these primarily definitional problems out of the way, I want to address first some of the ancient and admittedly complex and very special problems that the concept of consciousness poses for any psychological theory. I shall not propose any radical solutions but rather that the problem of the private datum can be approached reasonably and analytically, rather than frantically or mystically. Next, I want to sketch some of the possible uses of consciousness in cognitive theory, followed by some suggestions for the adaptive functions of consciousness. Finally, in the last section, I want to address the broader problem of the flow of consciousness and its relations to limited capacity, with particular attention to special states of consciousness.

Consciousness:
A Special Problem for Mental Theory

The individual experiences feelings, attitudes, thoughts, images, ideas, beliefs and other contents of consciousness, but these contents are not accessible to anyone else. Briefly stated, that is the special problem facing psychologists. There are no evasions possible. It is not possible to build a phenomenal psychology that is shared. A *theory* of phenomena may be shared but the private consciousness, once expressed in words, gestures, or in any way externalized is necessarily a transformation of the private experience. No theory external to the individual, that is, one that treats the organism as the object of observation, description, and explanation, can at the same time be a theory that uses private experiences, feelings, and attitudes as data (see Gray, 1971). Events and objects in consciousness can never be available to the observer without having been restructured, reinterpreted, and appropriately modified by structures that are specific to the individual doing the reporting. These structures may even be specific to the kinds of experiences, feelings, and attitudes that are reported. The content of consciousness, as philosophers and psychologists have told us for centuries, is not directly available as a datum in psychology.

How then are we to deal with the contents of consciousness? Can the perennial problem of private datum and public inference at least be stated concisely in order to indicate the magnitude of the problem and possible directions for future development?

We are faced with a phenomenon that might be called the uncertainty principle of psychology. Adrian (1966) for example, noted: "The particular difficulty that the questioner may influence the answer recalls the uncertainty principle in physics, which limits the knowledge we can gain about any individual particle [p. 242]."

There are two related problems in the study of consciousness. The first is more fundamental than the question that Adrian addresses. It is not only the case that the nature of the interrogation may affect the reported content of consciousness, but, more basically, the act of examination itself may affect the individually observable conscious contents. This conjecture is reasonable even at the level of processing capacity, since the conscious act of interrogating one's conscious content must occupy some part of the limited capacity. As a result the available content is altered by the process of interrogation.

Given that the act of interrogation changes the content of consciousness, the source of that inquiry becomes of secondary importance. The second problem to be faced is the fact that the contents of consciousness are not simply reproducible by some one-to-one mapping into verbal report. Even if these contents were always couched in language, which they surely are not, some theory of transmission would be required. As a result we are faced with the individual's observation of the contents of his consciousness on the one hand, and on the other with the psychologist's theoretical inference about those contents, based on whatever data, including introspective reports, are available. Both of these knowledges may be used as relevant to the construction of a psychology of cognition, though it may in principle be impossible to determine, in any exact sense, the relation between these two interpretations of consciousness.

Private experiences are important aspects of the fully functioning mental system. It is possible to get transformed reports about those events and it should be possible to develop appropriate theories that relate contents of consciousness, their transformations, and their report. However, it is not possible to build a theory that makes direct predictions about private experience since the outcome of those predictions cannot be inspected by the psychologist/observer.

This position does admit the development of private theories, by the individual—about himself. To the individual his experience *is* a datum, and as a consequence his theories about his own structures are, within limits, testable by direct experience. These individual, personal theories of the self are both pervasive and significant in explaining human action, but they cannot, without peril, be generalized to others or to the race as a whole (see Mandler & Mandler, 1974).

We note, therefore, that people's reports about their experiences, their behavior and their actions are very frequently, and may always be, fictions or theories about those events. However, it is only those reports that are available to us. Even the introspecting individual who says that his experience conforms to certain predicted aspects is making statements about derived correspondences resulting from mental transformations. Indirect scientific predictions about experiences are possible, but the test of those predictions is one step removed from the actual experiences, as are all predictions about the values of theoretical entities. If the behaviorist revolution, with all the negative influences it has had on the development of a fully theoretical psychology, has had one positive effect, it is this realization that even the complete acceptance of the importance of private experience does not thereby make it a possible end point for a scientific theory.

Some Uses of Consciousness

One of the important processes in which consciousness intervenes is in the testing of potential action choices and the appraisal of the situational givens. The relation between choice and consciousness, as we have seen, has motivated much of the recent research. The analysis of situations and appraisal of the environment, on the other hand, goes on mainly at the nonconscious level, which will be discussed in greater detail later. In any case, the outcomes of these analyses may be available in consciousness and the effect of potential actions on the present situation can be estimated and evaluated. Consciousness is a field in which potential choices are given the opportunity to be evaluated against potential outcomes. This delay produces reflective consideration and may in fact be responsible for greater "freedom" of action (see Mandler & Kessen, 1974).

Much of what is often considered to be the meaning of the common sense term "thinking" is what takes place in consciousness when the outcome of different structures, and even in some cases their composition, are evaluated and decisions are made. It is possible for the cognitive system to call for the testing of specific outcomes while temporarily blocking output from the system as a whole, to compare the consequences of different outcomes and to choose outcomes which produce one or another desired alternative. The notion of choice would be entirely within the context of modern choice theories (e.g., Luce, 1959; Tversky, 1972), and the choice itself, of course, would go through some "unconscious" cognitive structures before a "decision" is made. However, consciousness permits the comparison and inspection of various outcomes so that the choice systems which may in fact be "unconscious" can operate on these alternatives.

It appears that one of the functions of the consciousness mechanism is to bring two or more (previously unconscious) mental contents into direct juxtaposition. The phenomenal experience of choice, as a matter of fact, seems to demand exactly such an occurrence. We usually do not refer to a choice unless there is a "conscious" choice between two or more alternatives. The attribute of "choosing" is applied to a decision process between two items on a menu, several possible television programs, or two or more careers, but not to the decision process that decides whether to start walking across a street with the right or left foot, whether to scratch one's ear with a finger or the ball of the hand, or whether to take one or two sips from a cup of hot coffee. I would argue that the former cases involve the necessity of deciding between two or more choices presented to a choice mechanism at the same time, whereas the latter involve only the situationally predominant action. However, these cases may be transferred to the conscious choice state if and when certain conditions of possible consequences and immediate adaptability supervene. Given a hot cup of coffee so labeled, I may "choose" to take one very small sip, or I may "choose" to start with my right foot in a 100-meter race, given certain information on its advantage to my time in the distance. In other words, consequences and social relevance determine which choices are conscious. More important, however, the mechanisms of choice (including the various theories of choice behavior) are not conscious. It is presumably the operation of these mechanisms on material in the conscious state that give the epiphenomenal experience of free choice, the appearance that someone (the agent) is doing the choosing. He or she is, but by the operation of unconscious mechanisms, which therefore give the appearance of voluntary choice among the conscious alternatives. Mental mechanisms "choose" among both conscious and unconscious events.

It might be noted that the so-called mentalism that philosophers talk about often refers to these "thought" processes, the outcome of unconscious mental processes that are evaluated in the "conscious" system. However, to mistake conscious mental events for much more complex nonconscious structures is surely in error and leads to the kind of naive mentalism shown in the works of some philosophers of the mind.

Evaluative activities often act on conscious content, but evaluative activities also may take place at an "unconscious" level. Clearly many cognitive structures that lead to certain outcomes and the anticipation of these outcomes (a scanning ahead of a particular structure) may switch the system from one structure to another. However, these changes are not available to inspection, and are only available to indirect inspection by the process of hypothesizing their constitution and testing these hypotheses.

If the only difference between these two kinds of evaluative actions and choices is that some take place in consciousness and others do not, the end result would be a rather puny achievement for so imposing a mechanism as consciousness. I would propose initially two arguments for the distinction between conscious and unconscious evaluations and choices. First, many relational processes operate primarily, if not exclusively, on conscious content. I have already indicated this particular argument in the case of simple choice. However, there are other relational operators that seem to do their work primarily on conscious content. In addition to choice, these include evaluation, comparison, grouping, categorization, and serial ordering. In short, practically all novel relational orderings require that the events to be ordered must be simultaneously present in the conscious field. This applies to choice, as well as to relational concepts stored in memory, for example. Needless to say, there are many relational judg-ments that do not require conscious comparisons. To say that "a dog is an animal" makes uses of established structures and does not require a new relational operation. However, to say that "Rex looks like a cross between a dachshund and a spaniel" would presumably require conscious juxtaposition. Once relations (by they superordinate, subordinate, oppo-sites, or whatever) have been established and stored, subsequent evalua-tions are frequently unconscious.

The second argument for the importance of consciousness suggests that choice and other processes that operate on conscious content are dependent on those structures that can enter the conscious state. Only those structures that can become conscious can be subjected to choice activities. Thus, situ-ational and social relevance determine the content of consciousness and the "ideational" operations that can be performed on the individual's reality.

The Possible Adaptive Functions of Consciousness

One may look at some of these uses also from the point of view of their adaptive significance. Probably because of the unpleasantness of the past 50 or 60 years relatively little has been said about the adaptive func-tions of consciousness. Miller (1962) has described them in general terms and Gray (1971) has called for a more intensive look at the evolutionary significance of conscious systems. In general, however, American psycholo-gists particularly have shied away from looking at the functional signifi-cance of consciousness. This is at least surprising, since we are faced with a characteristic of the human species that is without exception. Given the rather weak evidence that psychologists have accepted as indicants for the evolutionary significance of such vague concepts as aggression and intelli-gence, why avoid a phenomenon as indisputably characteristic of the spe-cies as consciousness? Partly, the answer lies in the behaviorist dogma that consciousness is epiphenomenal and, by implication, has no adaptive sig-nificance. It is in part in opposition to that dogma that I want to suggest some possible directions in which speculations and investigations about the adaptiveness of consciousness might go.

There is a variety of functions that the consciousness system may per-form, all of which may be said to have evolutionary significance and all of which have varying degrees of evidence for their utility and theoretical significance:

1. The first, and most widely addressed function of consciousness con-siders it as a scratch pad for the choice and selection of actions systems. Decisions are made often on the basis of possible outcomes, desirable out-

comes, and appropriateness of various actions to environmental demands. Such a description comes close to what is often called "covert trial and error" behavior in the neobehaviorist literature. This function permits the organism more complex considerations of action-outcome contingencies than does the simple feedback concept of reinforcement, which alters the probability of one or another set of actions. It also permits the consideration of possible actions that the organisms has never before performed, thus eliminating the overt testing of possible harmful alternatives. In this sense the process is similar to the TOTE system of Miller, Galanter, and Pribram (1960).

2. Within the same general framework as the first function, consciousness is used to modify and interrogate long-range plans, rather than immediate-action alternatives. In the hierarchy of actions and plans in which the organism engages, this slightly different function makes it possible to organize disparate action systems in the service of a higher plan. For example, in planning a drive to some new destination one might consider subsets of the route, or, in devising a new recipe, the creative chef considers the interactions of several known culinary achievements. Within the same realm, consciousness is used to retrieve and consider modifications in long-range planning activities. These, in turn, might be modified in light of other evidence, either from the immediate environment or from long term storage.

3. In considering actions and plans consciousness participates in retrieval programs from long-term memory, even though these retrieval programs and strategies themselves are usually not conscious. Thus, frequently, though not always, the retrieval of information from long-term storage is initiated by relatively simple commands—in program language, rather than machine language. These may be simple instructions such as, "What is his name?" or, "Where did I read about that?" or more complex instructions, such as, "What is the relation between this situation and previous ones I have encountered?" This process has the adaptive function of permitting simple addresses to complex structures.

4. Comments on the organism's current activities occur in consciousness and use available cognitive structures to construct some storable representation of current activity. Many investigators have suggested that these new codings and representations always take place in consciousness. Such processes as mnemonic devices and storage strategies apparently require the intervention of conscious structures. Certainly many of them, such as categorization and mental images, do. Once this new organization of information is stored, it may be retrieved for a variety of important purposes.

First, in the social process consciousness provides access to the memory bank which, together with an adequate system of communication, such as human language, has tremendous benefit to cooperative social efforts. Other members of the species may receive solutions to problems, thus saving time if nothing else; they may be appraised of unsuccessful alternatives, or, more generally, participate in the cultural inheritance of the group. This process requires selection and comparison among alternatives retrieved from long-term storage, all of which apparently takes place in consciousness.

Second, both general information, as well as specific sensory inputs, may be stored in either propositional or analogue form. The rerepresentation at some future time makes possible decision processes that depend on comparisons between current and past events, and the retrieval of relevant or irrelevant information for current problem solving.

5. Another aspect that consciousness apparently permits is a "troubleshooting" function for structures normally not represented in consciousness. There are many systems that cannot be brought into consciousness, and probably most systems that analyze the environment in the first place have that characteristic. In most of these cases only the product of cognitive and mental activities are available to consciousness; among these are sensory analyzers, innate action patterns, language-production systems, and many more. In contrast, many systems are generated and built with the cooperation of conscious processes, but later become nonconscious or automatic. These latter systems may apparently be brought into consciousness, particularly when they are defective in their particular function (see also Vygotsky, 1962). We all have had experiences of automatically driving a car, typing a letter, or even handling cocktail party conversation, and being suddenly brought up short by some failure such as a defective brake, a stuck key or a "You aren't listening to me." At that time, the particular representations of actions and memories involved are brought into play in consciousness, and repair work gets under way. Thus, structures that are not species specific and general but are the result of experience can be inspected and reorganized more or less easily.

Many of these functions permit the organism to react reflectively rather than automatically, a distinction that has frequently been made between humans and lower animals. All of them permit more adaptive transactions between the organism and its environment. Also, in general, the functions of consciousness permit a focusing upon the most important and species relevant aspects of the environment. The notion that attentional mechanisms select personally relevant materials and events is commonplace in attentional research. The processes that define such relevance are generally unknown, although we can assume that an adaptive function of selection into consciousness exists. However, there remains the unexplored mystery of the processes of information reduction that select some aspect of the surround.

The need for a rapid reduction of all the sensory information available to an organism at any given point in time and space is obvious. If we were conscious of all the information available at the sensory surface, we would never escape from the confusion generated by our environment. Consciousness (or attention) is highly selective. The sensory systems themselves are, of course, selective in the first instance. The evolutionary process has generated organisms that register only a limited amount of the information available in their environment. How these limitations from the environment to the sensory surface have developed has been the subject of some biological speculations. The reduction from the sensory surface to consciousness is even more spectacular, but we have few clues for the evolutionary reason of this reduction. We know that it exists (e.g. Miller, 1956; Mandler, 1974), and attention theorists have been concerned primarily with the filtering mechanisms that reduce the sensory information to the few chunks of information that reach consciousness. However, why that number should be 5 or 6 or 7, rather than 3 or 12 is still shrouded in mystery.

THE LIMITATION OF CONSCIOUS CAPACITY AND THE FLOW OF CONSCIOUSNESS

One of the most perplexing results of experimental studies of consciousness has been the counterintuitive notion that consciousness seems to be discrete, relatively short, and quite transient. How does this contrast with consciousness in the common discourse? It seems to be continuous, flowing, extending without break throughout our waking hours, and just as flowing and continuous in our dreams. William James aptly called it "the stream of thought, of consciousness, or of subjective life." How can we reconcile these two impressions?

Before tackling that particular problem, consider the role of consciousness in our perception of time, or better, duration. For this purpose, I shall adopt the theory of time duration proposed by Ornstein (1969). This review relates the time experience to "the mechanisms of attention, coding, and storage" (Ornstein, 1969, p. 48). Ornstein's central thesis is that storage size is the basis for the construction of the duration of an interval. The notion of storage size derives directly from recent organizational theory that emphasizes the compact organization of information in memory and experience. The more different unrelated units the greater the storage size, the more highly organized the units, objects, or events are, the fewer are the units or chunks and the smaller is the storage size. As storage size of the material in consciousness increases, the duration experience lengthens. What changes storage size are increases or decreases in the amount of information received, changes in the coding or chunking of input, or, as Ornstein has shown experimentally, influencing the memory of the interval after it has passed. As Ornstein summarized in a later book (1972) "the more organized . . . the memory . . . the shorter the experience of duration [p. 87]."

Generally, then, the experience of duration (in consciousness) is one possible construction drawing on immediately pressing factors (such as attentiveness) but primarily on our stored long-term memory. Duration is constructed—first in the momentary consciousness, and second in the retrieval of events and codes that are recalled during the "construction" of a past interval. The contents of consciousness thus determine the experience of duration. Restricting these contents shortens duration, expanding them, for example, by increasing the complexity of an experience lengthens duration. Viligance, which increases expectancy of some event, lengthens duration; Ornstein uses the example of the "watched pot." On the other hand, condensing some experience into a very brief code ("I made breakfast") condenses the duration. Ornstein notes, as have others, that our Western linear mode of constructing duration is not the only mode and that present centeredness is not only possible but, in fact, the mode for other cultures than ours. The concatenation of limited conscious capacity, on the one hand, and the same consciousness serving as a vehicle for constructing experience of duration, on the other, brings us back to the disjunction between discrete consciousness and the flow of consciousness.

There is in principle no objection to constructing a flow model of consciousness out of the discrete units of attention or consciousness. The metaphor that comes to mind is a simplistic view of modern conceptions of light, which may be described either in terms of particles or in terms of waves. Again borrowing from physics, we then may metaphorically speak of the quantum of consciousness on the one hand and the flow of consciousness on the other. Another possible metaphor is that of the illusion of moving pictures that consist of individual frames. Neither metaphor probably does justice to the phenomenon, as no metaphor ever does. In particular, it is likely that instead of individual quanta or frames, the flow of consciousness frequently may involve the successive sampling of materials across a continuous retrieval of connected material from long-term storage. Such a phenomenon would depend on the retrieval strategies being used on long-term storage as well as on the nature of the material being sampled. In the case of consciousness of externally generated events, for example, somebody else's speech, the overlapping moving model may be the most appropriate, whereas in attempting the retrieval of a specific chunk of knowledge, the retrieval may be discontinuous.

Because of the limited capacity characteristics of discrete consciousness, I shall use the figure of speech of the conscious frame. We still carry with us the unsolved problem of the content of that slice of consciousness. For the time being we can only allude to the probability that it involves units or chunks of unitary aggregates of information.

Regardless of one's view of the conscious frame as sampling discrete, overlapping, or continuous elements of mental content or environmental input, our view requires a continuous interchange between long-term storage and the conscious state. In the case of an exclusively internal dialogue between the two, material is brought into consciousness and then returned to long-term storage either in essentially unchanged form or after some operations may have been performed on it while in consciousness. Thus, the memory of a friend brought into consciousness may be combined with a new insight that he resembles a recent acquaintance, and then the information is returned with the new relationship coded with it. Or information from storage is brought (within consciousness) in conjunction with new information currently being processed from the environment, for example, "Joe has grown a beard" and then returned to storage newly coded. Many experimental studies of memory require exactly this retrieval from storage and combination, in consciousness, with new information, such as that the word belongs to a particular list or category, or occurs at a particular serial position. I should note, of course, that the distinction between internal and external information is not a very clean one. Clearly, external events do not enter into consciousness as "pure" perceptions, rather they are coded and identified in terms of existing preattentive structures before they enter consciousness.

In general this position joins the long tradition of cognitive and phenomenological psychologists in asserting the importance of the role of consciousness in developing knowledge of oneself and the environment. I do not think that consciousness is primary or sufficient; it is one mode of processing. Just because some evaluation or knowledge does not enter consciousness does not permit a pejorative evaluation of such "automatic" or "unconscious" processing.

Conscious Stopping

One special reason why the view of the conscious frame is useful is that it permits a consideration of the special conditions when the flow of consciousness stops, single frames enter into consciousness, and remain there. Experimental psychologists have paid some attention to this phenomenon, as in the concept of maintaining or primary rehearsal, in which material is repeated but does not enter into long-term storage (Craik & Watkins, 1973; Woodward, Bjork, & Jongeward, 1973). However, the major source of knowledge of this phenomenon comes from esoteric psychologies and meditative methods.

The best objective presentation of these methods is once again provided by Ornstein (1972). He reviews meditation techniques dispassionately and positively. However, in reading Ornstein's description of these methods, a recurrent theme may be discerned. The achievement of the special kinds of conscious states that are claimed to occur seem to depend, without exception, on the unique attempt to stop the flow of ordinary consciousness—to concentrate on the frame, to hold it fixed in the focus of consciousness. The very difficulty of achieving the initial, apparently trivial, exercises of these techniques suggest the difficulty of stopping the flow. It requires total attention to a single, restricted set of limited thoughts or perceptions. In Zen, the exercises start with counting breaths, and then go on to concentrate on the process of breathing. Yogic meditation uses the *mantra,* "sonorous, flowing words which repeat easily." Some of the Sufi practices are seen as an "exericse for the brain based on repetition." The Christian mystic St. John of the Cross says (quoted in Ornstein, 1972): "Of all these forms and manners of knowledge the soul must strip and void itself and it must strive to lose the imaginary apprehension of them, so that there may be left in it no kind of impression of knowledge, nor trace of thought. . . . This cannot happen unless the memory can be annihilated in all its forms, . . . [pp. 119–120]." Or, as Ornstein points out, many prayers are monotonous, repetitive chants. In summary, "[The] common element in these diverse practices seems to be the active restriction of awareness to one single, unchanging process, and the withdrawal of attention from ordinary thought" (Ornstein, 1972, p. 122). Again: "The specific object used for meditation is much less important than the maintenance of the object as the single focus of awareness during a long period of time . . . [p. 122]."

I suggest that the "object of the single focus" must be no more than a frame of consciousness, that in fact it is restricted by the very limits that the limited capacity mechanism has been shown to exhibit. One could not mediate on an event that, at first, contains more than five to seven chunks. The observations that Ornstein and many others have reported suggest that it is in fact possible to stop the flow of consciousness to keep a single frame of consciousness in focus for extended periods of time. However, such an experience should in fact be a very *different* form of consciousness; the normal form is the flow. We thus become aware of this new consciousness, though only after the extensive practice it requires. However, we must also experience a very different content of consciousness. Given that the single "object" is held in consciousness, many new and different aspects of it then may be discovered.

Consider the possibility that at first any such object consists of several related qualities (or chunks). Presumably as these various attributes are related one to the other, the new relations form a more compact perception; the number of chunks, as it were, is reduced. In turn, this opens up the possibility of new chunks or attributes entering into the single frame. New relationships are discovered and again coalesce. Under these circumstances we may go through a process of structuring and restructuring, of discovering aspects of objects or events that would not normally be available during the flow of consciousness. Once this ability has been achieved, one should, in principle, be able to use the special consciousness to stop the flow of events, examine new nuances, and then continue. Thus, a limited set of attributes within a single frame is available at first; then new aspects enter and old ones drop away. The complexities of a rose, a face, or a cake "become conscious." This seems, in fact, to be taking place in what Ornstein calls the "opening up" of awareness, which follows the "turning off" phase and which provides the individual with a different state of comprehension of ongoing actions and events. Again, to quote Ornstein (1972): "The concentrative form turns off the normal mode of operation and allows a sensitivity to subtle stimuli which often go unnoticed in the normal mode. . . It also produces an *aftereffect* of 'fresh' perception when the practitioner returns to his usual surroundings [p. 136]." All I wish to add to Ornstein's insightful discussion is the possibility that modern psychology may define the process wherein this attentiveness occurs and also the processes which generate new perceptions and sensitivities. Meditative techniques provide us, in this fashion, with new insights into a mechanism that otherwise seems rather mundane and restrictive. There need not be anything mysterious about meditation, nor anything pedestrian about an information processing analysis of consciousness.

The enriching of knowledge though meditative experiences or, as we might call it, conscious stopping, should be put into the proper context of the ordinary, normal means of enriching experience. Without doubt, we enrich our experience and knowledge about the world around us without resorting to meditation. We can, without special preparation, perceive new facets about the world, about other people, even about ourselves as we gain new perspectives, new ways of structuring out experience. One of the main differences between the normal and the meditative enrichment is that the former deals with an open system; the latter deals with a closed one. Our enrichment in knowledge and appreciation of a lover, a novel, a science, an occupation occurs always in new contexts, sometimes widely different, sometimes only minutely so. However, the relationship between the object or event and ourselves is changed continuously by our mutual relations with the rest of the world. The new information, in a way, is always acquired in new contexts. What seems to distinguish this usual accretion from the meditative one is that the latter is a closed system; we are restricted to those relationships among qualities and attributes that are given in that object or situation. This restriction of possible relations presumably provides not only the illusion but possibly also the reality of depth of perception which the special experience provides. In contrast, artists and scientists, for example, apparently achieve the same depth of perception of special objects or events without the meditative experience.

Ornstein's notion that the experience of duration is constructed, based on the storage size of the cognitive structures that constitute an interval, may be applied directly to the flow and frame aspects of consciousness. In the open-system flow, time experience is constructed across frames out of cognitive structures that will, to varying degrees, occupy the capacity of the limited-capacity frame. Consider listening to a lecture on difficult, but interesting material. As the speaker proceeds, information is transmitted at a great rate, taking up the full capacity of each frame of consciousness. In Ornstein's terms, storage of information is near a maximum. As a result, the duration experience increases. In contrast, the redundant speaker makes fewer demands on each frame, the very ability to approach a difficult subject slowly and cumulatively permits us to use less of the full capacity of the frame, or, as another possibility, the capacity is filled less frequently in physical time and fewer frames are expended. In any case, the experience of duration is more extended in the former than in the latter case.

It is interesting to speculate that Ornstein's storage metaphor may be directly translated into the frame locution. Since consciousness is necessary for the transfer of information to long-term storage, complex (many chunks and relations) information requires more frames for the transfer function, as does rapidly presented information (more chunks per unit physical time). It appears that the storage metaphor is quite consistent with the frame-flow notion of consciousness. In the latter mode the construction of time depends on the sheer number of frames of consciousness activated or utilized during a specified interval. Parenthetically this position also indicates the independence of the conscious frame from physical time. The specious present, the limited-capacity mechanism, does not have a time constant. Frames are replaced under a variety of conditions, all of which seem to depend on using up their capacity, a new perceptual dimension, another class of stimulation, a sudden demand for focusing (attention), and many others will demand a shift to another content of consciousness, which is perceived as another *moment* of consciousness.

Finally, we may note the rather drastic changes in time perception that take place as a result of meditative experience. Given that the flow of frames is radically altered, one would naturally expect a similar and unusual change in duration experiences. The direction can be either way. Holding a single unit of consciousness and impeding the flow may collapse the duration experience, whereas the eventual ability to manipulate the flow of consciousness may change the usual duration experience with its apparently rather constant rate of change into a more variable ebb and flow of "short" and "long" durations. Instead of the flow of frames during normal states, during meditation the change from one conscious content to another occurs infrequently in physical time. The slow changes in perceptual structures which I suggested earlier for the meditative phase thus produce unusual duration experiences.

It is intriguing to speculate that the action of hallucinogenic or "mind-expanding" drugs has a similar locus and effect. Changes in perceptual processes coexist with changes in the experience of duration. It has been argued that these drugs often produce in the instant the experiences that meditative methods generate with extensive practice. It is possible that some drugs in fact slow the flow of conscious frames, and that some of the lasting effects of these drugs may be due to structural changes in control of the flow of consciousness.

CONCLUSION

The concept of consciousness was abandoned as a proper object of experimental study some 60 years ago. The reasons were manifold. The introspective method erred in assuming that consciousness could be made the datum of psychology or that verbal report was a royal road to its exploration. The failure of introspection both engendered behaviorism and failed to provide any viable alternatives. Others, like the Gestalt school and the French and English enclaves, successfully defended their views of the conscious organism, but had, for theoretical reasons, little grounds to mount a major analytic attack. The return of American psychology to a theory-rich as well as experimentally rigorous stance has given us the opportunity to develop the proper theoretical tools to return consciousness to its proper place in a theory of thought, mind, and actions. Most of the early steps that have been taken have been necessarily preliminary models and developments of experimental methods. My primary aim in these pages has been to try to point to the directions that these preliminary steps are taking. Granted that this has been a personal view at the current stage, it will have been successful if it generates discussion and investigation and, eventually, theory, which will define and specify the role that consciousness plays in man's transactions with his world.

ACKNOWLEDGMENTS

This chapter is part of a forthcoming book on *Mind and Emotion*. Its preparation was supported in part by grants from the National Science Foundation (GB 20798) and the National Institute of Mental Health (MH-15828). I am indebted to my students and colleagues at the Center for Human Information Processing for listening and reacting to my preliminary meanderings on the topic of consciousness. I am in great debt to my colleage Jean M. Mandler, whose patient and insightful critiques went far beyond the requirements of connubial duty. Both Ulric Neisser and C. R. Gallistel critically and creatively reacted to an earlier version—and I hope that this chapter does justice to their valuable assistance.

REFERENCES

Adrian, E. D. Consciousness. In J. C. Eccles (Ed.), *Brain and conscious experience.* New York: Springer Publ., 1966.

Craik, F. I. M., & Lockhart, R. S. Levels of processing: A framework for memory research. *Journal of Verbal Learning and Verbal Behavior,* 1972, **11,** 671–684.

Craik, F. I. M., & Watkins, M. J. The role of rehearsal in short-term memory. *Journal of Verbal Learning and Verbal Behavior,* 1973, **12,** 599–607.

Festinger, L., Burnham, C. A., Ono, H., & Bamber, D. Efference and the conscious experience of perception. *Journal of Experimental Psychology Monograph,* 1967, 74, No. 4.

Gallistel, C. R. Motivation as central organizing process: The psychophysical approach to its functional and neurophysiological analysis. In *Nebraska symposium on motivation: 1974.* Lincoln, Nebraska: University of Nebraska Press, 1974.

Garner, W. R. *The processing of information and structure.* Hillsdale, New Jersey: Lawrence Erlbaum Associates, 1974.

Gray, J. A. The mind-brain identity theory as a scientific hypothesis. *Philosophical Quarterly,* 1971, **21,** 247–252.

LaBerge, D. Acquisition of automatic processing in perceptual and associative learning. In P. M. A. Rabbitt & S. Dornic (Eds.), *Attention and performance V.* London: Academic Press, 1974.

Luce, R. D. *Individual choice behavior: A theoretical analysis.* New York: Wiley, 1959.

Mandler, G. From association to structure. *Psychological Review,* 1962, **69,** 415–427.

Mandler, G. Memory storage and retrieval: Some limits on the reach of attention and consciousness. In P. M. A. Rabbitt & S. Dornic (Eds.), *Attention and performance V.* London: Academic Press, 1974.

Mandler, G., & Kessen, W. The appearance of free will. In S. C. Brown (Ed.), *Philosophy of psychology.* London: Macmillan, 1974.

Mandler, J. M., & Mandler, G. Good guys vs. bad guys: The subject–object dichotomy. *Journal of Humanistic Psychology,* 1974, **14,** 63–87.

Miller, G. A. The magic number seven, plus or minus two: Some limits on our capacity for processing information. *Psychological Review,* 1956, **63,** 81–97.

Miller, G. A. *Psychology: The science of mental life.* New York: Harper and Row, 1962.

Miller, G. A., Galanter, E. H., & Pribram, K. *Plans and the structure of behavior.* New York: Holt, 1960.

Natsoulas, T. Concerning introspective "knowledge." *Psychological Bulletin,* 1970, **73,** 89–111.

Neisser, U. *Cognitive psychology.* New York: Appleton-Century-Crofts, 1967.

Ornstein, R. E. *On the experience of time.* Harmondsworth: Penguin, 1969.

Ornstein, R. E. *The psychology of consciousness.* San Francisco: Freeman, 1972.

Piaget, J. *The origin of intelligence in the child.* London: Routledge & Kegan Paul, 1953.

Posner, M. I. Short-term memory systems in human information processing. *Acta Psychologica,* 1967, **27,** 267–284.

Posner, M. I., & Boies, S. J. Components of attention. *Psychological Review,* 1971, **78,** 391–408.

Posner, M. I., & Keele, S. W. Time and space as measures of mental operations. Paper presented at the Annual Meeting of the American Psychological Association, 1970.

Posner, M. I., & Klein, R. M. On the functions of consciousness. In S. Kornblum (Ed.), *Attention and performance IV.* New York: Academic Press, 1973.

Posner, M. I., & Warren, R. E. Traces, concepts, and conscious constructions. In A. W. Melton & E. Martin (Eds.), *Coding processes in human memory.* Washington, D.C.: Winston, 1972.

Schachtel, E. G. *Metamorphosis.* New York: Basic Books, 1959.

Shallice, T. Dual functions of consciousness. *Psychological Review,* 1972, **79,** 383–393.

Sperling, G. Successive approximations to a model for short-term memory. *Acta Psychologica,* 1967, **27,** 285–292.

Tversky, A. Elimination by aspects: A theory of choice. *Psychological Review,* 1972, **79,** 281–299.

Vygotsky, L. S. *Thought and language.* Cambridge, Mass.: MIT Press, 1962.

Woodward, A. E., Jr., Bjork, R. A., & Jongeward, R. H., Jr. Recall and recognition as a function of primary rehearsal. *Journal of Verbal Learning and Verbal Behavior,* 1973, **12,** 608–617.

DISCUSSION: SECTIONS I AND II

POSNER: I'd like to encourage people from the audience to start off with any questions they'd like to ask members of the panel; and the panel to chime in as they like.

THEIOS: I'd like to ask Dr. Estes a question. He reviews the research done by Reicher and Wheeler and talked about his own data from this task. And in this task the subject is briefly shown a word or letter string and then he has to indicate whether one of 2 letters appeared in that work or in that string and he's cued for position. The question I have for Dr. Estes is what evidence do we have that in briefly presented words the subject even encodes the position of the letters? What I'm getting at is, in dealing with words, which you might think of as whole entities, why should letter position be important at all?

ESTES: We know that letter position *is* important because transposition errors are related in an orderly manner to distance from the probe stimulus. Why position *should be* important is a broader question. I think it's a matter of the task, in part. There could be experiments set up, I would guess, in which the letter position actually would not be relevant. One simple possibility that comes to mind is to vary the procedure of the Reicher type experiments, not as we did by using a probe, but by using a yes/no query: "Did a target letter appear anywhere in the display"? And although we have no data on it, since other things seem to fit into the orderly pattern, I would surmise that a subject could respond at that level. Processing the input information to the level of activating a character name would yield a yes/no response, presumably independently of linguistic context. If the probe includes position, then the question being put to the subject is, "What letter occurred in this position?," and he has to take together a number of sources in memory; the letter representations, any group representations that were activated, and the positional information in order to answer the joint question, which does have spatial relevance. The subject in the Reicher (1969) experiment is not asked "Which of these two letters occurred anywhere?"; he's asked, for example, "Which of these two letters occurred in position 3?" My interpretation is that the subject takes the task on faith and therefore he inhibits responding until he has collated the joint information that he has regarding identity and position to give him a basis for deciding what letter he thinks he saw in the indicated position. We could change the task and I don't see why it wouldn't be possible to set up the task so as to get responses on the basis of item without position.

THEIOS: It would seem to me that if words are recognized as patterns of letters and not letter by letter then it seems that if the experiment assumes that a word recognition is done letter by letter and if we take the position that a word is a whole entity, a pattern of characters, then the only way the subject could give you the correct response is to have him know the word and then recompute from what he knows about spelling.

BJORK: There's some evidence relevant to that matter. Wheeler (1970) took latencies in his experiment. In spite of the fact that single letters in words were better recognized than single letters by themselves, subjects were slower in the word conditions than they were in the single-letter conditions.

ESTES: They could be recomputing the spelling.

BJORK: I don't know, but something is taking a little longer time in the word case than in the single letter case.

ESTES: We could add that in the detection experiments where the differences in accuracy of identification between words, nonwords, and single letters disappears, the differences in reaction time disappear also.

MANDLER: I want to ask Bill Battig why he's upset. What theoretical position predicts the kind of consistencies you didn't find? I don't know of any. You're surprised you didn't find them, which says that somebody ought to have predicted them and I don't know who would predict them. So the first question is: Where did it say that you should have found what you didn't find? Second: I think if we're looking at cognitive processes we ought to investigate these processes. A serial list is not a cognitive process, neither is a paired associate list. In other words, if I'm interested in how people seriate I would investigate seriating rather than serial lists. We have inherited this business of looking at tasks rather than at processes, so that people go around saying, "I'm interested in paired associate learning or serial list learning." What the cognitive tradition says is, "We're interested in serial processing, visual processing, imaginal processing, etc." Then you set up a task in which you get that type of behavior or that kind of processing. Therefore, it is not at all surprising if you give them a mess of a task that you get a mess of different kinds of results. My question has two parts: first: Who would have predicted what you didn't find? and, second: Isn't it the case that cognitive theory looks at different kinds of problems than the ones you were looking at?

BATTIG: The answer to your first question is that I'm delighted to hear somebody say that because I don't see anything inherent in cognitive or any other kind of theorizing, particularly from the information-processing point of view, that would be at all inconsistent with what I was finding. However, if I look at specific theories I cannot find a single one that invokes the possibility that it works sometimes, but not others. That's just not the form and way in which the theories are stated. Maybe it's implicit in those theories that that is the case. If that's true, and if the effect of my analysis would be to make that more explicit, then my purposes are served. Now, as far as your other question is concerned, unless you were going to argue that somehow if you want to study serial processing that you don't use a task whereby subjects have to seriate, I guess I don't understand the question. You seem to be implying that if I'm studying serial learning of a list of items of some kind, that serial learning is such a mess that we can't study seriation, and that there's some other way that I can do it.

MANDLER: First, we know that all sorts of processes go into learning a list that happens to be presented serially. From a cognitive point of view a seriation process has to do with problems of serial ordering: for example, the kinds of things that Restle is doing. Then you have a theory that says that certain patterns should occur under certain circumstances; and you can set up an experiment to test a prediction from that particular theory of serial ordering. But, just because you present one item after another doesn't mean you're going to be studying seriation from a theoretical point of view. That's the confusion we have inherited: if you study a list that is presented one at a time at a one second rate you're necessarily studying serial learning. What you're in fact studying is that processes occur when items are presented in that particular order. Seriation, on the other hand, is a theoretical process that has to do with certain cognitive processes.

BATTIG: I understand that and I haven't limited studying seriation to doing it within serial learning tasks either. We have looked at the same thing in free recall tasks and find it operates quite extensively there, for example. And so if your question is that what we should be studying is the processing and not limiting it to a particular task, I could only agree. But we have to select a task to study whatever it is we're going to study, and it seems to be the real problem is to find out to what extent the processing is task dependent. The reason why we use particular tasks such as serial learning is because we do know something of the multiple types of processing that may go on in those tasks. Previously we had tried various kinds of experiments where we tried to develop our own new tasks; where we would build in particular modes of processing for our subjects to use. The main thing we found out from such experiments was that subjects didn't use what we built in to these tasks. In terms of the tasks we're using now, they are tasks wherein we felt we knew more about the processes subjects actually used, so it was a good place to start; but it's certainly not the ending point. Certainly processing should not be tied to a particular task, and we have never assumed that because a particular task is called a certain thing, that means that a particular type of processing is going on. One thing that our research has shown is that there are multiple types of processing going on in all the tasks we have worked with. Thus the question I would raise is whether there are any tasks, that anybody here has used, where you can say that the task is limited to one particular type of processing and that's all that's involved.

POSNER: Ben (Murdock), you said it isn't likely that we go back to when we were 10 years old, one episode at a time.

MURDOCK: Yes.

POSNER: It is likely, from your model, that we do it over the last 180 items in your experiment.

MURDOCK: Yes.

POSNER: Where does this model end and something else take over?

MURDOCK: That's a good question. It seems to me that if we have one process with very short lags and we have other processes with longer lags we probably have yet additional processes with much longer lags of the order of days, weeks, and years so that I can't even speculate what they are. So the answer to your question is that I simply don't know. We simply haven't gone beyond 64-item lists and lags of a couple of hundred. If somebody has the temerity to do so, let them stay with it.

ESTES: Don't you find it a little unsatisfying, Ben (Murdock), in that it would seem to require the individual to know the answer before he knows how to process? You ask him to find something in memory: if the item is very recent, he's supposed to find it by process 1; if it's a little further back, by process 2; and if it's still further back, by process 3. Unless he remembers the occurrences of the event before he begins the search, does he know which process to use?

MURDOCK: One of the models of short-term scanning that's got some supports is a model that Dave Burrows and Ron Okada (1973) have been working on where several processes go on in parallel. And they've got quite a bit of evidence to suggest that you can scan, say, for the semantic characteristics of items at the same time you're looking for the name match, for, instance. And if that's the case then several processes could go on simultaneously in our experiments and in real life.

ESTES: They wouldn't even necessarily be different processes; it could be that the same process acts on different aspects of the name.

BJORK: If you look at the first item tested, is performance in your system assumed to be a function of only the number of events intervening between the input and test of the tested item?

MURDOCK: You mean look only at the first item tested regardless what its serial position was?

BJORK: Let's say we test the item 10 back (counting backwards) from the end of a list that is either 12 items long, 20 items long, or 30 items long. Does reaction time or probability of saying yes vary?

MURDOCK: The probability of saying yes (the hit rate) falls off as the list length increases, and the scanning rate gets faster as list length increases. Whether these are correlated or any more than a correlation, I don't know.

BJORK: But let's assume the conveyor-belt metaphor. OK?

MURDOCK: Yes.

BJORK: The last item should be the last item, no matter how many precede it.

MURDOCK: You mean the last item presented and tested first?

BJORK: Yes.

MURDOCK: OK.

BJORK: It's hard to see how performance should vary with how many items you presented earlier; the last item is right there on the belt.

MURDOCK: That's true.

BJORK: And if I understand the decay or degradation mechanism, it is time dependent.

MURDOCK: Well, I didn't mean to imply that it was decay in the traditional sense. The data certainly suggest an interference sort of notion. So the more items that have followed it . . .

BJORK: But, when we are talking about the tenth item back, nine items have followed that item independent of how many items have preceded it.

MURDOCK: That's right. Now you're asking is the performance on that item then a function of the number of items that preceded it. The answer is yes.

BJORK: The answer seems different depending on whether I assume the conveyor-belt analogy you gave us or the model you propose—which I thought was based on the analogy. That is what has me confused.

MURDOCK: All right. What I didn't explain in terms of the model is how the scanning rate will vary. It seems to me unlikely that any kind of scanning process could be a template-matching operation. A more reasonable possibility is to talk about some sort of feature match. So that perhaps what you do is select a few features from the probe and that is what it means to say that you encode the probe; you select a few features and then you compare those features against the items in memory. Now it could be that the number of features you select is smaller the longer the lag range you're going to have to encompass. . .

MURDOCK: And the fewer features there are the more likely you will be to miss an old item, but on the other hand, the faster you can go. Now that would be consistent with the conveyor-belt type of model and consistent with the data.

HUMPHREYS: Did I understand you to say that you have not looked at your data in terms of the location of the probe item in the study list for each of the possible locations of this item in the test list?

MURDOCK: No, I said that the way I present the data, when I show you the lag latency functions, those are combined over different input/output combinations. Now, I have looked at them separately and that's essentially what I showed you in that graph (Fig. 12) where there was a 4-msec and a 6-msec slope for study and test positions. So I can't say that they're exactly the same, but the differences between them are quite small.

HUMPHREYS: Your data then differs from other data that has recently been published. Schulman (1974) seems to find no decay or degradation of familiarity as a function of later presentations, just as a function of time.

MURDOCK: He does find it in some of his data and he doesn't in other data. . . You've got to remember that we use a fairly fast presentation rate and, as the presentation rate slows down, the whole retention function gets flatter. And I've looked quickly at the recent Schulman (1974) paper and I don't think my data is really inconsistent with his. Such differences that do exist are attributive to different paradigms, and some of his data is forced choice, too.

HUMPHREYS: Your method of computing lag causes the proportion of study and test items in these lags to systematically vary with list length. So that a moderate lag in a long list might be made up predominantly of study items while the same lag in a shorter list would have to be made up of both study and test items. Could these changes in the proportion of study and test items cause the change in your estimates of scanning rate as a function of list length.

MURDOCK: The distribution of study items and test items changes systematically over the course of testing. And the whole point of selecting the lag function is that it's the critical variable as far as accuracy is concerned, and it provides the cleanest way of summarizing a large amount of data. That's why. I think it's a significant variable if not the relevant variable.

MACEY: I have a more fundamental problem. You said your tape-recorder notion of memory is not new and in agreeing with that, isn't there recent evidence by Hintzman that suggests that such a model is not accurate?

MURDOCK: The best evidence against it is the Hintzman, Block, and Summers (1973) article where they show that, in fact, when subjects miss the list of an item they can still identify, with a fair degree of accuracy, the serial position of the item within the list. That's the only strong negative evidence against this model. Most of the evidence is quite consistent.

MACEY: I beg to disagree with you on that point. Why then can't a person tell how far apart two intervening events are unless they are given the words first. He can't do that.

MURDOCK: Because now you're talking about repetitions and I haven't said anything about the effect of repetitions.

MACEY: No, different words. Why can't he judge the number of frames that occur? Or the number of inches it takes?

MURDOCK: Well, if we're talking about judgments of recency, indeed he can.

MACEY: No, judgments of spacing, of distance between events. . . . He can't do it for different words, but he can do it for the same word repeated twice or related words.

MURDOCK: If you take the data on absolute judgments of recency you'll find the two-alternative forced choice can be perfectly predicted from the absolute judgments, which says he can. Now, with this Hintzman and Block (1973) data, which says he can't, we have discrepancies in the data, which we have to resolve. My feeling is that such data as I'm familiar with seems to suggest that the subjects can do this quite well and, in fact, you can fit models for this data, and I have.

POSNER: Let me ask Mark Mayzner about firing color detectors from forms moving around in a circle. Does the color phenomena depend on the particular phosphor or scope used?

MAYZNER: I would think not. I base that on the fact that we found it on a couple of scopes having different phosphors. If you remove the illusory movement and increase the rate at which the inputs are displayed so that they appear simultaneous, color vanishes. Or, if you display them at a much slower rate so it's clearly sequential and you see all of them, there is no color.

POSNER: You didn't give us a hint as to how you interpret the mechanism which might underlie this. Do you have any hints at all?

MAYZNER: No, other than what I said . . .

BJORK: Do you think it's the color wheel business?

MAYZNER: No, I think it's totally different, because Benham's top, which is what I think you're referring to, is color being generated by changes in gradients produced by alternating black and white inputs to the visual system, and the color that is produced there occurs in the spatial location in space where the black and white gradients or sectors occur. Whereas, in the display we were talking about here, the color is totally within the confines of the displayed input where there is no change in energy gradients of any kind whatsoever. In a control condition we used a cardboard mask; put it over the cathode-ray tube (CRT) so that only part of the display shown was a tract where the Xs appeared. This was to insure that there was no ancillary phosphoric excitation that might relate to your question as well. The subject is brought into the room in blackness so he has no idea that there is any cardboard on the display and in that situation, the interior of this illusory movement created by the X moving around the perimeter produces this variety of colors and then when you turn the lights on and he sees the cardboard on the cathode-ray tube where the color seems to have appeared, he looks at you and says, "I don't believe it."

BJORK: Benham's top is a structure that doesn't radiate?

MAYZNER: No, no, they do not radiate. They're concentric, half of Benham's top is black and half is white and on the white sector, there are black concentric rings that are different arcs from the center of the circle. We have another display that I didn't get into at all that has some of the properties of Benham's top. We have another display that I didn't get into at all that has some of the properties of Benham's top. We display a very complex array of vertical lines that are moving horizontally across the display, vertically, and diagonally, in both orientations. And depending on the display order, you get varying blanking of the total number of lines displayed. Now, in that situation, once you have the display going, if you take cardboard masks of any shape you wish and place them over the illusory movement grid again in darkness, that cardboard will immediately show colors. So that region where there is no energy coming off the CRT, but there are an enormous number of lines in vertical, horizontal, and diagonal movement occurring, color is perceived in that region.

POSNER: Before George (Mandler) gets away, I have to ask whether he, certainly unlike me, could be aware of 5 plus or minus 2 different things at the same time.

MANDLER: I think the psychophysical evidence is that you can.

POSNER: I wonder why you wish to collapse the concept of short-term memory, which is another alternative way of handling the psychophysical data, with the concept of the focus of conscious attention. *I* seem to shift my attention from one item to another, though keeping maybe 5 plus or minus 2 ready for certain kinds of tasks.

MANDLER: Numerosity judgments, for example, can keep only about 5 dots in conscious attention, but not 8 or 9. If you give people 5 dots and you ask them how many there are, they'll tell you. If you go above 8, they're going to start estimating.

POSNER: Isn't that an artifact of the people like the old psychophysicists not having knowledge of the rapid scanning processes of 5, or 10 or 15 msec per item.

MANDLER: But why does it break down at 5 or 6? Just because they don't have the knowledge?

POSNER: They begin to lose their place.

MANDLER: Lose their place in a random array?

POSNER: Right. You start counting the same one over and over. That's been one explanation, but the subjective experience is that you see those 5 dots. As soon as you go over 8 you get a scanning effect.

BJORK: I want to ask one of Bill (Estes). It's an appealing notion that a word provides a structure that helps keep the order of the letters in the word, but what bothers me about that notion is that there has to be some accurate processing of the relative positions of the letters to get to the point that it becomes a word. I get bothered as I try to think of the stages of the processing that would go on; it seems like the wordiness of a word is assumed to have an influence before that wordiness is deduced—it's a familiar kind of problem.

ESTES: Well, I don't think so, Bob . . . if we think in terms of the levels of processing on that slide, if you still can recall it. Starting at different times, but ultimately occurring in parallel, we have units at the feature, letter, and letter group levels possibly being activated as a result of the same display. Now in the case of a string of random letters, it would be quite rare that groups of adjacent letters in any display would match familiar groups in memory. However, in the case of a word, it'll be considerably more likely that some of the adjacent letter pairs or trigrams in the display will find matches with relatively highly available structures in memory and thus will provide additional information to keep from getting the target letter out of place.

BJORK: Do you expect latency differences in the pointer experiments between the word case and the single-letter case? Or the nonword case?

ESTES: It's a fair question and I can't give you a fair answer. I think the answer is no, but you can't take it at full value as a theoretical deduction because I have seen the data and know that the trend is in this direction. That lack of difference fits with many other things in suggesting that although the onsets of the processes yielding these matches at various levels must be staggered if they run in parallel, it's not necessarily the case that an operation at one level must be completed before an operation at the next level can begin.

POSNER: Mark, one of the hypotheses underlying the sequential blanking notion has been a kind of analogy to impossible movement. I was wondering, in working on the parameters of sequential blanking, whether they run along together with the parameters necessary to produce the appearance or motion.

MAYZNER: If you look at a very large number of different sequential displays: of 5 elements, 10 elements, 20 elements; with different display orders and different display rates it's very easy to conjure up at certain values, rate and order—subjective feelings of apparent movement, impossible kinds of movements, all sorts of effects of this kind. I think the danger is in assuming that impossible movement is the only explanatory construct for blanking or metacontrast.

POSNER: Could you mention a couple of the alternative hypotheses that you entertain for the blanking phenomena?

MAYZNER: Well, the one that we've entertained the most seriously is that the elements which arrive in the system later; with chair, for example, where you miss the h, i and see the c, a, r; because of their spatial and temporal relationship to the earlier elements create a lateral inhibitory field that in some way is analogous to the type of inhibitory field discussed by Ratliff (1965) . . . that this is the basic underlying physiological substructure that underlies this phenomena. Now, some of the evidence for this is the mapping of that field that we did with single point sources of light. You can map out very clearly a region where you say inhibition, in some sense, or masking or blanking or whatever term you want to use, is occurring, and outside that region it is not occurring. Just as with metacontrast, if you exceed certain spatial or temporal ranges, the effect is gone.

ESTES: How, Mark (Mayzner), does that accommodate the fact that some of these recent studies, mentioned in your paper, among other places, show a rather conspicuous divergence between the subjective experiences reported by the subjects and the results of matching and recognition tests? In cases where the subject reports that he didn't see any letters in certain positions, a recognition test may nonetheless show that he had that information in memory. Then the blanking must result from processes occurring above the part of the visual system where lateral masking occurs. Let me get another part of the question out and then you can answer the whole thing. Is it possible that, in addition to or instead of having something to do with masking at the visual level, this failure to see letters in certain positions is closely related to the fact that we habitually don't see smeared images during the movement of our eyes in reading; that we habitually don't see a blank or the blind spot in the visual field? Could it be that under these rather unusual conditions, the lower levels of the visual field system are not actually failing to process what comes in from those locations. Rather, the whole system doesn't have any adequate way of dealing with this input and is keeping it from reaching higher levels (denying it access to consciousness?) just as you suppress input from the blind spot during reading?

MAYZNER: Well, I guess I would answer that this way: that until one can predict for, let's say, a 10 element display and a given display order that we have not yet examined previously, what elements might or might not be missing? I would not be confident in any theoretical account. I'm not even satisfied with the account that I described earlier in terms of lateral inhibition. Because one, you have the findings of Pollack (1972) and Cumming (1973) where using more refined psychophysical procedures, they are picking up information from these errors. So what I think is happening, in a more general sense, is that you are looking at a very complicated processing system and we have to look much more before we're going to be in a position to spell out the rules by which it works.

POSNER: The lesson might be that "looking" in the sense of subjective report isn't going to solve this. In a sense, you need to push on converging operations with more refined techniques rather than just getting more data from subjective experience.

MAYZNER: I think that's true.

THEIOS: I have a question for Dr. Mayzner. In your phenomenon of reduction in color, how big was the area in the internal part of the circle or the box?

MAYZNER: I would say about 2 inches by 2 inches. The effect is not crucially dependent on the size. It could have been 3×3 or 1×1.

THEIOS: Is there a gradient of color going toward black in the middle of the circle?

MAYZNER: That whole area is one color in the square.

THEIOS: Uniform brightness?

MAYZNER: Yes. Now in the circle it's quite different there; you either have a uniform color or the subjects will very often report the "Blades of a propeller" with 4 of the blades being black and these correspond to the location of the Xs as they move around the perimeter and the intermediate regions showing the color.

THEIOS: One other thing, you said that people could report different colors and that if a group of people were looking at it, they each might report a different color. If a single person watches this display, can you predict the order in which the colors would appear?

MAYZNER: No.

POSNER: I have to ask Bill Battig a question because I think he struck a blow for human kind. All the memory people that I've listened to lately say even though psychologists have shown that you shouldn't just do primary rehearsal, the subjects continue to do just that. Now, you show that your subjects seem to adopt a much more optimal strategy. Psychologists say that you shouldn't have too much interference, and subjects do adopt a way of isolating each particular item by a different method. Now, I wondered whether you had any observations as to why subjects seem to be adopting such an optimal strategy. One way of talking about it is saying that they're inconsistent and another way of talking about it is to say they've adopted an overall strategy, which is to reduce the total amount of interference in learning.

BATTIG: Yeah, I didn't go into that except at the very end, but I think you're exactly right. Probably the reason subjects used different processing for different items is because this does serve as a technique for reducing and minimizing interference. If you process several items, I don't think that each individual item gets processed completely differently from each other. I think there's some subgrouping that goes on. But in most of our lists they are long enough to produce substantial interference at the level of the whole list. One way, certainly, of coping with such intralist interference is to adopt different modes of processing for different parts of the list. I think that does go on and we do have some evidence that under conditions where that is optimal, subjects who do it, also perform better.

POSNER: At higher levels of practice do your subjects become less consistent or more consistent?

BATTIG: That's a question we really haven't gotten to yet. We have only gone as far as three successive lists, and the results were inconclusive on that point. Some of our evidence indicates that they do become more consistent, while other evidence indicates that they don't, and I suspect this depends primarily upon whether or not they can hit upon an efficient general strategy. This strategy is probably a more complex one that may be hierarchial in some sense. Therefore with the rather crude measures we're using, we probably don't get at some of the distinctions, some of the processing differences that may be involved. I would suspect that there may be conditions under which a practiced subject will probably develop complex but consistent strategies, but that's sheer speculation at this stage. What we'd need to do and what we're hoping to do next year are some longitudinal investigations where we get some really experienced subjects and see to what extent we can push their processing strategies around, and to what extent they will hit on consistent optimal strategies over a long period of time.

LYNNE REDER: Sometimes did you ask them for their strategies as they were learning the list?

BATTIG: Yes.

REDER: And you said you got some that were 60%?

BATTIG: Yes.

REDER: Did you correlate performance with the percentage strategies?

BATTIG: Yeah. We've tried that and the closest thing we get to anything that makes sense is that under conditions where the subject is better off to adopt a particular strategy, he performs better by using that strategy more consistently. However, where we've looked at whether a particular type of strategy usage correlates with performance, such relationships have been quite small.

KINTSCH: Would you tell us how you put consciousness into your system? You obviously don't want to equate it with focal attention, but how do you view the relationship of consciousness in the automatic processing that you've been describing?

POSNER: Well, I view it as a way of gaining control over particular strategies. So that on one hand we have a limited capacity system, but the crucial question of the system is not just its limited capacity system, but that it can assemble executive routines or strategies, which can allow you to perform nonhabitual processing on the subset of information that is selected out for special treatment. What it cannot do, and I'm not quite sure whether this is consistent with Bill's model or not, is to cut off processing of unrelated items.

ESTES: I don't know, but that you seem to be sidestepping, Mike (Posner). Granted the distinction between your automatic processing level, which is essentially parallel, and a limited capacity system that operates perhaps higher order programs, in a sense, why do you bring consciousness into the picture? Is there some tangible basis for associating consciousness with the limited capacity, presumably higher level systems?

POSNER: Well, I think there is. If you look at dichotic listening results or if you look at the Conrad results cited in my paper, you find very sophisticated semantic processing when the subject cannot report to you anything about the pathway activated. Starting with the limited capacity idea, we have developed converging operations such as the ability to report verbally and control intention which converge on the same mechanism. This constellation of things converging on one mechanism seemed to be reason to identify the operation of that mechanism with what we call being conscious.

ESTES: It seems rather unlikely to me that there is something different about these limited capacity processes because they're conscious or that the higher-order, executive operations necessary proceed differently when the individual is aware of them than when he is not. Perhaps these processes give rise to what we call conscious experience as an epiphenomenon. It may turn out that consciousness will always slip through all the converging operations and appear only as a byproduct; an aspect of experience that is more likely to be produced when limited capacity processes are involved than when only habitual ones are operative.

POSNER: I don't think I'd object to that.

SOLSO: On that note of harmony, let's end. Thank you.

REFERENCES

Burrows, D., & Okada, R. Parallel scanning of semantic and formal information. *Journal of Experimental Psychology,* 1973, **97,** 254–257.

Cumming, G. Perceptual analysis of letters masked by meta-contrast. Unpublished doctoral thesis, Department of Psychology, Oxford University, Oxford, England, 1973.

Hintzman, D. L., & Block, R. A. Memory for the spacing of repetitions. *Journal of Experimental Psychology,* 1973, **99,** 1, 70–74.

Hintzman, D. L., Block, R. A., & Summers, J. J. Modality tags and memory for repetitions: Locus of the spacing effect, *Journal of Verbal Learning and Verbal Behavior,* 1973, **12,** 229–238.

Pollack, I. Visual discrimination of "unseen objects": Forced-choice testing of Mayzner-Tresselt sequential blanking effect. *Perception & Psychophysics,* 1972, **11,** 121–128.

Ratliff, F. *Mach bands: Quantitative studies of neural networks in the retina.* San Francisco, California: Holden Day, 1965.

Reicher, G. M. Perceptual recognition as a function of meaningfulness of stimulus material. *Journal of Experimental Psychology,* 1969, **81,** 275–280.

Schulman, A. I. The declining course of recognition memory. *Memory & Cognition,* 1974, **2,** 14–18.

Wheeler, D. D. Process in word recognition. *Cognitive Psychology,* 1970, **1,** 59–95.

SECTION III

9

MEMORY REPRESENTATIONS OF TEXT

Walter Kintsch
University of Colorado

The purpose of this contribution is to explore the processes involved in text memory and, at the same time, to emphasize what appears to me a striking continuity between memory for word lists and memory for text. The parallels that I want to point out between list learning data and the results of research with texts are potentially important: if they are, indeed, indicators of common processes and not merely superficial similarities, the study of texts can be built upon the solid base of facts and the relatively advanced theoretical understanding which exist in list learning research. This, I claim, would be a vast improvement over the alternative accepted by disconcertingly many psycholinguists today: that the theory and data of "verbal learning" are essentially irrelevant to the study of memory and comprehension of sentences and texts.

I have recently suggested a model of episodic memory for list learning situations, as well as a theory for the representation of meaning in psychology (Kintsch, 1974). In this chapter I shall try to bring together these two separate proposals by extending the memory model to account for text memory. I shall assume that the encoding and storage operations in memory are basically the same, whether the material to be learned consists of word lists or prose paragraphs; differences are entirely due to the nature of the material involved. With word lists, processing is necessarily restricted to lower levels of analysis. Syntactic and semantic processing is possible only in a very limited way (though even this degenerate processing often plays an important role in list learning studies). Text comprehension, on the other hand, involves complex processes at the syntactic and semantic levels. In Section II I shall try to indicate what these processes are like, and what, according to the theory, the end product of this analysis consists of. Many problems which arise in text comprehension will be neglected here; attention will be focused on the multiple memory representations which arise in the process of text comprehension. A similar theoretical approach has been used previously by other authors, for instance in short-term memory research by Craik and Lockhart (1972) and in letter matching tasks by Posner (1969). Indeed, one may view the present work as an extension of Posner's work to textual materials. Section III describes the nature of the multiple memory representations that arise during comprehension of a text, and Section IV discusses the pattern matching procedures by means of which a subject determines whether a given test statement is or is not identical with a portion of his memory for a text. These sections are straightforward extensions and derivations from the theoretical ideas that will be presented in the first two sections of this chapter.

I. A MODEL FOR EPISODIC MEMORY

It is necessary, first of all, to outline the model of episodic memory presented in Kintsch (1974) that forms the basis for the present discussion. Actually, this is not a model in the strict formal sense, but rather a broad theoretical framework that serves to bring together some specific submodels and a wide variety of empirical results by means of a few key concepts and processing assumptions. Only those aspects of the model will be discussed that are directly relevant to the experimental work to be reported below. Specifically, this means that we are only concerned with the recognition subsystem of the model, and not with various forms of recall. Since the model is a two-process theory which makes rather sharp distinctions between recognition processes and recall processes, this permits a considerable simplification.

The experimental task of immediate interest is a recognition experiment for words. A list of words is presented visually, and later on the same words, together with distractor words, are again shown to the subject, who is asked to identify each word on the test list as either "old" or "new." How can this process of item recognition be described theoretically? The following are the main assumptions of the theory:

1. The written word is represented by a set of visual elements.
2. Corresponding to each word there is a word concept in semantic memory, consisting of various types of elements, including visual elements.

3. All these elements become available in working memory during the study phase of the experiment.
4. Most of these elements are rapidly lost, except for a subset which is selected to form a stable memory trace, called a memory episode.
5. On a recognition test, the test item is processed in the same way as the learning item, and its "oldness" is determined by means of a pattern match with the earlier memory episode.

It is not possible to provide a full description of this process here, but a few explanations are in order. A word is represented in semantic memory as a collection of elements, for example, visual, auditory, imaginal, motor, and meaning elements. These elements may be complex themselves and internally structured (this is best seen in the case of the meaning elements, the propositions discussed below). The formation of a memory episode for some word W in context CX consists of selecting a sample of elements from those available (elements representing the actual stimulus, elements contributed from memory, plus elements representing the context), and storing it in memory. Specifically, suppose that a subject is asked to remember the word W_i, presented visually, as a part of an experimental list. It is assumed that the visual stimulus consists of a set of visual elements, which are matched with a corresponding set of visual elements in the subject's memory, leading to the identification of the stimulus as the word W_i. This process is one of pattern completion, whereby the visual stimulus pattern is enriched from memory by other sensory, motor and semantic information about the word in question. All of this information is available at one time in the subject's working memory, but it is lost rapidly due to interference from new stimulus elements, with the exception of a subset of elements selected to form a permanent memory episode. This selection is biased rather than random, in that the momentary contents of short-term memory determine the ultimate composition of the memory episode. Elements common to more than one word held in short-term memory are favored by this bias. This selection bias assures that shared semantic features as well as other similarities among items, such as rhymes, are encoded preferentially. It also assures that stable context information is included in the memory episodes, which is crucial for later experimental performance, where the subject must not only make a recognition response, but decide whether or not a particular word has been experienced before in a given context.

Once a memory episode M_i has been formed, a re-presentation of word W_i can be recognized as such: the visual stimulus is processed in the same way as before and a test episode M_i^* is formed, that is identified via a pattern match with M_i (unless the composition of M_i and M_i^* are too different, which may occur when the selection processes operated under different biases because they occurred in different contexts). Recall, in contrast, must involve more than simple pattern matching operations. A recall cue (instructions and the experimental environment in the case of free recall) provides access to related memory episodes via pattern matching, but, unless these episodes are connected to the to be recalled memory episodes via a system of cross references, retrieval is impossible.

The theory is, therefore, a generation–recognition theory, but it does not involve tagging of semantic structures. Instead, these semantic structures are copied in episodic memory during the learning phase. Again, as in previous work, differences in the retrieval operations in recognition and recall are emphasized. The portions of the theory that are most important in the present context are the concepts of pattern completion and pattern matching; the representation of words as sets of elements at various levels—visual, auditory, semantic, etc.; the notion that these elements are rapidly lost from memory, unless specifically selected for inclusion in a memory episode; and finally that recognition tests involve the same kind of elaboration via pattern completion as occurred during original learning, with the effect that multilevel test representations may be matched with memory episodes or with traces from the subject's working memory, if these are still available.

II. SOME REMARKS ON TEXT BASES

The main concern of my research in the past few years has been the development of a formal representation for the meaning of texts which could serve as a basis for psychological experimentation on textual materials. A full account of this work is contained in Kintsch (1974), and I shall review only those aspects of the theory that are crucial for the work to be reported here.

The meaning of a text is to be represented by a text base. Text bases are constructed from propositions. A proposition is an n-tuple of word concepts, one of which serves as a predicator and the others as the arguments of the proposition. Semantic memory specifies which n-tuples form acceptable propositions by listing for each word concept the classes of arguments which it can take when used as a predicator, together with special conditions and restrictions concerning such uses. Text bases are ordered lists of propositions that are connected and structured by mean of a repetition rule: according to the theory, the repetition of the same argument in successive propositions gives continuity to a text base and distinguishes it from a random collection of propositions. At the same time, argument repetition determines the structure of a text, which in general, is equivalent to a connected graph.

TABLE 1
A Sample Text Base and Corresponding Texts

1	(GO,STANLEY,AFRICA) &	
2	(DOUBT,STANLEY,3) &	
3	(DEAD,LIVINGSTONE) &	
4	(CONSEQUENCE,1,2)	

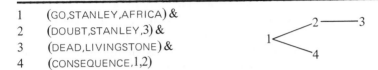

a. Stanley went to Africa because he doubted that Livingstone was dead.
b. Since Stanley doubted that Livingstone was dead, he went to Africa.
c. Stanley doubted that Livingstone was dead. As a consequence of this, Stanley went to Africa.
d. Stanley doubted that Livingstone was dead. Therefore, he went to Africa.
e. Because of Stanley's doubts about Livingstone's death, he went to Africa.
f. Because of doubts about Livingstone's death, Stanley went to Africa.

Table 1 shows a very brief text base, consisting of four propositions. For ease of exposition, I have written each proposition on a separate line and numbered the lines. In this way, one can refer to any of the propositions by the corresponding number. Thus, the second proposition reads STANLEY DOUBTED whatever the proposition on line 3 says (in this case, that LIVINGSTONE was DEAD). Note that the predicator of a proposition is written first. The fourth proposition has as a predicator the abstract word concept CONSEQUENCE, which may be realized in the text, for instance, by the sentence connective *because*. The word *because* is, of course, not the only way in which one can express the relation CONSEQUENCE in English. I could have used just as well *so-that, therefore, for, due to, since, thus, as a result, consequently, hence, as,* or *while,* to name just some of the possibilities available. Sentences (*a*)–(*d*) illustrate some of these. All of these sentences are possible texts that can be derived from the text base given in Table 1. It is, of course, not claimed that all of these versions are equally good, or that speakers would generate them randomly. Considerations such as what is new information and what is given in a particular communication situation will determine the speaker's choice of surface structure, as will other considerations, such as frequency of use of various expressions, or social context (one rarely uses *hence* informally). At the semantic level, however, all of these texts are equivalent. The pharaphrases (*a*)–(*d*) were obtained merely by varying the way in which the CONSEQUENCE relation was expressed. It is, of course, also possible to vary the expressions for some of the other propositions, and sentences (*e*) and (*f*) show two examples. Sentence (*f*) illustrates the fact that although text bases are unambiguous, texts frequently are not: it is not clear in (f) who doubted—Stanley, or someone else?

Table 1 also indicates the structure of the text base, which follows from the order of the propositions in the list and the pattern of argument repetitions: Proposition 1 is superordinate, Propositions 2 and 4 are directly subordinated to it (because the argument STANLEY is repeated in Proposition 2, and the whole first proposition is repeated as an argument in Proposition 3), and Proposition 3 is subordinated to Proposition 2 (it is, in fact, one of the arguments of Proposition 2). How does one know that (GO, STANLEY, AFRICA) should be listed first in this text base? If all one had was this brief text base, a nonarbitrary answer would not be possible; however, suppose these four propositions constitute the beginning of a story about Stanley's trip to Africa; in that case, the choice of (1) as the superordinate proposition would be well motivated. In general, however, the theory has nothing to say about where proposition lists come from, including their order. It treats proposition lists as given, and investigates how adequate they are as representations of meaning, and how useful they are for purposes of experimenting with textual materials.

In this chapter I shall not be concerned so much with the properties of text bases in themselves, but rather with the relationship between text bases and texts. Two aspects of this problem must be strictly separated. First, there is the question of the formal procedures that permit the generation of text from text bases and the construction of text bases from a given text. Second, there is the question how people speak and understand texts. I shall briefly comment on the first question before concentrating upon the second.

The problem of parsing a text and of deriving an abstract representation of its meaning is central to several current efforts in artificial intelligence. Although it is an extremely complex problem, some impressive, though partial, successes have been reported. No work has been done concerning this problem within the present approach. Instead, I have tried to circumvent it by starting from text bases and deriving texts from them. This latter problem is much simpler and better understood. Essentially, it is a linguistic problem and has been explored in some detail within generative grammar and generative semantics. At the risk of boring the linguistically sophisticated reader (and alienating the linguistically disinterested), I would like to show by means of a few textbook examples how this process of text generation from a text base proceeds. It is, after all, important to demonstrate that the relation between texts and text bases is not an arbitrary one, even at the present stage of knowledge.

As a very simple example, let us take two of the propositions from Table 1 and explore how a linguist would derive from them possible surface structures. Consider the two-proposition base (DOUBT,STANLEY,(DEAD,LIVING-STONE)). The linguistic structure that follows directly from these two propositions looks something like

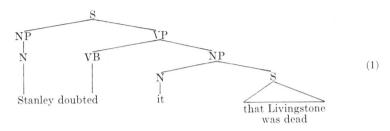

(1)

From this structure, linguists obtain by means of a transformation called it-deletion the following sentence:

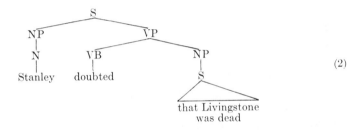

(2)

Alternatively, by applying first the passive transformation and then it-deletion, we get

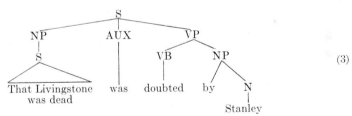

(3)

A third example can be obtained by following the passive transformation with an extraposition transformation:

(4)

Thus, we have obtained three different paraphrases of (DOUBT,STAN-LEY,(DEAD,LIVINGSTONE)). The example is simple, and the linguistic rules needed happen to be well understood, which is not the case for all possible text bases, but I think the problems involved are relatively secondary for the psychologist. Much more important is the second, psychological part of the original question: how does a real speaker generate text from text bases, and how does he construct text bases from texts?

The generation problem is not of immediate interest here because only comprehension but not generation is involved in the studies reported below. Note, however, that McNeill's contribution in this volume addresses itself to some aspects of text generation.

Although I have no work of my own to report concerning the question of how listeners or readers construct text bases, there exists a fairly rich literature that yields at least some tentative answers. It is clear, for instance, that syntactic processing plays a significant role in text comprehension. There are two lines of evidence to support this claim. First, there are a number of studies, using a variety of experimental methods, that have provided evidence that during comprehension subjects break down the constituents of a sentence in much the same way as a linguistic analysis would. This is, for instance, indicated by the transition error analyses of Johnson (1968), the recall data of Jarvella (1971), and the click studies from Fodor and Bever (1965) to Seitz and Weber (1974). Second, Kintsch and Monk (1972) have found that paragraphs based upon the same text base could be made easy or hard to read, depending upon the syntactic complexity of the expressions used. While these studies attest to the important role of syntactic analysis during comprehension, they say little about how this analysis is performed. There are, however, other results that indicate that syntactic processing does not consist in running off linguistic transformation rules in reverse; indeed, it appears that it is not done with algorithmic procedures at all, but through the use of various heuristics. This argument has been stated most clearly by Bever (1970). People do not follow general rules that invariably will uncover the text base underlying a given text, but they use fallible strategies to infer meaning from words, relying on syntactic, semantic, as well as pragmatic cues. For instance, Fodor and Garrett (1967) have shown that sentences containing relative clauses are easier to understand when the clause is marked by a relative pronoun than when the pronoun is absent. Apparently, the relative pronoun served the subject as an important cue to the sentence structure. Similarly, Hakes (1972) has demonstrated that sentences containing *that*-complement constructions became more difficult to comprehend when the *that* did not appear in the surface structure, in spite of the fact that the text base of the sentence remained unchanged. Bever (1970) showed that subjects tend to assume that the first unmarked noun phrase in a sentence is its main clause, so that sentences for which this heuristic did not apply proved to be hard to understand.

At the same time, it is clear that the syntactic analysis of a text does not proceed independently but interacts with the semantic processing of the text. Fodor, Garrett, and Bever (1968) demonstrated that the lexical complexity of verbs, as indexed by the number of different constructions permitted by the verb, influenced the ease with which a sentence could be processed. Bever (1970) argued that in cases where the semantic constraints among the words in a sentence are strong, syntactic processing would be superfluous. As an example, a reader who has arrived at the sequence of word concepts STANLEY, GO, and AFRICA can immediately form the corresponding proposition because it is really the only possibility. Data reported by Rosenberg (1968) indicate that this is indeed the case: for sentences with strong semantic constraints among the words, such as *The brave soldier fought the cruel war,* Rosenberg found no evidence that these sentences were parsed into their syntactic constituents during learning, while poorly integrated sentences, such as *The rich soldier liked the green house,* were learned more slowly and with an error pattern that indicated that subjects were chunking the sentence according to its syntactic structure.

Finally, it must be noted that the syntactic and semantic analysis of a text interacts with pragmatic, contextual factors. It has long been known that in cases where the situational constraints are powerful, subtle and detailed messages can be communicated by the most elliptic remarks. Olson (1970) has reported some experimental work in support of this conclusion.

The construction of a text base from a text appears, therefore, to involve multiple parallel processes. Each one of them seems to be heuristic in nature rather than algorithmic, one serving as a check on the other. What is important here is that this processing must give rise to a hierarchy of memory traces, ranging from the actual words used in the text, to a syntactic grouping of the word string, to the identification of semantic and pragmatic relationships in the text, to intermediate constructions involving only portions of the text, up to the final propositional base as the end product of the comprehension process. The next section of this chapter will be concerned with the memory consequences of this multiplicity of traces during text processing.

III. MEMORY FOR TEXT

The model for episodic memory described in Section I can be readily extended from word lists to texts. In the former case, episodic memory units correspond to words; in the latter, a paragraph becomes the unit of episodic memory. In Section II we represented the meaning of a paragraph by a propositional text base and described the processing involved in constructing such a text base from a text. It is assumed here that all processes involved in text comprehension yield their own specific memory traces which will be subject to the same kind of encoding and storage operations as the traces arising from the processing of a word list. The difference between text memory and list memory is not in the memory system at all, but in memory content, because more elaborate processing traces occur during text comprehension.

The first two columns in Table 2 list the processing levels involved in text comprehension as well as the corresponding memory traces. I have assumed here, for the sake of concreteness, that the text was presented visually. Note that the first four levels remain unchanged whether the task is one of list learning or text comprehension. In either case, the processing begins with a stimulus set which consists of a set of contextual elements CX, and a set of visual elements G_i, each representing the graphemic features of the ith word in the list or text. The visual stimulus elements G_i are matched with a set of graphemic elements $S_{graph,i}$ representing the reader's knowledge of the visual appearance of the ith word. (How this match is performed need not concern us here; the operation involved may be quite complex.) What is important for present purposes is the outcome of this match: by means of a process of pattern completion, not only the graphemic elements $S_{graph,i}$ become available, but also all other information known (that is, stored in semantic memory) about the word in question. The graphemic stimulus set is now enriched with auditory elements $S_{aud,i}$ specifying the sound and pronunciation of the word, imaginal elements $S_{imag,i}$ providing information about the visual appearance of the object or action represented by the word, motor cues $S_{mot,i}$ which may be a part of the knowledge about the word, and meaning elements $S_{sem,i}$, which indicate its meaning by specifying the relationship of the word concept corresponding to the ith word to other word concepts in the language. The meaning elements S_{sem} are propositions just like those used in text bases.

The results of this pattern completion process is shown, in part, in Table 2. The graphemic stimuli G_i are replaced by $G_i \cup S_{graph,i}$, that is, to the particular graphemic cues of the stimulus word is added the reader's knowledge about how one writes this word. The auditory elments $S_{aud,i}$ may play a role in reading, though their use is clearly optional (Gibson et al., 1970). They are very frequently used in list-learning tasks, because of the particular requirements of many short-term memory experiments. In order to keep Table 2 from becoming too unwieldly, the only other type of cues listed are the meaning elements S_{sem}, but it should be obvious that

TABLE 2
An Outline of Stages of Comprehension in Reading, the Memory Traces Arising from These Processes, and Their Temporal Characteristics

Processes	Memory trace	Decay rate	Probability of inclusion in a memory episode
1 Context processing	CX		High
2 Graphemic analysis	$G_1 \cup S_{\text{graph},1}, \ldots, G_n \cup S_{\text{graph},n}$	1 sec	Low
3 Auditory processing (optional)	$S_{\text{aud},1}, \ldots, S_{\text{aud},n}$	2–4 sec	Low, but used for rehersal
4 Word identification	$S_{\text{sem},1}, \ldots, S_{\text{sem},n}$	30 sec	Low
5 Syntactic-semantic analysis of word string	Surface structure of text	?	Low
6 Intermediate linguistic analysis	Intermediate structures and transformations	?	Low
7 Text base formation	$P_1 \& P_2 \& \ldots P_k$	?	High

imaginal and other types of elements can be easily fitted into this scheme if required. Meaning elements are of particular importance in many list-learning situations, and they are, of course, crucial, in text comprehension.

The difference between text memory and list memory consists in what is done with the $S_{\text{sem},i}$'s. Not much can be done in the case of lists, though even there semantic similarity among words determines the way in which these words will be encoded, and semantic relations among words figure prominently in the construction of a retrieval scheme for the list (see Kintsch, 1974 for details). Texts, on the other hand, are processed as described in the previous section. First, there will be a parsing of the word string into its syntactic constituents, together with a grouping according to the semantic constraints involved. I have indicated this processing on line 5 of Table 2. This is followed by further analysis of the string, involving transformations of some of the constituents identified earlier and the identification of the relations among these constituents. Line 6 of Table 2 indicates this stage of processing. While the first analysis of the word string was still closely tied to the actual surface structure of the text, at this stage intermediate structures between the surface form and the eventual text base are elaborated. Often inferences must be made, and presumably changes are made in the propositions derived from the text as the reader attempts to form a coherent, properly ordered proposition list. This list is the end product of the comprehension process, the text base.

The text base, as well as the memory traces generated in its construction, provide the raw materials for the operation of encoding and storage in memory. But before these questions can be considered in Sections III.B and III.C, a few remarks should be made about the nature of the processing hierarchy depicted in Table 2.

A. Parallel Processing

The levels of processing described above, from the pattern match on the basis of graphemic stimuli to the ultimate formation of a text base, are not to be thought of as sequential stages where earlier processes proceed independently of later ones, but are parallel and interactive. The outcome of the pattern match depends, in part, on higher level, semantic processing (the biasing mechanism built into the model achieves this result); which word concept will be selected if a word has several meanings depends upon how well it fits into the developing text base; which semantic constraints are used depends upon syntactic cues, etc. It is, furthermore, not necessary that a lower level process be completed at all. One may perceive a word without noticing a (misprinted) letter or one can read a text rapidly without becoming aware of each word. Examples mentioned in Section II show how a semantic analysis may shortcut syntactic processing.

As experimental support for these claims, let me merely cite two well-corroborated findings. At the level of letter recognition, letters may be identified faster when they form part of a word than when they are presented alone. For the conditions under which these effects hold, and an explanation which I think is compatible with the present theses, see the chapter by Estes in the present volume. At a higher level of processing, Meyer and Schvaneveldt (1971) have observed that subjects can determine faster that two strings of letters are words if the words are related associatively than if they are unrelated. Both findings indicate that processes at visual and meaning levels proceed in parallel and interactively, rather than sequentially.

B.   Trace Decay

The first memory assumption is that traces decay unless selected for storage in a memory episode. "Decay" is used here in a neutral sense, not contrastive with interference. This assumption merely says that not every process that occurs in perception and comprehension has permanent effects, and as such is quite uncontroversial. However, I also claim that decay rates for different types of traces differ, and, in general, are ordered so that the lower level traces decay more rapidly than the higher level traces. This claim can only be partially documented.

Experimental evidence exists for the loss of graphemic and auditory traces, as indicated in Table 2. The 1-sec decay time for graphemic traces is inferred from Sperling's work (Sperling, 1963), and the 3–4-sec estimate for auditory traces from Darwin, Turvey, and Crowder (1972). Both of these numbers are suspect, however, because they depend very strongly upon the experimental tasks used. In some tasks much longer decay times have been reported, and I am not certain which values are the right ones to consider here.

Decay of traces at the word level appears to be considerably slower. The retention of unrelated words has been the subject of much research on short-term memory, and we know, for instance, that word triplets are lost in about 18 sec in the absence of rehearsal, whereas the recall of single words is hardly impaired at all in the same period of time (Murdock, 1961). The value of 30 sec, which is listed in Table 1 as the decay time for word strings, is, therefore, only an approximation (for a review, see Murdock, 1974, p. 268).

I have put question marks in Table 2 for the rate of memory loss for linguistic structures, and for propositional information. The latter problem is complicated by the fact that the propositional information is usually what is selected for permanent memory storage, but it should be possible to devise incidental tasks where this would not be the case. The length of time that linguistic structures persist in memory is one of the experimental questions considered here.

Are there any plausible reasons for the retention rates for different types of traces to differ as assumed here? Suppose that the loss of memory traces is caused by interference of the following kind. Memory traces are conceived here as sets of elements. If A is such a set, and $a \in A$ is not selected for inclusion in the memory episode, a is lost from the set A with some probability whenever the element a is used in some other context. Graphemic and auditory features would be lost quickly in this manner, but the larger a unit becomes, the less likely would be its reappearance in a different context, interference would be reduced, and the loss from memory retarded. The reason for the forgetting would, therefore, be interference among identical elements.

C. Memory Episodes

The central assumption of the model is that a subset of elements is selected from those available in working memory and is stored permanently in memory as a "memory episode," $M,$ and nonselected elements in working memory are lost as described above. There are two important points to be made concerning the formation of memory episodes. First, any type of elements — graphemic, auditory, imaginal, semantic, etc. — may be selected for permanent storage, in addition to context elements which will always be included, because they are necessary for contextual recognition. Second, the selection is not random, but context biased.

The evidence for the first assumption is extremely strong. It is certain that graphemic and visual information may be stored in long-term memory. In reading a text, such information is probably of secondary importance, though. Much of it would already be decayed before the reader reaches the end of a paragraph. Nevertheless, it is well known how surprisingly useful incidental knowledge can be, such as, where on a page a certain phrase occurred (e.g., Rothkopf, 1971). Also, in some situations graphemic cues are processed with high priority, for example, the type font reversals used by Kolers (1973), where memory about how a text was written proved to be as good as memory for the text itself.

Auditory elements may also form parts of permanent memory episodes. In reading their role is secondary, as has been mentioned above, but in the case of spoken texts such information would be as important as the visual-graphemic elements in reading.

The actual words used in a text may also become part of memory episodes. This claim needs no experimental proof, since everyone knows that although one frequently remembers only the meaning of what one has read, often particular words are remembered, too. In the same way, long-term memory for phrases, surface form of sentences, and presumably also for the products of intermediate stages of the sentence comprehension process is possible. The main content of a memory episode consists, however, of meaning elements, simply because in reading or listening the meaning of a message is usually considered its most important aspect.

The kind of memory episode that is formed after reading a short paragraph is indicated in the last column of Table 2. It consists primarily of the text base that the reader has constructed on the basis of the paragraph (which may, of course, be a very incomplete and inaccurate copy of the original text base), plus context elements to identify where and when this text had been experienced, plus a sprinkling of other types of elements— graphemic, visual, acoustic, word, and syntactic. It must be emphasized again that this is the usual state of affairs, but that these normally neglected elements will be stored in addition to meaning or even in place of it, if they somehow appear important. A strange type face in reading or an accent in listening are unusual in experiments, and the subject must assume that they have something to do with the point of the study. A list of unrelated active and passive sentences is equally unusual, and the alert subject cannot help noticing that sentence voice is the important variable in such an experiment, and therefore carefully encodes syntactic features with each sentence. On the other hand, if we instruct a subject to read a text so that he later can make inferences about it, nonpropositional elements probably will be neglected.

There is a second process that determines what gets selected for inclusion in a memory episode, and that is the biasing process, which insures that common elements among memory episodes are preferentially encoded. The operation of this bias has been outlined in Section I, and there is no need to go into further details here. In summary, then, we have distinguished two separate influences that determine which elements from the many available in working memory are selected for encoding in episodic memory: a control process which assigns selection probabilities to the different levels of elements according to task demands, and a biasing mechanism which selects particular elements within each level.

In concluding this section I would like to point out the similarity of the present view of sentence memory with Miller's kernel-plus-footnote hypothesis (e.g., Miller, 1962). Clearly, propositions play a similar role as Miller's kernels, and the memory traces from the linguistic analyses that had to be performed to understand text are obvious counterparts of Miller's syntactic footnotes. However, kernels are syntactic concepts, while propositions derive from a semantic analysis. Furthermore, Miller's syntactic footnotes were obligatory and entirely predictable from transformational grammar; we leave open the possibility that syntactic analysis may not be performed at all in some cases, and may be only partial in others, and, in any case, involve entirely different operations than the transformations specified by transformational grammar. One might, therefore, prefer Miller's original theory over the present one for its specificity; but it is exactly those specific assumptions that did not hold up well to experimental test. In contrast, the situation with respect to vagueness and specificity is reversed when it comes to a comparison between Miller's kernels and the propositions of the present theory: the notion of a kernel sentence was never sufficiently elaborated and the semantic concept of a proposition may go some way toward fulfilling the expectations that were raised among psychologists when they first heard about "kernels."

IV.   ANSWERING QUESTIONS ABOUT A TEXT FROM MEMORY

After letting a subject read a text at his own pace, the experimenter removes the text and asks the subject to respond yes or no to a simple test statement. He is to answer "yes" if the test statement has been a part of what he had just read, and "no" otherwise. In order to force the subject to respond to the meaning of the test statement and not simply to whether or not some of the words used had appeared in the text, false statements are always constructed from words actually used in the text, so that they form a novel sentence that asserts something that is not true with respect to the content of the text. For the moment, let us assume that sentences requiring a yes answer are lifted verbatim from the text. The task is simple, and practically all sentences should be answered correctly by the experimental subjects. The dependent variables of interest are the response latencies for correct yes answers. False sentences are included merely for methodological reasons, and no theoretical predictions concerning them will be made.

The content of the subject's memory at the end of the reading has been described in the previous section. Briefly, we have a multiplicity of traces, from visual to semantic, each decaying at its own rate, plus a stable but highly selective memory episode concerning the text. In this situation the test statement appears, and the question is this: How does the subject arrive at his response?

The basic theoretical mechanism that is required is again the pattern matching procedure described in Section I. It is, however, complicated because there is not just one pattern to be matched, but a whole hierarchy of patterns. As the subject reads and comprehends the test statement, he goes through the same processes as in the reading of the original text, as a result of which graphemic, auditory, lexical, syntactic and propositional memory traces are formed. Thus, a pattern match is possible at any of these levels. It is assumed that these matches are performed in parallel. A response occurs when a match is successful at any level.

If lower-level memory traces are still available, the time required for a match is generally less than if the match can be performed only at the highest, propositional level. There are two reasons for this prediction. First, the test statement must be processed in the same way as any text: it takes time to elaborate the graphemic stimulus trace via processes of pattern matching and pattern completion, and a lower-level trace of the test statement may already be matched to some unit in episodic memory while processing at higher levels is still going on. Second, suppose that the time required for a pattern match is a random variable and equal for all types of matches. If several matches occur in parallel, a response can occur when the first one of these produces a result. Therefore, the average reaction time for several parallel processes will be less than for a single one. Specifically, if a test statement is presented right after reading a short paragraph, it can be expected that traces in working memory from the actual words used as well as from the syntactic analyses performed would still be available, in addition to the meaning of the text. A test statement may be recognized by means of a pattern match with any one of these traces, and hence recognition should be relatively fast. On the other hand, if the presentation of a test statement is sufficiently delayed, and if during the delay interval the subject performs other reading tasks that are likely to interfere with traces in working memory, only the elements encoded in episodic memory will be available for a match, and the reaction time should be correspondingly slower.

Posner's well-known experiments on letter matching on the basis of physical and name identity can be interpreted within this framework (Posner, 1969). Posner reported that matches on the basis of physical identity of letters were about 80 msec faster than name matches if the two letters followed each other immediately. The superiority of physical matches over name matches decreased, however, as the interval between the two letters was lengthened, and disappeared when the second letter was delayed by 2 sec. One possible interpretation of these results is that initially physical matches were performed on the bases of the visual trace of the letter, but that this trace decayed rapidly so that after a 2-sec delay all matches had to be performed on the basis of the name code. Posner also showed that name and physical codes could be manipulated separately. For instance, subjects were able to retain the visual trace to some extent, which implies that even at these low levels of analysis the control processes postulated by the present theory may be effective.

In Section V I shall present some experimental results which test some implications of the present theory. These studies may be regarded as paragraph analogues of Posner's letter matching tasks, and they demonstrate that qualitatively similar results may be obtained at different levels of memory. The theory just outlined provides an integrative framework for these findings, and, most importantly, relates them to the standard memory literature.

V.   MATCHES AT LINGUISTIC AND PROPOSITIONAL LEVELS

One way to obtain some empirical evidence concerning the questions raised here is to ask people to respond to test statements for which we know that only a propositional representation is available, and to compare response times with responses to statements for which the whole array of different memory traces is available. In working with even moderately long texts, the strictly visual and auditory memory traces which have a decay time of only seconds, can safely be neglected. Matches at these levels are out of the question because by the time the subject has finished reading a paragraph, that type of information has already been lost for most of the text. What we are concerned with, then, are the lexical, linguistic, and propositional traces. Subjects are expected to respond faster if they have all three types available than when a match must be made at the propositional level. We have tried two ways to make sure that matches must occur at the propositional level. In one case, long delays were used, and it was assumed that whatever the decay rate for lexical or linguistic information might be, such traces would be lost, and that therefore responses must be based upon propositional traces. In addition, we arranged texts in such a way that our subjects had available only propositional information in the first place; the information was obtained not through reading, which gives rise to a multiplicity of traces, but via inferences. Thus, test statements that referred to information that the subject had to infer could be compared with explicitly presented statements. I shall discuss this experiment first.

The study was done with Jan Keenan and is reported in Kintsch (1974). The main problem of the experiment was to arrange texts in such a way that one could be sure that the reader would make certain inferences. An example of how we tried to achieve this is shown in Table 3. The same 8-proposition text base is expressed in two ways. In one case, Proposition 4, (CAUSE,(DISCARD,CIGARETTE),FIRE), is explicitly contained in the text as *The discarded cigarette started a fire.* This is the explicit version of the paragraph. In the implicit version this statement is missing. However, unless a reader infers this fact from his knowledge about forests, burning cigarettes, and fires, the two sentences of the paragraph are discontinuous and make no sense as a text. To encourage the subjects to infer the implicit

TABLE 3
An Eight-Proposition Text Base and Two
Corresponding Textual Versions.[a]

1	(DISCARD,CIGARETTE) &
2	(CARELESS,DISCARD) &
3	(BURN,CIGARETTE) &
*4	(CAUSE,1,FIRE) &
5	(DESTROY,FIRE,FOREST) &
6	(SIZE,FOREST,ACRE) &
7	(VIRGIN,FOREST) &
8	(MANY,ACRE)

Explicit: A carelessly discarded burning cigarette started a fire. The fire destroyed many acres of virgin forest.

Implicit: A burning cigarette was carelessly discarded. The fire destroyed many acres of virgin forest.

[a]The proposition omitted in the implicit paragraph is marked with an asterisk.

proposition we instructed them specifically that each paragraph told one connected story, and should be understood in this way. After reading a text, therefore, we expected all subjects to have stored in memory Proposition 4, but those who read the explicit paragraph to have stored, in addition, lexical and linguistic traces not available to the readers of the implicit passage.

In the experiment we used 12 pairs of paragraphs such as that presented in Table 3. The test statement was always based on the critical proposition. There were also 10 pairs of longer paragraphs (between 34 and 123 words), for which more than one question was asked. In addition to test statements that referred to the critical propositions, there were textual statements concerning explicit statements in both versions. These could be used to check on the general comparability of the two paragraph versions, and also provided the necessary false test statements.

The 40 subjects who participated in the experiment were tested individually. The general procedure consisted of the following sequence of events. A slide with one of the paragraphs appeared; the subject read at his own rate and pressed an advance button when he finished; the test statement appeared on the next slide, and the trial was terminated by the subject's "true" or "false" response (made by depressing appropriate response keys). Subjects were instructed to "work as fast as you can, but the most important thing is that you understand what you read, not speed," and "answer true or false based on the information which is implied or stated in the paragraph."

The results of the analysis confirmed the predictions made here. Reaction times to the test statements were shorter when they referred to explicit information than when they referred to implicit information. For short paragraphs, explicit test statements required 3.8 sec on the average for a response, while implicit statements required 4.2 sec. For the long paragraphs, the corresponding values were 4.3 and 4.8 sec. This difference was significant statistically, $F(1, 38) = 4.03$, at the .051 level. In an analysis over paragraphs rather than subjects, average response times were greater for the implicit statements on 32 of the 36 questions (subject differences are, however, confounded in this comparison because a between-group design was used). Control questions that referred to explicitly presented material in both versions of the paragraphs did not differ significantly (4.5 sec for the explicit, 4.4 sec for the implicit version of the paragraphs). Thus, it appears that the paragraphs were generally comparable.

The experiment was replicated with one important modification: test statements were not given immediately after reading, but after a 15-min delay filled with an interferring verbal task, which we hoped, would be sufficient to erase from memory any lexical–linguistic traces about the paragraphs and force all subjects to answer the test statements on the basis of propositional memory, thus cancelling the advantage for the explicit statements.

Three of the short and four of the long paragraphs used before were employed again. In addition, eight dummy paragraphs were included as a warm-up task and to provide false test statements. Forty subjects read all 15 paragraphs as before, and were told that they would be questioned about them later. After reading, a subject participated for 15 minutes in a sentence memory task which was designed to interfere with lexical–linguistic memory traces. Finally, he answered "true" or "false" to the test statements from the paragraphs. Statements were presented in random order. The paragraphs were selected in such a way that their topics were quite distinct, so that subjects did not experience any difficulty in deciding to which paragraph a question referred.

Short paragraphs had a mean response time of 4.1 sec for both explicit and implicit statements, while long paragraphs had a mean of 5.2 sec for explicit and 5.4 sec for implicit statements. An analysis of variance revealed no significant differences for the explicit–implicit comparisons. We may, therefore, conclude that we were successful in eliminating nonpropositional levels of memory by means of the 15-min delay used, and that subjects were responding on the basis of propositional memory in this experiment, irrespective of whether a statement had been explicit or implicit.

A third experiment by Gail McKoon and Jan Keenan replicated and extended these findings. Eight different paragraphs were used, which were longer (116–160 words) than those of the earlier experiments. Four questions were asked about each paragraph: two were true test statements referring either to an explicit or implicit proposition from the paragraph, and two were false statements, also referring either to explicit or implicit material. Again 40 subjects served in the experiment, which was computer controlled with oscilloscope displays. Four delays were used between reading of a text and answering the test statements: 0 sec, 30 sec, 20 min, and 48 hr. The first and third delay intervals replicated our earlier work; the 30-sec delay interval was included to determine whether the memory traces responsible for the facilitation of the response immediately after reading are lost or weakened within that time period. If short-term memory is involved, we would expect just that to happen. The 48-hr interval was included to check the hypothesis that propositional memory is quite stable and would show little change during that interval. The 30-sec and 20-min intervals were always filled with a rehearsal prevention task (unscrambling sentences appearing on the scope).

The results of this study confirmed the earlier ones. First, there was no significant difference in response times between 0 delay and 30-sec delay, in this way ruling out short-term memory as a causal factor for the effects obtained. Furthermore, there was no significant difference between performance after 20 min and 48 hr (though this statement must be regarded with care, since the data are not very clear in this respect, and the lack of a significant difference may merely reflect a lack of statistical power). On the other hand, explicit statements were again answered faster at 0- and 30-sec delays (4.0 sec for explicit and 4.8 sec for implicit statements $F(1, 554) = 11.4$), while the difference between these two types of statements was no longer statistically significant with 20-min and 48-hr delays (4.8 sec for explicit versus 5.1 sec for implicit statements, $F(1, 554) = 1.54$). Thus, the data are again in accord with the theory outlined here. After short delays, subjects have available both propositional and lexical–linguistic representations of a text and can decide relatively rapidly whether test statements are true or not by means of matches at the lexical–linguistic level. After long delays, or for test statements that were never explicitly presented, only the propositional level is available, and matches require somewhat longer. It should, perhaps, be noted that in all cases subjects were quite able to respond correctly: the proportion of correct responses was always high and only slightly greater for explicit statements than for implicit statements, presumably reflecting a (small) decrease in the likelihood that a reader will successfully encode a proposition that required an inference as compared to one that is directly represented in a text.

There are other ways of obtaining evidence concerning processing at different memory levels in statement verification tasks. One possibility is to compare subjects' performance on a true–false task with performance on mere recognition tasks. The former is more likely to involve the propositional level, whereas determination of whether a sentence was or was not part of a previous text need not. Some data that we have collected are quite suggestive in this respect. They come from experiments that were designed for quite different purposes, which means that they are not ideal for testing the present hypothesis, but the results are worth noting.

The studies in questions were done with Dorothy Monk and are also reported in Kintsch (1974). There are two parallel experiments. In the first one, 16 paragraphs (biographies of American presidents) were used. Four paragraphs each were of length 20, 40, 80 and 120 words. After reading each paragraph, a subject was shown a test sentence on a slide and asked to respond "true" or "false" to it, as fast as he could. Test statements were always seven words long. True statements paraphrased a statement made approximately in the middle of the paragraph. The wording of the test statement was fairly close to the original text, except that nouns were substituted for all pronouns, word order was rearranged, and some words used in the text were deleted. False statements were constructed by combining words from the text in such a way that a grammatical, plausible sentence resulted that clearly contradicted facts asserted in the paragraph.

A second experiment used the same procedure, except that 20 new paragraphs were adapted from the same source (we feel that it is crucial for this type of work to use as many different paragraphs as possible), and the test statements as well as the response requirement were slightly changed. The paragraphs were written in such a way that they contained, somewhere near their middle, a seven-word sentence that could be lifted from the text and used verbatim as a test statement. Furthermore, subjects in this experiment were instructed to respond "yes" only if a statement was a verbatim repetition of a sentence in the text, and "no" otherwise.

It seems reasonable that under these circumstances the subjects who were asked to make true–false judgments would base their responses upon matches at the propositional level, whereas the subjects making yes–no recognition decisions would work at a word-linguistic level. They were, after all, required to respond "yes" only to verbatim repetitions, and, although there were in actual fact no true but nonverbatim test sentences, it appears likely that subjects relied mainly on surface structure matches. Thus, one would expect response times in the true–false experiment to be generally longer than in the yes–no recognition experiment. This was clearly the case. The mean response time for true–false judgments was 5.8 sec, but only 4.0 sec were required for the yes–no judgments. Since both subjects and texts were different in the two studies, and because of the differences in the nature of true test statements, this finding is not unambiguous, but, as far as we can trust it, it certainly agrees with the claims made here.

The main purpose of the experiments under discussion was, however, a different one, namely to investigate whether the speed with which a test statement can be answered depends upon the length of the paragraph. The answer to that question turns out to be quite interesting in the present context. Not only was there a statistically significant relationship between paragraph length and response speed in both experiments, it also appeared that the rate of scanning was faster for those paragraphs where the scanning operation was performed at the surface structure level than for those where the scanning occurred at a propositional level. In the true–false task each word in the paragraph added 11 msec to the response time, whereas only 4 msec were required in the yes–no task. We have, however, recently performed some experiments that seem to indicate that it is not paragraph length per se which influences response times in these experiments, but the position of the test statement in the text hierarchy. With longer paragraphs, it becomes more likely that a test statement refers to a highly subordinate proposition, while the level of subordination of test statements tends to be less for shorter paragraphs. For the moment, at least, the whole question of exactly how a subject searches through a paragraph for information concerning some test statement must remain open. But even though it is impossible to say, at this stage of our investigations, how information in a text is located and what precisely the role of paragraph length is, the results reported above are quite suggestive: decision times are faster when the subject operates at a lexical–linguistic level than when he operates at a propositional level, and scanning times are also faster in the former case. As has been stressed before, these claims are a little suspect because they are based upon comparisons between two rather different experiments, but they are still worth mentioning here, because they fit in very well with the levels of processing approach of this chapter.

VI. POSTSCRIPT: LIST LEARNING AND TEXT LEARNING

In the first two sections of this paper, two theoretical developments have been described that occurred quite independently. The first is a model for episodic memory, and its main purpose is to provide a coherent framework for the rich empirical results that are available today from the laboratory investigation of memory. What characterized this investigation was its concern with memory for word lists, rather than for texts. It has sometimes been claimed that, therefore, the results of this research effort are irrevelant to our understanding of comprehension and memory of texts, and hence useless for the development of an educational technology. List-learning research, it is said, is strictly of academic interest, in the worst sense of that expression. It would be unfortunate, indeed, if that were true, both because a large body of data and a sophisticated research methodology would suddenly become pointless and forgotten (an event not without precedent in the history of our science), and equally because psycholinguistic research would have to start anew without a historical foundation (wasting its time rediscovering phenomena and blind alleys long familiar in the verbal learning research).

In what way can one say that memory theory and psycholinguistics have been brought together in the work reported here? Primarily, in that the theory outlined here is a straightforward extension of a recognition model for list-learning experiments. As is made quite clear by Table 2, the list-learning model can, in fact, be regarded as a submodel of the present one: list memory and text memory do not differ in the memory processes assumed, but entirely in terms of the greater number of qualitatively distinct processing levels that are involved in reading a text, in contrast to reading a word list. Each of these processing levels generates its own memory trace, and I have tried to investigate how the existence of these multiple traces may affect performance in one particular laboratory situation.

Experimental results have confirmed some of the deductions made from the theory. Basically, what I have been trying to show was that matches made at a lexical–linguistic level are faster than matches at a propositional level, much like, in a letter-matching task, physical matches are faster than name matches. We found several ways to manipulate the likelihood that matches occur at a particular level, either the lexical–linguistic or propositional one. First, we compared verification times for test statements explicitly presented in a text and verification times for statements inferred during reading. After brief delays, when the explicitly presented statements were still represented by multilevel traces, the expected results were indeed obtained. Second, we have shown that the advantage of explicit over implicit test statements is lost if a 15–20-min delay is interposed between reading and test. Presumably, this reflects the fact that after such a delay, only the more stable propositional traces are available any more. Third, we observed that subjects respond faster when asked to determine whether a test statement is a verbatim copy of one made in a paragraph than when they are asked to determine whether a test statement was true or false with respect to some text. Again, we assumed that in the latter case processing occurred mainly at the propositional level, while in the yes–no recognition task matches must be made at a lexical–linguistic level.

Clearly, these results leave open many questions about memory for text. But perhaps the kind of framework developed here will prove useful in future studies of text memory, and the levels-of-processing approach advocated by several participants of this symposium may provide a bridge between research on text memory and the existing work on list memory.

ACKNOWLEDGMENTS

This research was supported by Grant MH 15872 from the National Institute of Mental Health. I thank Eileen Kintsch, Jan Keenan, and Gail McKoon for critical comments on various drafts of this chapter.

REFERENCES

Bever, T. G. The cognitive basis for linguistic structures. In J. R. Hayes (Ed.), *Cognition and the development of language.* New York: Wiley, 1970.

Craik, F. I. M., & Lockhart, R. S. Levels of processing: A framework for memory research. *Journal of Verbal Learning and Verbal Behavior,* 1972, **11,** 671–684.

Darwin, C. J., Turvey, M. T., & Crowder, R. G. An auditory analogue of the Sperling partial report procedure: Evidence for brief auditory storage. *Cognitive Psychology,* 1972, **3,** 255–267.

Fodor, J. A., & Bever, T. G. The psychological reality of linguistic segments. *Journal of Verbal Learning and Verbal Behavior,* 1965, **4,** 414–420.

Fodor, J. A., & Garrett, M. Some syntactic determinants of sentential complexity. *Perception & Psychophysics,* 1967, **2,** 289–296.

Fodor, J. A., Garrett, M., & Bever, T. G. Some syntactic determinants of sentential complexity. II: Verb structure. *Perception & Psychophysics,* 1968, **3,** 453–461.

Gibson, E. J., Shurcliff, A., & Yonas, A. Utilization of spelling patterns by deaf and hearing subjects. In H. Levine & J. P. Williams (Eds.), *Basic studies in reading.* New York: Basic Books, 1970. Pp. 57–73.

Hakes, D. T. Effects of reducing complement constructions on sentence comprehension. *Journal of Verbal Learning and Verbal Behavior,* 1972, **11,** 278–286.

Jarvella, R. J. Syntactic processing of connected speech. *Journal of Verbal Learning and Verbal Behavior,* 1971, **10,** 409–416.

Johnson, N. F. Sequential verbal behavior. In T. R. Dixon & D. L. Horton (Eds.), *Verbal behavior and general behavior theory.* Englewood Cliffs: Prentice Hall, 1968. Pp. 421–450.

Kintsch, W. *The representation of meaning in memory.* Hillsdale, New Jersey: Lawrence Erlbaum Associates, 1974.

Kintsch, W., & Monk, D. Storage of complex information in memory: Some implications of the speed with which inferences can be made. *Journal of Experimental Psychology,* 1972, **94,** 25–32.

Kolers, P. A. Remembering operations. *Memory & Cognition*, 1973, 1, 347–355.

Meyer, D. E., & Schvaneveldt, R. W. Facilitation in recognizing pairs of words: Evidence of a dependence between retrieval operations. *Journal of Experimental psychology*, 1971, **90**, 227–234.

Miller, G. A. Some psychological studies of grammar. *American Psychologist*, 1962, **17**, 748–762.

Murdock, B. B., Jr. The retention of individual items. *Journal of Experimental psychology*, 1961, **62**, 618–625.

Murdock, B. B., Jr. *Human memory: Theory and data*. Hillsdale, New Jersey: Lawrence Erlbaum Associates, 1974.

Olson, D. R. Language and thought: Aspects of a cognitive theory of semantics. *Psychological Review*, 1970, **77**, 257–273.

Posner, M. I. Abstraction and the process of recognition. In G. H. Bower & J. T. Spence (Eds.), *The psychology of learning and motivation*. Vol. 3. New York: Academic Press, 1969. Pp. 44–100.

Rosenberg, S. Associative and phrase structure in sentence recall. *Journal of Verbal Learning and Verbal Behavior*, 1968, **7**, 1077–1081.

Rothkopf, E. Z. Incidental memory for location of information in text. *Journal of Verbal Learning and Verbal Behavior*, 1971, **10**, 608–613.

Seitz, M. R., & Weber, B. A. Effects of response requirements on the location of clicks superimposed on sentences. *Memory & Cognition*, 1974, **2**, 43–46.

Sperling, G. A model for visual memory tasks. *Human factors*, 1963, **5**, 19–31.

10
COMPUTER SIMULATION OF A LANGUAGE ACQUISITION SYSTEM: A FIRST REPORT

John R. Anderson
Human Performance Center
University of Michigan

This research is concerned with understanding language acquisition. The approach is different from the typical one. Generally, research in this area has asked, "What are the detailed facts of language acquisition?" and theories have been advanced which attempted to account for these facts. I have been principally focusing on one gross fact about language acquisition—that languages are learned at all. What I have been doing is trying to identify what algorithms are capable of language acquisition, attempting to simulate these algorithms by computer, and only later testing the psychological predictions of these algorithms. In this paper I attempt to do a number of things relevant to this enterprise. First, I review some of the significant work on language induction to convince the reader that it is far from a trivial matter to construct an algorithm that can induce a language. I also argue that natural languages are learnable because the learner can take advantage of strong constraints on the possible relations between a sentence and its semantic referent. A computer simulation program called LAS.1 is described in detail which makes use of some of these constraints. It enjoys some success in a language-induction situation. Then I discuss in more general terms some ideas about the basis for making generalizations in learning natural language. Finally, an experiment is reported which tests one of the claims of LAS.1 about language learnability.

FORMAL RESULTS ON GRAMMAR INDUCTION

Probably the most influential paper in the field is by Gold (1967). He provided an explicit criterion for success in a language-induction problem and proceeded to determine formally which learner–teacher interactions could achieve that criterion for which languages. Gold considers a language to be *identified in the limit* if after some finite time the learner discovers a grammar that generates the strings of the language. He considers two information sequences — in the *first* the learner is presented with all the sentences of the language, and in the *second* the learner is presented with all strings, each properly identified as sentence or nonsentence. Then Gold asks this question: Suppose the learner can assume the language comes from some formally characterized class of languages; can he identify in the limit which language it is? Gold considers the classical nesting of language classes—finite cardinality languages, regular (finite state), context free, context sensitive, and primitive recursive. His classic result is that if the learner is only given positive information about the language (i.e., the first information sequence), then he can only identify finite cardinality languages. However, given positive and negative information (i.e., the second information sequence), he can learn up to primitive recursive languages.

The proof that the finite state class is not identifiable with only positive information is deceptively simple. Among the finite state languages are all languages of finite cardinality (i.e., with only finitely many strings). At every finite point in the information sequence the learner will not know if the language is generated by one of the infinite number of finite cardinality languages that includes the sample or an infinite cardinality finite state grammar that includes the sample. Logically, it could be either.

It is similarly easy to prove that any language in the primitive recursive class can be induced, given positive and negative information. It is possible to enumerate all possible primitive recursive grammars. Assume an algorithm that proceeds through this countably infinite enumeration, looking at one grammar after another until it finds the correct one. The algorithm will stay with any grammar as long as the information sequence is consistent with it. Any incorrect grammar G will be rejected at some finite point in the information sequence—either because the sequence contains, as a negative instance, a sentence generated by G, or as a positive instance, a sentence not generated by G. Since the correct grammar has some finite position in the enumeration, the algorithm will eventually consider it and stay with it. Gold's proofs are technically better than the above, but these will do for present purposes.

The algorithm outlined in the second proof may not seem very satisfactory. For instance, the position is astronomical of English grammar in an alphabetic ordering of all possible context-sensitive grammars using English morphemes as terminal symbols. However, Gold also proved that there is no algorithm uniformly more effective than this enumeration technique. That is, given any algorithm one can pick some context-sensitive language and information sequence for which the enumeration algorithm will be faster.

Thus, Gold leaves us with two very startling results with which we must live. First, only finite cardinality languages can be induced without use of negative information. This is startling because children get little negative feedback and make little use of what negative feedback they do get (Brown, 1973). Second, no procedure is more effective than blind enumeration. This is startling because blind enumeration is clearly hopeless as a practical induction algorithm for natural language.

The basic problem is that the class of all context-sensitive languages is just too large and amorphous for a learner possibly to identify an arbitrary choice from this class, given an arbitrary information sequence. There has to be more structure to the language-learning situation and the learner has to take advantage of this structure. This structure can be essentially of three sorts:

1. The class of possible languages can be much more restricted than the class of context-sensitive languages.

2. The learner can make certain assumptions about the information sequence. For instance, he may expect to see certain kinds of grammatical structures early or see certain structures used with some constant probability.

3. There may exist information other than the sentences in the information sequence. This information may serve to provide valuable clues as to the structure of the language.

These three sorts of ideas have been used in those past induction algorithms that have had some success in language-learning situations.

For instance, Pao (1969) formalized an algorithm for finite-state grammar induction that did not require the number of states to be known in advance. A sample set of sentences was provided that utilized all the rules in the grammar. A minimal finite-state network was constructed that generated exactly the sample set of sentences. Then an attempt was made to generalize by merging nodes in the network. The algorithm checked the consequences of potential generalizations by asking the teacher whether sentences added by these generalizations were actually in the target language. Pao's work is particularly interesting because she extended these induction procedures to context-free languages. Apparently unaware of Woods' (1970) work, she developed a network formalism very similar to his. She found that such augmented network grammars could be induced by her algorithms if she provided punctuation information indicating where transitions between networks occur. Basically such punctuation information amounts to indicating the sentence's surface structure. Interestingly, Saporta, Blumenthal, Lackowski, and Rieff (1963) found that humans learned artificial context-free languages more easily when surface structure was indicated by spacing. I also make use of the Woods' network formalism and a similar punctuation idea.

Crespi-Reghizzi (1970) also obtained encouraging results when his induction program was given information about sentence surface structure. He was interested in the induction of operator-precedence languages that are a subset of context-free languages. For a special subset of operator-precedence languages he was able to define an algorithm that worked with only positive information. Except for finite cardinality languages, this is the only available report of success with just positive information.

I think the work of Pao and Crespi-Reghizzi have promising aspects. They have shown that relatively efficient, constructive algorithms are possible for interesting language classes if the algorithms have access to information about the sentences' surface structure. The problem with their work is that this information is provided in an ad hoc manner. It has the flavor of "cheating," and certainly it is not the way things happen with respect to natural language induction. There is also a sense in which the work of Pao, Crespi-Reghizzi, and others is irrelevant to the task of inducing a natural language. They have, as their goal, the induction of the correct syntactic characterization of a target language. However, this is not what natural language learning is about. In learning a natural language the goal is to learn a *map* that allows us to go from sentences to their corresponding conceptual structures or vice versa.

The importance of semantics has been very forcefully brought home to psychologists by a pair of experiments by Moeser and Bregman (1972, 1973) on the induction of artificial languages. They compared language learning in the situation where their subjects only saw well-formed strings of the language versus the situation where they saw well-formed strings plus pictures of the semantic referent to these strings. In either case, the criterion test was for the subject to be able to detect which strings of the language were well formed—without aid of any referent pictures. After 3000 training trials subjects in the no-referent condition were at chance in the criterion test, whereas subjects in the referent condition were essentially perfect.

THE ROLE OF SEMANTICS

Results like those of Moeser and Bregman have left some believing that there is some magic power in having a semantic referent. However, there is no necessary advantage to having a semantic referent. The relationship between a sentence and its semantic referent could, in principle, be an arbitrary primitive recursive relation. Inducing this relation is at least as difficult as inducing an arbitrary primitive recursive language. For the formally trained reader there is a proof of this claim in the Appendix. The consequence of this fact is that inducing a semantic relation between language and referent is not a tractable problem unless it is assumed that there are strong constraints on the form of this relation. My research is aimed at identifying these constraints and constructing algorithms that can take advantage of the constraints.

How does this semantic referent facilitate grammar induction? There are at least three ways. First, rules of natural language are not formulated with respect to single words but with respect to word classes like noun or transitive verb which have a common semantic core. Therefore, semantics can help determine the word classes. This is much more efficient than learning the syntactic rules for each word separately. Second, semantics is of considerable aid in generalizing rules. A general heuristic employed by LAS (Language Acquisition System) is: if two syntactically similar rules function to create the same semantic structure, then they can be merged into a single rule. Third, there is a nonarbitrary correspondence between the structure of the semantic referent and the structure of the sentence that permits one to punctuate the sentence with surface-structure information. The nature of this correspondence will be explained later.

Siklóssy's Work

One attempt to incorporate semantics as a guide to grammar induction was by Siklóssy (1971). He attempted to write a program that would be able to learn languages from the language-through-pictures books (e.g., Richards, Jasuilko, & Gibson, 1961). The books in this series attempt to teach a language by presenting pictures paired with sentences that describe the depicted situations. Siklóssy's program, *Zbie*, used general pattern-matching techniques to find correspondences between the pictures (actually hand-encoded picture descriptions) and the sentences. The program does use information in the picture encodings to help induce the surface structure of the sentence, somewhat in the manner of LAS. However, it remains unclear exactly what use *Zbie* makes of semantics or what kinds of languages the program can learn. The displayed examples of the program's behavior have very few examples of it making generalizations. As we will see, a program must have strong powers of generalization if it is to learn a language. The few examples of generalization work as follows: Suppose *Zbie* sees the following three sentences:

> John walks.
> Mary walks.
> John talks.

On the basis of this distributional evidence, *Zbie* will generalize and assume that *John* and *Mary* constitute one word class and *walks* and *talks* constitute another. Thus, it would recognize *Mary talks* as an acceptable sentence although it never studied this sentence.

Siklóssy also provides no discussion of how his program's behavior relates to that of a human learning a language. The one example of an attempt to simulate child language learning is Kelley (1967). His program attempted to simulate the initial growth of child utterances from one word, to two words, to three words. Kelley claims to be making use of semantic information, but he never specifies its role in the program's performance. The details of the program are not explained. In his examples, the program never gets to the point of producing grammatical sentences, and it is unclear whether it could.

I think all the preceding induction programs underestimate or ignore the potential for generalization that exists in natural language. Suppose a non-English learner saw Sentences (1)–(3) along with the information that indicated their semantic structure:

(1)   The boy kicked the girl.
(2)   The girl thanked a man.
(3)   The dog bit a fireman who kicked a cat.

Further, suppose the learner were presented Sentences 4–6 and asked to judge their acceptability.

(4)   The boy thanked a man.
(5)   A cat bit the fireman.
(6)   The girl who thanked the boy kicked the cat.

After studying Sentences (1)–(3), none of these test sentences would be accepted by any previous induction program. Yet I would not be surprised if our non-English learner accepted some or all of these sentences. In Sentence (4), *The boy,* the subject of Sentence (1), is being generalized to go with the predicate of Sentence (2). This is presumably because the learner sees *no semantic difference* between the role of *girl* in Sentence (2) and *boy* in Sentence (1). If the learner accepted Sentence (5), it would be because he had generalized the object noun phrase, *a cat,* from the relative clause of Sentence (3) to the subject noun phrase of the main sentence. In Sentence (6), the relative clause is being generalized from an object noun phrase modifier to a subject noun phrase modifier.

These examples are hypothetical. It may turn out that some of these are not made in natural language learning. They illustrate, however, the kind of radical generalizations that I think are necessary to natural language learning. These generalizations are examples of what I call *semantics-induced equivalence of syntax*. Basically, this refers to the fact that the same syntactic devices tend to be used to signal similar semantic relations in different linguistic contexts. This permits the learner to generalize syntactic knowledge across contexts. There is no logical reason why a language should have this redundancy in its structure, but natural languages do. The problem of natural language learning is half-solved when we recognize that this redundancy exists. However, the other half of the problem is not solved so easily. That is, one must understand the nature of those redundancies to the point where one can specify effective learning algorithms. Most of the remainder of this chapter is taken up with reporting what progress I have made so far in this task.

RATIONALE FOR THE RESEARCH APPROACH

Most of the research effort has been devoted to developing a program called LAS (an acronym for Language Acquisition System). I will describe a first-pass version of the program that has as its only serious goal success in a nontrivial language acquisition situation. This emphasis on adequacy is justified in light of the evidence reviewed about the serious logical problems in the task of language induction. It is worthwhile to know how languages can be learned at all before turning to the question of how humans learn languages.

This project does have the ultimate goal of providing a faithful simulation of child language acquisition. One might question whether a system constructed just to succeed at language learning will have much in common with the child's acquisition system. I strongly suspect it will, provided we insist that the system have the same information-processing limitations as a child and provided its language-learning situation has the same information-processing demands as that of the child. The consideration underlying this optimistic forecast is that learning a natural language imposes very severe and highly unique information-processing demands on any induction system, and consequently, there are very severe limitations on the possible structures for a successful system. A similar argument has been forcefully advanced by Simon (1969) with respect to the information-processing demands of various problem-solving tasks.

The current version of the program LAS.1 works in an overly simplified domain and makes unreasonable assumptions about information-processing capacities. Nonetheless, it predicts many of the gross features of generalization and overgeneralization in child language learning. It is terribly "off" in other aspects. It turns out that many of its failures of simulation can be traced to the unrealistic assumptions it is making about task domain and information-processing abilities. These assumptions were made to make the first-pass task more tractable. I remain optimistic that, as the unrealistic assumptions are removed, the program will begin to provide an adequate simulation.

It is probably inevitable that the question will be asked as to whether it is really worthwhile to invest in the resources necessary to construct a computer program. Could not the model just be specified conceptually? The reason why this is not possible has to do with the complexity of any theory that addresses the details of natural language. There is no other way to test the predictions of such a theory or to assure that it is internally consistent. The experience with transformational grammars handwritten for natural language is that they have hidden inconsistencies (Friedman, 1971). The computer is a tool essential to developing and testing complex theories.

THE PROGRAM LAS.1

Overview of LAS

LAS is an interactive program written in Michigan LISP (Hafner & Wilcox, 1974). The program to be described is LAS.1, an early version of LAS. The LAS program is in a constant state of change as new ideas for grammar induction are tried out. Therefore, LAS.1 represents a short period in the history of LAS. The program accepts as input lists of words, which it treats as sentences, and scene descriptions encoded in a variant of the HAM propositional language (see Anderson & Bower, 1973). It obeys commands to speak, understand, and learn. The logical structure of LAS is illustrated in Fig. 1. Central to LAS is an augmented transition network grammar similar to that of Woods (1970). In response to the command *Listen,* LAS evokes the program UNDERSTAND. The input to UNDERSTAND is a sentence. LAS uses the information in the network grammar to parse the sentence and obtain a representation of the sentence's

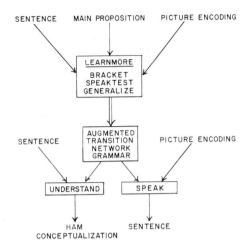

FIG. 1. A schematic representation giving the input and output of the major components of LAS: LEARNMORE, SPEAK, and UNDERSTAND.

meaning. In response to the command *Speak,* LAS evokes the program SPEAK. SPEAK receives a picture encoding and uses the information in the network grammar to generate a sentence to describe the encoding. Note that LAS is using the same network formalism both to speak and understand. The principal purpose of SPEAK and UNDERSTAND in LAS is to provide a test of the grammars induced by LEARNMORE.

The philosophy behind the LEARNMORE program is to provide LAS with the same information that a child has when he is learning a language through ostension. It is assumed that in this learning mode the adult can both direct the child's attention to what is being described and focus the child's attention on that aspect of the situation being described. Thus, LEARNMORE is provided with a sentence, a HAM description of the scene, and an indication of the main proposition in the sentence. It is to produce as output the network grammar that will be used by SPEAK and UNDERSTAND. It is possible that the picture description provides more information than is in the sentence. This provides no obstacle to LAS's heuristics. In this particular version of LAS, it is assumed that it already knows the meaning of the content words in the sentence. With this information BRACKET will assign a surface structure to the sentence. SPEAKTEST will determine whether the sentence is handled by the current grammar. If not, additions are made to handle this case. These additions generalize to other cases so that LAS can understand many more sentences than the ones it was explicitly trained with.

The SPEAKTEST program constructs a parsing network adequate to handle all the sentences it was presented with. Also it makes many low-level generalizations about phrase structures and word classes. This permits

LAS to analyze successfully or generate many novel sentences. However, many essential grammatical generalizations are left to be made by the program GENERALIZE. Principally, GENERALIZE must recognize that networks and words occurring at various points in the grammar are identical. Recognition of identical grammars is essential to identifying the recursive structure of the language. GENERALIZE is a program that is only called after fairly stable networks and word classes have been built up. It is only at this point that it is safe to make these critical generalizations.

The HAM.2 Memory System

LAS.1 uses a version of the HAM memory system (see Anderson & Bower, 1973) called HAM.2. HAM.2 provides LAS with two essential features. First, it provides a representational formalism for propositional knowledge. This is used for representing the comprehension output of UNDERSTAND, the to-be-spoken input to SPEAK, the semantic information in long-term memory, and syntactic information about word classes. HAM.2 also contains a memory searching algorithm MATCH1, which is used to evaluate various parsing conditions. For instance, the UNDERSTAND program requires that certain features be true of a word for a parsing rule to apply. These are checked by the MATCH1 process. The same MATCH1 process is used by the SPEAK program to determine whether the action associated with a parsing rule creates part of the to-be-spoken structure. This MATCH1 process is a variant of the MATCH process described by Anderson and Bower (1973, Chs. 9 and 12), and its details are not discussed here.

However, it would be useful to describe here the representational formalisms used by HAM.2. Figure 2 illustrates how the information in the sentence *A red square is above the circle* would be represented with the HAM.2 network formalisms. There are four distinct propositions predicated about the two nodes X and Y: X is red, X is a square, X is above Y, and Y is a circle. Each proposition is represented by a distinct tree structure. Each tree structure consists of a root proposition node connected by an S link to a subject node and by a P link to a predicate node. The predicate nodes can be decomposed into an R link pointing to a relation node and into an O link pointing to an object node. The semantics of these representations are to be interpreted in terms of simple set-theoretic notions. The subject is a subset of the predicate. Thus, the individual X is a subset of the red things, the square things, and the things above Y. The individual Y is a subset of the circular things.

One other point needs emphasizing about this representation. There is a distinction made between words and the concepts that they reference. The words are connected to their corresponding ideas by links labeled W.

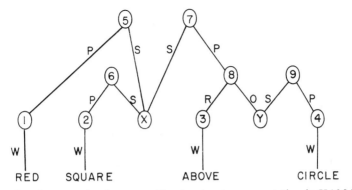

Fɪɢ. 2.   An example of a propositional network representation in HAM.2.

Figure 2 illustrates all the network notation needed in the current implementation of LAS. There are a number of respects in which this representation is simpler than the old HAM representation. There are not the means
for representing the situation (time + place) in which such a fact is true
or for embedding one proposition within another. Thus, we cannot express
in HAM.2 such sentences as *Yesterday in my bedroom a red square was
above the circle* or *John believes that a red square is above the circle.*
Representations for such statements are not needed in the current LAS
project because we are only concerned with representing information that
can be conveyed by ostension. In ostension, the assumed time and place
are here and now. Concepts like *belief,* which require embedded propositions, are too abstract for ostension. In future research LAS will be extended beyond the current ostensive domain. At that point, complications
will be required in the HAM.2 representations; however, when starting
out on a project it is preferable to keep things as simple as possible.

There are a number of motivations for the associative network representation. Anderson and Bower (1973) have combined this representation
with a number of assumptions about the psychological processes that are
used with the network representations. Predictions derived from the Anderson and Bower model turn out to be generally true of human cognitive
performances. (However, many of the specific details of HAM's representation have never been tested empirically.) The principal feature that rec-
ommends associative network representations as a computer formalism
has to do with the facility with which they can be searched. Another advantage of this representation is particularly relevant to the LAS project. This
has to do with the modularity of the representation. Each proposition is
coded as a network structure that can be accessed and used, independent
of other structures.

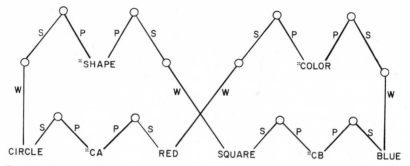

FIG. 3.   An example of a HAM structure encoding both categorical information and word-class information.

Thus far, I have shown how the HAM.2 representation encodes the episodic information that is the input to SPEAK and the output of UNDERSTAND. It can also be used to encode the semantic and syntactic information required by the parsing system. Figure 3 illustrates how HAM.2 would encode the fact that *circle* and *square* are both shapes, *red* and *blue* are both colors, *circle* and *red* belong to the word class *CA, but *square* and *blue* belong to the word class *CB. Note that the word-class information is predicated of the words, whereas the categorical information is predicated of the concepts attached to these words. The categorical information would be used if some syntactic rule only applied to *shapes* or only to *colors*. The word-class information might be evoked if a language arbitrarily applied one syntactic rule to one word class and another rule to a different word class. Inflections are a common example of syntactic rules that apply to arbitrarily defined word classes.

HAM.2 has a small language of commands that cause various memory links to be built. The following four are all that are currently used:

(1)   (Ideate X Y):   create a *W* link from word *X* to idea *Y*.
(2)   (Out-of X Y):   create a proposition node *Z*. From this root node create an *S* link to *X* and a *P* link to *Y*.
(3)   (Relatify X Y):   create an *R* link from *X* to *Y*.
(4)   (Objectify X Y):   create an *O* link from *X* to *Y*.

These commands will appear in LAS's parsing networks to create memory structures required in the conditions and actions. Often rather than memory nodes, variables (denoted X1, X2, etc.) will appear in these commands. If the variable has as its value a memory node, that node is used in the structure building. If the variable has no value, a memory node is created and assigned to it and that node is used in the memory condition.

To illustrate the use of these commands, the following is a listing of the commands that would create the structure in Fig. 2:

    (Ideate red 1)
    (Ideate square 2)
    (Ideate above 3)
    (Ideate circle 4)
    (Out-of X 1)
    (Out-of X 2)
    (Out-of X 8)
    (Objectify 8 Y)
    (Relatify 8 3)
    (Out-of Y 4)

The Network Grammars

LAS uses an augmented network grammar similar to that of Woods (1970). Augmented transition networks are modified finite-state networks that, because of their modifications, have considerably more computational power. In the form proposed by Woods they have the power of a Turing machine, which is to say that they are really too powerful as models of human linguistic competence. The network grammar is composed of sequences of parsing arcs. Associated with each arc is a condition and action. The condition tests whether some property is true of the sentence, and the action creates a piece of semantic structure. A sentence is accepted by the network grammar if some path can be found through the network in which all the conditions are satisfied by the sentence. The meaning of the sentence is represented by the semantic structure created by all the actions along that path.

To pass a particular condition on an arc in a network it is sometimes necessary to pass control to some other network and pass through that network analyzing a subphrase of the sentence. Thus, one network can call another. It can, in fact, call itself. This gives the network formalisms the recursive power associated with context-free grammars. LAS's network grammars have certain context-sensitive features that will be discussed with respect to the SPEAK and UNDERSTAND programs.

To illustrate LAS's network formalisms I present the grammars for a couple of test languages that have been used in the LAS project. The first, GRAMMAR1, is a simple artificial grammar. The second, GRAMMAR2, is a more complex grammar for a subset of English. They are defined by the rewrite rules in Table 1. GRAMMAR1 was designed to be maximally different from English word order. The sentences of GRAMMAR1 are to be read as asserting that the first noun phrase (NP) has the relation speci-

TABLE 1
The Two Test Grammars

GRAMMAR1			GRAMMAR2		
S	→	NP NP RA	S	→	NP is ADJ
		NP NP RB			NP is RA NP
NP	→	SHAPE (COLOR) (SIZE)			NP is RB NP
SHAPE	→	square, circle, etc.	NP	→	(the, a) NP* (CLAUSE)
COLOR	→	red, blue, etc.	NP*	→	SHAPE
SIZE	→	large, small, etc.			ADJ NP*
RA	→	above, right-of	CLAUSE	→	that is ADJ
RB	→	below, left-of			that is RA NP
					that is RB NP
			SHAPE	→	square, circle, etc.
			ADJ	→	red, big, blue, etc.
			RA	→	above, right-of
			RB	→	below, left-of

fied by the last word to the second noun phrase. For purposes of readability, the words of these languages are English but they need not be. GRAMMAR1 is a finite language without recursion. In contrast, in GRAMMAR2 the NP element has an optional CLAUSE which can recursively call NP, generating a potential infinite embedding of construction. In both grammars, it is assumed that *above* and *below* are connected to the same idea and also *right-of* and *left-of* are connected to a single idea. The words differ in the assignment of their NP arguments to subject and object roles. Thus, the difference between the word pairs is syntactic. This is indicated by having the words belong to two word classes RA and RB. Thus, UNDERSTAND with GRAMMAR2 would derive the same HAM representation in Fig. 2 for the sentences *The red square is above the circle* and *The circle is below the red square*. It would have been possible to generate distinct representations for these two sentences. I think this would have been less psychologically interesting. Basically, the network grammar makes the inferences that *A below B* is equivalent to *B above A* and encodes the latter.

Figure 4 illustrates the parsing networks for the grammars. It should be understood that these networks have been deliberately written in an inefficient manner. For instance, note in GRAMMAR1 that there are two distinct paths in the main START network. The first is for those sentences with RA relations and the second for those sentences with RB relations.

If a sentence input to UNDERSTAND has an RB relation, UNDERSTAND will first attempt to parse it by the first branch. The two noun-phrase branches will succeed, but the relation branch will fail. UNDERSTAND will have to back up and try the second branch that leads to RB. This costly back-up is not really necessary. It would have been possible to have constructed the START network in the following form:

$$\text{START} \xrightarrow{\quad NP \quad} X \xrightarrow{\quad NP \quad} Y \begin{array}{c} \overset{\varepsilon^{RA}}{\nearrow} \text{STOP} \\ \underset{\varepsilon_{RB}}{\searrow} \text{STOP} \end{array}$$

In this form the network does not branch until the critical relation word is reached. This means postponing until the end the assignment of noun phrases to subject and object roles in the representations of the sentence's meaning. The above network was not chosen because we wanted a more demanding test of the back-up facilities of SPEAK and UNDERSTAND.

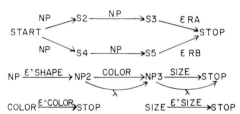

FIG. 4.   The network grammers used by LAS.1.

Table 2 provides a formal specification of the information stored in LAS's network grammars. A node either has a number of arcs proceeding out of it (1a) or it is a stop node (1b). In speaking and understanding, LAS will try to find some path through the network ending with a stop node. Each arc consists of some condition that must be true of the sentence for that arc to be used in parsing (understanding) the sentence. The second element is an action to be taken if the condition is met. This action will create a piece of HAM conceptual structure to correspond to the meaning conveyed by the sentence at that point. Finally, an arc includes specification of the next node to which control should transfer after performing the action. An action consists of zero or more HAM memory commands (rule 3). A condition can consist of zero or more memory commands also (rule 4a). These specify properties that must be true of the incoming word. Alternatively, a condition may involve a push to an embedded network (rule 4b). For instance, suppose the structure in Fig. 3 were to be spoken using GRAMMAR1. The START network would be called to realize the *X is above Y* proposition. The embedded NP network would be called to realize the *X is red* and *X is square* propositions. In pushing to a network two things must be specified — NODE, which is the embedded network, and VAR, which is the memory node at which the main and embedded propositions intersect. In the example the memory node is *X*. The element *t* in rule 4b is a place-holder for information that is needed by the control mechanisms of the UNDERSTAND program. The three rules 6a, 6b, and 6c specify three types of arguments that memory commands can have. They can either directly refer to memory nodes, or refer to the current word in the sentence, or refer to variables that are bound to memory nodes in the course of parsing. Figure 5 provides the encoding of the network for GRAMMAR1.

Note that there tends to be a one-to-one correspondence between HAM propositions and LAS networks. That is, each network expresses just one proposition and calls one embedded network to express any other propositions. This correspondence is not quite perfect in GRAMMAR1 or GRAMMAR2, but the grammars induced by LEARNMORE necessarily have a perfect correspondence.

These grammar networks have a number of features to commend them. SPEAK and UNDERSTAND use the same network for sentence comprehension and generation. Thus, LAS is the first extant system to have a uniform grammatical notation for its parsing and generation systems. In this way, LAS has only to induce one set of grammatical rules to do both tasks. Such networks are modular in two senses. First, they are relatively independent of each other. Second, they are independent of the SPEAK and UNDERSTAND programs that use them. This modularity greatly simplifies

TABLE 2
Formal Specification of the
Network Grammar

NODE	→	ARC*	(1a)
		stop	(1b)
ARC	→	CONDITION ACTION NODE	(2)
ACTION	→	COMMAND*	(3)
CONDITION	→	(COMMAND*)	(4a)
		push VAR *t* NODE	(4b)
COMMAND	→	FUNCTION ARG ARG	(5)
ARG	→	memory node	(6a)
		word	(6b)
		X1, X2, X3, X4, X5	(6c)
FUNCTION	→	out-of, objectify,	
		relatify, ideate	(7)

```
(DEFPROP START PATH
  (((PUSH X1 T NP) ((OUT-OF X1 X5)) S2 )
   ((PUSH X1 T NP) ((OBJECTIFY X5 X1)) S4 )))
(DEFPROP S2 PATH
  (((PUSH X2 T NP) ((OBJECTIFY X5 X2)) S3 )))
(DEFPROP S3 PATH
  (((((IDEATE WORD X4) (OUT-OF WORD *RA)) ((RELATIFY X5 X4)) STOP )))
(DEFPROP S4 PATH
  (((PUSH X2 T NP) ((OUT-OF X2 X5)) S5 )))
(DEFPROP S5 PATH
  (((((IDEATE WORD X4) (OUT-OF WORD *RB)) ((RELATIFY X5 X4)) STOP )))
(DEFPROP NP PATH
  (((((IDEATE WORD X4) (OUT-OF X4 *SHAPE)) ((OUT-OF X1 X4)) NP2 )))
(DEFPROP NP2 PATH
  (((PUSH X1 T COLOR) NIL NP3 )
   ( NIL NIL NP3)))
(DEFPROP NP3 PATH
  (((PUSH X1 T SIZE) NIL STOP )
   (NIL NIL STOP)))
(DEFPROP COLOR PATH
  (((((IDEATE WORD X4) (OUT-OF X4 *COLOR)) ((OUT-OF X1 X4)) STOP )))
(DEFPROP SIZE PATH
  (((((IDEATE WORD X4) (OUT-OF X4 *SIZE)) ((OUT-OF X1 X4)) STOP )))))
```

FIG. 5. The LISP commands creating GRAMMAR1.

LAS's task of induction. LAS only induces the network grammars; the interpretative SPEAK and UNDERSTAND programs represent innate linguistic competences. Finally, the networks themselves are very simple, with limited conditions and actions. Thus, LAS need consider only a small range of possibilities in inducing a network. The network formalism gains its expressive power by the embedding of networks. Because of network modularity, the induction task does not increase with the complexity of embedding.

One might question whether it is really a virtue to have the same representation for the grammatical knowledge for both understanding and production. It is a common observation that children are able to understand
sentences before they can generate them. LAS would not seem to be able
to simulate this basic fact of language learning. However, there may be
reasons why child production does not mirror comprehension, other than
that different grammatical competences underlie the two. The child may
not yet have acquired the physical mastery to produce certain words. This
clearly is the case, for instance, with Lenneberg's (1962) anarthric child
who understood but was not able to speak. Also the child may have the
potential to use a certain grammatical construction but instead uses other
preferred modes of production. The final possibility is that the child may
be resorting to nonlinguistic strategies in language understanding. Bever
(1970) has presented evidence that young children do not understand passives but can still act out passives when they are not reversible. It seems
the child can take advantage of the conceptual constraints between subject,
verb, and object. The child's grammatical deficit only appears when he
is asked to act out reversible passives. Similarly, Clark (1974) has shown
that young children understand relational terms like *in, on,* and *under* by
resorting to heuristic strategies. It is clear that we also have the ability
to understand speech without knowing the syntax. For instance, when Tar-
zan utters *food boy eat,* we know what he must mean. This is because
we can take advantage of conceptual constraints among the words.

The study of Fraser, Bellugi, and Brown (1963) is often cited as showing that comprehension precedes production. They found children had a
higher probability of understanding a sentence (as manifested by pointing
to an appropriate picture) than of producing the sentence. However, there
were difficulties of equating the measures of production and comprehension. Fernald (1970), using different scoring procedures, found no difference. Interestingly, Fraser and co-workers did find a strong correlation
between which sentence forms could be understood and which could be
produced. That is, sentence forms that were relatively easy to understand
were relatively easy to produce. A common base for comprehension and
production would produce such a correlation.

The SPEAK Program

SPEAK starts with a HAM network of propositions tagged as to-be-
spoken and a topic of the sentence. The topic of the sentence will correspond to the first meaning-bearing element in the START network. SPEAK
searches through its START network looking for some path that will express a to-be-spoken proposition attached to the topic and that expresses
the topic as the first element. It determines whether a path accomplishes

this by evaluating the actions associated with a path and determining if they create a structure that appropriately matches the to-be-spoken structure. When it finds such a path it uses it for generation.

Generation is accomplished by evaluating the conditions along the path. If a condition involves a push to an embedded network, SPEAK is recursively called to speak some subphrase expressing a proposition attached to the main proposition. The arguments for a recursive call of PUSH are the embedded network and the node that connects the main proposition and the embedded proposition. If the condition does not involve a PUSH, it will contain a set of memory commands specifying that some features be true of a word. It will use these features to determine what the word is. The word so determined will be spoken.

As an example, consider how SPEAK would generate a sentence corresponding to the HAM structure in Fig. 6, using GRAMMAR2, the English-like grammar in Fig. 5. Figure 6 contains a set of propositions about three objects, denoted by the nodes G246, G195, and G182. Of node G246 it is asserted that it is a triangle, and that G195 is right of it. Of G195 it is asserted that it is a square and that it is above G182. Of G182 it is asserted that it is square, small, and red. Figure 7 outlines the control structure of the generation of this sentence from GRAMMAR2. LAS enters the START network intent on producing some utterance about G195. That is, the topic is G195 (it could have been G246 or G182). The first path through the network involves predicating an adjective of G195, but there is nothing in the adjective class predicated of G195. The second path through the START network corresponds to something LAS can say about G195—it is above G182. Therefore, LAS plans to say this as its main proposition. First, it must find some noun phrase to express G195. The substructure under G195 in Fig. 7 reflects the construction of this subnetwork. The NP network is called, which prints *the* and calls NP1, which retrieves *square* and calls CLAUSE, which prints *that, is* and *right-of* and recursively calls NP to print *the square* to express G246. Similarly, recursive calls are made on the NP1 network to express G182 as *the small red square*.

The actual sentence generated is dependent on choice of topic for the START network. Given the same to-be-spoken HAM network, but the topic G246, SPEAK generated *A triangle is left-of a square that is above a small red square*. Given the topic G182, it generated *A red square that is below a square that is right-of a triangle is small*. Note how the choice of the relation words *left-of* versus *right-of* and of *above* versus *below* is dependent on choice of topic.

It is interesting to inquire about the linguistic power of LAS as a speaker. Clearly, it can generate any context-free language since its transition net-

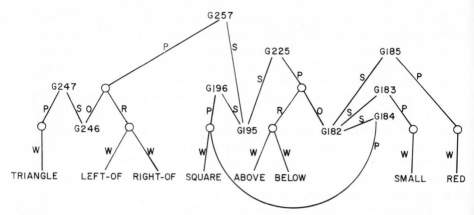

FIG. 6. This to-be-spoken HAM network is given as input to the SPEAK program.

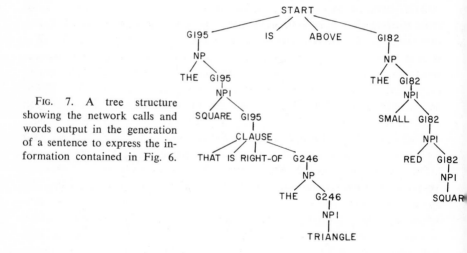

FIG. 7. A tree structure showing the network calls and words output in the generation of a sentence to express the information contained in Fig. 6.

works correspond, in structure, to a context-free grammar. However, it turns out that LAS has certain context-sensitive aspects because its productions are constrained by the requirement that they express some well-formed HAM conceptual structure. Consider two problems that Chomsky (1957) regarded as not handled well by context-free grammars. The first is agreement of number between a subject NP and verb. This is hard to arrange in a context-free grammar because the NP is already built by the time the choice of verb number must be made. The solution is trivial in LAS—when both the NP and verb are spoken, their number is determined by inspection of whatever concept in the to-be-spoken structure underlies the subject. The other Chomsky example involves the identity of selectional restrictions for active and passive sentences. This is also achieved automatically in LAS, since the restrictions in both cases are regarded simply as reflections of restrictions in the semantic structure from which both sentences are spoken.

Although LAS can handle those features of natural language suggestive of context-sensitive rules, it cannot handle examples like languages of the form $a^n b^n c^n$, which require context-sensitive grammars. It is interesting, however, that it is hard to find natural language sentences of this structure. The best I can come up with are respectively type sentences, e.g., *John and Bill hit and kissed Jane and Mary, respectively*. This sentence is of questionable acceptability.

The UNDERSTAND Program

The search in SPEAK for a grammatical realization of the conceptual structure was limited to a search through a single network at a time. Search terminated when a path was found that would express part of the to-be-spoken HAM structure. Because search is limited to a single parsing network, the control structure was simply required to execute a depth-first search through a finite network. In the UNDERSTAND program it is necessary, when one path through a network fails, to consider the possibility that the failure may be in a parsing of a subnetwork called on that path. Therefore, it is possible to have to back into a network a second time to attempt a different parsing. For this reason the control structure of the UNDERSTAND program is more complicated. The UNDERSTAND program and its control structure were written by Carol Hafner, a computer science student at Michigan.

Perhaps an English example would be useful to motivate the need for a complex control structure. Compare the two sentences *The Democratic party hopes to win in '76* with *The Democratic party hopes are high for '76*. A main parsing network would call a noun-phrase network to identify the first noun phrase. Suppose UNDERSTAND identified *The Democratic party*. Later elements in the second sentence would indicate that this choice was wrong. Therefore, the main network would have to reenter the noun-phrase network and attempt a different parsing to retrieve *The Democratic party hopes*. When UNDERSTAND reentered the noun-phrase network to retrieve this parsing, it must remember which parsings it tried the first time so that it does not retrieve the same old parsing. The complexities of this control structure are described in a more complete report (Anderson, 1974). Here I just overview the general structure of the program. The program tries to find some path through the START network that will result in a complete parsing of the sentence. It evaluates the acceptability of a particular path by evaluating the conditions associated with that path. A condition may require that certain features be true of words in the sentence. This is determined by checking memory. Alternatively, a condition can require a push to an embedded network. This network must parse some subphrase of the sentence. When LAS finds an acceptable path through a network, it will collect the actions along that path to create a temporary memory structure to represent the meaning of the phrase that LAS has parsed. Thus, for instance, given the sentence, *The square that is right-of the triangle is above the small red square,* LAS would parse it following the control structure of Fig. 7, retrieving the HAM structure in Fig. 6. That is, in LAS.1, understanding really is simply generation put in reverse. This is an example of a reversible transition network. Simmons (1973) has a similar idea but uses two different networks, one for generation and one for analysis. In exchange for this complexity, he gains the savings of only having to write one interpretative process both for understanding and generation.

It is also of interest to consider the power of LAS as an acceptor of languages. It is clear that LAS as presently constituted can accept exactly the context-free languages. This is because, unlike Woods' (1970) system, actions on arcs cannot influence the results of conditions on arcs, and, therefore, play no role in determining whether a string is accepted or not. However, what is interesting is that LAS's behavior as a language understander is relatively little affected by its limitations on grammatical powers. Consider the following example of where it might seem that LAS would need a context-sensitive grammar. In English noun phrases, it seems we can have almost arbitrary numbers of adjectives. This led to the rule in GRAMMAR2, where NP1 could recursively call itself, each time accepting another adjective. There is nothing in this rule to prevent it from accepting phrases like *the small big square* or other ungrammatical phrases. However, in practice this does not lead LAS into any difficulties because it would never be presented with such a sentence, due to the constraints on what a speaker may properly say to LAS.

General Conditions for Language Acquisition

Having now reviewed how LAS.1 understands and produces sentences, I will present the three aspects of the induction program: BRACKET, SPEAKTEST, and GENERALIZE. Before doing so, it is wise to state briefly the conditions under which LAS learns a language. It is assumed that LAS.1 already has concepts attached to the words of the language. That is, lexicalization is complete. The task of LAS.1 is to learn the grammar of the language, that is, how to go from a string of words to a representation of their combined meaning. Because LAS.1 is not concerned with learning word meanings, it cannot be a very realistic model for first-language learning. It is a somewhat more realistic model for second-language learning where many concepts can transfer from the first to the second language. Hopefully, later versions of LAS will deal with learning word meanings.

Another feature of LAS.1 is that it works in a particularly restricted semantic domain. It is presented with pictures indicating relations and properties of two-dimensional geometric objects. Actually, these pictures are given as encodings in the HAM propositional network representation. Along with these pictures LAS is presented sentences describing the picture and an indication of that aspect in the picture that corresponds to the main proposition of the sentence. From this information input, a network grammar is constructed. The semantic domain may be very simple, but the goal is to be able to learn any natural or natural-like language that may describe that domain.

A third feature to note about LAS's induction heuristics is that they are really set up to deal with word-order information in natural language. In principle, they could be extended to deal with inflectional information. However, they would lead to considerable morphemic overgeneralization. In fact, morphemic overgeneralization does run rampant in early child language acquisition (Brown, 1973). However, children do recover from these overgeneralizations and learn the inflectional contigencies of their language. As currently constituted, LAS does not provide a model of this later process of acquiring the correct morphemic rules.

If for this reason only, LAS is not a complete model of language acquisition. Later I will point out some ways in which it proves to be inadequate with respect to some aspects of word order. It is quite reasonable to suppose that LAS, as currently conceived, will not be able to handle all the details of language acquisition. However, if this program is going to be a useful step in the right direction, it will have to solve a significant portion of the problem of inducing a natural language. It is comforting that those difficulties for LAS which I have uncovered so far are aspects of natural language that are acquired late and with difficulty by the child.

BRACKET—THE GRAPH-DEFORMATION CONDITION

A major development in the LAS project has been the BRACKET program. This is an algorithm for taking a sentence of an arbitrary language and a HAM conceptual structure and producing a bracketing of the sentence that indicates its surface structure. This surface structure prescribes the hierarchy of networks required to parse the sentence. The basic assumption being used by the BRACKET program is what I have called the *graph-deformation condition.* It is assumed that one can derive from the HAM conceptual structure a language-free graph structure that is called the *prototype structure.* It is further assumed that the surface structure interconnecting the content words in the sentence must be isomorphic in its connectivity to the prototype structure. That is the surface structure of the sentence must be a graph deformation of the prototype structure. The best way to explain the graph-deformation condition is by an example. In the illustration I first assume that the prototype structure is just the HAM conceptual structure. Later I explain why something slightly different is required.

Consider part (a) of Fig. 8, which illustrates the HAM structure for the series of propositions in the English sentence *The red square is above the small circle.* Figure 8b illustrates a graph deformation of that structure giving the surface structure of the sentence. That is, the connections among the elements in Fig. 8b are the same as in Fig. 8a. The connections have only been rearranged spatially. Note how elements within the same noun phrase are appropriately assigned to the same subtree. Note that the proto-

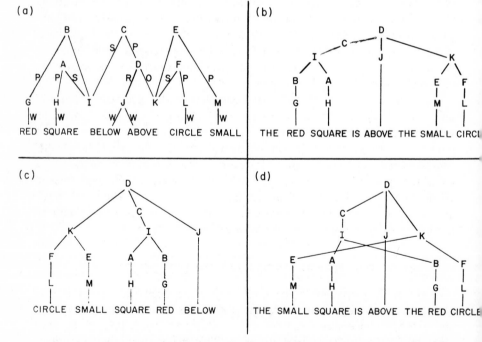

Fig. 8. The surface structures of the sentences in (b) and (c) are graph deformations of the HAM structure in (a). Part (d) displays a sentence for which no graph deformation of (a) will be a surface structure.

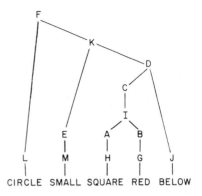

Fig. 9.   An alternate surface structure for the sentence in Fig. 8c.

type structure is not specific with respect to which links are above others and which are right of others. Although the HAM structure in Fig. 8a is set forth in a particular spatial array, the choice is arbitrary. In contrast, the surface structure of a sentence does specify the spatial relation of links. It seems reasonable that all natural languages have as their semantics the same order-free prototype network. They differ from one another in (*a*) the spatial ordering their surface structure assigns to the network and (*b*) the insertion of non-meaning-bearing morphemes into the sentence. However, the surface structure of all natural languages is derived from the same graph patterns. Fig. 8c shows how the prototype structure of Fig. 8a can provide the surface structure for a sentence of the artificial GRAMMAR1. All the sentences of GRAMMAR1 preserve the connectivity of the underlying HAM structure. By this criterion, at least, GRAMMAR1 could be a natural language.

However, certain conceivable languages would have surface structures that could not be deformations of the underlying structure. Figure 8d illustrates such a hypothetical language with the same syntactic structure as English, but with different rules of semantic interpretation. In this language the adjectives preceding the object noun modify the subject noun and vice versa. As Fig. 8d illustrates, there is no deformation of the prototype structure in Fig. 8a to achieve a surface structure for the sentences in the language. No matter how it is attempted, some branches must cross.

LAS will use the connectivity of the prototype network to infer what the connectivity of the surface structure of the sentence must be. The network does not specify the right–left ordering of the branches or the above–below ordering. The right–left ordering can be inferred simply from the ordering of the words in the sentence. However, to specify the above–below ordering, BRACKET needs one further piece of information. Figure 9 illustrates an alternate surface structure that could have been assigned to the string in Fig. 8c. It might be translated into English syntax as *Circular is the small thing that is below the red square.* Clearly, as these two structures illustrate, the prototype structure and the sentence are not enough to specify the hierarchical ordering of subtrees in the surface structure. The difference between Figs. 8c and 9 is the choice of which proposition is principal and which is subordinate. If BRACKET is also given information as to the main proposition, it can then unambiguously retrieve the surface structure of the sentence. The assumption that BRACKET is given the main proposition amounts, psychologically, to the claim that the teacher can direct the learner's attention to what is being asserted in the sentence. Thus, in Fig. 8c, the teacher would direct the learner to the picture of a red triangle above a small circle. He would both have to assume that the learner properly conceptualized the picture and that he also realized the aboveness relation was what was being asserted of the picture.

More on the Graph-Deformation Condition

I think that the graph-deformation condition has something of the status of a universal property of language. However, to make this claim viable, it is clear that something other than the HAM network will have to be adopted as the prototype structure. HAM's binary branching works well enough for the domain of discourse that I have been interested in so far, but it will not generalize to sentences that have verbs that take more than two noun-phrase arguments. Figure 10a shows how HAM would represent the sentence *John opened the door with a key.* This is decomposed into a set of subpropositions—*John turned the key which caused the door to be opened.* Because of the binary structure, certain elements are grouped together. In particular, *John* and *key* are closer together and *door* and *open* are closer together. If Fig. 10a were the prototype, LAS could not bracket a sentence that alternated words from the two subgroups. For instance, there is no deformation of the structure in Fig. 10a that would provide a bracketing for *John opened with a key the door.* Branches of the HAM structure would have to cross. This English sentence and other English sentences that violate the deformation condition for Fig. 10a have a semiunacceptable ring to them. However, this is almost certainly a peculiarity of English. Other languages permit free ordering of their noun phrases. What is needed for a prototype structure is something like the Fillmore (1968) case representation in Fig. 10b where all arguments are equally accessible from the main proposition node. The problem posed by the verb *open* is one posed by any verb that takes more than two noun-phrase arguments. HAM's representation rules out certain sequences of the verb and its arguments, while it is likely that all sequences can be found in some natural language. There are two ways to deal with

(a)

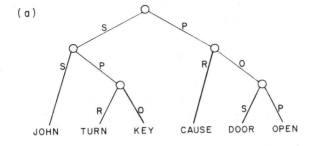

(b)

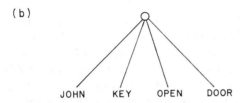

FIG. 10.   (a) HAM representation for the sentence *John opened the door with a key*. (b) The prototype structure that LAS would derive from (a).

this dilemma. One could resort to a memory representation like Fig. 10b. However, there are a number of significant considerations that motivate the HAM representation in Fig. 10a. Moreover, representations like Fig. 10b finesse one of the most interesting questions in language acquisition—how we learn the case structure of complex verbs. To address this question we need a representation that decomposes multiargument verbs into a representation like Fig. 10a, which exposes the semantic function of the case arguments. Learning the role of the verb *open* in the language then involves learning how to assign its noun-phrase arguments to a structure like Fig. 10a. Later versions of LAS will attempt to learn the case structure of verbs.

If we keep the HAM representations, then the graph-deformation condition cannot be applied directly to the memory representations. What is characteristic of multiargument verbs in a HAM structure is that the arguments are interconnected by causal relations as in Fig. 10a. Thus, BRACKET should be made to treat all the terminal arguments in such causal structures as defining a single level of nodes in a graph structure, all connected to a single root node. That is, BRACKET can derive from a HAM structure like Fig. 10a a prototype structure like Fig. 10b for purposes of utilizing the graph-deformation condition. BRACKET already does this to some extent in the current implementation.

The Details of BRACKET's Output

Thus far, only a description of how one would retrieve the surface structure connecting the content words of the sentence has been given. Suppose BRACKET were given *A triangle is left-of a square that is above a small red square.* A bracketing structure must be imposed on this sentence that will also include the function words. Given this sentence and the conceptual structure in Fig. 6, BRACKET returned

> (G257 (G246 G247 a triangle) is left-of (G195 G196
> a square (G195 G225 that is above (G182 G183 a
> small (G182 G185 red (G182 G184 square)))))).

The main proposition is *G257*, which is given as the first term in the bracketing. The first bracketed subexpression describes the subject noun phrase. The first element in the subexpression *G246* is the node that links the embedded proposition *G247* to the main proposition *G257*. The first two words of the sentence *A triangle* are placed in this bracketed subexpression. The next two words *is left-of* are in main bracketing. There are no embedded propositions corresponding to these two. The remainder of the output of BRACKET corresponds to a description of the element *G195*. The first embedded proposition *G196* asserts this object is a square and the second proposition, *G225*, asserts that *G195* is above *G182*. Note that the *G225* proposition is embedded as a subexpression within the *G196* proposition. The last element in the *G225* proposition is

> (G182 G183 a small (G182 G185 red (G182 G184
> square))).

This expression has in it three propositions *G183, G185, G184,* about *G182*.

The above example illustrates the output of BRACKET. Astractly, the output of BRACKET may be specified by the following four rewrite rules:

(1)   S → proposition element*
(2)   element → word
(3)   element → (topic S)
(4)   element → (Topic S element)

That is, each bracketed output is a proposition node followed by a sequence of elements (rule 1). These elements are either rewritten as words (rule 2) or bracketed subexpressions (rules 3 and 4). A bracketed subexpression begins with a topic node that indicates the connection between the embedded and embedding propositions. The elements within an expression are either non-meaning-bearing words or elements corresponding to subject, predicate, relation, and object in the proposition. Note that BRACKET induces a correspondence between a level of bracketing and a single proposition. Each level of bracketing will also correspond to a new network in LAS's grammar. Because of the modularity of HAM propositions, a modularity is achieved for the grammatical networks. When a number of embedded propositions are attached to the same node, they are embedded within one another in a right-branching manner (rule 4).

The insertion of nonfunction words into the bracketing is a troublesome problem because there are no semantic features to indicate where they belong. Consider the first word *a* in the example sentence above. It could have been placed in the top level of bracketing or in the subexpression containing *triangle*. Currently, all the function words to the right of a content word are placed in the same level as the content word. The bracketing is closed immediately after this content word. Therefore, *is* is not placed in the noun-phrase bracketing. This heuristic seems to work more often than not. However, there clearly are cases where it will not work. Consider the sentence *The boy who Jane spoke to was deaf*. The current BRACKET program would return this as

((The boy (who Jane spoke)) to was deaf).

That is, it would not identify *to* as in the relative clause. Similarly, non-meaning-bearing suffixes like gender would not be retrieved as part of the noun by this heuristic. However, there is a strong clue to guide bracketing in such cases. There tends to be a pause after morphemes like *to*. Perhaps such pause structures could be called upon to help the BRACKET program decide how to insert the nonmeaning-bearing morphemes into the bracketing.

Non-meaning-bearing morphemes pose further problems besides bracketing. Consider a sequence of such morphemes in a noun phrase. That sequence could have its own grammar that, in principle, might constitute an arbitrary recursive language. The semantic referent of the sentence could provide no clues at all as to the structure of that language. Therefore, we would be back to the same impossible language-induction task that we characterized in the introduction. Hence, it is comforting to observe that the structure of these strings of non-meaning-bearing morphemes tends to be very simple. There are not many examples of these strings being longer than two words. Thus, it seems that the languages constituted by these non-meaning-bearing strings are nothing more than very simple finite cardinality languages that pose, in themselves, no serious induction problems. The various stretches of non-meaning-bearing morphemes in a sentence could also have complex interdependencies, thereby posing serious induction problems. Again it does not seem to be the case that these dependencies exist. Therefore, it seems that the structure of natural language is simple just at those points where it would have to be for a LAS-like induction program to work.

In concluding this section I should point out one example sentence that BRACKET cannot currently handle. They are *respectivley* sentences like *John and Bill danced and laughed, respectively.* The problem with such a sentence is that underlying it is the following prototype structure:

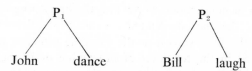

Thus, *John* and *dance* are close together and so are *Bill* and *laugh.* However, the sentence intersperses these elements in just such a way to make bracketing impossible. There are probably other examples like this, but I cannot think of them. Fortunately, this is not an utterance that appears early in child speech, nor is it a particularly simple one for adults. Of all the grammatical constructions, the *respectively* construction is the one that most suggests the need to have transformational rules in this grammar.

AN EXAMPLE OF GRAMMAR INDUCTION

The function of SPEAKTEST is to test whether its grammar is capable of generating a sentence and, if it is not, appropriately to modify the grammar so that it can. SPEAKTEST is called after BRACKET is complete. It receives from BRACKET a HAM conceptual structure, a bracketed sentence, the main proposition, and the topic of the sentence. As in the SPEAK program SPEAKTEST attempts to find some path through its network that will express a proposition attached to the topic. If it succeeds, no modifications to the network are made. If it cannot, a new path is built through the network to incorporate the sentence.

The best way to understand the operation of SPEAKTEST is to watch it go through one example. The target language it was given to learn is illustrated in Table 3. This is a very simple language, basically GRAMMAR1 of Fig. 4. It has a smaller vocabulary to make it more tractable. The reason for choosing this language is that it is of just sufficient complexity to illustrate LAS's acquisition mechanisms. In addition, LAS[1] has learned GRAMMAR2, also given in Fig. 4.

---

[1] The version of LAS that learned GRAMMAR2 is not identical with LAS.1. In particular, it does not use the same form of left generalization. The difficulties left generalization poses for noun-phrase induction are discussed later.

TABLE 3
Test Grammar to Be Learned

		Example sentences
S	→ NP NP RA	square red triangle small above
	NP NP RB	triangle triangle blue small left-of
NP	→ SHAPE (COLOR) (SIZE)	
SHAPE	→ square, triangle	
COLOR	→ blue, red	
SIZE	→ large, small	
RA	→ above, right-of	
RB	→ below, left-of	

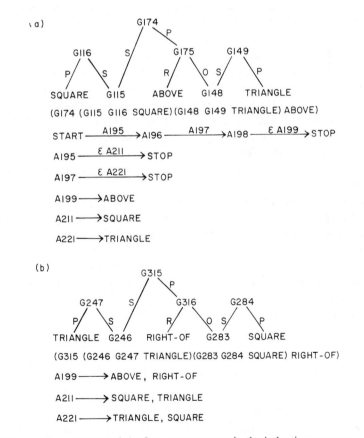

Fɪɢ. 11. LAS's treatment of the first two sentences in the induction sequence.

Figure 11 illustrates LAS's handling of the first two sentences that come in. The first sentence is *Square triangle above*. This sentence is returned by BRACKET as

(G174 (G115 G116 square) (G148 G149 triangle) above).

G174 refers to the main proposition given as an argument to LEARNMORE. Since this is LAS's first sentence of the language, the START network will, of course, completely fail to parse the sentence. It has no grammar yet. Therefore, it induces the top-level START network in Fig. 11a. A listing of the exact arc information induced is given below the graphical illustration in Fig. 11a. Since the first two elements after *G174* in the bracketed sentence are themselves bracketed, the first two arcs in the network will be pushes to subnetworks. The third arc contains a condition on the word *above*. The restriction made is that it be a member of the word class *A199*. This class was created for this sentence and only contains the word *above* at this point. Having now constructed a path through the START network, SPEAKTEST checks the subnetworks in that path to see whether they can handle the bracketed subexpressions in the sentence. This is accomplished by a recursive call to SPEAKTEST. For the first phrase, SPEAKTEST is called, taking as arguments the network *A195*, the phrase (G116 square), and the topic *G115*. In network *A195* the word class *A211* is created to contain *square*, and in network *A197* the word class *A221* contains *triangle*. These two subnetworks should be the same in a final grammar, but LAS is not prepared to risk such a generalization at this point.

Note in this example how the bracketing above provided by BRACKET completely specified the embedding of networks. The first element *G174* was the main proposition. The second element (G115 G116 square) was a bracketed subexpression indicating that a subnetwork should be created. Similarly, the third expression indicated a subnetwork. The last element *above* was a single word and so could be handled by a memory condition in the main network.

The second sentence is *triangle square right-of*. This is transformed by BRACKET to

(G315 (G246 G247 triangle) (G283 G284 square) right-of).

Because of the narrow one-member word classes this sentence cannot be handled by the current grammar. However, SPEAKTEST does not add new network arcs to handle the sentence. Rather, it expands word class *A119* to include *right-of*, word class *A211* to include *triangle,* and word class *A221* to include *square.* The grammar is now at such a stage that LAS could speak or understand the sentences *triangle square above* or *square square right-of* and other sentences that it had not studied. Thus, already the first generalizations have been made. LAS can produce and understand novel sentences.

This illustrates the type of generalizations that are made within the SPEAKTEST program. For instance, consider the generalization that arose when SPEAKTEST decided to use the existing network structure to incorporate *triangle,* the first word of the second sentence. This involved (a) using the same subnetwork *A195* that had been created for *square* and (*b*) expanding the word class *A211* to include *triangle.* Both decisions rested on semantic criteria. The network *A195* was created to analyze a description of a node attached to the main proposition by the relation *S. Triangle* was a description of the node *G246*, which is related by *S* to the main proposition. On the basis of this identity of semantic function, LAS assigns the parsing of *triangle* to the network *A195*. Within the *A195* network the word class *A211* contains words that are predicates of the subject node. *Triangle* has this semantic function and is therefore added to the word class.

In making these generalizations, SPEAKTEST is making a strong assumption about the nature of natural language. Words or phrases with identical semantic functions at identical points in a network have identical syntax. This is the assumption of *semantic-induced equivalence of syntax.* It is another way in which semantic information facilitates grammar induction. It clearly need not be true of an arbitrary language. For instance, decisions made in the subject noun phrase might in theory condition syntactic decisions made in the object noun phrase. Because of its heuristics in SPEAKTEST for generalization, LAS would not be able to learn such a language.

Figure 12 illustrates LAS's network grammar after two more sentences have come in. Sentences 3 and 4 involve the relations *below* and *left-of.* LAS treats these as syntactic variants of *above* and *right-of*, which differ in their assignment of their noun-phrase arguments to the logical categories subject and object. Therefore, LAS creates an alternative branch through its START network to accommodate this possibility.

Figure 13 illustrates the course of LAS's learning. Altogether LAS will be presented 14 sentences. Subsequently, it will have to make three extra generalizations to capture the entire target language. Plotted on the abscissa is this learning history, and along the ordinate we have the natural logarithm of the number of sentences the grammar can handle. This is a finite

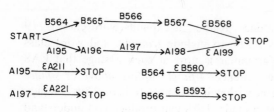

FIG. 12.   LAS's grammar after studying

1. square triangle above
2. triangle square right-of
3. square triangle below
4. triangle square left-of

In the grammar, word class A199 contains *above* and *right-of;* word class B568 contains *below* and *left-of;* word classes A211, A221, B580, and B593 each contain *square* and *triangle.*

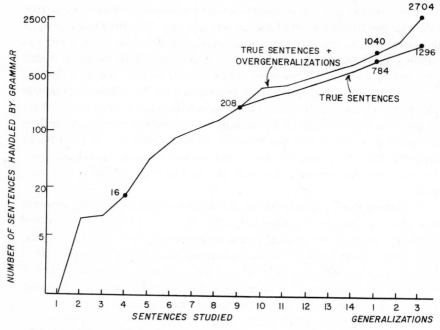

FIG. 13.   The growth in the number of sentences accepted by LAS's grammar over the course of its learning history.

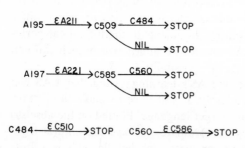

FIG. 14.   Additions to LAS's grammar after studying

5. square red triangle blue above
6. triangle large square small right-of
7. triangle red triangle red above
8. square small triangle red right-of
9. square blue triangle large right-of

Word classes C510 and C586 both contain *small, blue, large,* and *red.*

328

language, unlike GRAMMAR2, and therefore the number of sentences in the language will always be finite. As can be seen from Fig. 13, by the fourth sentence LAS's grammar is adequate to handle 16 sentences.

LAS's grammar after the next five sentences is shown in Fig. 14. These are LAS's first encounters with two-word noun phrases. All five sentences involve the relations *right-of* and *above* and therefore result in the elaboration of the *A195* and *A197* subnetworks. Consider the first sentence, *square red triangle blue above,* which is retrieved by BRACKET as

(C329 (C270 C271 square (C270 C272 red)) (C303
C304 triangle (C303 C305 blue) above) C270).

Consider the parsing of the first noun phrase. Note that the adjective (C270 C272 red) is embedded within the larger noun phrase. This is an example of the right embedding that BRACKET always imposes on a sentence. This will cause SPEAKTEST to create a push to an embedded network within its *A195* subnetwork. As can be seen in Fig. 14, the existing are containing the *A211* word class is kept to handle *square.* Two alternative arcs are added—one with a push to the *C484* network and the other with a NIL transition. Within the *C484* network the word class *C510* is set up, which initially only contains the word *red.*

This illustrates the principle of left generalization in LAS.1: Suppose a network contains a sequence of arcs A_1, A_2, . . . , A_m. Suppose further a phrase assigned to the network requires arcs X_1 . . . , X_m, . . . , X_n to be successfully parsed. If arcs A_1, A_2, . . . , A_m have the same semantic function as required of arcs X_1, X_2, . . . , X_m, then the parsing of the first m elements in the phrase is assigned to the existing arcs A_1, . . . , A_m. After arc A_m two alternate paths are built. A NIL arc is added to permit the phrases that used to be parsed by A_1, . . . , A_m. Also arcs X_{m+1}, . . . , X_n are added to handle the new phrase. LAS is making the generalization that any sequence of constituents parsable by A_1, . . . , A_m can be placed in front of any sequence of elements parsable by X_{m+1}, . . . , X_n. Left generalization may be seen as an elaboration of semantics-induced equivalence of syntax.

Figure 15 shows a more conservative way that LAS might have made this generalization. Instead of network 15a, it might have set up network 15b. In network 15b a new word class X has been set up to record just those words that can be followed by an adjective. Networks 15c and d illustrate how left generalization can and does lead to overgeneralization in natural language. Suppose a child hears phrases like *The boy, A dog, The foot,* etc. He would set up a network that would accept any article followed by any noun. Suppose he then hears *The boys.* This would be

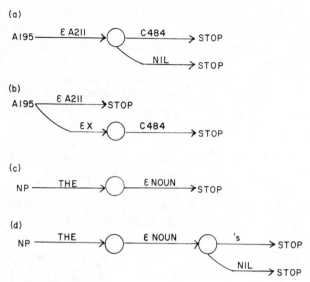

Fɪɢ. 15.   Some possible network grammars.

represented in LAS as *The + boy + 's*.[2] Because of left generalization LAS
would construct the network illustrated in Fig. 15d. In this network LAS
has incorporated the generalization that *foots* is the pluralization of *foot*.
This sort of morphemic generalization is, of course, a notorious overgeneralization in child language (e.g., Ervin, 1964). What is distinctive about
such morphemic rules is that there are a number of alternatives and no
semantic basis to choose among them. Because of its principle of semantics-
induced equivalence of syntax, LAS will overgeneralize in those situations.
Children may be operating under a similar rule.

Figure 16 shows LAS's treatment of the last five sentences in the training
sequences. These involve some three-word noun phrases and also expansion of the noun phrases on the branch of the START network for RB
relations. As can be seen from Fig. 13, at the point of the 14th sentence
LAS has expanded its grammar to the point where it will handle 616 sentences of the target language. Actually the grammar has produced some
overgeneralizations—it will accept a total of 750 sentences. LAS has encountered phrases like *square, square small, square red,* and *square red
small.* From this experience, LAS has generalized to the conclusion that
the sentences of the language consist of a shape, followed optionally by
either a size or color, followed optionally by a size. Thus, the induced

[2] To accomplish this I would have to put some mechanism in LAS that would
segment words into their morphemes.

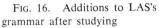

FIG. 16.   Additions to LAS's grammar after studying

10. square blue small triangle right-of
11. triangle red square blue left-of
12. triangle small square red small below
13. square blue triangle blue large left-of
14. square red large triangle red large below

Word class D714 includes *small;* D1054 includes *red, blue,* and *small;* D1117 includes *blue* and *red;* E905 includes *small* and *large;* and E1395 includes *large.*

C484 —ε C510→ D713 —D692→ STOP
                      ↘NIL→ STOP

B566 —ε B593→ D1116 —D1095→ STOP
                      ↘NIL→ STOP

B564 —ε B580→ D1044 —D1023→ STOP
                      ↘NIL→ STOP

D1023 —εD1045→ E1394 —E1368→ STOP
                      ↘NIL→ STOP

D1095 —εD1117→ E904 —E884→ STOP
                      ↘NIL→ STOP

D692 —ε D714→ STOP

E884 —ε E905→ STOP   E1368 —εE1395→ STOP

grammar includes phrases like *square small small* because size words were found to be acceptable in both second and third positions. Interestingly, this mistake will not cause LAS any problems. It will never speak a phrase like *square small small* because it will never have a to-be-spoken HAM structure with two *smalls* modifying an object. It will never hear such a phrase, and thus UNDERSTAND can not make any mistakes. This is a nice example of how an over general grammar can be constrained successfully by considerations of semantic acceptability.

The problem of learning to sequence noun modifiers has turned out to be a source of unexpected difficulty. In part, the ordering of modifiers is governed by pragmatic factors. For instance, one is likely to say *small red square* when referring to one of many red squares, but *red small square* when referring to one of many small squares. Differences like these could be controlled by ordering of links in the HAM memory structure. Later in this paper I will provide a fuller description of the problems created by such overgeneralization.

GENERALIZE

After taking in 14 sentences LAS has built up a partial network grammar that serves to generate many more sentences than those it originally encountered. However, note that LAS has constructed four copies of a noun-phrase grammar. One would like it to recognize that those grammars are the same. The failure to do so with respect to this simple artificial language only amounts to an inelegance. However, the identification of identical networks is critical to inducing languages with recursive rules.

A list is kept of all the networks created by SPEAKTEST. Once the structure of these networks becomes stable, GENERALIZE is called to determine which networks are identical. It compares pairs of networks looking for those that are identical. The criterion for identification of two networks is that they have the same arc paths. Two arcs are considered identical if they have the same syntactic conditions and semantic actions. Consider what LAS would do if it had the following embedding of networks for English noun phrases:

$$NP \to \text{the NOUN}_1$$
$$\to \text{the ADJ}_1 \text{ NP}_1$$
$$NP_1 \to \text{NOUN}_2$$
$$\to \text{ADJ}_2 \text{ NP}_2$$
$$NP_2 \to \text{NOUN}_3$$
$$\to \text{ADJ}_3 \text{ NP}_3$$
$$NP_3 \to \text{NOUN}_4$$

That is, there are four networks, NP, NP_1, NP_2, and NP_3, whose structures are indicated by the above rewrite rules. It is assumed that LAS has only experienced three consecutive adjectives and therefore SPEAKTEST has only three embeddings. The critical inductive step for LAS is to recognize $NP_1 = NP_2$. This requires recognizing the identity of the word classes $NOUN_2$ and $NOUN_3$ and the word classes ADJ_2 and ADJ_3. This will be done on the criterion of the amount of overlap of words in the two classes. It also requires recognition that network $NP_2 = NP_3$. Thus, to identify two networks may require that two other networks be identified. The network NP_3 is only a subnetwork of NP_2. So in the recursive identification of networks, GENERALIZE will have to accept a subnetwork relation between one network like NP_2 which contains another like NP_3. The assumption is that with sufficient experience the embedded network would become filled out to be the same the embedding network. After NP_1 has been identified with NP_2, HAM will have a new network structure given below where NP* represents the amalgamation of NP_1, NP_2, and NP_3:

$$NP \to \text{the NOUN}$$
$$\to \text{the ADJ NP*}$$
$$NP* \to \text{NOUN*}$$
$$\to \text{ADJ* NP*}$$

FIG. 17. The final grammar at the end of the induction sequence. B568 includes *below* and *left-of;* A199 includes *above* and *right-of;* B593 includes *square* and *triangle;* D1117 includes *blue, red, large,* and *small;* E905 includes *large* and *small.*

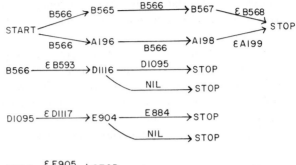

Note that new word classes NOUN* and ADJ* have been created as the union of the word classes NOUN$_2$, NOUN$_3$, NOUN$_4$, and of the classes ADJ$_2$, ADJ$_3$, respectively.

GENERALIZE was called to ruminate over the networks generated after the first 14 sentences. GENERALIZE succeeded in identifying *A195* with *A197*. As a consequence, network *A195* replaced network *A197* at the position where it occurred in the START network (see Fig. 12). Similarly, network *B566* was identified with and replaced *B564*. Finally, *B566* was identified with and replaced *A195* throughout the START network. The final effective grammar is illustrated in Fig. 17. It now handles all the sentences of the grammar. It handles more sentences than the grammar that was constructed after the fourteenth sentence. This is because the noun-phrase network *B566* has been expanded to incorporate all possible noun phrases. Before the generalizations, none of the networks—*B564, B566, A195,* or *A197*—were complete. The network *B566* became complete through merging with *B564* and *A195*.

At this point, LAS now has a grammar adequate to speak and understand the target language. There are two major assumptions that LAS is making about the relation between sentence and referent that permit it to be successful with these types of languages. The first is the assumption of the correspondence between the surface structure of the language and the semantic structure. This is critical to BRACKET's identification of the surface structure of the sentence which is, in turn, critical to the proper embedding of parsing networks. Second, there is the assumption of a se-mantics-induced equivalence of syntax. This played a critical role in the generalizations of both SPEAKTEST and GENERALIZE. It was noted with re-spect to pluralization that such generalizations can be in error and that children also tend to make such errors. However, I would want to argue that, on the whole, natural language is not perverse. Therefore, most of those generalizations will turn out to be good decisions. Clearly, for languages to be learnable there must be some set of generalizations that are usually safe. The only question is whether LAS has captured the safe generalizations.

The importance of semantics to child language learning has been suggested in various ways recently by many theoreticians (e.g., Bloom, 1970, 1973; Bowerman, 1973; Brown, 1973; Schlesinger, 1971; Sinclair-deZwart, 1973), but there has been little offered in the way of concrete algorithms to make explicit the contribution of semantics. LAS.1 is a first small step toward making this contribution explicit.

ASSESSMENT OF LAS.1

This concludes the explanation of the algorithms to be used by LAS.1 for language induction. In many ways the task faced by LAS.1 is overly simplistic, and its algorithms are probably too efficient and free from information-processing limitations. Therefore, the acquisition behavior of LAS.1 does not mirror in most respects that of the child. Later versions of this program will attempt a more realistic simulation. Nonetheless, I think LAS.1 is a significant step forward. The following are the significant contributions embodied thus far in LAS.1:

1. The transition network formalism has been interfaced with a set of simple and psychologically realistic long-term memory operations. In this way we have bridled the unlimited Turing-computable power of the Woods augmented-transition network.

2. A single grammatical formalism has been created for generation and understanding. Thus, LAS only needs to induce one set of grammatical rules.

3. Two important ways were identified in which a semantic referent helps grammar induction. These were stated as the graph-deformation condition and the semantics-induced equivalence of syntax conditions.

4. Algorithms have been developed adequate to learn natural languages with a simple semantics.

Future Directions

As mentioned earlier, the program LAS is not a fixed object. It is constantly being changed to try out new ideas. LAS.1, just described, represents the program's status during March, 1974. Sometime in the next year I hope to begin a complete reprogramming of the system to achieve a more realistic simulation. Among the goals are the following:

1. The program will incorporate realistic assumptions about short-term memory limitations and left-to-right sentence processing.
2. The program will learn the meaning of words.

3. The program should use semantic and contextual redundancy to partially replace explicitly provided HAM-encoding of pictures.
4. The program should handle sentences in a more complex semantic domain.
5. The program should be elaborated to handle such things as questions and commands as well as declarative sentences.

The interested reader may write to me for a paper setting forth these goals in some detail.

GENERALIZATIONS ABOUT NOUN PHRASES

This section is concerned with the possible bases for making generalizations about those linguistic units that correspond to noun phrases. The learner must identify which sequences of words constitute acceptable noun phrases. The learner could record, with each linguistic context, which noun phrases he has encountered in that context. He would only speak or accept those noun phrases. The problem with this, of course, is that the learner would never make the generalizations that are required if he is to learn a language on the basis of finite experience. So the question is how to devise an algorithm that will make adequate generalizations about the structure of noun phrases. There are two categories of generalization, which I will discuss separately. First, with respect to a noun phrase occurring at a particular point in the grammar, one can generalize from the acceptability of some sequences for that noun-phrase unit to the acceptability of other sequences. For instance, having seen *the red square* and *the green circle* as sentence subjects, it might seem reasonable to generalize to the acceptability of *the green square* and *the red circle* as subjects. The second sort of generalization involves the merging of rules for a noun phrase occurring at one point in the grammar with rules for a noun phrase occurring at another point. For instance, this occurred in the just-described induction sequence of LAS.1 when GENERALIZE was called to merge the four noun-phrase grammars into a single noun-phrase grammar.

Generalization within a Noun-Phrase Grammar

There are two principles of generalization that seemed useful and were used in LAS.1 for acquiring the structure of noun phrases. The first involves merging words that occur in the same serial position into a single word class. For instance, consider the following pair of phrases:

(1)   The tall boy
(2)   A short girl

On the basis of this experience, LAS.1 would build up a rule for noun phrases of the form (The,a) + (tall,short) + (boy,girl). Let us call this *ordinal generalization.* The second type of generalization is *left generalization.* After seeing (3) and (4)

(3)   The boy
(4)   The girl who cries

LAS will form the generalization that either *boy* or *girl* can be followed by the relative clause *who cries.*

Unfortunately, unbridled use of these principles can lead an induction program into error. Consider the pair of phrases (5) and (6):

(5)   Comfortable big pillow
(6)   White foam pillow
(7)   White big pillow

By the principal of ordinal generalization, an induction algorithm would conclude that (7) was acceptable, but it is not. The question of the ordering of adjectives in English has been studied extensively by Vendler (1968). He concludes that there is a relatively strict and complex ordering involving 19 classes of adjectives. Adjectives in a higher class must precede adjectives in a lower class if they both occur in a noun phrase. A phrase like (7) can be acceptable, but only in special circumstances where it can be interpreted as *the white one of the big pillows.*

These adjective classes are not at all arbitrary but are correlated with semantic features. It seems that the more noun-like the adjective class is, the closer it can occur to the noun. Thus, for instance, adjectives that refer to substance like *foam* follow adjectives that refer to absolute properties like *white,* which follow adjectives like *big,* which refer to relative properties, which follow adjectives like *comfortable,* which refer to features of the noun's use.

Perhaps, the way to deal with the problem of adjective ordering is to build into the induction routine a bias to look for semantically defined word classes and to learn the principles or ordering of these word classes. There is one potential problem with this move. Perhaps the phenomenon of adjective class ordering is not universal. The work on adjective ordering so far has been done only in English.[3]

---

[3] There are languages like Chinese in which, some claim, there is no adjective class. Such languages would be a trivial case for the proposed algorithm. The question is whether languages *with adjectives* have the Vendler class orderings.

It seems then, that the solution to the problem of adjective ordering is to increase LAS's use of semantic information. The proposal thus far is to have LAS identify word classes on the basis of semantic criteria and learn the ordering of the classes. It may even prove possible to give LAS strong information about the possible word orders. The nounness principle of ordering uncovered by Vendler for English may well be universal. If so, it could be built into LAS's induction routines.

Another interesting fact about noun phrases is that there is one class of words, nouns, that is obligatory whereas the adjective word classes are optional. The existence of such a noun class seems to be universal. There is no necessary reason why this should be so, but it does serve to create problems for LAS.1. Consider the following noun phrases:

(8)   The square
(9)   The red square
(10)   The red

After seeing (8) and (9), LAS.1 because of its principle of left generalization, would accept (10). There seems no semantic basis to prevent LAS from making this mistake. Phrase (8) conveys the information that there is an object that is square. Thus from (8) LAS learns *The + property* is acceptable. From (9) it learns that *red* is a property that may follow *the*. So naturally it assumes that it could refer to an object with just the property *red*. Therefore, it seems that LAS is going to have to enter the language-learning situation with the understanding that there is an obligatory noun class and attempt to identify which concepts the language puts into that class. It seems hard to believe that these will be the same words for all languages. I just cannot see any reason why a color concept like *red* could not have in some language the same status as a shape concept like *square* has in English.

Thus, the conclusion seems to be that the generalizations within noun phrases should not be concerned with absolute position; rather, they should be concerned with relative positional information. LAS should emerge with a set of semantically identified word classes, some of which are obligatory and some of which are optional. LAS should learn what is the ordering that the language places on these word classes.

Between Noun-Phrase Generalization

Noun phrases that occur at different points in the grammar have a lot in common. This is clearly the case in English where there is essentially just one grammar for noun phrases in all contexts. For languages inflected for case, however, there can be differences between noun phrases, depending on whether the phrase is subject, object, instrument, etc. However, even for these there is much in common between the different noun phrases. LAS, as seen in the example-induction sequence, has a tendency to create distinct networks for noun phrases occurring at different points in the grammar. It does not naturally take advantage of the redundancies.

In that example-induction sequence a solution was offered to the problem of how to detect the identity of networks occurring in distinct positions. A program GENERALIZE was constructed, which ruminated over the network grammars, trying to identify various networks with each other. While this solution was workable, it has always struck me as somewhat unpalatable from a psychological point of view.

Currently I am working on a different solution that, although awkward to simulate on a serial computer, seems more plausible. Whenever a push is made to a network grammar by SPEAKTEST, the to-be-analyzed phrase is not only parsed by that network, but a parallel attempt is made to parse it by all other grammar networks. This parallelism is costly to simulate on a serial computer, but it is quite compatible with our understanding of human cognitive functioning.

If it turns out that some other network can parse the phrase, then that network is merged with the one to which the push is made. This allows LAS to identify similar networks very quickly and merge them into a single network. Its most interesting aspect, though, is the claim it makes about our linguistic processing. Unlike the network grammars of Woods, a particular network is not just evoked when it is called by another. All networks are constantly active, ready to analyze a phrase whenever it comes in. Consider the following phrases:

(1)   The red *the tall house* . . .
(2)   The red *was kicked by the boy* . . .
(3)   The boy with a *which is above the square* . . .
(4)   The son of *in a serious problem* . . .

In (1) a noun phrase begins where it cannot in English. Similarly in (2) an illegally placed predicate begins; in (3), a relative clause; and in (4), a prepositional phrase. Yet in hearing these phrases I seem to have little difficulty in identifying the illegally placed constructions as noun phrase or predicate, etc. Such identifications would be impossible if our grammatical comprehension were being executed as in a Woods network. Noun phrases and other grammatical categories would only be recognized as such if they occur at legal points in a sentence. This may be one example of where the model suggested by a serial computer is considerably different from the human model.

A PREDICTION ABOUT LANGUAGE LEARNABILITY

One of the benefits of working with LAS is that it has suggested interesting questions about language processing and language acquisition. These are not questions that had occurred to me before working with an explicit process model. These are also not questions that can be informally answered by introspecting on one's own language processing or by observing children learning a natural language. LAS is an explicit language-processing mechanism and, as such, has limitations on what it can do. Therefore, it makes predictions about what sorts of situations should be impossible or difficult for our language-processing mechanisms. It requires controlled experimentation to assess these claims. I would like to describe briefly one such experiment to test a claim made by LAS about language learnability. This requires working with an artificial language. Before getting to the experiment, I should discuss the criticisms that have been made of past artificial language experimentation.

Criticisms of Experiments with Artificial Languages

For ethical reasons it is not possible to expose young children, just learning their first language, to an artificial language that LAS had identified as degenerate and probably not learnable. This means that all experimentation with artificial languages must be done either on older children already well established in their first language or on adults. Consequently, the first language may be mediating acquisition of the second language. There is evidence (see Lenneberg, 1967) that there is a critical initial period during which languages can be learned much more successfully than in later years. Lenneberg speculates that there is a physiological basis for this critical period. Thus, one might wonder whether the same processes are being studied with older subjects as with the young child. Personally, I also doubt that the mechanisms of language acquisition are entirely the same with the young child in first-language learning as with the older subject in second-language learning. However, it does seem probable that there should be considerable overlap in the mechanisms for the two situations. The reason for this belief has already been stated. Both for the adult and the young child, language acquisition presents largely the same set of severe and unique information-processing demands. The algorithms that deal with induction problems therefore are probably not very different in any system that successfully learns the language.

Other criticisms (e.g., Slobin, 1971; Miller, 1967) of studies of artificial language learning focus on the fact that these languages are artificial. Natural language is much more complicated than an artificial laboratory language: it takes years to acquire it; it serves more complex functions; the child's motivations are more complex than the laboratory subject. However, these criticisms miss the whole point of laboratory experimentation which is to isolate and study significant aspects of a complex natural phenomenon. Another criticism of the past artificial-languages studies (e.g., Braine, 1963; Miller, 1967; Reber, 1969) is that they lack a semantic referent. Clearly, this makes an enormous difference to the sort of algorithms a subject can employ. The critical heuristics used by LAS would be useless without semantics. Moeser and Bregman (1972, 1973) have shown that the existence of a semantic referent has a huge effect on language acquisition.

An Experiment[1]

Critical to LAS's induction algorithm is that the graph-deformation condition be met in regard to the relation between the surface structure of the sentence and the prototype structure. That is, the surface structure must preserve the original connectivity of concepts. This graph deformation was tested in this experiment. The experiment uses the following grammar:

$$S \rightarrow NP\ PRED$$
$$NP \rightarrow Shape\ (Size)\ (Pattern)\ (CLAUSE)$$
$$CLAUSE \rightarrow te\ PRED$$
$$PRED \rightarrow Adj$$
$$\rightarrow NP\ Rel$$
$$Shape \rightarrow square,\ circle,\ diamond,\ triangle$$
$$Size \rightarrow large,\ small$$
$$Pattern \rightarrow striped,\ dotted$$
$$Adj \rightarrow red,\ broken$$
$$Rel \rightarrow above,\ below,\ right\text{-}of,\ left\text{-}of$$

This is an expanded version of GRAMMAR1 described in Fig. 4. (The element *te* serves the function of a relative pronoun like *that*.) An example of a sentence in this language is *Square striped te triangle large te broken above circle dotted small right-of*. The experiment compares four conditions of learning for this language:

1. *No reference*. Here subjects simply study strings of the language trying to infer their grammatical structure.
2. *Bad semantics*. Here a picture of the sentence's referent is presented along with the sentences. However, the relationship between the sentence's semantic referent and the surface structure violates LAS's constraints. The

[1] I would like to thank Rebecca Paulson for conducting this experiment and performing the data analysis.

adjective following the ith shape will modify the $(n + 1 - i)$th shape in the sentence (where n is the number of noun phrases). For example, the adjectives associated with the first noun phrase modifies the last shape. Similarly, the ith relation describes the relation between the $(m + 1 - i)$th pair of shapes (where m is the number of relations). So, for instance, the second relation *right-of* describes the relationship between the first pair of shapes, *square* and *triangle*. The appropriate picture for the example sentence is given in Fig. 18a.

3. *Good semantics.* Here the adjective in each noun phrase modifies the noun in that phrase. Relations relate the appropriate nouns in the surface structure. The appropriate picture for the example sentence in this case is given in Fig. 18b. LAS could bracket sentences given this picture if it could guess the main proposition.

4. *Good semantics plus highlighting.* The picture in this condition is the same as that in condition (3), but the shapes in the main proposition are highlighted. In this condition LAS would be guaranteed of successfully bracketing the sentence because the main proposition is given. The picture for this condition is given in Fig. 18c.

In some ways this experiment is like Moeser and Bregman's (1973). However, here English words are used so that the subjects do not need to induce the language's lexicalization as well as its grammar. This corresponds to the situation faced by LAS.1. Moeser and Bregman's language was not a true context-free language but rather a finite-cardinality language. Essentially they contrasted (1) with (3) and found Condition (1) much worse. They did not have a condition like (2) where there was a semantics as elaborate as Condition (3), but where the relation between referent and sentence violated the graph-deformation condition. LAS would predict no difference between Conditions (1) and (2) and predict that both would be much worse than (3). Condition (4) should be better than Condition (3) if the subjects have any difficulty in guessing what the main proposition is. For this particular language, there is little doubt about what to choose as the main proposition. It is always the one whose relation or adjective is last in the sentence.

The basic procedure in the experiment involved having all subjects pass through eight blocks of study–test. In each block the subject studied six sentences with the semantics appropriate to his condition (if any). The sentences were presented to the subjects on cards with pictures given below, depicting the appropriate semantic information. Subjects in the no-semantics condition had just the sentence printed on the card. Subjects were given 30 sec to study each sentence. After studying the six sentences the subjects were given a test booklet that contained on separate pages six pairs of

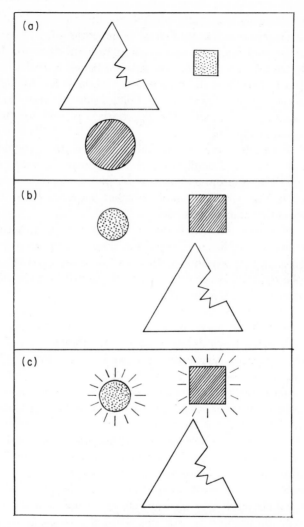

FIG. 18.   Three different semantic referents for the same sentence. Part (a) was used in the bad semantics condition; Part (b) in the good semantics condition; Part (c) in the good semantics plus highlighting condition.

sentences without any picture referents. The subject's task was to indicate which sentence of each pair was grammatically well formed for the language studied. Subjects were given 30 sec to make their decision for each sentence pair. Subjects in all conditions studied and were tested with the same set of sentences. The only variation between conditions was the information that accompanied the sentences on the study trials. The study and test sentences were randomly generated with the constraint that they mention at least two objects and no more than four objects.

The test pairs were of two sorts. There were pairs that tested for some minimal syntactic contrast. Thus, a subject might have to choose between:

A. Square striped large triangle te red above
B. Square large striped triangle te red above

The second sort of test presented a correct sentence with some unrelated sentence that had a gross semantic defect. So a subject might see:

C. Circle large te triangle small below above
D. Square striped large triangle te red above

In this example C is wrong semantically because *above* requires to noun-phrase arguments and only one is given (*triangle* is an argument for *below*). Subjects found the two types of tests to be of approximately equal difficulty. Therefore, I will present data pooled over the two test types.

Figure 19 provides a summary of the main results of the experiment. It is based on data collected from eight subjects in each condition. In Fig. 19, the data are classified by whether they came from the first or second half of the experiment, and by the condition. Plotted in percent correct choice on the test pairs. In all conditions subjects were able to pick up on some regularities and perform better than chance (50%). However, subjects were much worse in the bad-semantics and no-semantics conditions than in the two good-semantics conditions. Also subjects in the bad- and no-semantics conditions showed little improvement from the first to the second half of the experiment whereas subjects in the good-semantics conditions showed considerable improvement.

Subjects with good semantics plus highlighting of main propositions are nonsignificantly worse than subjects without highlighting. The difference is completely due to the two subjects in the highlighting condition who performed very poorly. It seems that these two subjects did not understand the intention of the highlighing information. Perhaps, subjects in the good-semantics condition were able to guess what the main proposition was. If so, providing them with this highlighting information would be of no help. I am currently planning to do an experiment where the main proposition will be completely ambiguous.

Many readers may not be surprised by the better learning in the good-semantics conditions. Hopefully, the significance of this outcome is clear. It shows that semantics is important to induction of the syntactic structure of a natural language. However, it also shows that semantics is useless if the relation between the semantic referent and the syntactic structure

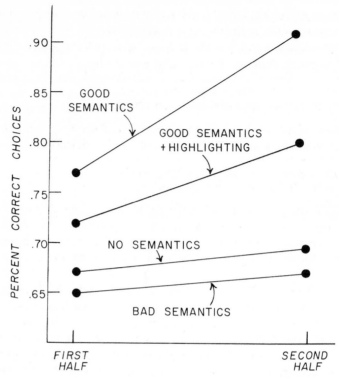

F<small>IG</small>. 19.   Performance in grammaticality judgment task as a function of semantic condition and half of the experiment.

is arbitrary. The surface structure of the sentence must be a graph deformation of the underlying semantic structure. Failure to appreciate the contribution of semantics to language induction and failure to understand the nature of this contribution of semantics to the induction process have been fundamental in the stagnation of attempts to understand the algorithms permitting language induction. These facts may be obvious when pointed out, but they have been unavailable to the linguistic theorists for fifteen years.

SUMMARY

This contribution reports what has been accomplished and gives some of my ideas after nine months of work on the problem of language acquisition. The approach to this problem has been strongly influenced by the formal theory of language. For instance, the work of Gold, reviewed in this paper, is of fundamental importance and should be understood by anyone interested in the induction of any complex skill. Attempting to stay in a rigorous framework, I have been trying to understand the nature of the critical role of semantics in language induction.

I have become convinced that natural languages are in no way a random selection from the set of all possible languages. This idea is not new. It was advanced by Chomsky (1965) to account for why children seem to have the success they do in language acquisition. However, Chomsky seems to have thought that there were purely syntactic constraints on the forms of natural language. The only possible role he saw for semantics was one of motivating the learner. As he wrote (Chomsky, 1962):

> . . . it might be maintained, not without plausibility, that semantic information of some sort is essential even if the formalized grammar that is the output of the device does not contain statements of direct semantic nature. Here, care is necessary. It may well be that a child given only the input of nonsense elements would not come to learn the principles of sentence formation. This is not necessarily a relevant observation, however, even if true. It may only indicate that meaningfulness and semantic function provide the motivation for language learning, while playing no necessary part in its mechanism, which is what concerns us here [p. 531].

It is now clear, however, that many of the constraints on language, and many of the potential generalizations, are only possible when we make use of the language's semantics. It seems hard to specify any strong properties that directly constrain the syntactic form of a natural language. It seems these constraints only come indirectly by making reference to semantic information. These constraints and potential generalizations often seem obvious when pointed out. Therefore, I find myself attempting to discover and formalize the obvious. What is remarkable is how slow a task this is proving to be. It is unfortunately not the case that we are naturally aware of the powerful constraints that shape the language that we speak. It seems that it is only in attempting to simulate the language-learning process that I am coming to understand what is a natural language.

APPENDIX

The following gives an outline of a proof to demonstrate that an algorithm that could induce an arbitrary primitive recursive (pr) relation between a sentence and its semantic referent could be used to induce an arbitrary primitive recursive language. This result is important because, in light of Gold's work, we know there can be no satisfactory algorithms for inducing an arbitrary pr language. This establishes, then, that the relation between a sentence of a natural language and its referent is clearly subject to some strong constraints. I am indebted to Clayton Lewis for help with the structuring of this proof.

The basic idea of the proof is to assume that there is some fixed set of possible semantic referents for all natural languages. We make only weak assumptions about the nature of this set of referents. Thus, the proof is not specific to a particular semantic theory. We are assuming that a particular natural language corresponds to some function that maps these semantic referents into sentences of the language. We show that an algorithm that could induce any such pr functions could be used to induce the recognition function for a pr language. The proof involves identifying each string in a language-free manner with an arbitrary semantic referent. We then attempt to induce a semantic function between the language-free semantic equivalent of a string and another string that indicates whether the first is grammatical. This semantic function can serve as the basis of a recognition function.

1. First, by Gödelization we can associate with each semantic referent a unique integer, and with each string of words in the language a unique integer. The semantic relation is given by a function F which maps the integer equivalent of the semantic referent into the integer equivalent of the sentence.

2. Provided that the set of possible referents is a primitive recursive set, there is an effective ordering of these referents. Let Num (x) be the function that gives the position of the semantic referent denoted by integer x in the enumeration. Let Expand (n) be a function that gives the nth semantic referent. The first function is pr, and we will assume that the set of semantic referents is such that the second function is also pr.

3. Let the recognition function for a language L be $R_L(y)$ which has the value 1 if the string of words corresponding to y is a sentence in L and the value 0 otherwise.

4. Let Conc (x,t) be a function that, if t has the value 1, returns as its value the integer equivalent of a string represented by integer x concatenated with a special symbol. Otherwise, its value is just x. Let Detect (y) be a function that detects whether the special symbol is concatenated onto the string represented by y. Both of these functions are pr.

5. Among the possible pr functions that map a referent x onto a sentence is the following:

$$F_L(x) = \text{Conc}(\text{Num}(x), R_L(\text{Num}(x))).$$

That is, this function retrieves the position n of the referent represented by x in the ordering and checks whether the string corresponding to n is in the language L. If it is not, F_L outputs n; otherwise, it outputs n', the integer equivalent of n concatenated with the special symbol.

6. Suppose we have an algorithm A that can identify any pr relation between the set of referents and a language. It must be able to identify F_L. From A it is possible to construct an algorithm A^* that will identify any pr language. The inputs to A^* will be integer equivalents of strings and 1's and 0's to indicate whether the strings are in the language. The following is a description of A^*:

   i. Given x representing some string it computes Expand $(x) = y$ which corresponds to the xth semantic referent.
   ii. If x is grammatical it computes $z = $ conc $(x,1)$. Otherwise $z = x$.
   iii. It provides as input to algorithm A, y a semantic referent and z a sentence.
   iv. Eventually A, given this input, will induce the function F_L. This is a pr function mapping referents onto sentences.
   v. A^* can construct R_L from F_L as follows:

$$R_L(x) = \text{Detect}(F_L(\text{Expand}(x))). \qquad \text{Q.E.D.}$$

ACKNOWLEDGMENTS

This research is supported by grant GB-40298 from NSF to the author. I have had the good fortune of interacting with some very bright graduate students at Michigan—Ross Bott, Carol Hafner, Clayton Lewis, and Lynne Reder. While they may not have found all the flaws in my ideas, this paper is certainly freer from error because of them. Each of these students also has suggested ideas that I have incorporated into the paper.

REFERENCES

Anderson, J. R. Computer simulation of a language-acquisition system: A first report. Unpublished manuscript, University of Michigan, 1974.

Anderson, J. R., & Bower G. H. *Human associative memory*. Washington: Winston, 1973.

Bever, T. G. The cognitive basis for linguistic structures. In J. R. Hayes (Ed.), *Cognition and the development of language*. New York: Wiley, 1970.

Bloom, L. *Language development: Form and function in emerging grammars*. Cambridge, Massachusetts: MIT Press, 1970.

Bloom, L. *One word at a time*. The Hague: Mouton, 1973.

Bowerman, M. *Early syntactic development*. Cambridge, England: University Press, 1973.

Braine, M. D. S. On learning grammatican order of words. *Psychological Review*, 1963, **70**, 323–348.

Brown, R. *A first language*. Cambridge, Mass.: Harvard University Press, 1973.

Chomsky, N. *Syntactic structures*. The Hague: Mouton, 1957.

Chomsky, N. Explanatory models in linguistics. In E. Nagel, P. Suppes, & A. Tarski (Eds.), *Logic, methodology, and philosophy of science: Proceedings of the 1960 International Congress*. Stanford, California: Stanford University Press, 1962.

Chomsky, N. *Aspects of the theory of syntax*. Cambridge, Massachusetts: MIT Press, 1965.

Clark, E. V. Non-linguistic strategies and the acquisition of word meanings. *Cognition: International Journal of Cognitive Psychology*, 1974, in press.

Crespi-Reghizzi, S. The mechanical acquisition of precedence grammars. Report No. UCLA-ENG-7054, School of Engineering and Applied Science, University of California at Los Angeles, 1970.

Ervin, S. M. Imitation and structural change in children's language. In E. H. Lenneberg (Ed.), *New directions in the study of language*. Cambridge, Mass.: MIT Press, 1964. Pp. 163–189.

Fernald, C. Children's active and passive knowledge of syntax. Paper presented at the meeting of the Midwestern Psychological Association, 1970.

Fillmore, C. J. The case for case. In E. Bach and R. J. Harms (Eds.), *Universals in linguistic theory*. New York: Holt, Rinehart & Winston, 1968.

Fraser, D., Bellugi, U., & Brown, R. Control of grammar in imitation, comprehension, and production. *Journal of Verbal Learning and Verbal Behavior*, 1963, **2**, 121–135.

Friedman, J. *A computer model of transformational grammar*. New York: American Elsevier, 1971.

Gold, M. Language identification in the limit. *Information and Control*, 1967, **10**, 447–474.

Hafner, C., & Wilcox, B. LISP MTS programmer's manual. (Mental Health Research Communication 302 and Information Processing Paper 21) Ann Arbor: University of Michigan, 1974.

Kelley, K. L. Early syntactic acquisition. (Report No. P-3719) Santa Monica, Cal.: The Rand Corp., 1967.

Lenneberg, E. H. Understanding language without ability to speak: A case report. *Journal of Abnormal and Social Psychology*, 1962, **65**, 419–425.

Lenneberg, E. H. *Biological foundations of language*. New York: Wiley, 1967.

Miller, G. A. *The psychology of communication* New York: Basic Books, 1967.

Moeser, S. D., & Bregman, A. S. The role of reference in the acquisition of a miniature artificial language. *Journal of Verbal Learning and Verbal Behavior*, 1972, **11**, 759–769.

Moeser, S. D., & Bregman, A. S. Imagery and language acquisition. *Journal of Verbal Learning and Verbal Behavior*, 1973, **12**, 91–98.

Pao, T. W. L. A solution of the syntactic induction-conference problem for a nontrivial subset context-free languages. Report No. 70-19, The Moore School of Electrical Engineering, University of Pennsylvania, August, 1969.

Reber, A. S. Transfer of structure in synthetic languages. *Journal of Experimental Psychology*, 1969, **81**, 115–119.

Richards, I. A., Jasuilko, E., & Gibson, C. *Russian through pictures*. Book I. New York: Washington Square Press, 1961.

Saporta, S., Blumenthal, A. L., Lackowski, P., & Reiff, D. G. Grammatical models of language learning. In R. J. DePiertro (Ed.), *Monograph Series on Language and Linguistics*. Vol. 16. Report of the 14th Annual Round Table Meeting on Linguistic and Language Studies, 1963. Pp. 133–142.

Schlesinger, I. M. Production of utterances and language acquisition. In D. I. Slobin (Ed.), *The ontogenesis of grammar*. New York: Academic Press, 1971.

Siklóssy, L. A language-learning heuristic program. *Cognitive Psychology*, 1971, **2**, 479–495.

Simmons, R. F. Semantic networks: Their computations and use for understanding English sentences. In R. C. Schank & K. M. Colby (Eds.), *Computer models of thought and language*. San Francisco: Freeman, 1973.

Simon, H. A. *The sciences of the artificial*. Cambridge, Mass.: MIT Press, 1969.

Sinclair-deZwart, H. Language acquisition and cognitive development. In T. E. Moore (Ed.), *Cognitive development and the acquisition of language*. New York: Academic Press, 1973.

Slobin, D. I. On the learning of morphological rules: A reply to Palermo and Eberhart. In D. I. Slobin (Ed.), *The ontogenesis of grammer. New York: Academic* Press, 1971.

Woods, W. A. Transition network grammars for natural language analysis. *Communications of the ACM*. 1970, **13**, 591–606.

11
SEMIOTIC EXTENSION

David McNeill[1]
Institute for Advanced Study
Princeton, New Jersey

The purpose of the theory given here is to describe the conceptual basis of speech production — that is, to describe the way speakers build up utterances as they generate and find ways to interrelate concepts. Although this theory is intended to explain the speech production of adults as well as children, it is, for reasons that will become evident in the course of the exposition, necessarily presented first in terms of ontogenesis. This presentation, therefore, except in its final sections, concentrates on the development of speech production in children.

To set the stage, however, it is important to describe briefly the overall approach. A central claim is that the speech production mechanisms of adults are relatively narrow in their most direct conceptual adaptation and are not fundamentally different from the mechanisms available in young children, whose mental functioning is at the sensory–motor and early representational levels. However, these initially limited mechanisms are borrowed by the higher level conceptual processes of adults; such borrowing I am calling "semiotic extension."

Relying on the semiotic extension of the basic speech mechanisms, speech production is organized around conceptual units formed at the sensory–motor level, that is, around such conceptual entities as Objects, Actions, States, and Events, regardless of the level of the mental processing

[1] On leave from the University of Chicago, Committee on Cognition and Communication.

behind the content being expressed. Even abstract content, where there may not be real objects, actions, states, or events at all, must be organized into these sensory–motor structures. According to the theory given here, speech cannot be produced in any other way than from the use of sensory–motor schemas as a guide, even though the speaker's mental processes may be organized at operational levels much different from the level of sensory–motor functioning.

The structure of speech seems to be quite directly adapted to the organization of information at the levels of sensory–motor and early representational intelligence. It is at these cognitive levels that the concepts of Objects, Actions, States, and Events are first differentiated. Intelligence here is geared to the practical understanding of concrete situations. As Piaget (1962) says, ". . . it is precisely the sensory-motor schemas evolved during the first year of life which ensure the gradual organization of the object, of space, and of constancy of form and dimensions [p. 77]." Speech, in turn, appears to be exceptionally good at describing concrete situations, an intuition that has been discussed in many places (and constitutes a cornerstone of the empiricist doctrine of language).

The semiotic extension, however, since it takes speech beyond its level of direct adaptation, creates two opposed tendencies in the relationship of language to thought. First, the original mechanisms are enriched far beyond the level of thought they are directly adapted to. It is only such enrichment that makes speech useful at all beyond concrete situations. Second, the extended use of the basic speech mechanisms makes distortions possible in the process of thought itself, higher levels of mental functioning conforming too directly to the structure of the speech mechanisms. The most extreme versions of this second tendency are codified in the Whorfian hypothesis. However, it is the lack of any direct adaptation between speech and the higher levels of mental functioning that creates these distortions, and such distortion is the inevitable accompaniment of enrichment. Although, for example, it may be a philosophical error which arises from the use of language, to regard abstract concepts such as an image as entities, it is an error created from the process of semiotic extension, without which it would be impossible to speak of these abstractions at all.

THE STUDY OF PERFORMANCE

The approach taken here stresses performance entirely. Without entering a discussion of exactly what the relation between competence and performance might actually be, and whether such a dichotomy can be maintained precisely, it is possible to indicate with a few remarks what range of problems is considered as being within the performance domain:

1. Knowing the order of words, for example, that in English declarative sentences, Agent precedes Action, does not explain how a speaker organizes an utterance in which the relevant words occur in this order; these topics are sharply separated, and the second, only, is a topic of performance.

2. Logical structures do not necessarily have validity as models of processing (although they have validity in other ways). The logical structure of a negative sentence, for example, can be analyzed as corresponding to a falsified assertion. "I don't require you to stand on your head" corresponds to: False [I require you to stand on your head]. This analysis can be defended on a variety of grounds which relate to one's knowledge of the structure of negation and the syntax of English negative sentences. However, it does not follow that at any stage in the utterance of "I don't require you to stand on your head" the positive assertion was generated along with the predicate, False.

On the contrary, this would be a most implausible claim. The intuitions of a speaker cannot be dismissed entirely in deciding what are reasonable hypotheses. These intuitions do not seem to include anything that corresponds to the generation of an appropriate logical analysis in the case of negation (and in numerous other cases). Rather, the negative element is integrated into the structure of the sentence from the moment it appears at all in the flow of processes leading to speech.

3. Linguistic relationships do not necessarily correspond to processing relationships. Pronouns representing definite noun phrases (NPs), for example, are required to be transformationally recoverable. This means that a pronominal NP in the surface structure of a sentence must be derived from a source NP in the underlying structure that does not include a pronoun. One motivation behind this recoverability is that the referent of a definite pronoun in a sentence is in general always known. "George knew that he would be late" is ambiguous, but the ambiguity is between two well-defined alternative derivations of "he," neither of which has a pronoun as the source. This transformational structure corresponds to the speaker's intuition that pronouns have definite referents, but it suggests an implausible mechanism if it is assumed to describe the processes that supposedly take place during speech production. It should not suggest, for example, that at an intermediate stage of producing one of the senses of the sentence above, the proper name "George" or some other index (not the pronoun) which keeps the referential correlations straight, is generated. While it is

undoubtedly the case that a speaker knows the definite referent of the pronoun he utters in such a sentence, it is implausible to claim that, because he knows this, he generated a nonpronomial underlying form first. It is more plausible to be guided again by intuition, and to say that the pronoun appears in pronomial form from the first in the production of the sentence.

PRODUCTION MECHANISMS

Lashley (1951) believed that one function of structure in the production of speech is that it controls the serial order of events in the action of speaking. By means of a structural schema, the speaker is able to organize elementary linguistic units (phonemes, syllables, words, phrases, whatever they may prove to be) into a strict sequential order, and do this as part of a single integrated action. In part, the speed of the action seems to require such an overall organization. Given the central-to-peripheral conduction delays involved, there is not enough time to maintain the sequence of action over feedback loops at the speeds with which it is performed (12 phonemes and 5 or 6 syllables per second are typical). Wickelgren (1969) has challenged Lashley's conclusion, that the speed of production requires the operation of organizational schemas, but there is indirect evidence apart from the rate of speech production for the operation of organizational schemas at least at the word and syllable levels (Kozhevnikov & Chistovich, 1965).

The notion of an organizational schema (Lashley) or syntagma (Kozhevnikov and Chistovich) will prove to be most useful. It is important therefore to grasp what problem is referred to when these terms are introduced into the discussion. (They will be treated as synonymous.) Each utterance must be produced in some particular order. This is trivially true, since only a single order is physiologically possible in a given utterance. This inevitable physiological requirement, however, is at least one factor that creates the necessity for an organizational schema. If we were equipped with a large number of independent production channels, say 10 or 20 separately programmed vocal tracts, we could transmit messages with great explosions of signs and not worry about selecting concrete sequences of them. (Whether such outbursts could be perceived is another question.) Since this is not possible, we must organize a serial order of elements to speak at all. The problem is one of choice and arrangement, which words are to precede and which to follow. Linearity creates this necessity for organization. We are guided by a variety of grammatical rules for establishing certain orders, but even when no rule applies (as in nongrammatical sequences), there must be an order, hence an organizational schema. The notion of an organizational schema is thus more general than the notion of a grammatical rule (in the linguistic sense).

A characteristic of organized action sequences is that they are performed as integrated wholes (Lashley, 1951). In the case of speech, the basis for integration seems to be associated with the organization of meaning. A syntagma, according to Kozhevnikov and Chistovich (1965), is "one meaning unit, which is pronounced as a single output [p. 74]." A syntagma thus unites the structure of meaning with the organization of articulation, and explains the latter (in part) by reference to the former. This process can be investigated in a preliminary way, as described below. A related idea is that of the phonemic clause (Trager & Smith, 1951; Boomer, 1965), except that the concept of a phonemic clause overlooks completely the essential correlation with semantic organization. From the point of view of the production process, the phonemic clause considers only the side of the syntagma that has to do with the integration of action. A phonemic clause in English, for example, conversational pronunciation of "How could they think to do it," has one primary stress, one terminal juncture, and one unified stress and pitch pattern: properties that describe a single integrated action sequence within the English phonological system. To bring this characterization into contact with actual production processes it is necessary to restore the opposite side of the syntagma, having to do with meaning.

A review of what is known of the organization of the syntagma, however, really cannot go very much further than this. The most recent research is almost completely limited to the syllabic speech level and levels still more microscopic (Kozhevnikov & Chistovich, 1965; Fromkin, 1968, 1971; MacKay, 1972). Very little can be said about the organization of speech processes at a semantic or conceptual level. One reflection of this imbalance appears in a model proposed by Fromkin. She was trying to sketch the entire flow of information processing from the conception of meaning to the final articulation of phoneme sequences. The model is presented (Fromkin, 1971) in the form of a flow chart, and looks a little like those maps Bostonians are said to have drawn of the United States. As one gets closer to how sequences of phonemes might be produced, the amount of detail greatly increases, but the formation of conceptual structure is confined to a single unanalyzed box, and its relation to sentence structure to two others.

But the difficulty in Fromkin's model is not merely an absence of detail at the semantic and syntactic levels. More important, there is an error of theoretical principle. The model supposes that, in the course of producing speech, semantic and syntactic structures are generated and stored before any lower level processes take place. This sequence of steps is quite implausible for the general case in producing meaningful utterances. For many speakers, normal speech seems to be uttered *as* it is organized. The conceptual arrangements behind speech can be worked out at nearly the same time the sentence is produced, certainly not always a phrase or sentence in advance. Of course, articulation can be delayed, and some speakers may do this routinely when they speak carefully, but what is inconsistent with Fromkin's model is that articulation should not be always delayed.

Intuition confirms that speech can be produced as it is organized. An experiment by Marslen-Wilson (1973) demonstrates this directly and convincingly. He found a group of subjects who could consistently shadow speech with very short latencies, about 200 msec behind the input (a lag of a syllable approximately), and yet speak clearly and shadow accurately on the whole. Of 111 "constructive errors" made by these subjects (a constructive error is one in which the shadower adds words, or changes them, or changes parts of words to make new words), 108 were still semantically and syntactically appropriate word choices within the context. An example occurred when a subject inserted "that" while shadowing "It was beginning to be light enough so I could see . . . ," or said "He heard that the brigade . . ." when shadowing "He heard at the brigade . . ."

That is, the shadowers made lexical selections that fit the structure of the sentence as it had been developed up to the point of the error. Clearly, in view of the short latencies involved, the shadowers had been able to speak sentence structures as they assembled them, at least from the level where semantic content is constrained.

ONTOGENESIS

Children's speech is relatively rich at an early stage with the means for making concrete descriptions. The semantic relationships which appear in the organization of adult utterances (Actor, Action, Recipient, and others) arise quite early in children's speech and have obvious utility in describing events, actions, states and objects. These early utterances are typically closely associated with practical situations and depend on the child's mode of cognitive functioning at this stage (Sinclair-deZwart, 1973). This early use by children of the same basic semantic relations that are central to adult speech, implies the existence of an isomorphism between the basic adult language structures and the child's cognitive functioning. The sense in which there can be such an isomorphism forms the substance of the ontogenetic theory given here. This theory, in turn, suggests certain insights into the mode of functioning that takes place during adult speech production. In essence, the explanation of why languages are excellent instruments for concrete description is to be found in the ontogenesis of speech and its relation to cognition.

Children begin to produce utterances that contain more than one word at a characteristic stage of mental development: it occurs upon the transition from the sensory–motor period when the child's knowledge of the world has been successfully organized into action schemas, to the representational period when these schemas begin a process of interiorization (Piaget, 1962). This correlation has been discussed by Brown (1973) and Bloom (1973). There is an explanation (given below) of why children are unable to produce combinatorial utterances before the process of interiorization has begun. To give it, however, and in general to present the ontogenetic theory here, it is necessary to provide examples of children's mental development during the sensory–motor and the early representational periods. In addition, these examples will illustrate what is meant by the term "action schema."

The clear differentiation of objects, actions, and places that is characteristic of adult thought, is achieved by young children only after a lengthy developmental process during which rudimentary action schemas are differentiated and coordinated. In the sensory–motor period, the child's cognitive functioning is interconnected with the means he has for organizing action, as illustrated in the following examples:

(5 *months.*) The child is looking at two celluloid parrots, which earlier had been in her bassinet but now hang some distance off, and kicks her legs. This movement had made the parrots jump and rattle before, and is the baby's schema, to which the sight of the parrots is assimilated. The schema is the meaning of the parrots for the child, i.e., she understands them in terms of an action she knows how to perform with them (Piaget, 1952, p. 160).

(*11 to 14 months.*) The adult opens and closes his eyes. The child has a schema for opening and closing her mouth at this stage, but none independently for her eyes (she does not know where her eyes are, cannot find them with her hands, etc.), but she imitates the adult by opening and closing her mouth. Thus, unfamiliar movements can be assimilated to schemas which control other familiar movements. There is here the beginning of a differentiation between the overt performance of an action and the schema for this action (Piaget, 1962, p. 36).

(*16 months.*) The child is trying to open a match box with a sliding lid to obtain a chain hidden inside. As she struggles with the box she opens and closes her mouth several times. Thus, she pictures the desired activity to herself, using an action schema that relates to movements of her mouth, but to represent a movement of an external entity which has not actually occurred. There is a further degree of abstraction here, away from the literal content of the action schema (Piaget, 1962, p. 65).

Such action schemas are the source of meaning to the child for events involving herself and the world as she experiences it. During the first year, there is an elaboration of sensory–motor schemas. New ones appear, more general ones differentiate into more specific ones, and there is a process of coordination whereby schemas interact and relate to one another; thus, the child's thought processes gain in scope, precision and flexibility.

In the second year, there is a further process that Piaget calls "interiorization." As a result of this process, which extends well into the representational period, the schema remains in close contact with action structurally, but the actual performance of the motor movements associated with the action schema become less and less important. The schema is differentiated from the overt action. The final result of the process is a kind of internal imitation to which Piaget gives the name "image." It is not important for my purposes here whether such internal imitations are called "images" in the sense of this term in philosophical and other psychological discussions. What is significant is the idea that the essential structural properties of action schemas are preserved even though the overt performance of the action has dropped away. The action becomes "mentally representable" (Sinclair-deZwart, 1973),

The emergence of patterned speech coincides with this process of interiorization. The following chart shows the interrelation:

	single words	word patterns	
Language	─────────────────────────────→		
Sensory–motor schemas	──────────────────────→		
	exterior	transition	interior
Zone	A	B	C

The boundaries between Zones A, B, and C, and those between single words and word patterns, not to mention the correlations between speech and cognition, cannot be precise. Nevertheless, judging both from the examples in Piaget (1962), as well as the ages over which the initial interiorizations take place (about 14–24 months), which approximate those of the single word period (about 12–20 months), it is roughly the case that word patterns emerge in a child's speech as the interiorization of action schemas is taking place. And as the process of interiorization proceeds, the scope of the child's grammatical organization increases.

At the time corresponding to Zones A and B, linguistic usage is closely linked to the performance of action. This has been noted by many investigators (e.g., Werner & Kaplan, 1963; Gruber, 1973; Greenfield, Smith, & Laufer, 1972; Piaget, 1962). Single-word utterances accompany actions that are in progress. For example, "bow wow" referred to anything (horses, hens, people, dogs, etc.) the child saw from the balcony where she first used the word to refer to an actual dog (Piaget, 1962, p. 216). The action does not necessarily have to be one performed by the child. The child's perception of an action by another person or thing is assimilated to a schema of the child's own (as in the match box example, above). The child just mentioned, for example, used "daddy" to refer to anyone who stretched out his arms or who lit a pipe.

If one disregards the dynamic aspect of action schemas, considering only the external conditions with which the schemas are connected, it is theoretically possible to extract a set of perceptual features that corresponds to the data assimilated to the schema. According to a recent argument by E. Clark (1973) the child links the words he uses to a subset of the perceptual features with which these words are associated in adult usage. The principal evidence for her argument consists of referential overextensions by the child (e.g., the overextension of "bow bow" or "daddy," above) which can be seen as proceeding along a variety of perceptual dimensions (such as size, movement, shape). There is no fundamental inconsistency between this argument of Clark's based on the abstraction of perceptual features, and the view assumed above, that single-word utterances relate to action schemas. Such an abstraction, however, overlooks that the process behind the child's use of words is essentially active. This results in a simplification that is perhaps appropriate for some purposes, but is inadequate for the argument of this paper; this argument makes fundamental use of the dynamic aspect of sensory–motor schemas.

Piaget places great emphasis on the development of symbolic relationships at the representational stage. It is this development, Piaget argues, that makes interiorization possible, and through this, language as well as symbolic play and deferred imitation. Through symbolic relationships, words call forth past schemas, which in turn provide meaning to current perceptions. This "symbolic function" is fundamental. It opens the way for the creation of a novel process, the formation of syntagmas, which is crucial in the emergence of patterned speech. There is the absolute necessity for the child to organize his production of utterances where they consist of two or more distinct words. In addition to symbols, the child must have the capability of forming syntagmas. The connection between the child's cognitive functioning and his linguistic development, is by far the clearest in this process.

A phenomenon that occurs at the beginning of patterned speech demonstrates the importance of the development of syntagmas. Many children, as they leave the single-word period, start to produce successions of two or more single-word utterances (Greenfield et al., 1972; Rodgon, 1972; Bloom, 1973). These are not yet true sentences. Often the two words have a semantic connection that can be recognized, but the words are not part of a single integrated utterance for the child. Some examples from several of the children who participated in Rodgon's study are the following ("duration" refers to the total duration of the utterance in seconds):

Utterance	Duration
open matches	3.15
doggie byebye	3.90
open purse	3.75
doggie woof-woof	2.05
dah awgone	3.40
book baby	4.50
dah awgaw	1.65
awgaw bip	1.95
byebye daddy	3.30

Each word has an independent intonation pattern and is followed by what for an adult would be a terminal juncture; hence they are not part of a single phonemic clause. There is also a long and variable pause between the two words. The child appears to be unable to form a single syntagma for the whole utterance.

This difficulty might reflect some weakness in the child's processes of controlling articulatory movements, which affects his ability to map the syntagma into speech sounds. However, these same children, on other occasions in this period, successfully formed syntagmas, and produced utterances that possess the phonological and temporal properties of one integrated action. Some examples of these utterances from the same children studied by Rodgon, are as follows:

Utterance	Duration
this is nice	1.35
my shoe	1.05
go baby	1.20
don't doll	1.50
book down	0.75
open book	0.90
bye book	0.90
bye bye cow	1.20
bye daddy	1.50

The alternation between this integration and the punctation shown above during this period is complete: there is either a phonemic clause including temporal patterning, or there are two clearly successive utterances. The impression is strongly given that the child does something qualitatively different when he produces a single, integrated utterance. That a wider range of semantic relationships is reflected in the integrated utterances than in the successive ones will be taken up in a later section.

The necessity of considering the developmental basis of the syntagma therefore cannot be overlooked. It emerges with the advent of the symbolic function and can be observed in intermittent use in the speech of individual children. It appears to be crucial in the child's ability to produce patterned speech.

As mentioned earlier, the syntagma is the minimal unit of speech production based on meaning; it is a meaning unit pronounced as a whole (Kozhevnikov & Chisovich, 1965); it thereby unites the organization of speech with the organization of meaning. There is, at the end of the sensory–motor period of development, a unique and natural basis for the evolution of the syntagma, which exists at no other time in development. Given this basis, moreover, it is possible to see why the emergence of the syntagma is withheld until the interiorization of action schemas has begun.

The production of speech must itself be organized by schemas for action. The intonational patterning, timing, and other properties of fluent speech are all tied together by such action schemas. The schemas for these integrated speech actions should not be fundamentally different in kind from the schemas for other types of action sequences. It is the lack of any fundamental difference, the lack of any necessary difference of logical form, between the action schemas providing the child's cognitive understanding at this stage and the action schemas by which speech may be organized, that constitutes the basis upon which organized speech can occur at all. What is necessary is that the child should be able to use the action schema for cognition to organize the action schema for speech. If there is not a fundamental difference in kind between the two kinds of schemas, the schema for the utterance can line up with the schema for the content to be expressed; the latter then will guide and organize the former, and this process makes the syntagma. The structure for the action that is schematized in the child's mode of representing the world at this stage can be used to give structure to the production of utterances that describe this world.

EVIDENCE FOR THIS ARGUMENT

During the production of speech, young children apparently are influenced by the organization of sensory–motor schemas, in that speech orders can be seen to reflect necessary sequences of action. Children have a strong tendency to express the locative relation, for example, in the following order: Object–Location, or Action–Location. This tendency has been documented in the speech of children learning English (Bloom, 1970; Bowerman, 1973), Finnish (Bowerman, 1973), Hungarian and Serbo-Croatian together (Slobin, 1973), and Luo, a language spoken in Kenya (Blount, 1969). Now, the action of placing an object in a certain location necessarily occurs in a sequence that includes the location in the last place, after the object and the action (which are not inherently ordered). If this action sequence is systematized into a schema as the basis of the child's conception of place, locative utterances will tend to be produced in the observed Object– or Action–Location order.

The conceptualization of place does not always derive from the motion of transporting an object, however, since the object can be observed already in place. In this case, where there is no movement, there can be no basis in the child's action schema for a preferred word order. Reversals of the object–location order are rare for English speaking children, but those that occur at all, always seem to involve location without the logical possibility of movement, as in this example from Bloom (1970, p. 56): the child, looking at a photograph in a magazine of a flower on the toe of a bare foot, said, "foots flower." This order contrasts with such utterances as "sweater chair," which was said as the same child placed a sweater on a chair.

The important distinction between movement and nonmovement locatives is not whether a movement actually occurs, but whether one could logically occur in the situation. The child's syntagma for a nonmovement locative such as "foots flower," presumably must be based on an interiorized action schema in the same way as is the syntagma for "sweater chair." The syntagma for the nonmovement Locative, however, rests on a schema that necessarily lacks an intrinsic order of execution. Sequence is undetermined, so that word order should be variable from utterance to utterance as other factors come into play. In the examples given by Bowerman (1973) for an English speaking child, those which logically could not have involved a locative movement were half in one order and half in the other (Bowerman, 1973, p. 290):

Object–Location	Location–Object
ear outside	there cow
mess here	here mess

On the other hand, no reversals occur in the locatives where movement logically could have occurred, and the schema would have an intrinsic sequence of action (no contextual observations are reported):

Object–Location

Kendall bed (= is in bed)
Kendall water
Kendall pool
lotion tummy
    (= is on tummy?)
towel bed (2 times)
Kendall innere
Kendall innere bed
Kendall down
pillow here (a pillow is some-
    thing that might have been
    moved in contrast to "mess,"
    above)

Similar differences appear in the speech of one of Bowerman's Finnish speaking subjects, Seppo, at a developmental level comparable to Kendall's (a mean length of utterance of about 1.4). Bowerman's other subject was observed at a more advanced level where factors other than action schematic effects could be expected to play a greater role. For Seppo, at this stage, location was expressed with the words meaning "away," "here," "there," and also by various nouns that referred to the places where actions or other objects could be located. I have found 25 examples in Bowerman's Appendicies E and G (coverning Seppo's speech at mean length of utterance 1.42) in which a locative meaning appears to have been involved. Seven of these mention the location first, but none are clear counterexamples to the proposed principle of locative ordering. Four do not seem to be integrated utterances involving a syntagma ("away . . . closed"), one logically does not seem to involve a movement ("house fast train," which describes a picture of a house with a train in the background—assuming this was a locative utterance), and two involve prolocatives, which Bowerman reports (1973, p. 53) were initially used in a nondirectional sense, hence are not based on movement.

It should be noted that there are no grounds in the order of events for these speech preferences for the Object–Location order. It is possible to notice a location before one sees the object, supporting a Location–Object order, or the location after this object, supporting an Object–Location order, and neither order seems inherent to the locative situation. Inherent sequences can be determined with perfect regularity only in an action with an intrinsic sequence of performance. Even when there is a series of events, such as someone standing up and walking to a particular place, the order as perceived can easily be reversed in memory, and presumably is, under the influence of the law of recency; hence the perception of sequences would not provide immutable models for utterances whose word order is determined and fixed; but there can be no alteration of the order of events in an action schema. (This point corresponds to the nonreversibility of preoperational thought.)

FURTHER EVIDENCE FOR THE ARGUMENT

When the semantic relations are Actor and Action, all children except Samoan (Kernan, 1969) strongly prefer the word order: Actor–Action (Bloom, 1970; Blount, 1969; Bowerman, 1973). There is a necessary sequence in the performance of any action where the actor is ego, since the intention to act must precede the action itself. Further, insofar as the actions of other people or the actions of objects are assimilated to the same action schemas as organize ego's own actions, this order preference would extend to all Actor and Action sequences, as has been reported. (There is a corresponding tendency to view inanimate objects as having intentions at this stage of development; see Piaget, 1969.) If the preference for the Actor–Action order should be reversed, this presumably would happen because of a failure to extend the schema from ego's own actions when the actor is not ego. Sinclair-deZwart (1973) has in fact cited several examples of utterances with the Action–Actor order produced by French speaking children, but each occurred when the Actor was someone other than ego.

On the other hand, there is nearly equal use of the Action–Object and Object–Action orders in the speech of some of the same English and Finnish speaking children (Bowerman, 1973). Of 23 Action and Object sentences reported for Kendall, the English speaking child, 13 were Action–Object (including four that may have been successive single words) and 10 were Object–Action. For Seppo, the Finnish-speaking child, there were 47 Action–Object and 26 Object–Action sequences (Bowerman, 1973, Table 14). Now, there is no basis in the actual performance of an action for an ordering of the action and its object. (Object in this case does not mean a physical object, but the conceptualization of the object of an action.) The object upon which the action operates is not separable from the action; it does not become the object of the action until the action (or the intention to act) occurs. Thus, the action schema relating actions and objects is indeterminate for word order. The idea of the action, if there is an object, indivisibly includes the idea of the object as an aspect of the action; for example, "thread break" (Kendall).

In contrast to this indeterminancy, however, when the same action schema organizes a syntagma that includes Actor and Object, without the action being mentioned, a necessary sequence in action once again appears, because intentions must precede actions (which create the objects of actions). This, I believe, explains the widely noted puzzle: that Actor–Object sentences without verbs are ordered in the speech of young children as Actor–Action sentences are, but not necessarily as Action–Object sentences are.

OTHER INFLUENCES ON WORD ORDER

When possessive relations involve alienable possessions, for example, "Kendall rocking chair," there is again an association of word order with action, at least in the speech of English-speaking and Finnish-speaking children (Bloom, 1970; Bowerman, 1973). The order is Possessor–Possessed, corresponding to the necessary action sequence involved when the possessor manually takes the (alienable) possessed into possession. A high proportion of the available examples in Bloom's and Bowerman's descriptions of child speech show the Possessor–Possessed order. The possessive relation, however, introduces a second factor. With English- (and, presumably, Finnish-) speaking children, inalienable possessions also are encoded in the Possessor–Possessed order (e.g., "pig tail," meaning "the pig's tail"), although there can be no corresponding action sequence in these cases. The explanation of the Possessor–Possessed order with inalienable possession is not completely clear, but almost certainly is connected, for English at least, with the fact that the main conceptual form of children's possessive in the early stages is the alienable type (Brown, 1973). Thus, generalizations are possible from the initial alienable possessive, which could be based on action schemas, to the inalienable possessive, when these appear, which could be based on semantic similarity plus the identity of the word order sequences for the two types in the adult speech the children hear.

The basis of the semantic similarity can itself involve an intrinsic action sequence that is the same with alienable and inalienable possession. In their behavior, young children will refer to their body parts, concrete inalienable possessions of which they are aware, by a form of manipulation. They do not merely utter the word "foot," for example, but reach down with their hands and grasp their foot. This action sequence is plausibly connected to the child's conception of possession, and its occurrence in this situation shows that a schema for possession based on movement could be extended to the domain of inalienable possessions. The comparability of action forms provides a basis for the Possessor–Possessed word order with both the inalienable as well as the alienable types of possession, since in both, there is an intrinsic sequence with the object possessed in last place.

It is obvious that there must be interactions between the schematic influences on word order, which arise from the child's mode of cognitive functioning, and the influences from the adult speech the child hears. The child's syntagmas for speech production are based on numerous kinds of information. It is not clear how these interactions work in detail, but it appears that any departure from the schematic sequence will be toward an order that is dominant in the speech the child hears, and any departure from the dominant word order will occur when there is no possible schematic order.

Children learning Luo, for example, use the order Possessed–Possessor for both the alienable as well as the inalienable possessive relation (Blount, 1969). The explanation is that, in Luo, possession is conveyed entirely by suffixation. Whether Luo children ever use simple noun–noun sequences for possession, in which the Possessor–Possessed sequence would be possible, is not known, but none is reported for the stage at which Blount was able to make observations. Nevertheless, the case of Luo is perhaps not different in principle from the English speaking child's use of the opposite Possessor–Possessed order to describe inalienable possession. In both situations, there is a discernible effect of the adult speech model on the child's construction of syntagmas, which goes beyond the effects of the child's own sensory–motor schemas. Similarly, when schemas are indeterminate for order (such as the schema for Object and Action), some children (Kendall, Seppo) form syntagmas in either direction, controlling the order from various sources, some of which can be found in adult speech. For example, some but not all of Kendall's Object–Action utterances expressed the action with just the particle half of a separable verb, for example, "Hat on" from "Put the hat on." The source of word order here is a particular lexical sequence in adult speech which offered an ambiguous model. Since the action schema does not determine the word order either, the Object–Action order was utterable for the child (and may have been favored by perceptual salience). Other children take over the dominant word order of Action–Object (as did Bowerman's other Finnish subject, Rina, and Bloom's three subjects). With still other children, processes of topicalization can determine the starting point of speech. These different situations illustrate some aspects of the variety of forces that influence word order in addition to schematic sequences.

Considering, then, the influence of necessary sequences in the performance of action on word order in speech, there is support for the theory that the child's first syntagmas are organized by means of the interiorized action schemas by which he understands and interprets the world. According to this theory, the child "lines up" the schema for the utterance with the action schema that represents the content to be expressed, and in this way is guided to produce an utterance that expresses the right content. When the cognitive schema has an intrinsic sequence, the utterance will tend to be produced in the same sequence. If the cognitive schema is indeterminate for sequence, the corresponding utterances will be produced in sequences determined by a variety of other factors, some of which might change from time to time. There will be a strong effect of the dominant adult word order. In all cases, nevertheless, the possibility of forming the syntagma is based on a necessary relationship with the structure of the child's sensory–motor schemas.

EMERGENCE OF PATTERNED SPEECH

From the point of view described above, organized speech is a new form of action for the child. Rather than performing actual overt hand movements, bodily adjustments, etc., organized and given meaning by sensory–motor action schemas, the child now assembles utterances based on these same schemas. In a deep sense, patterned speech is a form of action continuous with earlier actions; but it is also a new departure, a convergence of vocalizations with sensory–motor representations, which has not occurred before.

The emergence of patterned speech depends on the interiorization of action schemas, which in turn is produced from the child's development of the symbolic function, because the action schemas that guide speech have to be mentally representable. The speech action replaces, as it were, the original action in the process of forming the syntagma. Like any overt action, the action of speech can not be differentiated from the underlying action schema that guides it; therefore, the original action based on the action schema must be differentiated in order for patterned speech to occur. Even adults find it extremely difficult to perform an overt action and describe their performance in speech at the same time. If the action is an unfamiliar one for which there are no well established interiorized schemas (e.g., putting together a novel object, such as an aquarium heater), adults seem to find it nearly impossible to speak and perform simultaneously (see the section on gestures, below). They may revert to single word utterances, thus failing to integrate a syntagma at all, or introduce small asynchronies between patterned speech and the corresponding parts of the action, thus basing speech on an interiorized schema once again. In both these resolutions, adults reflect the fundamental inconsistency of speech that is being guided by an action schema when the action itself is not differentiated from the schema. There is nothing surprising about this difficulty if speech is viewed as a form of action based on other action schemas. The same difficulty would exist no less forcefully for young children for whom the action of speech is a new development.

The emergence of patterned speech production, therefore, waits until the process of interiorization has differentiated action schemas from actual overt action. Then, the child's speech can be based on a fully mental version of the action schema. Note that this explanation of the empirical connection between interiorization and the emergence of patterned speech depends crucially on the hypothesis proposed here, namely, that the syntagma is initially formed by aligning two action schemas, one for speech with one for cognitive organization. Without this hypothesis, there is merely the correlation between the interiorization process and the onset of patterned speech, but by taking into account the necessity of the syntagma and its basis in the child's intellectual functioning, this correlation is explained.

Nevertheless, it is necessary to refine the description of these connections between overt action, speech, and action schemas. These relationships are not merely mechanical. It is entirely possible, for example, to perform overt activities and produce speech describing these activities, and this is not limited to adult speakers. As mentioned above, the greatest difficulties in combining speech with action appear for adults with unfamiliar actions, actions whose own organization is tentative. Well understood actions, walking, standing up, tying a shoe lace, etc., can be combined with speech, although even here the combination is difficult (shown by the action and speech both being slower than normal, etc.). The explanation of the successful combination of speech with action must lie in the reorganization of familiar actions that takes place on higher levels as actions are interiorized. This is a process that occurs in a child as he reaches higher levels of mental functioning, passing to the representational level from the sensory-motor level, but also in adults as they master new skills. Piaget describes it as follows: ". . . the series of successive physical actions, each given momentarily, is completed by representative systems capable of evoking in the form of an almost simultaneous whole, past or future actions or events as well as present ones and spatially distant as well as near ones" (Piaget, 1972, p. 27).

There is a kind of snapshot of the entire integrated action when this is interiorized as a pattern, which pattern includes the significant parts of the action, how they are interrelated, and their sequence. It is for this reason, presumably, that familiar actions are difficult to start at arbitrary points, e.g., retying a shoe lace after it has been untied half way. The schema for an action sequence can be invoked only as a whole in which steps are not readily extricated from other steps to which they are related.

Thus an organizational schema can support two action sequences, speech and nonspeech, but the integration of action sequences into whole patterns of inextricable parts is the fundamental step in the organization of speech.

The conceptual content of speech, when this is grasped in terms of interiorized action schemas by young children, becomes a direct pattern for speaking, evoked as a whole. The same is true of adult speech, thanks to the process of semiotic extension, described below. In both children and adults, speech is an action organized by another action schema.

A prediction that can be obtained from this view is that new sentence patterns first emerge in a child's speech on a schema by schema basis. As different action schemas become interiorized, word patterns should appear that are based on each one. I know of no data that bear directly on this prediction. It does lead to a new interpretation of certain phenomena, however, that are not otherwise explained and can be mentioned as being consistent with the prediction. In the first place, there is the gradual spread of syntactic patterning throughout a child's speech, once word patterns have appeared at all. Nearly every observer of the single word period reports scattered two-word patterns (pronounced as an integrated unit) which occur several months "before" patterned speech sets in. These would be, according to the present view, based on the first of the sensory–motor schemas to become interiorized. It is consistent with this explanation, that such early word patterns seem to have a narrow range of use based on just one or two schemas. For example, Bloom (1973) reports the following utterances from the speech of Allison at 16 months, 3 weeks, some 4 months before the beginning of what Bloom deemed to be productive syntax, all of which are based on the related ideas of recurrence and disappearance:

> more cookie
> car away
> more baby
> there mama (apparently expressing recurrence)
> more cow
> more pig
> (These examples exclude the mysterious word "widə".)

Another phenomenon that can be interpreted if word patterns develop schema by schema, is the fact noted earlier, that the true word patterns from Rodgon's (1972) study covered a wider range of semantic relationships than successive single word utterances did. In the true word patterns, seven different relationships seem to have been represented (Possession, Location, Deixis, Agent, Rejection, Object, and Disappearance), compared to only two relationships with successive single word utterances, both of which were also included in the true word patterns (Object and Disappearance). Rodgon's subjects were selected to be at a more advanced and transitional stage than Allison was at 16 months, and would have successfully interiorized a wider range of cognitive schemas.

According to the theory suggested here, then, the line between single-word speech and patterned speech is necessarily indistinct. Whether a particular schema occurs in a child's speech during this stage as a word pattern or as a single-word utterance depends in part on the extent of progress the schema has made toward interiorization.

The action of speech has properties of its own, which for English at least are recognized in the description of the phonemic clause (Trager & Smith, 1951). Apparently, there are initially independent lines of development for this phonological integration and for the interiorization of action schemas. The two converge for the first time in the formation of the syntagma. This initial independence can actually be seen in the speech of some young children. There is babbling with recognizable intonation patterns, and this shows an aspect of the integration of speech action that is associated with the phonemic clause but without any organized cognitive content to go along with it. There is also the production of semantically related successive single words described earlier, and this shows an integration of semantic content but without a sufficient organization of the child's speech action. For patterned speech to occur, according to the theory given here, a phonological pattern must be assimilated and guided by a cognitive schema, which demands both cognitive interiorization and phonological integration. Recent studies of infant vocalization have traced the beginnings of phonological organization well back into the first year of life; the child's interiorized sensory-motor schemas have long been known to have their origins there; however, organized patterned speech becomes possible only when the syntagma itself can be formed, long after these first steps.

Another implication of the theory given here is that the development of patterned speech emerges continuously from the single word period that precedes it. From the point of the view of the child, the two periods may be indistinguishable. Patterned speech is an action based on other action schemas. Single word speech is continuous with patterned speech in that it, too, is an action based on other action schemas, but does not become patterned speech because the action schemas on which meaningful speech rests are not yet fully differentiated from overt actions. It is not possible yet to "line up" speech with the representation of information except in the limited and somewhat spasmodic way we recognize as single word speech. Nevertheless, there are the same intimate connections between speech and sensory-motor intellectual functioning as described earlier, which integrate single word utterances into semantic structures, in many cases apparently the same structures as involved in patterned speech

(Greenfield *et al.*, 1972). During the single word period itself, utterances are typically produced in the context of an actual ongoing action, thus demonstrating directly the fusion of speech with action that is eventually elaborated into patterned speech.

Gruber (1973), for example, found that a significant part of the single-word usage of a child he studied was accompanied by one of two gestures: demands which were uttered in conjunction with a characteristic movement of the arms, and displays which were produced with a different and equally characteristic movement. Greenfield *et al.* (1972), tracing the emergence of case relations in the single-word period, found many examples of single-word utterances produced by the child together with a variety of actions. For example, when the child's mother asked, "Do you want to get up?" the child (13 months, 16 days) replied, "up," and reached upward. At 16 months, 18 days, a second child said "mil" (milk) as he reached for the milk. At 18 months, 4 days, a child who had just turned off the fan, said "ban" (fan). Single words are also used in an instrumental sense connected with an action: for example, "poon" (spoon) as the child watched another child eating with a spoon. Examples such as these exist in abundance. As Greenfield *et al.* (1972) say, "The child begins by combining words with nonverbal aspects of an event [p. 59]."

In a similar vein, successive single-word utterances are closely associated with action schemas which also control the performance of a concurrent overt action. In the following example from Bloom, the child's speech consists of a series of words pronouned (without phonological integration) during the performance of a complex action sequence in which several objects are being manipulated in relation to each other (Bloom, 1973, p. 50):

(Child picking up blanket; handing it to M.)	Blanket/Cover
M: Blanket? Cover?	
(Child touches doll's head)	Head
(Child touching doll's head, lifting doll to her own head)	Head
(Child touching doll's head in front of her)	Head
M: Head?	Cover

Examples such as these show that single word utterances are characteristically produced as the accompaniment of an ongoing organized activity. According to the theory of speech production given here, the syntagma grows out of this basis in action, depending crucially on the persistence of the structure and dynamics of action schemas as the process of interiorization takes place.

Bruner has proposed on several occasions (e.g., Bruner, 1974) that the origin of language in children must be sought in the way the child organizes patterns of action jointly with adults. This certainly is an approach with which the theory above would agree, but there are differences in formulation which distinguish the two points of view. These arise in particular over Bruner's account of action patterns in terms of analogies to the linguistic concepts of sentence positions and privileges of occurrence. I find no clear sense in which the child can be said to learn positions and privileges of occurrence in action sequences, beyond a much more global necessity of producing certain actions in particular irreversible directions. In these cases, nothing about position must be learned; the privileges of occurrence of agent–action, alienable possessor–possessed, or object–location are taken care of automatically. In other cases, where independent learning of position is necessary, because there may not be intrinsic action sequences, as in action–object, nonmotion locative, and inalienable possessor–possessed, there are apparently not privileges of occurrence in speech either until linguistically based regularities have become established; this may not occur, in some cases, until a point well past when the child first expresses the relation in speech. Thus the empirical necessity of Bruner's hypothesis is far from obvious.

SEMIOTIC EXTENSION

It is my thesis that the speech mechanism described in the preceding sections for the beginning stages of speech also operates in the speech production of adults. The speaker's cognitive operations change extensively with development, and there is a major development of syntactic processes that greatly increase the flexibility and complexity of the sentence forms the adult speaker commands, but the basic mechanism for organizing syntagmas described above persists through all these changes. This mechanism remains one in which the syntagma is formed from an alignment of two action schemas, one for speech and one for cognition. According to this thesis, the speech process remains directly adapted to the sensory–motor and representational levels of thought. But there is, in addition, a "semiotic extension" of the basic speech mechanisms, in which the speaking process, although adapted to the sensory–motor and representational levels of cognitive functioning, is extended to express quite different and more abstract levels of operational thought. The semiotic extension is the basis of contact between adult conceptualization and the sensory–motor processes of speech production.

It is for this reason that adult speakers, although capable of forming complex utterances by generating concepts and interrelations of concepts, organize their utterances, however complex, as arrangements of Objects, Actions, States, Events, etc. The operational concepts which may be the utterance's actual content fall into one or more of these sensory–motor structures semiotically extended; according to this theory, in order to speak at all, speech must be generated with a syntagma at the level of an action schema, and when thought is not itself at this level, this requires a semiotic extension.

Various traces appear in adult speech showing the continued operation of the original syntagmatic mechanisms through a process of semiotic extension, for example, pauses and hesitations that occur at positions within the conceptual structure that can be identified as the semiotic extension of action schemas. A different and more direct trace, however, is the formation of spontaneous gestures during speech, which is discussed here.

GESTURES

Far from being mere embellishments, spontaneous gestures can be seen to arise directly from the operation of the speech mechanisms themselves. They are a vestige of the original representation of content in action schemas. As syntagmas are formed by aligning action schemas, but the actual content may be at a higher level of mental functioning, the tendency exists to respond during the organization of the syntagma by representing the content also at the sensory–motor level. These representations are the sources of many gestures. They arise from the semiotic extension of the fundamental sensory–motor basis of speech.

Consistent with this origin of gestures is the developmental fact that, for some children if not for all, gesturing in the intended sense appears only gradually during the period when the semiotic extension is initially being set up, between ages 3 and 5. Before this, there are no or few gestures as opposed to practical movements to achieve some physical effect. (Remember, the theory is that gestures arise from the semiotic extension, not from the interiorization of action schemas.)

The observations reported here are made with adult speakers who were given various tasks designed to produce speech related to one or another level of mental functioning, sensory–motor to formal operational.

At the sensory–motor level, the subjects were asked to assemble a moderately complex object (an aquarium) and describe each movement as they made it. In another task at the same level, they were asked to stand up and sit down, and to describe each phase of these movements as they made them. In a third task they tied and described tying a bow knot. Note that these tasks do not exactly simulate the production of speech by children in the early stages of word patterning. They come closer to simulating the period before this, when action schemas have not yet been interiorized, except that the adult speakers, unlike children, were expected to produce word patterns as well as perform overt movements.

Nevertheless, although the subjects attempted to act and describe their actions at the same time, it turned out to be essentially impossible for them to produce patterned speech as an accompaniment of action in the task of assembling a complex unfamiliar object. The subjects did, in fact, simulate some of the events that occur when children make the transition from single words to word patterns.

In the following example, there is a momentary reversion to single-word speech ("R" is the right hand; "L" is the left; a small vertical mark shows where a movement or posture began relative to the speech; the line between vertical marks shows the duration of the movement or posture relative to the speech):

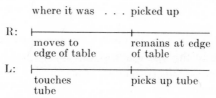

The utterance of "picked up" was delayed until the action of picking up with the left hand had already been launched. Considering just this one utterance, the conditions are the same as in children's single word speech: a word is uttered as an integral part of an action but is not integrated into a phonemic clause. The overt action could not serve as the basis for a continuous utterance.

More commonly, adults in this situation change the language–thought relationship to the next higher level, that is, to the representational level, by speaking and acting in alternation, thereby actually simulating the transition to patterned speech. In this method of coping with the difficulty of speaking and acting simultaneously, the speech is related to an interiorized action schema. The following is an example:

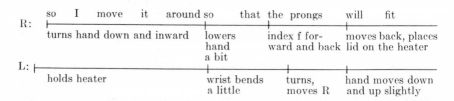

The portion of the utterance that describes the action, "so I move it around," is produced before the performance of the action itself, which happens to coincide with a later part of the utterance, "so that the prongs." This part, in turn, is produced in advance of the action it relates to when the lid is placed on the heater. By generating speech from an interiorized anticipatory schema in this way, while performing the action itself from a later exteriorized schema, it becomes possible for the adult to speak and act at the same time. (The task is still quite difficult even with this separation of speech and action.)

With the simpler and more routine tasks of standing up and sitting down or tying a knot, adult subjects can describe their actions as they perform them. The correlation of speech and action is different in these cases from the examples just shown. In the simple cases, presumably, a single action schema simultaneously underlies both the production of the utterance and the performance of the overt action, and this makes the speech and action very tightly correlated in time. The following example is from a subject tying a bow knot:

```
         with my    right    hand    make    a    loop
    R:   ├─────────────────┼──────────────────┼─────────┤
         turns hand down and  hand moves forward
         outward, up and back while turning to R

    L:   ├───────────────────┼──────────────┼──────────────┤
         hand turning       hand           hand turns in
         under              stationary     toward self
```

As the speaker makes a loop in the string (this is the kind of knot tied in shoe laces), she says "my right hand makes a loop." The movement could conceivably have started with the utterance of "with," one syllable earlier. This amount of asynchrony is very nearly the largest observed in these tasks; very often the action and the utterance precisely coincide at the moment of onset (offsets are more difficult to locate). For example,

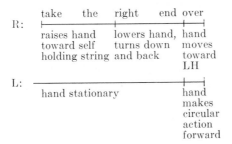

Every segment of the action is accompanied by a new component in the description: "take," "right," and, especially, "over."

These sensory–motor tasks provide the base line for the other tasks intended to evoke speech–thought interrelations at different points along the semiotic extension. When there is a real action, and subjects are able to describe it at all as they perform it, there is, as shown, a close temporal correlation between speech and action. At higher levels of intellectual functioning, there is no longer an overt action performed, but the production of speech still depends on syntagmas put together at the sensory–motor level. The extension of the actual semantic content of the utterance to the syntagma can produce gestures. One would expect these vestigial actions, from this reasoning, to be as closely correlated in time and form as real actions are in the sensory–motor tasks.

The following example involves mental paper folding (Shepard & Feng, 1972), a task in which the subject imagines folding a paper cutout (represented by a drawing) into a cube. This task very strongly evokes gestures of a highly iconic kind, as the speaker performs approximations of the manipulations he would have performed on a real paper cutout. The task thus accomplishes the purpose of recreating on a sensory–motor level the mental processing that is taking place on the representational level. The temporal correlations here often are extremely close, as the following example shows:

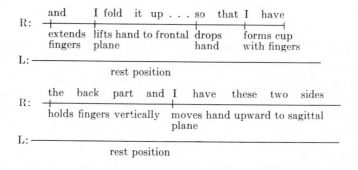

Each representation of action in this example is accompanied by a description and a synchronous gesture iconically related to the action. When the speaker says, "I fold it up," he raises his hand to the plane occupied by the imaginary folded paper; as he says "the back part," he holds his fingers vertically, etc. Throughout, there are parallel and synchronous gestures. Typically, the synchronization is especially clear at the onsets. On the other hand, the conjunctions ("and" and "so that") are not regularly associated with the occurrence of gestures: only the first of the two "ands" is produced with a gesture, "so that" is accompanied by an actual disappearance of gestures, and the second "and" simply coexists peacefully with a gesture that continues from before.

This example is typical in showing that gestures are initiated with the onset of the speech associated with action schemas (in the example shown,

Objects and Actions), but not reliably with syntactic formatives, such as conjunctions. The correlation of gestures with the semiotic equivalent of action schemas exists also when the content of speech is relatively abstract. In such utterances, the gestures are less often obviously iconic, although even abstract content offers possibilities for iconic relationships, but there is no break in the correlation between the onset of the gesture and the organization of action schemas. The tendency to produce gestures does not seem to be at all reduced. That gestures should persist to the limits of the semiotic extension is not surprising, of course, if the speech mechanisms, even at these levels, remain sensory–motor. The following example comes from a scientific discussion, presumably at a level of mental functioning near formal operations:

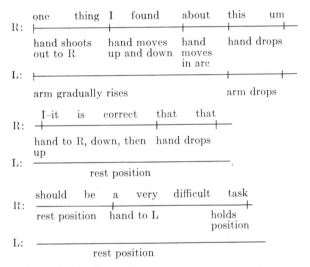

Some of these gestures are iconic, and all are correlated with the semiotic equivalent of sensory–motor schemas.

These correlations are often metaphorical, which process appears to be one method used within the semiotic extension for making contact between the action schemas of the syntagma and the actual intellectual content of the utterance. For example, "about" has a literal meaning connected with location. It is used in the example in an abstract sense, but the associated gesture, produced only when "about" was uttered, iconically represents the literal meaning (hand moving in an arc); this is a metaphorical connection upon which a semiotic extension might have been based. Similarly, "I found" was accompanied by an up and down hand movement that conceivably is related to an action–schema representation of the literal meaning of the verb, even though the speaker clearly had in mind a more abstract sense of "find."

The following list shows the type of action schema to which each gesture appears to have been related:

	Utterance	Gesture	Schema
Syntagma A	one thing	H to R	Object
	I found	H up and down	Action
	about	H in arc	Location
	this um	none	Object
Syntagma B	I–it is correct	H to R, down, up	State
	that	none	none
Syntagma C	that	none	Object
	should be	none	none
	a very difficult task	H to L and hold	State

When an action schema might have been involved in the organization of a syntagma, with two exceptions in this example ("this um," the second "that"), there is a gesture produced in synchrony with the corresponding part of the utterance. However, as shown in the earlier representational example, when a part of the utterance consisted of a grammatical formative (the first "that" and "should be"), that is, when a syntactic process was involved which does not relate to an action schema, a gesture was not produced.

The production of spontaneous gestures coincides with the expression of entire schemas in the flow of speech, not with such lesser units as words. This is true of all the tasks, including discourse at the operational level, and shows, graphically and concurrently in the behavior of the speaker, how speech is built up concept by concept at each level of thought, and how concepts remain in contact with action schemas at the level of the syntagma within the semiotic extension. At the representational level, for example, a gesture coincided with the part of the utterance that expressed an Object ("the back part and"), and a different gesture coincided with the next part of the utterance expressing an Action ("I have these two sides"). In the operational example, gestures coincide with single words when these also express whole schemas ("about"), but when an entire phrase expresses a schema there is still a single gesture ("a very difficult task").

At the same time, the basis of speech organization does not correspond consistently to such syntactic entities as the syntactic clause or phrase. Recent attempts to describe the performance of speech production in terms of these syntactic categories appear to be misguided. In the operational example, a clause, "that should be a very difficult task," was uttered without any gesture until the concept of a State starts to be expressed, at which moment a gesture begins. Similarly, syntactic phrases are broken up by distinct gestures, each of which corresponds to a concept. When a VP in the operational example, "found about this," was uttered, it was broken into three components: the verb, which fell out of the VP to join the preceding subject NP and express the concept of an Action; "about" which expresses Location; and "this" which expresses Object. In the representational example, verbs are also produced with the subject to express an Action concept, rather than with the rest of the VP ("I have/the back part and"). Thus, the controlling factor appears to be the schema the subject and verb express together and not the NP–VP phrase structure. The speaker seems to proceed from concept to concept with various nonconceptual syntactic processes being recruited by the process of conceptual construction.

CONCLUSION

While this study of gestures cannot prove the argument proposed here, it does, at the very least, show an intimate connection between the production of speech by adults and the representation of conceptual structures on a sensory–motor level; this is a connection of the kind anticipated by the theory discussed in this paper.

ACKNOWLEDGMENTS

Preparation of this paper was supported by a grant from the Sloan Foundation, a fellowship from the Guggenheim Foundation, and by research grants from NSF and NIE.

REFERENCES

Bloom, L. *Language development: Form and function in emerging grammars.* Cambridge, Massachusetts: MIT Press, 1970.

Bloom, L., *One word at a time—The use of single word utterances before syntax.* The Hague: Mouton, 1973.

Blount, B. G. Acquisition of language by Luo children. Working Paper No. 19, Language Behavior Research Laboratory, University of California, Berkeley, 1969.

Boomer, D. S. Hesitations and grammatical encoding. *Language and Speech,* 1965, **8**, 148–158.

Bowerman, M. F. *Early syntactic development: A cross-linguistic study with special reference to Finnish.* Cambridge, England: Cambridge University Press, 1973.

Brown, R. *A first language.* Cambridge, Massachusetts: Harvard University Press, 1973.

Bruner, J. The ontogenesis of speech acts. Unpublished paper. Oxford University, 1974.

Clark, E. V. What's in a word? On the child's acquisition of semantics in his first language. In T. E. Moore (Ed.), *Cognitive development and the acquisition of language*. New York: Academic Press, 1973.

Fromkin, V. A. Speculations on performance models. *Journal of Linguistics*, 1968, **4**, 47–68.

Fromkin, V. A. The non-anomalous nature of anomalous utterances. *Language*, 1971, **47**, 27–52.

Greenfield, P. M., Smith, J. H., & Laufer, B. Communication and the beginning of language: The development of semantic structure in one-word speech and beyond. Unpublished monograph, Harvard University, 1972.

Gruber, J. S. Correlations between the syntactic constituents of the child and the adult. In C. A. Ferguson and D. I. Slobin (Eds.), *Studies of child language development*. New York: Holt, 1973.

Kernan, K. T. The acquisition of language by Samoan children. Unpublished doctoral dissertation, University of California at Berkeley, 1969.

Kozhevnikov, V. A. & Chistovich, L. A. *Speech, articulation, and perception*. Washington, D.C.: U.S. Department of Commerce, Joint Publication Research Service, 1965.

Lashley, K. S. The problem of serial order in behavior. In L. A. Jeffress (Ed.), *Cerebral mechanisms in behavior*. New York: Wiley, 1951.

MacKay, D. G. The structure of words and syllables: Evidence from errors in speech. *Cognitive Psychology*, 1972, **3**, 210–227.

Marslen-Wilson, W. Linguistic structure and speech shadowing at very short latencies. *Nature*, 1973, **244**, 522–523.

Piaget, J. *The origin of intelligence in children*. New York: International Universities Press, 1952.

Piaget, J. *Play, dreams, and imitation in childhood*. New York: Norton, 1962.

Piaget, J. *The child's conception of the world*. Totowa, New Jersey: Littlefield, Adams, & Co., 1969.

Piaget, J. *The principles of genetic epistemology*. New York: Basic Books, 1972.

Rodgon, M. M. An investigation into the nature of holophrases and the beginnings of combinatorial speech. Unpublished doctoral dissertation, University of Chicago, 1972.

Shepard, R. N., & Feng, C. A chronometric study of mental paper folding. *Cognitive Psychology*, 1972, **3**, 228–243.

Sinclair-deZwart, H. Language acquisition and cognitive development. In T. E. Moore (Ed.), *Cognitive development and the acquisition of language*. New York: Academic Press, 1973.

Slobin, D. I. Cognitive prerequisites for the development of grammar. In C. A. Ferguson & D. I. Slobin (Eds.), *Studies of child language development*. New York: Holt, 1973.

Trager, G. L., & Smith, H. L. *Outline of English structure*. Norman, Oklahoma: Battenburg Press, 1951.

Werner, H., & Kaplan, B. *Symbol formation: An organismic-development approach to language and the expression of thought*. New York: Wiley, 1963.

Wickelgren, W. A. Context-sensitive coding, associative memory, and serial order in (speech) behavior. *Psychological Review*, 1969, **76**, 1–15.

12

THE CONSTRUCTION AND USE OF REPRESENTATIONS INVOLVING LINEAR ORDER

Tom Trabasso and Christine A. Riley
Princeton University

The problem of how we represent information about the world is central to cognitive psychology. The representation and operations upon it tell us how the person solves a problem, remembers a sentence, answers a question or makes a decision. An internal representation is a symbol structure, containing elements that are related to one another in some defined way, is constructed by the person in response to task demands and stored in memory for related purposes. The representation is constructed by processing stimuli and can be used to construct other representations, access descriptive information and retrieve properties of elements in response to inferential and other questions.

In this contribution, we shall be concerned with two questions on this problem. First, how do people construct internal representations from partial information? Second, given that the representation has an assumed structure, how does the person access and use it in solving a problem?

Specifically, we shall be concerned with how people derive knowledge of a linear ordering of events from pairwise relations among them. For example, how do we know that the first six students in a class are ordered in intelligence from the brightest first, as John, Paul, Fred, George, Henry and Tom from the information that

> John is brighter than Paul;
> Paul is brighter than Fred;
> Fred is brighter than George;
> George is brighter than Henry; and
> Henry is brighter than Tom?

In addition, once we know the linear order, how do we use it to make inferences such as Paul is brighter than Henry or answer a question, "Who is brighter, George or Paul?"

The choice of the transitive inference problem is not accidental. Study of the ordered syllogism has historically been of interest to investigation of intelligence (Burt, 1919), cognitive development (Piaget, 1921), social dominance (DeSoto & Bosley, 1962), reasoning (Hunter, 1957; Huttenlocher, 1968), psycholinguistics (Clark, 1969), reading of prose (Frase, 1972), and integration or assimilation of information in language contexts (Barclay, 1973; Bransford & Franks, 1971; Potts, 1972). We shall discuss the relevance of our work to these other investigations in appropriate sections below.

PROBLEM ORIGINS:
THE DEVELOPMENT OF TRANSITIVE REASONING

Our own concern with the problem began with an examination of the three-term series problem as studied and used by developmental psychologists to diagnose the mental abilities of children. Given the information that a quantity A, was greater than another quantity B $(A > B)$, and that $(B > C)$, one could, if one had knowledge of transitive relations, deduce that $A > C$. For example, Piaget (see Piaget, Inhelder, & Szeminska, 1960) investigated how well children could use measuring objects as middle terms in making quantitative comparisons of the type: the chair (A) is taller than one's body (B) whereas one's body (B) is taller than the table (C); therefore, the chair (A) is taller than the table (C), even though one could not compare them directly. If asked to justify his response, the child who presumably understood transitivity would argue that it is so of logical necessity, that is, "It has to be."

Piaget's (1970, pp. 29–30) explanations vary but a failure in the task may be, from his viewpoint, interpreted as either a failure to coordinate the terms, an inability to appreciate the reversible nature of the asymmetrical relations, that is, $A > B$ and $B < A$, or a failure to seriate long series of asymmetrical, transitive relations.

Peter Bryant and Tom Trabasso (1971) examined this diagnostic problem from a viewpoint where other factors such as coding or memory could lead to success or failure and misclassification of the child. A child could fail to make a correct inference if he *forgot* or did not properly encode both premises so that a failure in memory necessarily leads to a failure in logic. (A success in memory does not imply a success in reasoning, however.) In addition, a child could succeed for reasons other than formal reasoning. For example, if he codes and remembers *only* that A is tall,

	TRAINING		TESTING		
			2	3	4	5

	TRAINING		TESTING			
			2	3	4	5
	1 < 2, 2 > 1	1	TE	E	E	E
	2 < 3, 3 > 2	2		T	I I	E
	3 < 4, 4 > 3	3			T	E
	4 < 5, 5 > 4	4				TE

FIG. 1. Schematic outline of training and testing relations for five-term series problems.

T = TRAINING PAIR
E = END - ANCHORED PAIR
I I = INFERENCE PAIR OF STEP - SIZE I

then he can answer the question without coordinating the three terms. Bryant and Trabasso (1971) developed a procedure for training pairwise relations and testing inferences which allowed measurement of (1) retention for the premises or original, pairwise relations upon which children were trained; (2) inference tests involving end-anchor elements; and (3) inference tests with response assignments controlled (see Smedslund, 1969).

The Bryant and Trabasso (1971) procedures are schematized in Fig. 1. We use numerals to stand for the quantities where 1 is shortest and 5 is tallest.

The training consisted of first showing the child a pair of colored sticks that appear to be of equal height, asking the child, for example, "Which is longer (or which is shorter), the red stick or the blue stick?," recording his choice and then giving him feedback. The feedback was either "visual" and consisted of showing the child the actual difference between the pair or "linguistic" wherein only the relation was stated, for example, "Yes, the red stick is longer" or "No, the blue stick is shorter."

Training was done in two phases. In the first phase, one pair at a time was trained in a choice-discrimination task, asking both comparative questions. When the child mastered that pair, the next pair in the ascending (or descending) order was trained. When the four pairs were sequentially learned, training in the second phase was given wherein all four pairs were presented in a blocked, randomized order.

After the child met a criterion of 24 successively correct choices, he was tested without feedback on all possible pairs, using both positions and questions. These tests are summarized as a matrix in the right-hand side of Fig. 1. We note that the main diagonal tests (1, 2), (2, 3), (3, 4) and (4, 5), marked with a T, yield information on how well the children retrieved ordered information from the premises. The first-row and last-column tests, (1, 3), (1, 4), (1, 5), (2, 5) and (3, 5), marked with an E, yield information on the degree of end anchoring and that test (2, 4) is

TABLE 1
Summary Information on 16 Conditions
Using Five-Term Problems

Case	Source	Median age of Ss	Feedback in training	$N = Ss$ x tests per test pair
1	Bryant and Trabasso (1971)	4.6	Visual	20 x 4 = 80
2	Bryant and Trabasso (1971)	5.6	Visual	20 x 4 = 80
3	Bryant and Trabasso (1971)	6.6	Visual	20 x 4 = 80
4	Bryant and Trabasso (unpublished)	4.6	Visual	17 x 4 = 68
5	Bryant and Trabasso (unpublished)	4.6	Visual	17 x 4 = 68
6	Bryant and Trabasso (1971)	4.6	Linguistic	25 x 4 = 100
7	Bryant and Trabasso (1971)	5.6	Linguistic	25 x 4 = 100
8	Bryant and Trabasso (unpublished)	4.6	Visual	25 x 4 = 100
9	Lutkus and Trabasso (1974)	MA = 5	Visual	20 x 4 = 80
10	Lutkus and Trabasso (1974)	MA = 6	Visual	20 x 4 = 80
11	Riley and Trabasso (1974)	4.6	Linguistic	20 x 4 = 80
12	Riley and Trabasso (1974)	4.6	Visual	20 x 4 = 80
13	Riley and Trabasso (1974)	4.6	Linguistic-one comparative	7 x 4 = 28
14	Riley and Trabasso (1974)	4.6	Visual-one comparative	11 x 4 = 44
15	Riley and Trabasso (1974)	4.6	Linguistic-inferred relations	40 x 4 = 160
16	Riley and Trabasso (1974)	4.6	Visual-inferred relations	40 x 4 = 160

the critical, inference test. Since there are no terms between Sticks 2 and 3 in (2, 3) and between Sticks 3 and 4 in (3, 4), no inferential steps are required while the (2, 4) test involves one intervening stick or "coordination." We shall refer to these distances as Steps 0 or 1.

Since the initial study by Bryant and Trabasso (1971) we have carried out six studies involving some sixteen conditions (cases) using these procedures. The ages, subjects, questions and feedback varied across the studies and the 16 cases are summarized in Table 1.

You will note that the ages (and mental ages) range from 4 to 7 years since we were interested in what Piaget calls "preoperational" children, that is, those who were not supposed to be able to perform such inferences. We have already pointed out the two kinds of feedback. When, in Cases 13 and 14, one comparative was used, the relations were always expressed as "longer" (or "shorter") throughout the series. In Cases 15 and 16, both relations occurred *across* the series, for example, $A > B$, $C < B$, $C > D$, and $D < E$ and the child had to infer $B < A$, etc.

TRAINING RESULTS: SERIAL POSITION EFFECTS

The two phases of training yielded quite different results. In the first phase, the children learned each pair quite rapidly, averaging slightly more than half an error per pair. Table 2 gives some representative data for seven cases studied.

The ease of learning these pairs was surprising to us given the fact that the child was learning four successive discriminations, some members of which had two responses associated with them. Apparently, this was not a factor in the initial training. It was a factor in the second, randomized pair training phase. Here marked serial position effects occurred with the middle pairs, (2, 3) and (3, 4), showing the most errors. Examples from seven cases are shown in Table 3.

This pattern of errors could arise for several reasons and their occurrence bears upon the first question: how does one construct a representation of linear order from pairwise information? We, however, shall post-

TABLE 2
Mean Number of Errors Per Pair of Sticks in Reaching Criterion (Phase I)

	Pair				
Case	(1, 2)	(2, 3)	(3, 4)	(4, 5)	
1	.55	.75	.75	.45	
2	.40	.25	.50	.45	
3	.60	.25	.30	.60	
9	.70	.70	.85	.60	
10	.70	.70	.80	1.10	
11	1.00	1.25	1.10	1.40	
12	.15	.45	.30	.25	
Total mean:	.59	.62	.66	.69	.64

TABLE 3
Mean Number of Errors Per Pair of Sticks
in Reaching Criterion (Phase II)

| Case | Pair | | | |
	(1, 2)	(2, 3)	(3, 4)	(4, 5)
1	.60	.60	1.05	.70
2	.00	.10	.45	.10
3	.20	.10	.70	.40
9	2.50	4.50	3.45	1.65
10	1.90	5.90	8.70	2.20
11	3.10	4.10	5.35	2.55
12	.35	.90	.90	.15
Total mean:	1.24	2.17	2.94	1.11
Proportion total errors:	.17	.29	.39	.15

pone their discussion until after presentation and consideration of the test results.

TESTING RESULTS: MEMORY AND INFERENCE CORRELATIONS

Table 4 summarizes the test results in terms of the proportion of correct responses to all tests for the sixteen cases. The columns in Table 4 are arranged according to degree of correct responding with the best performance tests on the right. In general, the transitive test (2, 4) is approximately equal to one of the premises (2, 3) or (3, 4), which, in turn, lag behind the "short" anchor tests [(1, 2), (1, 3), (1, 4)] followed by the "long" anchor tests [(2, 5), (3, 5), (4, 5)] with the (1, 5), "both" anchor test, showing the best retrieval.

As concerns the memory and inference hypothesis, there was a strong correlation between success on the premises (2, 3) and (3, 4) with performance on the inference test (2, 4) ($r = .87$, $p < .01$). This correlation was also marked with performance on end-anchor pairs ($r = .92$, $p < .01$). Thus, retention of the premises was strongly related to ability to answer inferential questions.

A demonstration of the relationship may be observed in Cases 4 and 5 and compared with Cases 1, 2 and 3. Cases 1, 2, and 3 involved children

TABLE 4
Proportion of Correct Responses for All Test Pairs: 16 Conditions Using Five-Term Series Problems

Case	Transitive pair Step 1	Premises Step 0		Short anchors			Long anchors			Both anchors
	(2, 4)	(2, 3)	(3, 4)	(1, 2)	(1, 3)	(1, 4)	(2, 5)	(3, 5)	(4, 5)	(1, 5)
1	78	90	92	91	94	92	93	96	96	98
2	88	92	86	100	100	100	100	96	100	98
3	92	98	94	100	100	99	100	99	99	100
4	84	94	94	96	100	94	97	94	88	98
5	93	100	96	100	98	100	98	100	100	100
6	82	87	89	94	88	90	93	98	98	97
7	85	97	87	98	95	98	95	92	98	97
8	94	87	90	93	96	98	99	97	97	99
9	79	70	83	89	91	96	94	96	98	98
10	83	78	69	88	98	92	96	94	96	98
11	68	79	66	85	76	80	75	81	91	86
12	88	91	81	98	90	88	91	90	99	93
13	71	57	54	75	59	61	61	71	75	57
14	73	68	59	71	71	75	77	82	82	77
15	56	53	54	60	61	56	59	50	61	59
16	61	61	56	69	68	60	72	63	69	65
Weighted average 1–16:	77.9	79.9	77.0	86.3	85.5	84.4	86.4	84.8	88.6	87.4
Weighted average 1–12:	84.6	88.5	85.5	94.3	93.7	93.9	94.3	94.4	96.8	96.8

in England, aged 4–6 years, who were trained with visual feedback. One can note that the proportion of successes on $(2, 4)$ increases with age from .78 to .92. In an unpublished study, Bryant and Trabasso retained and retested 17 4-year-olds from Case 1. These children were retrained and retested twice with feedback on the original pairs during testing; no feedback was given on inferential tests. These data are summarized in Cases 4 and 5. We note the continued increase in proportion of correct responding on all tests with the attendant increase on inference tests $(2, 4)$ from .78 to .84 to .92. In fact, the data on the 4-year-olds in Case 5 may be compared to that for 6-year-olds in Case 3. They are virtually indistinguishable. The claim here is not that we turned 4-year-olds into 6-year-olds; rather, by allowing 4-year-olds to code and retrieve the premises of the five-term series problem as well as 6-year-olds, their performance on inference tests was increased exceptionally and was nearly perfect (13 out of 17 children made no errors on four tests).

One other comment is in order. There is some question as to whether Cases 13–16 should be included with Cases 1–12 since Riley and Trabasso (1974) showed that the children in these studies either did not learn the original pairs or performed for the most part at chance levels because of other, systematic solutions which led to a disproportionate number of errors at $k = 2$ (see below).

STOCHASTIC RETRIEVAL MODELS

If one scans the relation between performance on the transitive test $(2, 4)$ and the retrieval of premises [tests $(2, 3)$, $(3, 4)$], one notes that for several cases $(1, 3, 4, 5, 6, 7)$ the transitive test proportion is below the others. This observation rules out prediction via Luce's choice axiom

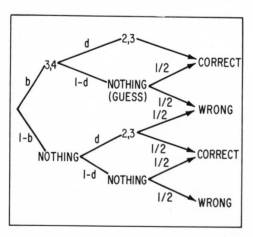

Fig. 2. Tree diagram for a model of retrieval for ordered pairs and perfect coordination on transitive tests.

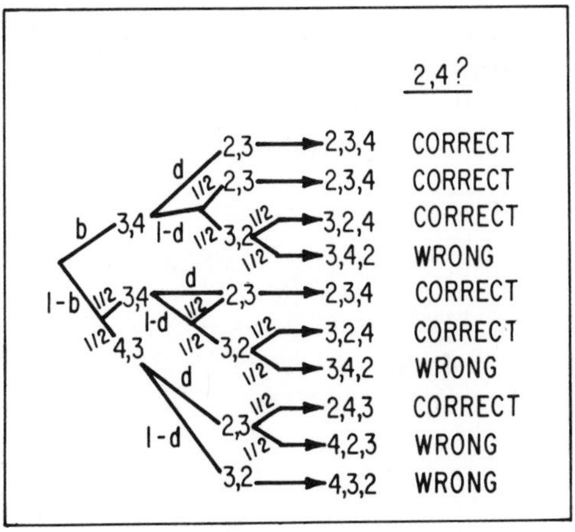

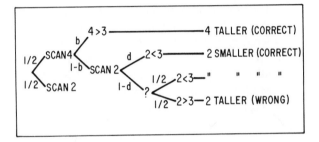

FIG. 3. Tree diagram for a model of retrieval for ordered pairs and imperfect coordination on transitive tests.

FIG. 4. Tree diagram for a model of incomplete memory search for relational information on one term of a transitive test pair.

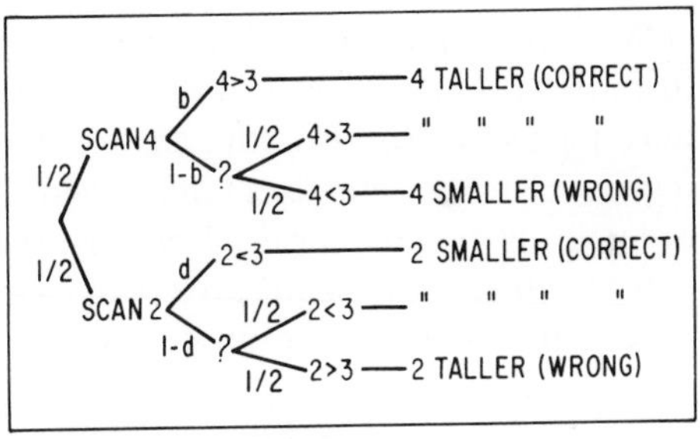

FIG. 5. Tree diagram for a model of exhaustive memory search for relational information on either term of a transitive test pair.

(see Hoffman, Trabasso, & Friedman, 1974) for transitive relations since success on the transitive test should be greater than or equal to the maximum proportion on the premises. It also led us to consider some retrieval models that might account for the relation and to provide answers on the question of how one uses a memory representation to answer questions.

We note the strong correlation between performance on pairs $(2, 3)$ and $(3, 4)$ with pair $(2, 4)$. Four stochastic models were explored with respect to this relation. These models are represented via tree diagrams in Figures 2, 3, 4 and 5. All four models allow independent prediction of performance on the transitive test $(2, 4)$ from knowledge of performance on the premise tests $(2, 3)$ and $(3, 4)$. Let b be the probability of retrieving the *ordered* information on the $(3, 4)$ test and d be the probability of retrieving $(2, 3)$. Then the observed probability of a correct response for each premise is

$$P(3,4) = b + \tfrac{1}{2}(1 - b) \tag{1}$$
$$P(2,3) = d + \tfrac{1}{2}(1 - d), \tag{2}$$

where $\tfrac{1}{2}$ is the guessing probability of the order when retrieval fails. Solving Eqs. (1) and (2), the estimates for b and d are

$$\hat{b} = 1 - 2P(3,4) \tag{3}$$

and

$$\hat{d} = 1 - 2P(2,3). \tag{4}$$

The first model, depicted in Fig. 2, assumes that the child when presented with the inference test pair $(2, 4)$, independently retrieves the ordered pairs $(2, 3)$ and $(3, 4)$, and coordinates them perfectly. If he fails to retrieve one pair, he guesses the answer to the question. This model predicts $P(2, 4) < \min. (P(2, 3), P(3, 4))$.

Multiplying the probabilities across the branches and summing those for correct responses, we find

$$P(2,4) = bd + \tfrac{1}{2}(1 - bd) \tag{5}$$

A coordination model is shown in Fig. 3. As before, the child is assumed to retrieve independently order information on the premises. Here, if he fails, instead of guessing the answer, he first generates (guesses) the missing premise (or premises) and then coordinates their relations into an ordered set of three terms. Here errors are not due to a failure to coordinate. Rather, they would arise from errors in memory and from guessing the wrong order for the missing premises. For this model, the prediction equation is

$$P(2,4) = (3b + 3d + 3 - bd)/8. \tag{6}$$

The models depicted in Figs. 4 and 5 differ from those above in terms of depth of search. In Fig. 4, the child, when confronted with the colored sticks in pair $(2, 4)$, is assumed to select one of the sticks as a retrieval cue at random. He then scans his memory for order information on that stick in relation to the question. Thus, if the question is "Longer?" and he scans Stick 4, he will find the Stick 4 is longer with probability b and be correct. However, if he fails to find anything on Stick 4, he guesses its relation to Stick 3, and terminates his search by indicating which stick has the relation that matches the relation in the question. Thus, only one stick is searched in memory. The prediction equation for the model in Fig. 4 is

$$P(2,4) = (b + d + 2)/4. \tag{7}$$

Whereas in Fig. 4, search was terminated after searching only one stick, Fig. 5 shows a model where the search on each stick as a retrieval cue is exhaustive. If the child fails to find a relation on one stick, he then searches his memory for information on the other. The response rule is the same as that for the model in Fig. 4. The predicted probability of a correct response on an inference test for the model in Fig. 5 is

$$P(2,4) = (1 + b + d - bd)/2. \tag{8}$$

We estimated the values of b and d, using Eqs. (1) and (2) and their corresponding observed values in Table 4 for each of the sixteen cases. These estimates then were used in Eqs. (5)–(8) to predict the observed $P(2, 4)$. These predictions are summarized in Table 5 which gives the observed $P(2, 4)$ for each case and the predicted $P(2, 4)$ minus the observed $P(2, 4)$ for each model. Model 1 is that shown in Fig. 2, Model 2 is that shown in Figure 3, etc.

Comparing the models across the sixteen cases shows that they *all* do about equally well on average. Model 1 has the best predictions for six out of the first seven cases. Models 1 and 2 do best when the retention and inferential performance is high or well above chance (8 out of 11 cases). Conversely, Models 3 and 4 do better when performance is poorer overall. These data, although not conclusive, favor the idea that when coordination occurs, overall performance is better.

We also asked how well the stochastic models predicted individual differences in the conditions, that is, how well they could predict the distributions of the number of children making 0, 1, 2, 3 or 4 successes on the four test questions. The distribution is assumed to be binomial with $N = 4$ and $p = $ predicted $P(2, 4)$. The observed and predicted (in parentheses) numbers of children making k correct responses are given in Table 6 for the best-fitting models of Table 5.

In general, the models predict the shape of the distributions quite well. The only obvious failure is Case 15 and this was one of those instances where the children were observed to have used a strategy that would yield an abnormal number of correct answers at $k = 2$ (see Riley & Trabasso, 1974). Hence, the stochastic models can predict the distribution of correct responses or individual differences reasonably well.

Although the stochastic models showed reasonable success in capturing some aspects of the data, the data did not allow us a clear choice among them. Furthermore, their predictions were limited to the relationship be-

TABLE 5
Observed Proportion Correct Responses on Inference Tests and Deviations from Predicted Values for Four Stochastic Models

	Inferential test	Predicted–observed values			
		Model			
Case	$P(2, 4)$	1	2	3	4
1	.78	.06*	.13	.13	.20
2	.88	−.08	.00*	.01	.10
3	.92	.00*	.04	.01	.08
4	.84	.05*	.10	.10	.15
5	.93	.03*	.05	.05	.07
6	.82	−.03*	.05	.06	.15
7	.85	.00*	.07	.01	.14
8	.94	−.15	−.06	−.06	.03*
9	.79	−.16	−.05	−.02*	.11
10	.83	−.22	−.13	−.10	.03*
11	.68	−.09	.01*	.04	.18
12	.88	−.13	−.03	−.02*	.09
13	.71	−.20	−.25	−.16	−.11*
14	.73	−.20	−.16	−.10	−.01*
15	.56	−.06	−.13	−.02	.01*
16	.61	−.10	−.11	−.02*	.05
Average deviation:		.10	.09	.06	.09

*Best-fitting model.

tween performance on the transitive test (2, 4) and the premises (2, 3) and (3, 4). They did not handle two other important features: the serial position effect and the other, end-anchor test results. This led us to another research strategy.

WHAT OCCURS IN TRAINING: THE SERIAL-POSITION EFFECT

The first question of interest is on *how* a child constructs a representation of pairwise information. The data bearing on this question are those having to do with the serial-position effect (see Table 3) and a study by Riley and Trabasso (1974), in which it was found that the children learned fastest and showed the best performance on tests where they were trained with *both* comparative terms.

TABLE 6
Observed (and Predicted) Number of Subjects
Making k : Correct Test Responses

			Number correct (k)				
Case	Best model	p	0	1	2	3	4
1	1	.84	0 (0)	2 (.3)	3 (2.3)	6 (7.7)	9 (9.8)
2	2	.88	0 (0)	0 (.1)	2 (1.3)	6 (6.4)	12 (12.2)
3	1	.92	0 (0)	0 (0)	1 (1.0)	4 (4.9)	15 (14.5)
4	1	.88	0 (0)	0 (.1)	3 (1.0)	4 (5.4)	10 (10.5)
5	1	.96	0 (0)	0 (0)	2 (.2)	2 (2.4)	13 (14.4)
6	1	.79	0 (0)	0 (.7)	3 (4.2)	11 (10.4)	12 (9.7)
7	1	.85	0 (0)	0 (.3)	4 (2.5)	6 (9.3)	15 (12.9)
8	4	.97	0 (0)	0 (0)	0 (0)	6 (2.4)	19 (22.5)
9	3	.77	0 (0)	1 (.1)	3 (1.0)	4 (5.9)	12 (13.0)
10	4	.86	0 (0)	2 (.2)	3 (1.7)	5 (7.0)	10 (11.2)
11	2	.69	1 (.2)	2 (1.7)	6 (5.5)	4 (8.1)	7 (4.5)
12	3	.86	0 (0)	1 (.2)	2 (1.7)	3 (7.1)	14 (10.9)
13	4	.60	0 (.2)	2 (1.0)	0 (2.4)	2 (2.4)	3 (.9)
14	4	.74	0 (.1)	0 (.6)	4 (2.5)	4 (4.6)	3 (3.3)
15	4	.57	2 (1.4)	2 (7.3)	23 (14.4)	10 (10.8)	3 (4.2)
16	3	.58	2 (1.2)	5 (6.7)	14 (14.2)	11 (13.3)	8 (4.7)

Two possibilities suggest themselves. First, the children learn each pair
as an ordered set: (1, 2), (2, 3), (3, 4), (4, 5). Since pairs (1, 2) and
(4, 5) each contain a member which has only one comparative associated
with it, then ease of learning these pairs should be facilitated. Pairs (2, 3)
and (3, 4) would cause problems since all three members have double
functions. Factors such as "response competition" would produce higher
error rates and the serial-position effect.

Riley and Trabasso (1974) suggested an "ends-inward" process model,
which yields a linear order (1, 2, 3, 4, 5). This model is not unlike that
of Feigenbaum and Simon (1962) (see also DeSoto & Bosley, 1962; Wishner, Shipley, & Hurvich, 1957) with the exception that we are dealing with
pairs of events rather than single items or the mapping of responses onto
continua (see Bower, 1971, for a discussion of serial-position effects where
subjects learn associations to locations on physical continua).

In our situation, the child is first assumed to isolate end-anchor members
(Sticks 1 and 5). This can be done by finding that stick which is *only*
taller (longer), then that stick which is *only shorter*. This isolation may

involve linguistic factors of two kinds: the longer term is faster because it is "unmarked" (Clark, 1969), it is more frequent or better known to the child, and the child is using a strategy by isolating that stick which is only long or only short. In addition, *absolute* length can play a role, especially when the feedback is visual.

Once the ends are isolated, the child might use a linear, spatial image (either left–right or top–bottom as first suggested by DeSoto, London, & Handel, 1965), placing the shortest on one end and the longest on the other.

Once end-anchor items are mapped onto the spatial dimension, the pairs are first ordered and entered into the array. This is done by first ordering the end pairs $(1, 2)$ and $(4, 5)$, entering Sticks 2 and 4 into the array. Then one orders pairs $(2, 3)$ and $(3, 4)$, entering Stick 3 into the array. If one associates errors with each of these steps, one will obtain the serial-position effect in the acquisition of a linear ordering.

With 5 sticks or a five-term series problem, one cannot discriminate between the learn-ordered-pairs versus learn-a-linear-order strategies. In order to provide a discrimination, one needs more pairs, say five. That is, suppose there are six sticks and five pairs: $(1, 2)$, $(2, 3)$, $(3, 4)$, $(4, 5)$, $(5, 6)$, then the assumption that the child learns only the pairwise relations predicts that pairs $(2, 3)$, $(3, 4)$ and $(4, 5)$ would be equal in difficulty. The ends-inward strategy predicts $(3, 4)$ to be the last pair acquired. This difference was one reason which led us to use a more extended array than we had used in the earlier studies.

WHAT OCCURS IN TESTING?

The two process models described in the preceding section assume that different representations of the ordered information are stored in memory. In one, the subject stores separate pairs; in the other, he stores a linear order that may have a spatial referent. The stochastic models in Figs. 2–5 are indifferent on the kind of representation that is stored since *all* assume that the subject accesses ordered information on pairs and a failure to have entered a member of a pair into the array or to have not learned the order of a pair would both contribute to failure in retrieval. However, if one asks the question in terms of *speed* of retrieval, a different class of models is suggested. Suppose that the person has stored the pairs separately and he coordinates them at the time of testing. Disregarding end-anchor effects, if each retrieval and coordination requires time, then the fastest retrieval times would be for the original, adjacent pairs. The next slowest set would be for those one step apart [e.g., $(2, 4)$ or $(3, 5)$] and the slowest would be for those furthest apart [e.g., $(2, 5)$] or requiring two coordinations.

Alternatively, if the problem is to access an underlying scale or a linear array, then *distance* between members of a test pair should be inversely proportional to speed (see Moyer & Landauer, 1967). Ignoring end-anchor effects once again, the expectation would be that the fastest time would occur for pair (2, 5), followed by pairs (3, 5) and (2, 4) with the slowest times occurring for the original pairs (2, 3), (3, 4) and (4, 5). These expectations led to the following experiment by Trabasso, Riley, and Wilson (1975).

REACTION-TIME EXPERIMENTS:
SIX-TERM SERIES PROBLEMS

The basic paradigm used by Trabasso, Riley, and Wilson (1975) is illustrated in Fig. 6. In the task there are six colored sticks of different lengths. Stick 1 is the shortest and Stick 6 is the longest. Following the procedure of Bryant and Trabasso (1971) described previously, a subject is first trained to make relational choices of longer or shorter on each of five adjacent pairs of sticks. On choice trials, the subject can use only the color coding to predict the length relation; in training he is given feedback (either visual or linguistic). In order to record both accuracy and speed of choice, the subject's response is to press a window in front of the stick he thinks is the longer (or shorter). The time from when the question is asked and the colors are simultaneously presented until he makes a choice is recorded on a clock and serves as our main datum of interest.

Following training on the premises or the adjacent pairs, the subject is tested on all possible pairs without feedback. The matrix in the right-hand side of Fig. 6 when filled with the reaction times tells us three pieces of information. The main diagonal (T) shows us the time to decide relations on training (adjacent) pairs. The first row and last column (indicated

	TRAINING		TESTING				
			2	3	4	5	6
	1 < 2, 2 > 1	1	TE	E	E	E	E
FIG. 6. Schematic outline of	2 < 3, 3 > 2	2		T	I1	I2	E
training and testing relations	3 < 4, 4 > 3	3			T	I1	E
for six-term series problems.	4 < 5, 5 > 4	4				T	E
	5 < 6, 6 > 5	5					TE

T = TRAINING PAIR
E = END-ANCHORED PAIR
Ii = INFERENCE PAIR OF STEP-SIZE i, i = 1, 2

by E) tell us whether or not there are end-anchor effects. The off-diagonal entries (indicated by I) tell us how fast subjects responded to inference tests. Distance or the number of inferential steps between sticks vary here from $I = 0$ [pairs $(2, 3)$, $(3, 4)$, $(4, 5)$], to $I = 1$ [pairs $(2, 4)$ or $(3, 5)$], to $I = 2$ [pair $(2, 5)$].

Trabasso, Riley, and Wilson (1975) studied three main groups of subjects, ages 6, 9, and college years, respectively. There were two training conditions, one with visual feedback (Condition V) and one with linguistic feedback (Condition L). A third condition omitted training by presenting the subjects with a *display* of sticks, arranged in order by size and asking the same set of questions (Condition D). The display condition was used as a converging operation and was assumed to mimic an internal, spatial array.

Six-Term Training Results:
Serial-Position Effects

The serial-position data for the training conditions favor the idea that the subjects constructed linear orders from the pairwise relations. The findings are summarized in Fig. 7 and Table 7. Figure 7 shows the trial-block

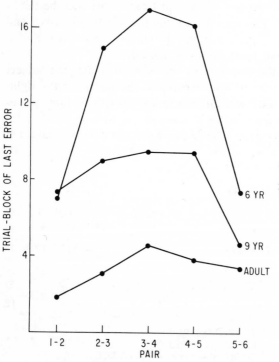

Fig. 7. Serial position curves on errors in training adjacent pairs (Data from Trabasso, Riley, & Wilson, 1975.)

TABLE 7
Relative Percent Trials To Criterion
for Each Pair in Training[a]

| | PAIR | | | | |
Age	(1,2)	(2,3)	(3,4)	(4,5)	(5,6)
6	11	24	28	26	11
9	18	23	28	23	12
Adult	11	18	26	24	12
Observed average relative difficulty:	13	22	28	24	12

[a] Data from Trabasso, Riley, and Wilson (1975).

of last error per pair for each age group; Table 7 shows the serial-position curves relative to total errors. In all cases, pair $(3, 4)$ took the longest to learn; as shown by Table 7, the serial-position curves were quite comparable for the three groups.

Six-Term Test Results: Reaction Times and Distance

In all but one of the nine cases studied, the reaction times *decreased* as a function of distance between pairs. Excluding the end-anchor tests, Fig. 8 shows the choice reaction times for inferential steps of 0, 1, or 2. The only deviant point is the 0-step for the 6-year-olds who had linguistic feedback in training and who had a high error rate compared to the others (20% versus 5% for all other conditions). These data indicate that the subjects integrated the pairwise information into linear orders during training.

Test Results: End Anchors

Figure 9 shows the end-anchor effects. In general, choice reaction time was fastest when both anchors were present [pair $(1, 6)$], next fastest for long anchor questions (those involving Stick 6), and slowest for short anchor questions (those involving Stick 1). The latter is the unmarked comparative effect. Distance effects are clear with one exception: the three-step [pair $(2, 6)$] was slower than expected. We also note a congruence effect (Clark, 1969). When the question matched the end-anchor label, the reaction time was faster.

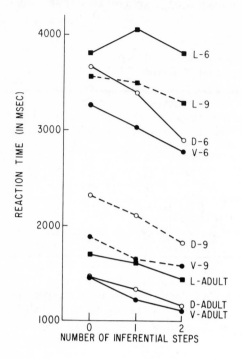

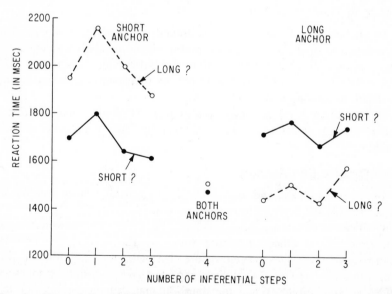

FIG. 8. Choice reaction times for answering test questions on pairs of terms requiring 0, 1, or 2 inferential steps: L = linguistic feedback in training; V = visual feedback in training; D = display of sticks. Numbers are ages of subjects: 6 = 6 years; 9 = 9 years; adults = college students (Data from Trabasso, Riley, & Wilson, 1975).

FIG. 9. Mean choice reaction time to answer test questions on pairs involving end-anchor effects as a function of comparative question and pair distance or number of inferential steps. (Data from Trabasso, Riley, & Wilson, 1975.)

LINEAR ORDER IS INDEPENDENT OF INPUT

Trabasso, Riley, and Wilson (1975) explored two other kinds of input and their effects on choice reaction times in testing. In two conditions with college students as subjects, they presented displays of six colored sticks without any size difference and asked the subjects to identify each end as the tallest or shortest stick and imagine that they were so ordered in height. These were called "distance display conditions." In another condition, subjects learned, by anticipation, the names of six colors in order. They were instructed to imagine that the first represented the tallest member and the last, the shortest member in a series of sticks that varied in height. Thus, the subjects had only spatial or linear order relations to use as reference. All three groups were tested on all possible questions without feedback in the choice–reaction-time experiment.

The test data from all three conditions resembled very closely the findings of the main experiment. All told, there were twelve cases and they are listed in Table 8. We looked for some convenient way of comparing all 12 cases in Table 8. The method we chose captures the *ordinal* relations among the reaction times for tests. For each case, the 15 test reaction times were ranked 1–15 from the fastest to the slowest. Then a coefficient of concordance was calculated, to see how well the cases agreed upon the relative order of the times. The degree of agreement was very substantial

TABLE 8
Twelve RT Conditions Studied By
Trabasso, Riley, and Wilson (1975)
Using Six-Term Series Problems

Case	Age	Condition
A	6	Train Visual Feedback
B	6	Size and Distance Display
C	6	Train Linguistic Feedback
D	9	Train Visual Feedback
E	9	Size and Distance Display
F	9	Train Linguistic Feedback
G	Adult	Train Visual Feedback
H	Adult	Size and Distance Display
I	Adult	Train Linguistic Feedback
J	Adult	Distance Display
K	Adult	Distance Display
L	Adult	Train Serial Order of Colors

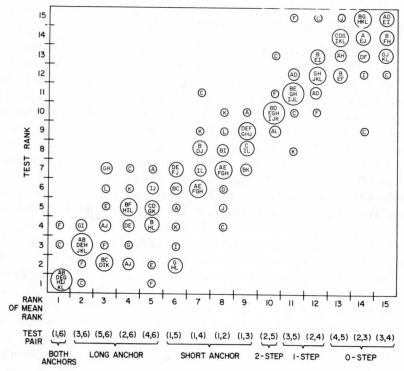

Fig. 10.   Rank orders of test pairs for twelve conditions ordered according to their average rank per pair over conditions. (Data from Trabasso, Riley, & Wilson, 1975.)

$(W = .89, p < .01)$; we represent the relation visually in Fig. 10, which shows the rank for each test for each case, ordered according to the average rank of a test across all cases. Of particular importance is the listed order on the ordinate of Fig. 10, ranging from both anchors [test (1, 6)] to the adjacent pairs [0-step or pairs (4, 5), (2, 3), (3, 4)]. The ordinal relations among the reaction times across all tests constitute the data for which we wish to account. An answer here provides the answer to our second main question, namely, how does one use an internal, linear order as a representation to make inferences or comparisons?

THE USE OF A LINEAR-ORDER REPRESENTATION

The central questions raised at the outset are directly concerned with how one is to account for two main results: (1) the serial-position effect in training (as seen in Tables 2 and 7); and (2) the relative order of errors (Table 4) and choice–reaction times (Fig. 10) in testing.

The first effect can be accounted for by a model for how one constructs a representation of linear order from partial, pairwise information. Here, as pointed out above, we have favored the "ends-inward" construction. At the same time, we must recognize that the person is not only seriating the Sticks 1, 2, 3, 4, 5, 6 but has associated with the locations linguistic or perceptual notions of length. These length "codes" could range from very tall (call it, Tall $+ +$) to very short (call it, Short $+ +$) but the codes could also be on one dimension (tallness or shortness), depending upon which property is called for by the question.

Given a correspondence between the linear order (1, 2, 3, 4, 5, 6) and a dimension, the person can use this mapping to make comparisons of one length with another. This representation relates to our second question, namely, how does one use it to answer questions or draw inferences. In one approach, the person first locates each term in the array, notes their relative order, assigns the appropriate label and chooses that term which is the subject of the relation. Specifically, given: "Which is longer, Red or Blue?," the person first locates the ordinal position of Red and Blue, outputting Red = 2 and Blue = 4. Then he notes that 4 is greater than 2, and it follows that Blue is longer than Red. Therefore, he chooses Blue. This resembles a "spatial strategy" since it depends upon locating the terms in the linear order and distance plays a role here.

Another method is to use the associations of the locations in the linear order with the comparative labels directly. That is, the person generates from the ordinal locations of the colors, associations of length and then compares the two colors, selecting the correct color on the basis of whichever one is stronger on that dimension. For example, if the question is "Which is shorter, Yellow or White?," the person notes that Yellow has x relative units of shortness whereas White has y relative units of shortness. He then chooses that color which has the greater relative unit. We shall now consider these process models and how well they predict the data.

ACCESSING A LINEAR ORDER: STRENGTH OR DISTANCE?

Suppose that each location, i, in a linear order has a code, C_i, for the underlying dimensional scale of length and each term, S_i, is a color name associated with C_i at location i. As the linear order or scale is developed in training, stick color S_i becomes maximally associated with C_i but retains some association with other labels. The strength of the association depends upon several factors, notably (1) the availability of the code (reflected in the unmarked/marked difference), (2) the ease of locating the S_i, and (3) the number of times S_i is associated with C_i, etc. These factors clearly favor the long end-anchor association.

TABLE 9
Associative Strengths for Generalization Model

| Linear order | Code | Stick | | | | | |
		S_1	S_2	S_3	S_4	S_5	S_6
1	C_1 Short + +	16	13	11	10	6	0
2	C_2 Short +	13	16	14	13	9	3
3	C_3 Short	11	14	16	15	11	5
4	C_4 Tall	10	13	15	16	12	6
5	C_5 Tall +	6	9	11	12	16	10
6	C_6 Tall + +	0	3	5	6	10	16
	Sum:	56	68	72	72	64	40

TABLE 10
Confusion Matrix for Generalization Model

| Stick | Code | | | | | |
	C_1	C_2	C_3	C_4	C_5	C_6
S_1	.285	.232	.196	.179	.107	.000
S_2	.191	.235	.206	.191	.132	.044
S_3	.153	.194	.222	.208	.153	.069
S_4	.139	.181	.208	.222	.167	.083
S_5	.093	.141	.172	.188	.250	.156
S_6	.000	.075	.125	.150	.250	.400

The S_i "generalize" to other codes as they are close to C_i (very short is similar to short etc.). We shall assume that this generalization declines monotonically from the maxmum associative strength at C_i.

These assumptions are illustrated in Table 9, using hypothetical numbers for the associative strengths. In this example, all codes are equally associated but their gradients vary with the steepest gradients occurring at the ends, especially for the long end anchor.

One could interpret Table 9 as reflecting degree of "confusability" of the codes with one another. In fact, by dividing each cell entry by its column sum, one can compute a color-code confusion matrix. This matrix is given in Table 10.

One of the alternative models above states that the person generates appropriate codes for the pair (S_i, S_j) and compares their strengths in order

TABLE 11
Summed Probabilities for Locating
A Pair of Codes:
Generalization Model

Stick	2	3	4	5	6
1	520	507	507	535	685
2		457	457	485	635
3			444	472	622
4				472	622
5					650

to decide an answer to a question. One rule for finding the strength of a coded relation is that following Luce's (1959) choice axiom which supposes that the probability of a code label C_i, to an eliciting stimulus S_i, is the ratio of the strength of C_i to that stimulus divided by the summed strengths of all the codes to that stimulus. Applying this rule to all the cell entries of Table 9 results in the confusion matrix of code probabilities shown in Table 10.

For a pair (S_i, S_j) let us assume that the ease of generating a pair of codes is directly related to the sum of the code probabilities. Table 11 shows these sums for all tests using the main diagonal probabilities in Table 10.

If we rank order the summed probabilities, 1–15, from the highest to the lowest and assume this rank order to be for speed, we note that the ranks of the test pairs closely approximate those for the tests in Fig. 10. These ranks are compared directly in Table 17, and the rank-order correlation is very high, $r = .96$. We note that there are a number of pairs of tied ranks. These are removed if we complete the model by another application of the choice axiom on strength comparisons between the pair members. For example, the ratio involving (2, 4) is greater than the ratio involving (2, 3) as that pair (2, 4) is decided more quickly than pair (2, 3) although the ease of generating their codes is the same. However, breaking ties does not improve the prediction very much and the bulk of the reaction times can be accounted for by the ease of finding codes on the scale.

Before we dismiss spatial imagery models (see Huttenlocher, 1968; DeSoto et al., 1965) in favor of associative strength models, we note that a spatial distance representation can be defined by subtracting the strengths between a pair of sticks for a given code or location in the linear order. The distance gradients for the sticks are given in Table 12.

This exercise shows that Murdock's (1960) theory of stimulus distinctiveness is isomorphic to Bower's (1971) stimulus-generalization model used to account for serial-position effects in mapping labels onto physical continua.

The spatial model says that in order to answer a test question, the person must first *locate* the stick colors in the array so that the ease of comparing their ordinal positions depends upon how discriminable each stick color is from every other one in the array. We follow Murdock's (1960) procedure and compute the relative discriminability of a stick by first summing its distance from all other sticks and then, applying the choice axiom, compute its relative discriminability by finding the ratio of its distance to the sum of all the distances in the array. The relative discriminability for each stick is shown in Table 12.

If the ease of locating a pair of sticks in the array is related to distance, then one would expect the sum of the relative discriminabilities to be inversely related to speed. The sum of the relative discriminabilities for each test pair is given in Table 13.

TABLE 12
Distances for Pairs of Sticks

Stick	1	2	3	4	5	6	Sum	Relative discriminability
1	0	3	5	6	10	16	40	.196
2	3	0	2	3	7	13	28	.137
3	5	2	0	1	5	11	24	.118
4	6	3	1	0	4	10	24	.118
5	10	7	5	4	0	6	32	.157
6	16	13	11	10	6	0	56	.275

TABLE 13
Summed Relative Discriminabilities or
The Probability for Locating a Pair of Sticks
Relative to All Other Pairs: Distance Model

Stick	2	3	4	5	6
1	333	314	314	353	471
2		255	255	294	412
3			236	275	393
4				275	393
5					432

TABLE 14
Relative Errors in Training[a]

Model	\(1, 2\)	\(2, 3\)	\(3, 4\)	\(4, 5\)	\(5, 6\)
	PAIR				
Distance	.18	.23	.25	.21	.14
Generalization	.19	.219	.224	.211	.15

[a] Relative errors are obtained by (1) finding the reciprocal for each of the main diagonal entries of Tables 13 and 11, respectively, and (2) normalizing the reciprocals for each table.

TABLE 15
Associative Strengths for Comparative Labels:
Category-Scale Model

Stick	Sum	Short sum	p (Short/S_i)	Long Sum	p (Long/S_i)
1	56	40	.714	16	.286
2	68	43	.632	25	.368
3	72	41	.569	31	.431
4	72	38	.528	34	.472
5	64	26	.406	38	.594
6	40	8	.200	32	.800

The rank order of these sums (1 = highest) is identical to that for the generalization model. Thus, one cannot discriminate between these interpretations. It is also the case that both models predict serial-position effects in training, that is, there should be a correlation between these effects and relative discriminabilities or relative strengths. Assuming that errors are inversely related to correct responses, the reciprocals of each main diagonal of Table 11 and 13, respectively, were normalized and are presented in Table 14. In Table 14 it can be seen that both models predict the kind of serial-position effects observed in Tables 3 and 7.

We would like to consider another plausible process model by which the person makes a transitive inference or arrives at a decision in the test series. In this model, the person *categorizes* the scale into long and short halves (as illustrated in Table 9). That is, locations 1–3 are "short" and locations 4–6 are "long." Given the comparative of the question, the person generates codes for each stick, compares the relative strengths of the codes and chooses that stick color which has the greater strength. Here we assume

TABLE 16
Code Probabilities for Associative Model
Averaged over Questions

Stick	2	3	4	5	6
1	547	579	599	656	759
2		532	552	608	722
3			521	582	695
4				561	677
5					622

TABLE 17
Observed and Expected Rank Order for Test RTs

	Pair	Observed rank	Generalization-distance	Association
Both anchors	1, 6	1	1	1
Long anchor	3, 6	2	4.5	3
	5, 6	3	2	6
	2, 6	4	3	2
	4, 6	5	4.5	4
Short anchor	1, 5	6	6	5
	1, 4	7	8.5	8
	1, 2	8	7	13
	1, 3	9	8.5	10
2 Step	2, 5	10	10	7
1 Step	3, 5	11	11.5	9
	2, 4	12	13.5	12
0 Step	4, 5	13	11.5	11
	2, 3	14	13.5	14
	3, 4	15	15	15
Correlation			.96	.89

that the strengths are hypothetically those in Table 9. The stick color is associated with a short or long code according to the relative strengths of associations to each half of the scale. For Stick 1, the sum for the short code is $16 + 13 + 11 = 40$; for the long code, it is $10 + 6 = 16$. Then the conditional probability of "short" given S_1 is $40/56 = .714$; the conditional probability of "long" given S_1 is $16/56 = .286$. This relative weighting of associative strengths yields two scales, one for each comparative code. The two resulting hypothetical gradients are shown in Table 15.

To apply this model to the test situation, we need a response rule for comparing strengths on a given scale. If the question is Shorter?, we use the short scale; if Longer?, the long scale. For pair $(1, 2)$, these ratios are $.714/(.714 + .632) = .530$ and $.368/(.286 + .368) = .563$, respectively. The average of these ratios for all test pairs is given in Table 16 (the average for $(1, 2)$ is $.547$).

Assuming that speed is directly proportional to the magnitude of the ratios, then we can rank order the probabilities in Table 16, 1 to 15, with $1 = $ highest, and compare the ranks to those obtained in Fig. 10. Table 17 shows the comparison.

Although the rank-order correlation is very high ($r = .89$), this model does not predict the order as well as the previous two models which depended more upon confusion than associative strength. The problem with the categorization–association model has to do with the short-anchor times being too slow. However, strengthening the short-anchor associations does not remove the problem since trade-offs will occur elsewhere in the calculations.

CONCLUSIONS

Our analysis suggests that children ranging in age from 4 to 10 years, mentally retarded adolescents, and college students use similar strategies of (1) constructing linear orders from pairwise, ordered information and (2) use this order to make inferences about comparative relations among the pairs. The construction of the linear order involves an "ends-inward" strategy with the linguistically unmarked "long" end being isolated first.

When tested for comparative relations among members, the subjects clearly use an underlying scale involving either strength or distance relations among the members and linguistic codes. In short, we believe that we have provided a mechanism for information integration and inference-making that cuts across a variety of situations and tasks.

Developmentally, we feel that we have identified a common set of mental operations for use by children or adults to perform transitive inferences. The fact that an older child or adult may justify his response, respond more quickly, etc. may simply be a result of a more strongly associated set of linearly ordered codes rather than any qualitative differences in cognitive abilities. That is, a child (or adult) may state that Red is longer than Blue for reasons of logical necessity because Red is more strongly associated with long than Blue. That is, he has knowledge, of a sort, of the decision rule used to make the judgment. Our findings indicate that seriation, that is, the creation of a linear order, is critical to making inferences or at least performing well on inference tests. If subjects do not construct a linear order, they are unlikely to be able to remember the pairwise relations or even to have ordered the pairs, and hence cannot deduce relations. The main problem we have isolated for young children in these tasks is *linguistic,* not logical. The relatively poorer performance has consistently been in those conditions where the feedback is only linguistic. We suggest that young children have difficulty isolating end anchors when the only clue is a single comparative, and when only one comparative question is asked, they reduce the comparative to labels (e.g., longer to long as in Riley & Trabasso, 1974). However, they do not have difficulty mapping these codes onto physical displays or integrating when they have referents for the terms. The developmental differences then lie in language and not in logic.

Critics of the Bryant and Trabasso (1971) study have suggested that strategies such as we have described here are irrelevant when applied to Piaget's model of cognitive development (see Youniss & Furth, 1973; De Boysson-Bardies & O'Regan, 1973). To argue that the research is irrelevent when it shows that children do not use the kind of logicomathematical structure assumed by Piaget would seem to beg the developmental question. Children and adults use similar, if not identical, cognitive operations here. The developmental differences lie in the domain of memory and language. Statements that negative findings are irrelevant would seem to prevent critical testing of the theory.

With respect to the study of three-term series in adults (see Clark, 1969; Huttenlocher, 1968), we suggest that both imaginal and linguistic factors are involved. Indeed, our model makes use of both factors (as well as others).

Our data also make contact with "assimilation theory" (Bransford & Franks, 1971; Barclay, 1973; Potts, 1972; Scholz & Potts, 1974). We hope that our demonstration leads to a fuller development for mechanisms by which disparate information is integrated and "false recognitions" or inferences are made.

Finally, the relation between reaction time and distance (Moyer & Landauer, 1967) may now be more clearly understood as a result of decision processes and operations on a linear order or associative strengths. Moyer's (1973) observation that people were faster to answer questions like "Who is larger, a dog or a squirrel?" than "Who is larger, a cat or a rabbit?" does not necessarily depend upon images. Rather, images could be constructed from the associated magnitudes of size stored with the lexical name of each animal.

In retrospect, the use of associative strength notions and response rules seems to have led us full circle back to the old problem of transposition (Spence, 1937). History has a way of repeating itself, at least in part.

ACKNOWLEDGMENTS

This research was supported by Research Grant No. 19223 from the National Institute of Mental Health, United States Public Health Service to T. Trabasso.

REFERENCES

Barclay, J. R. The role of comprehension in remembering sentences. *Cognitive Psychology*, 1973, **4**, 229–254.

Bower, G. H. Adaptation-level coding of stimuli and serial position effects. In M. H. Appley (Ed.), *Adaptation-level theory*, New York: Academic Press, 1971. Pp. 175–201.

Bransford, J. D., & Franks, J. J. The abstraction of linguistic ideas. *Cognitive Psychology*, 1971, **2**, 331–350.

Bryant, P. E., & Trabasso, T. Transitive inferences and memory in young children. *Nature*, 1971, **232**, 456–458.

Burt, C. The development of reasoning in school children. *Journal of Experimental Pedagogy*, 1919, **5**, 68–77.

Clark, H. H. Linguistic processes in deductive reasoning. *Journal of Experimental Psychology*, 1969, **76**, 387–404.

De Boysson-Bardies, B., & O'Regan, K. What children do in spite of adults' hypotheses. *Nature*, 1973, **246**, 531–534.

DeSoto, C. B., & Bosley, J. G. The cognitive structure of a social structure. *Journal of Abnormal and Social Psychology*, 1962, **64**, 303–307.

DeSoto, C. B., London, M., & Handel, S. Social reasoning and spatial paralogic. *Journal of Personality and Social Psychology*, 1965, **2**, 513–521.

Feigenbaum, E. A., & Simon, H. A. A theory of the serial position effect. *British Journal of Psychology*, 1962, **53**, 307–320.

Frase, L. T. Maintenance and control in the acquisition of knowledge from written materials. In R. O. Freedle & J. B. Carroll (Eds.), *Language comprehension and the acquisition of knowledge*, Washington, D.C.: Winston, 1972, 337–360.

Hoffman, S., Trabasso, T., & Friedman, M. Mental operations on number symbols by children. *Memory & Cognition*, 1974, **2**, 591–595.

Hunter, I. M. L. The solving of three-term series problems. *British Journal of Psychology*, 1957, **48**, 286–298.

Huttenlocher, J. Constructing spatial images: A strategy in reasoning. *Psychological Review*, 1968, **75**, 550–560.

Luce, R. D. *Individual choice behavior*, New York: Wiley, 1959.

Lutkus, A. D., & Trabasso, T. Transitive inferences in preoperational retarded adolescents. *American Journal of Mental Deficiency*, 1974, **78**, 599–606.

Moyer, R. S. Comparing objects in memory: Evidence suggesting an internal psychophysics. *Perception & Psychophysics*, 1973, **13**, 180–184.

Moyer, R. S., & Landauer, T. K. Time required for judgments of numerical inequality. *Nature*, 1967, **215**, 1519–1520.

Murdock, B. B., Jr. The distinctiveness of stimuli. *Psychological Review,* 1960, **67,** 16–31.

Piaget, J. Une forme verbal de la comparison chez l'enfant. *Archives de Psychologie,* 1921, 141–172.

Piaget, J. *Genetic epistemology.* Translated by Eleanor Duckwork. New York: Columbia University Press, 1970.

Piaget, J., Inhelder, B., & Szeminska, A. *The child's conception of geometry,* London: Routledge & Kegan Paul, 1960.

Potts, G. R. Information processing strategies used in the encoding of linear orderings. *Journal of Verbal Learning and Verbal Behavior,* 1972, **11,** 727–740.

Riley, C. A., & Trabasso, T. Comparatives, logical structures and encoding in a transitive inference task. *Journal of Experimental Child Psychology,* 1974, **17,** 187–203.

Scholz, K. W., & Potts, G. R. Cognitive processing of linear orderings. *Journal of Experimental Psychology,* 1974, **102,** 323–326.

Smedslund, J. Psychological diagnostics. *Psychological Bulletin,* 1969, **71,** 237–248.

Spence, K. W. The differential response in animals to stimuli varying within a single dimension. *Psychological Review,* 1937, **44,** 430–444.

Trabasso, T., Riley, C. A., & Wilson, E. G. The representation of linear order and spatial strategies in reasoning: A developmental study. In R. Falmagne (Ed.), *Psychological studies of logic and its development.* Hillsdale, New Jersey: Lawrence Erlbaum Associates, 1975.

Wishner, J., Shipley, T. E., & Hurvich, M. S. The serial-position curve as a function of organization. *American Journal of Psychology,* 1957, **70,** 258–262.

Youniss, J., & Furth, H. G. Reasoning and Piaget: A comment on Bryant and Trabasso. *Nature,* 1973, **244,** 314–315.

DISCUSSION: SECTION III

TRABASSO: Bob Solso has asked me to act as chairman for the discussion section and I'd like to open the discussion by asking either the panel members or the audience to pose questions for the members on today's panel.

ESTES: I'd be interested in what either David McNeill or John Anderson might have to say about the connection, or lack of it, between their approaches to speech production. In McNeill's presentation, the essentials are that the individual generates a sensory–motor schema for an action; the schema is a major way station that precedes and is partly responsible for the resulting speech production. This step in the process, superficially at least, is somewhat similar in Anderson's presentation. How close or how wide apart do you feel that you are in that aspect of speech production?

McNEILL: I was struck by the same similarity, in that the operations of the BRACKET program are rather like the alignment of sensory–motor schemas. An important difference is that the conceptual structure of this BRACKET program deals with propositions. Though it is true that you could describe sensory–motor schemas in a propositional format, that would be to miss the essential quality of the sensory–motor schema, which is closely connected to actual action. But the idea otherwise seems very similar and particularly the idea that the surface structure of speech will have certain necessary correlations with the underlying conceptual structure.

ANDERSON: I think child speech has more constraints than those required by the BRACKET program. For instance, there is nothing in the BRACKET program that would require that the subject come before the verb,

411

but this appears to be the case in child speech. On the other hand, such constraints do not appear in adult speech. The greater flexibility of the BRACKET program is required so that it is possible for LAS to acquire the full variety of sentence structure in adult speech. Perhaps McNeill was talking about an earlier stage in language organization than that for which LAS would be an appropriate mechanism.

McNEILL: In an aspect of this work that I haven't discussed, I've developed a notation for describing the conceptual arrangements behind adult speech. It rests upon the assumption that the BRACKET program rests upon, namely that there are nonarbitrary connections between the form of the surface structure and the form of the underlying conceptual arrangements. Adult conceptual structures can be seen as being continuous with the sensory–motor action schemas of children, but they are remotely connected to these action schemas by means of the semiotic extension. This means, however, that for adults as well as children, utterances can be constructed concept by concept, as the speaker moves from one action–schema concept or its abstract semiotic equivalent to another. You can, by describing the conceptual structure in this way, which is not arbitrary, account for a large fraction of the surface structure, for example, most word order sequences. These details of the surface can be seen as having been determined by the underlying conceptual arrangements. What details aren't then determined by the underlying conceptual arrangements appear to be determined by syntactic routines of great flexibility that can, essentially, convert almost any thinkable conceptual structure into actual surface structures.

ESTES: Is it the case that the machinery also works backwards, that in the understanding of speech, a sentence I hear denotes sensory–motor schemas as an essential part of the language production?

McNEILL: I don't know. I would doubt if there are many asymmetries between speech understanding and speech production, but I don't think you really have to organize a syntagma in all cases to understand. There are various kinds of perceptual heuristics of the kind Bever (1970) has described which seem to have as a common purpose that they avoid organizing a syntagma. You can indeed understand speech that way.

POSNER: Does your theory suggest that you could use a separate generative speech process other than the one describing the aquarium that you are building with less interference?

McNEILL: I did that and, of course, the obvious happened, and the interference is enormous. I had people stand up and describe that, and sit down and describe that, and then I had them sit down again and describe standing up. That throws into conflict two simultaneous, closely related action schemas. What they tended to do was to either describe what they were doing, but inversely, or do the inverse of what they were describing. Since the actions of sitting and standing are not perfect mirror images, this produced peculiar descriptions or peculiar behavior depending on which direction the influence came from. There is certainly tremendous conflict when you have very closely schemas being operated at the same time. This seems to me to be proof that the conceptual content of speech is intimately connected to schemas of action. In the case of doing something with the aquarium and trying to describe it by producing speech and the corresponding action somewhat asynchronously, that's still very difficult. My subjects all complained about having to do that. It's much easier to perform while not saying anything and then describe it or vice versa.

BJORK: I was wondering about something as I listened to you talk. Have you ever tried to describe something to somebody else with your hands in your pockets or behind your back? The point of such an exercise is to demonstrate how dependent we are on gestures in using speech. It is terribly difficult, at least initially. Suppose you have a subject describe something, in one case free to gesture, and, in another case, constrained from using his hands. I wonder if an analysis of his verbal behavior in the two cases would show certain kinds of equivalencies between gestures and words, or identify in some direct ways the functions served by gestures in terms of their formal properties.

McNEILL: I hadn't thought of it, I don't know what difference it would make. Some people find it incredibly difficult to speak without gesturing, though, in principle, it's possible and it's just the tendency to gesture that you have to suppress; there's not an inevitable connection between gesturing and the expression of speech.

BJORK: There is a kind of adaptation with practice. Initially it's incredible; your hands jerk of their own will, you do a lot of stammering, and so forth. But then one seems to develop a verbal pattern much more elaborate than normal speech, and . . .

McNEILL: I've observed people who speak this way (*he gestures*) and then they will say something. I assume what they are doing, in fact, is constructing the utterance silently as they perform the gesture and then they repeat it. They typically don't gesture as they repeat it.

CARLSON: It seems to me that Drs. Anderson and McNeill have discussed and talked about the acquisition and generation of language. Whereas, Drs. Bjork, Kintsch, and Trabasso have been talking about semantic memory, that is, the retention of language once it's acquired. I'd like you to comment on the relationship between those two general areas of inquiry.

TRABASSO: Some of us operate at the front end of the process and some of us operate near the back end. I have operated on the back end to a large extent. That is, I have been less concerned with the taking in of information, operating on it, and constructing representations from the input. Rather, the person has constructed a certain kind of representation which has some temporary or relative durability in memory. One uses that representation to solve a problem or answer a question or draw an inference. The front (acquisition) end of the process is assumed or given. This is analogous, in some sense, to the use of HAM structures in sentence memory by Anderson & Bower. One could have a HAM structure without any explanation or description as to how it was constructed. Given that HAM represents a sentence, as it does, then interesting questions follow. Can we find out whether or not a sentence is stored in a certain representation? Then one designs experiments on this question, but one needs a process model at the retrieval end of it. At least, that is how I interpret Anderson & Bower's approach. I don't recall that they, in their book, distinguish between the structure of the sentence and various retrieval plans nor did they have a parser for constructing representations. The question arises: Where and why the HAM representation? Is it a given? Is it innate or does it follow from a set of parsing routines?

ANDERSON: HAM is an important component of LAS. There is a lot of memory searching that is necessary in LAS and this searching is performed by the HAM MATCH algorithm.

ANDERSON: Until recently no concern has been with memory for sentences. I just assumed a particular HAM representation was an appropriate memory representation for a particular sentence. In this respect I was like Trabasso. However, I became upset about the degrees of freedom we have when we are allowed to choose our representation. It seemed that if HAM could not handle a phenomenon with the first representation thought of, the representation could be changed slightly to accommodate the phenomenon. Therefore, it seemed important to understand the mechanism that determined the representation for an input. It seems to me that the best way to do this is to understand how the mechanism evolved—that is, to study language acquisition.

BJORK: Well, I'm not going to worry about a question like that. I see McNeill, Anderson, and Kintsch as along the same kind of continuum certainly, but there's no particular problem of abstracting or growing a meaning structure that is reasonably well organized. There is a certain commonness of approach, I think, if you stretch it a little bit. That is, to some degree, with the possible exception of Tom's work, there is a levels of processing idea common to all of the work reported here; but the levels are defined differently. The idea that one goes through levels of analysis or overlapping stages seems to be an idea whose time has come in any number of ways. I'm struck by that similarity. That general framework, however, integrates everything only in a general way. Some of the efforts reported here are reasonably far apart. In my own case, I was tending to focus on memory for individual items, not sentences and so on. But still, in terms of the kind of operations that go on even during an effort to memorize a standard free-recall list, the organization built during that effort shares certain kinds of components, certain kinds of similarities with the kind of growth that's being talked about with more meaningful materials, propositions, and so on.

TRABASSO: I could have presented more along these lines also by having stressed the process model in acquisition of the linear order. I had suggested the ends-inward analysis of the partial information of pairs of ordered information. But, I think I was looking at a more static representation; that is, some representation that a person would develop for a problem solution, using representation in Allen Newell and Herb Simon's sense of the term. Perhaps that is not so much of interest, and one is now more interested in looking at whole systems where the process–structure distinction is not made. Allen Newell (1972) has an interesting discussion of the issue. Whether something is process or structure depends upon your point of view. The kinds of structures one observes, for example, in Kintsch's outline, shift and change, depending upon what information has been processed, is forgotten as well as what operations have occurred. Newell also points out that structure has an aspect of time to it. Things that seem to be more enduring are regarded as structure; things which seem to change fast are regarded as process. He also makes distinctions as to what is program and what is data. That is, one can have data which are structures, which are operated on by programs which, in turn, are processes. But you can also have compilers operating on programs and now the programs become data and the compilers become processes, etc. Today we seem to be emphasizing more the processing that seems to be involved. The outputs of these processes are "idealized" structures of different duration. I think that I tried to freeze things a little more by stressing the kind of structure one would evolve (namely, a linear order) to enable one to solve a limited set of problems.

BJORK: But as you kept getting close to the analysis of that problem, you seemed always to move away from it.

TRABASSO: From what?

BJORK: From the problem of specifying the internal representation and the use thereof. Take, for example, the association idea you proposed. I think a formally equivalent model is something like the following: the subject constructs a magnitude estimate for each item in an ordering, but there is variability in each estimate. That is, his representation of each item is characterized by a certain mean magnitude, but there is variation in that magnitude such that there is overlap among the magnitude distributions. Such a model will yield predictions identical to those of the association idea. At any rate, I am not sure that this structure vs. process business holds up in any sort of neat way in terms of sorting out theories.

POSNER: I want to ask David McNeill whether he feels that he has a radical theory. It seems that cognitive psychology has been getting more and more propositional models. Everyone says that they're not language, but most of the examples seem very linguistic in form. Now someone comes along that's working with language and he uses a sensory-motor representation that seems to be a very concrete representation. Does this make a radical?

McNEILL: I don't feel particularly radical. The idea is really old in the life span of our field. Piaget was making some of these proposals forty or fifty years ago. But, you're quite right, it doesn't correspond in any obvious way to what has become a common mode of representation which uses some form of propositional representation. I'm attempting to describe a particular level in the stream of processes leading up to speech and it is certainly not the bottom level where logical structures might best be described. I resist even attempting to use something as powerful as a propositional notation to describe the organization of a syntagma. I think that would miss some essential properties such as its close connection with actual organizational action processes. Of course, there may be deeper levels where information storage or cognitive activity finally leads up to the level of a syntagma, which is where the sentence itself begins to take shape, and perhaps one could profitably describe these levels in terms of propositions. You're quite right to point to this difference; I'm very much conscious of it.

MANDLER: It is not only the case that the idea is relatively ancient, as Dave (McNeill) says, but also that it is a well known general notion that is becoming popular as a way of looking at the world. I am talking about structuralism which is a nonpropositional set of theoretical ideas. We have missed a lot in American psychology by ignoring the structuralist, dialectic approaches. For example, the work of Weiss and von Holst, which is structuralist in conception, can teach us much about the organization of simple action sequences. Psychologists have paid too little attention to these developments whether they come from Piaget or from the biologists, though much of current theory is structuralist without acknowledging it. It would be useful if we started reading some of the basic literature, just as the linguists have, and some of the developmental psychologists. I don't think that these are radical notions, they are just outside the parochialism of American psychology.

TRABASSO: Would you care to distinguish what you mean by Structuralism versus Propositionalism? I'm not sure you can. Suppose I have a list of propositions, but contained in that list are also statements which relate propositions, so that I have a structure that lists the propositions, but I can also move from one proposition to another since other, structural relations are imbedded in my list of propositions.

MANDLER: There are ways in which propositional systems can easily be translated into structuralist notions, but I don't think that we have the time now to develop what Lévy-Strauss or Piaget mean by structuralism. Piaget published his development of the idea of structuralism in 1968, with the English translation in 1970, in which he discusses the historical and contemporary development of structuralism, and how relational structures are and have been used to represent systems from mathematics to simple action systems to cultural systems.

TRABASSO: Yes, but you were making an admonition here that we are not capturing something in our work that structuralism does.

MANDLER: No, I'm saying we're just not reading the literature that's all.

TRABASSO: Then, I would ask: Why aren't we reading this literature and who should we read?

MANDLER: We're not reading, for example, Weiss and von Holst.

TRABASSO: Why should we? What might it lead to which we are not already doing?

MANDLER: I recently had the opportunity to read an advance copy of an article by C. R. Gallistel in the forthcoming *Nebraska Symposium on Motivation,* which discusses the problem of the organization of action sequences from a physiological–biological point of view. I discovered that the biological literature has addressed Lashley's problem of the syntax of action much more directly than the psychologists have. There is a literature around Piaget, Lévy–Strauss, and de Saussure on the one hand, and Weiss and von Holst on the other, which would be useful for the problems we are addressing. Structuralism represents a movement which is holistic, concerned with systems of transformations that are self-regulating, and is an alternative to the traditionally atomistic and linear models that American psychologists are so fond of. It is not radical, and it is not new. It's just a bit outside traditional American psychology.

TRABASSO: Suppose, for example, you describe an action sequence. You could describe it in Piaget's terms as the internalization of the child's perception of the movement he makes towards an object. Now, why couldn't one make another description of that at some abstract or formal level which captures all the properties of action sequence and allows one to generate it? That is, can you find abstract representation, network representation, list representation which would give you the same outcomes as described by a structuralist? I fail to see where there is a real difference if you can write a formalism which captures features of both systems.

MANDLER: Of course it is possible, and at the present stage of development probably unprovable that analog systems and propositional systems are fundamentally different. It would be an interesting thing to do and why not try it; by all means, let's work on all of these alternatives. I didn't say we should do one thing and not others. The developments in linguistics and psycholinguistics suggest, however, that we are moving more toward a new way of looking at things.

McNEILL: It certainly is true things have changed in 10 years, but the early work in child language was concerned with a rather specialized problem: the description of competence and this clearly is not that. I don't know what the proper statement is to the relationship between competence and performance, though I'm committed to the idea that you must clearly distinguish the two, and that whatever relation Paiget and this kind of thinking has with respect to the organization of linguistic processes, it is a relation that is interpretable at the level of performance. A crucial step in my argument that has been missing from previous discussions of the influence of cognition on language, is the connection of action schemas with syntagmas. The influence of cognitive functioning on language is clearest at this level. It is much less clear where the influence has usually been discussed, namely, in the parallelisms of static linguistic knowledge (i.e., competence) with cognitive structure (e.g., Bloom, 1973). Now, the early child language work was self-conscious in avoiding many questions of linguistics performance and was consistent in avoiding questions of the cognitive basis of linguistic structures. The tendency in the field has been to get away from the competence side of the linguistic dichotomy or even to do away with the dichotomy. This second step seems to me nonsensical whereas the first is quite interesting. Considering questions of performance brings in the conceptual basis of language in a natural way, which is lost or obscured if the distinction between competence and performance is obliterated. The two are not the same. For example, it's a structural fact of English that passive sentences are related to active sentences in a certain way: the order of NPs is reversed, there is an auxiliary verb to carry tense, etc. However, the production of passive sentences can be explained on grounds which make no use of these specific structural relations: the first noun is the focus, the conceptual content is Receptive rather than Operative, etc. This creates a curious paradox in which the structural facts true of passive sentences play no part in the production of these same sentences.

TRABASSO: Dave, while I can't speak for you because I'm not inside your head, but having spent a semester looking at some work by developmental psychologists, I came away with the impression that when people began to look at semantics, to use case grammars to describe utterances of children, and the arguments by Bowerman and Schesinger on intentions or prior conceptualizations before speech, they were forced to begin to consider what the child knew prior to the onset of speech. Piaget is a reference here since he spent considerable time describing in some detail the child's knowledge of the world, especially the perceptual world, prior to the onset of speech. These structures may be the ones onto which language is mapped or those which determine what is spoken. I see you as fitting into this trend of thought.

McNEILL: Whether it was recognized as such, a part of what has been going on is a growing interest in questions of performance and a declining interest in questions of pure abstract competence. This hasn't always been perceived as such, but that's really what has taken place. This phenomenon has occurred in several fields at once: in developmental psycholinguistics, in psycholinguistics in general and also within linguistic theory. So there are now theories like generative symantics, where it's specifically argued that you can no longer draw a sharp distinction between competence and performance. There have been many influences, in fact, on the growing interest in questions of performance: artificial intelligence certainly has been one, and the growing acquaintance with Piaget has been another, as Trabasso points out. There is another aspect of this. Performance was a neglected topic ten years ago, in part because of the dangers of backsliding into behaviorism. At that time, it was generally true that questions of performance were in the domain of behaviorism. Within psycholinguistics now, however, behaviorism is no longer a tenable point of view. That has released questions of performance for serious consideration.

ANDERSON: We are only focusing on one aspect of the papers presented here. In Bjork's and Kintsch's work there has been discussion of levels of encoding and the relation of this concept to memory. I do not know why deeper levels of encoding are associated with better memory and I do not know what mechanism would produce this outcome. Walter was suggesting that deeper memory traces have slower decay rates associated with them. For instance, propositional traces decay more slowly than lexical traces. But consider experiments where some subjects study sentences and other subjects generate sentences. In both cases propositional traces are set up, but one might think the generation case involves deeper processing. Indeed, memory is better in the generation case. So it seems that even when propositional traces are being set up, the propositions are more durable when they result from deeper processes. Therefore, I do not think levels of encoding can simply be explained in terms of different decay rates for different types of traces.

Some further data came from experiments that Trabasso and I have been doing. These experiments are very much like the ones Kintsch has reported. We present subjects with a sentence like "The boy was hit by the girl" and have them verify whether that sentence is true in light of sentences they studied earlier. Originally, they either studied "The girl hit the boy" or "The boy was hit by the girl". As Kintsch found, subjects are faster when the test sentence physically matches the study sentence. In a test immediately after study this effect is of the order of 500 msec. but it diminishes to 200 msec after 30 sec of intervening activity. Kintsch might want to interpret this as indicating a fast decay of exact word information. A problem for this explanation is that the advantage for a physical match does not diminish after 30 sec. A 200-msec advantage for physical match is still found 20 min later. So, it seems that once out of range of short-term memory, lexical information does not decay rapidly. So why do we remember better what we process at deeper levels?

KINTSCH: I don't think that's a general, necessary statement to make it that way. I think it's a question of what cues the subject chooses to store in his long-term memory. Now usually when you are, say, reading a newspaper or reading a book, the important aspect to be remembered is the meaning. This is what is stored permanently. The other traces that are worked with in the process of comprehending this test are not regarded as important, not stored, and therefore they are lost. It becomes different when you go through a psychological experiment like yours where you give active and passive sentences. The likelihood is there that the subject, in this case, quite intentionally encodes the sentence not only with respect to meaning but also with respect to the actual words that are being used and the actual phrases that are being used in this situation. I gave the example of Koler's work, who found memory for upright and inverted typeface after two or three weeks. Clearly, one cannot say that it is only propositions that people can remember. They can choose to remember visual information, imagery information, any kind of information. It is usually the case that the meaning information is the important one and the one emphasized in the task.

MANDLER: It is a question of what you are going to process. To support what Walter (Kintsch) said, it depends what the subject thinks he is supposed to be doing. Arthur Graesser and I just finished a study in which we had two groups of subjects, both of which listened to passages that were purportedly excerpts from essays written by high school and junior high school students. Under one condition the subjects were asked to judge whether listeners could understand what the students were trying to get across. In the other condition the subjects were asked to judge whether the sentences of the passage were grammatically correct or not.

They were then given a forced-choice four-alternative recognition test for the sentences that had been presented. For the subjects in the first group the data show total confusion on surface characteristics of the sentences and, of course, excellent recognition of the semantic contents. The second group, who judged grammaticality, recognition of surface structure was essentially just as good as for meaning, which was as high as the recognition performance of the first group. In other words, the group who judged grammaticality processed surface structure as well as meaning. If you tell subjects what to do, they will do it and store the result. It isn't that meaning memory is necessarily better, but it is in the nature of the communication process that we process it first, more extensively, and most deeply. If however the situation requires that surface structure be stored, people will do that and will apparently do it just as well.

ANDERSON: We should not just look at sentence memory. Consider tasks where we just want subjects to remember single words. The subjects' recall is better if he is asked to study the words in a way that requires him to process the word's meaning. All the subject is asked to remember is the physical word and so you would think the subject would be better if he were instructed to focus on the physical features of the word. But this is not so.

KINTSCH: That's not usually true because an important part in any recall experiment is the organization of the list of words that the S can make. Usually, but not entirely, this organization is made on the basis of meaning. Let me report some other data that show that it is not universally true that the verbal traces on, let's say, the actual words used, are lost in 20 min. I think it depends upon the situation into which you put the subject: when we do it with separate sentences we get results exactly like yours. Jan Keenan (in preparation) has done a study where she tested the hypothesis that if the subjects have access to information at the word level or linguistic level, they can answer questions faster than if they only had access to it at a propositional level. She didn't put this information in a text, but used information that people have in their semantic memory like, "Chicago is the largest city in Illinois." You would answer true to this, I suppose. "Loyola is the largest private univeristy in Illinois" is another such statement except our subjects wouldn't know that. And so in one case the subjects read the sentence first, "Chicago is the largest city in Illinois" and then after a delay they were tested, responding "True/False" to that sentence. Let's look what happened in the immediate test. There is a tremendous facilitation, the prime sentences are much faster than the non-prime sentences. In fact, there is also a nice paraphrase effect. How can you paraphrase, "Chicago is the largest city in Illinois"?

KEENAN: "Chicago is the most popular city in Illinois?"

KINTSCH: Thank you. If you do that then the reaction time falls nicely in between these two levels. Now we then put in a 20-min delay between the priming and the actual test questions. According to our paragraph data these 20 min should have wiped out all the memory traces and whether a sentence had been primed or not, the response times should be the same. This wasn't the case at all. The advantage was diminished, but it wasn't gone at all. We did it again with an hour delay and the advantage was still there. I think the difference is in what the subject does when you give him a list of unrelated sentences at the beginning of an experiment: that is something the subject will encode and store in his memory. It will be there, even if you go out for 48 hr. We'll still find the priming advantage in this case. We haven't done the second part of the experiment, which is to put the same sentences into paragraphs so it will be an incidental task. In that case, what we expect is that the priming effect will be wiped out in 20 min or something like that. The reason is that if you read a paragraph of text and you're not forewarned about a particular sentence in it, you would not start encoding and storing it in long-term memory. Such a sentence would be just material in working memory and would be lost soon.

BJORK: There's an aspect of John's question that worries me and I don't think any of these replies have addressed that aspect. Consider the standard level-of-processing notion with respect to the processing of a single word presented visually. Initially some lower-level analyzers are assumed to start operating on figure-ground contrasts, angles, and such; and there's something that corresponds to a sensory trace — and then maybe there is a naming event of some kind, and eventually more idiosyncratic higher-level semantic associations are generated to the word, and so on. Now it's typically asserted that the lower-level traces are lost on the order of, at the very lowest levels, hundredths of milliseconds, intermediate levels, seconds, and so on. The question that concerns me is why? It is one thing to simply state that lower-level traces are lost a great deal more rapidly than higher-level traces, but it is another thing to say why that should be the case. We tend to accept that assumption fairly uncritically, I think, because it is consistent with a vague physiological representation we have in mind. One possible explanation, however, is that the different components of a memory trace are differentially susceptible to influence. At the lowest levels of a visual analysis, for example, the trace should be highly susceptible, on a rapid time scale, to destructive interference from subsequent input. As you get to higher-level components of the trace, that is, to more idiosyncratic, semantic associations, and so on, those components are, in fact, associations with something that already exits in a durable form in memory. The chances of destructive interference in the immediate future are much less. It might be that we could design a sequence of inputs to memory that would lead to very rapid kinds of processing interference at the higher levels. That is, it might be possible to produce loss of semantic content at exceptionally rapid rates if successive inputs were contrived to provide maximal destructive influence in the processing of such content.

KINTSCH: I'd like to comment on this. I don't have any solution to the question which you raise and I realize it's a very big problem, but the way I speculated about it was similar to what you were saying. It is, perhaps, a notion of interference. The larger the units with which we are working in memory become, the less likely that such a unit reoccurs and therefore interferes with something that is already at work in memory. But, the angle detectors and line detectors at the lowest visual level or the phonemes at the acoustic level reoccur very frequently and therefore tend to interfere with material that's held in memory. In contrast, when you come to propositional units, the likelihood that such propositional units will reoccur and interfere is lessened. This is a very vague speculation, but it is perhaps testable with the proper experiment.

TRABASSO: There is also a second point, namely, that you already have in long-term memory a lot of this information, which you're somehow using to interact with the incoming utterance.

BJORK: That is, become associated with things that are more durable already. That assumption, however, begs part of the question. Why did those things get durable?

MAYZNER: Could I raise an issue that's related to this? It seems to me a problem that very often gets lost. You've been talking a great deal about trace decay, traces being lost, traces interfering. How do you answer the question of: "Is this a loss, a decay, or is this a problem in retrieval?" It's there, but with the procedure you're presenting you're not able to retrieve it from wherever it happens to be lost.

KINTSCH: I don't have a satisfactory answer to that question, but, it seems to me on logical grounds that not everything that is elaborated or being worked on in a working memory could be stored. If one were making a computer simulation, one would just erase the working memory.

MAYZNER: But, I would have thought that, until I read Julesz's (1970) book on random dot stereograms where he found a few subjects and one of them, one girl in particular, was able to fuse the random dots over 24–48 hr, as I recall.

TRABASSO: You're talking about data based upon one subject that hasn't been replicated independently. If you want to show that sensory information is preserved for long, long periods of time, it can be reconstructed, and, in fact, is used to create an illusion; that's not a good experiment.

THEIOS: I'd like to direct that same question to John Anderson. How does your system deal with retrieval versus difficulty wiping out of memory?

ANDERSON: In our system, information can be wiped out during the first 30 sec. After that, all forgetting is due to interference of other material in the retrieval process.

THEIOS: In the very operation of putting it into the memory and giving it deep structure it is stripped of its surface structure.

ANDERSON: I don't think so. Many experiments show that the subjects have memory for surface structure at delays and at the same time for the sentences' meaning.

I do not think my original question has been satisfactorily answered. We cannot simply explain the advantage of propositional information by a slower decay rate or lesser interference. Lexical information suffers rapid loss over the first 30 sec. However, conditional on surviving the first 30 sec, that lexical information seems to be very durable.

KINTSCH: That's quite right, but the answer would be that what is not decayed in the first 30 sec is encoded permanently, just as propositional meaning information is, that is, stored away in a memory episode and is subject to retrieval difficulty, but not to any further memory loss. At that point, it has the same memory status as propositional information.

ANDERSON: So what you're saying is that lexical information has difficulty in being converted into a permanent form. Once converted, there is no difficulty in maintaining it.

MANDLER: John (Anderson), let me give you an example where we store surface structure permanently, namely in poetry. Poetry loses its purpose if you simply store deep structure. In poetry we store both surface structure and deep structure permanently and both of them are equally retrievable, not just 20 min, but years later. We don't make the kind of mistakes in poetry that we make in remembering simple prose. We don't tend to paraphrase poetry because we store surface structure. Sometimes we don't even store meaning which is even a better example. We store the surface structure—the rhythm—and sometimes lose meaning.

ANDERSON: But for unspecified reasons it is still harder to initially commit that surface structure to memory.

MANDLER: No, more frequent.

ANDERSON: If it is just more frequent, we cannot explain the levels of encoding phenomena. Mandler is saying there is a propensity to encode meaning. But consider tasks where subjects are told to focus on surface structure instead. That is, their natural propensity is changed by instructions. Why do they do worse under such instructions if there is no inherent difficulty in trying to remember form?

THEIOS: Well, you yourself said that the topic was very important, that whatever was under discussion was not as important, and that if you're dealing with poetry that puts you in the mode right there to deal with the surface structure and to encode that very well. There are mechanisms in your model that should account for poetry, I would think.

ANDERSON: No, there are not, but perhaps there should be.

KINTSCH: I think John's point is a very important one, but again it's hard to see what the answer to it is; for this whole viewpoint to work one must really assume that it is easier to store the meaning of a paragraph than the complete visual information. If we don't make this assumption than we could just as well always store the visual information and recompute everything from there. Now, why this is so, I don't really know. Perhaps it is the case that the amount of work involved in storing visual information is very much greater. A visual description of a page of text maybe more complicated than a propositional description of the meaning of what's being said on this page.

TRABASSO: Would it help to bring in recognition here? There are studies on long-term recognition for visual information. Isn't it possible to process very quickly large amounts of visual information, and recognize it quite well as in the running recognition paradigm? Perhaps a lot of sensory information is stored, but not retrieved? One may have to make these distinctions but I sense that you don't want to.

MAYZNER: Well that was the point I was trying to make before.

BJORK: George's question gets at a very tricky business and I'm not sure it's a good example, because there are cases where the surface structure is a structure that contains or orders the meaning. Let's take any little rhyme that helps you sort out some fact like, "I before E except after C." The advantage of such rhymes is that when incorrect information is inserted, the rhyme doesn't work. The surface structure of the rhyme embodies or organizes the meaning or content. It's struck me on occasion that rhyme or rhythm properties are an intrinsic part of the memory trace rather than an extrinsic surface characteristic of the nominal stimulus. Often in lecturing undergraduate courses in learning and memory on mnemonic techniques, I ask the class if they have noticed that the Sheraton Hotel people are trying to teach them a 10-digit number, and whether, in fact, the Sheraton people have succeeded. Did they succeed with anyone here? What's the number?

CARLSON: 800-325 and a double something.

BJORK: That's close. The actual number is 800-325-3535. Now, I didn't actually sing the number, and whenever students retrieve the number, they don't sing it either (one does not tend to come out and sing in a large undergraduate class); but they do say the number with the exact rhythmic clustering involved in the song. In fact, it is nearly impossible to retrieve the number from memory without that rhythm. It is as if the rhythm is a part of the memory trace.

FREUND: That example is a bad example because the 800 is superfluous if you know that 800 is a toll-free number.

BJORK: That, in part, is why it is a good example. The 800 is superfluous or chunkable, but it's part of the rhythm and in terms of the whole sequence 800-325-2525 (he sings it), the "eight, oh, oh," beginning is very important. It is very difficult to jump to the 325-2525 without saying the 800. The rhythm and the numbers become unified in a Gestalt-type of fashion.

TRABASSO: I've been making some semantic interpretations of nonverbal communications both within myself and across the room and so I think it's about time to end today's session. Thank you very much.

REFERENCES

Bever, T. G. The cognitive basis for linguistic structures. In R. Hayes (Ed.), *Cognition and the development of language.* New York: Wiley, 1970.

Bloom, 1973

Newell, A. A note on the process-structure distinctions in developmental psychology. In S. Farnham-Diggory :Ed.), *Information processing in children.* New York: Academic Press, 1972. Pp. 116–143.

Julesz, B. *Foundations of cyclopean perception.* New York: Wiley, 1970.

Piaget, J. *Structuralism.* New York: Basic Books, 1970.

AUTHOR INDEX

SUBJECT INDEX